A Recovery for All:

Rethinking Socio-Economic Policies for Children and Poor Households

Isabel Ortiz

Matthew Cummins

Editors

Division of Policy and Practice

Cover Design: Upasana Young
Cover and back photos:
© UNICEF/NYHQ1998-0529/Giacomo Pirozzi
© UN photo/Fred Noy
© UNICEF/NYHQ2011-0224/Roger LeMoyne
© UN photo/WFP

A Recovery for All: Rethinking Socio-Economic Policies for Children and Poor Households
Isabel Ortiz and Matthew Cummins (Editors)

© United Nations Children's Fund (UNICEF), Division of Policy and Practice, New York 2012
ISBN: 978-1-105-58755-9

Praise for *A Recovery for All*

"This book offers a critical review of the social effects of the ongoing crisis and underscores the need to prioritize children and vulnerable groups not only in social but also in macroeconomic decision making."

>José Antonio Ocampo, Professor, Columbia University; former United Nations Under-Secretary-General for Economic and Social Affairs, and former Minister of Finance of Colombia

"This book combines academic rigour and human compassion to reveal the multiple channels through which the global financial crisis has affected poor children and households around the world. It argues that such crises also represent moments of opportunity for progressive reform, and shows what needs to happen to end child poverty and tackle inequality."

>Duncan Green, Head of Research, Oxfam GB

"This compelling collection shows that children are the worst affected by economic crises, but this need not happen. It argues convincingly that protecting and increasing the public expenditures that matter most for children can also be the basis for sustained economic recovery."

>Jayati Ghosh, Executive Secretary, International Development Economics Associates (IDEAs), and Professor, Jawaharlal Nehru University, India

"*A Recovery for All* documents in vivid detail how high food prices, unemployment and austerity measures have led to increased hunger, poverty and social tensions. It offers alternatives for an effective policy response to protect the rights of people, especially children, affected by the crisis and calls for urgent debate in every country."

>Sakiko Fukuda-Parr, Professor of International Affairs, The New School, and Director of UNDP's Human Development Reports 1995-2004

"The crisis took a heavy toll on children and their families. People across the globe are demanding change with social justice. UNICEF is once again at the forefront of such demands, supported by careful documentation and analysis of the impacts of the crisis and responses on the most vulnerable. This book presents a powerful statement of these impacts; it also outlines feasible policy alternatives—supported by the United Nations system—that can foster an inclusive and sustainable *'Recovery for All.'*"

> Sarah Cook, Director, United Nations Research Institute for Social Development (UNRISD)

"Isabel Ortiz and Matthew Cummins have provided us with a devastating analysis of the impact of the global economic crisis on the welfare of children and their families everywhere. Following in the path laid down by an earlier generation of radical scholars working with UNICEF (*Adjustment with a Human Face*, 1987), this book not only lays bare the social consequences of the crisis but sets out clear realisable fiscal policies that, if acted upon globally and within countries, would ensure a *'Recovery for All.'* Are policymakers listening?"

> Bob Deacon, Emeritus Professor of International Social Policy, University of Sheffield, and founder of the journal *Global Social Policy*

"A recovery that leaves children behind is not only ethically unacceptable, but will also be economically damaging. With rigorous analysis of the available options and passionate defense of the rights of children, UNICEF demonstrates that a *'Recovery for All'* is at the same time the morally just policy and the economic framework that makes sense. A must-read for the policy-makers and the policy-sufferers, all of us, citizens."

> Roberto Bissio, Executive Director, Third World Institute, and Coordinator, Social Watch, Uruguay HQ

"Combining theoretical insights with sound empirical evidence, this book points to the dangers for employment, distribution, welfare and the status of children of fiscal conservatism and an overemphasis on austerity in a world in search of recovery from the Great Recession."

> C.P. Chandrasekhar, Executive Committee Member, International Development Economics Associates (IDEAs), and Professor, Jawaharlal Nehru University, India

"On top of the pre-existing unsolved structural global social crisis, poor and vulnerable households have since 2007 been hit by a relentless series of adverse shocks triggered by the food, fuel and financial crises. Finally when all their defenses were down and all their coping mechanisms were exhausted, they were hit by the effects by fiscal austerity measures. This book guides us through the effects of the multiple crises on the poor, but it also demonstrates convincingly that the fiscal space for a basic floor of social protection that would provide effective protection from the worst social fall-out of such crises can be found. The book reminds us that fiscal space is not a question of economic performance or state of development, it is first and foremost a question of political will. It is the lack of political will, i.e., our cruel indifference vis-à-vis avoidable ill health, hunger, destitution and deaths, that prevents us from reducing vulnerability of those who have no means to fend for themselves."

> Michael Cichon, Director of Social Security Department, International Labour Organization (ILO)

"UNICEF has shown itself to be a lead agency in producing carefully prepared papers in the area of their remit—children and poor families. This book rigorously examines the global crises that have created new poverty. UNICEF does not stay with a bleak picture but rather moves to examine a '*Recovery for all*' and argues there is fiscal space to achieve this. This is a fundamental text for those working in social policy and social development. All CSOs trying to make children's rights a reality and social protection a practical issue will find in this book strong evidence-based arguments and many updated figures. A very useful support!"

> Christian Rollet, President, and Denys Correll, Executive Director, International Council on Social Welfare (ICSW), Uganda HQ

"UNICEF's bold analysis, developed during the global financial and economic crisis, demonstrates that we must give up the addiction to preserve macroeconomic stability at any human cost. The addiction, an outdated orthodoxy, grows from the predominance of Ministries of Finance, and finance in general, in policymaking, and obscures the common good. European policymakers today would do well to learn the lessons here, before the North ignites another avoidable global crisis."

> Soren Ambrose, Advocacy Manager, ActionAid International, Kenya

"Much has been written about the global crises that started in 2008, from subprime mortgages to macroeconomic imbalances, from banking crises to Eurozone debt crisis. This outstanding and well-researched book will tell you what all this means for poor children across the world and for plain citizens such as you. Most importantly, it will tell you what are the alternative economic policies that can make a difference and support a '*Recovery for All*.' Read it—this book will give you hope."

Nuria Molina, Director of Policy and Research, Save the Children

"UNICEF's heart has always been in the right place—promoting children's rights. This publication reveals UNICEF's brains: Promotion of children's rights globally also requires rigorous analysis and fearless advocacy for equitable global economic and social policy."

Timo Voipio, Chair, OECD-DAC Network on Poverty Reduction (POVNET)

Foreword

From as early as 1947, UNICEF has recognized the importance of economic policy for children. In the 1960s, UNICEF became convinced that children would never receive the priorities they deserved unless their needs were fully integrated into national economic planning and with the help of some of the world's leading economists defined policies and a country-focused approach to do this.

The 1980s were years of debt, recession and structural adjustment, with serious and severe repercussions on people—and children—especially in Africa and Latin America. In 1982 and 1983, UNICEF organized a series of country assessments of how children were being affected by the triple economic onslaught—with the results pulled together in a publication, *The Impact of World Recession on Children*. Hans Singer, one of the UN's first and most eminent economists, analyzed how children in developing countries were suffering from a "a reverse shock-absorber effect," which multiplied the impacts of the downturns of recession in the North several fold in their repercussions on children in the South. Jim Grant, UNICEF's Executive Director at the time, became the leading international voice arguing the need for policy change—especially to respond to the immediate and urgent needs of children. By 1987, UNICEF had published its two volume study, *Adjustment with a Human Face*, a publication prepared by Giovanni Andrea Cornia, Frances Stewart and myself with inputs from UNICEF field offices in many parts of the world. This challenged the world to place long-term priorities for children before the short-term exigencies of adjustment.

Soon, UNICEF started moving from adjustment with a human face to development with a human face. By this was meant that the real problem was not so much to provide short-term protection to offset the setbacks of structural adjustment, but to get back to a positive path of development, in which concerns for children were fully incorporated into advancing human development, even where economic growth was still constrained by the international context and pressures. In 1990, UNICEF organized the World Summit for Children which re-iterated a call for a new approach to adjustment and agreed a larger core of goals. UNICEF developed the concept of "First Call for Children," essentially meaning that in bad times as in good, countries should ensure that children's priority needs should have a first call on resources—a principle accepted by most families for their own children but still only rarely recognized in national economic policy.

These principles from the 1980s and 1990s are just as important today, when UNICEF's concerns are focused on equity and how best to intensify its efforts to address new obstacles to the realization of children's rights. This volume follows in the best line of UNICEF's tradition, combining careful analysis with challenges to policymakers nationally and internationally. Millions of children and their families today are caught in a world crisis, with many countries experiencing high and unaffordable food prices, unemployment and austerity measures. These can have largely irreversible adverse impacts on children's survival and development, as UNICEF demonstrated 25 years ago with *Adjustment with a Human Face*. These documents are a contribution of UNICEF and its partners to international advocacy to highlight the risks to children and their families and to show the possibilities for policies that are inclusive and equitable toward *"A Recovery for All."*

> Sir Richard Jolly, Honorary Professor and Research Associate, Institute of Development Studies, University of Sussex, and former Assistant Secretary-General, UNICEF

Contents

Boxes, Tables and Figures

Boxes

Tables

Figures

Acknowledgements

This book would not have been possible without substantive comments and contributions from colleagues and partners worldwide. The authors would like to thank the following persons, in particular, by alphabetical order: Abdolreza Abbassian (Secretary of the Intergovernmental Group on Grains Trade and Markets Division, FAO), Soren Ambrose (International Policy Manager, ActionAid International), Alice Amsden (Barton L. Weller Professor of Development Economics, Massachusetts Institute of Technology), Roberto Benes (Regional Advisor, UNICEF Regional Office for the Middle East and North Africa), Henk-Jan Brinkman (Chief of Policy, Planning and Application Branch, Peacebuilding Support Office, UN, and former Chief of the Economic Analysis Service, World Food Programme), Anisuzzaman Chowdhury (Senior Economic Affairs Officer, UN-DESA), Michael Cichon (Director of Social Security Department, ILO), Michael Clark (Interregional Adviser, UNCTAD), Marva Corley (International Institute for Labour Studies, ILO), Sakiko Fukuda-Parr (Professor of International Affairs, The New School, USA), Krzysztof Hagemejer (Chief of Policy Development and Research, ILO), Degol Hailu (Economic Policy Advisor, UNDP), Gail Hurley (Policy Specialist, UNDP), International Monetary Fund (IMF) staff led by Sanjeev Gupta (Deputy Director, Fiscal Affairs Department), Anne Jellema (International Director of Policy, Action Aid International), Richard King (Economic Justice Researcher, Oxfam International), Gabriele Koehler (Institute of Development Studies and former senior staff at UNCTAD and UNICEF), Lisa Kurbiel (Senior Social Policy Specialist, UNICEF Mozambique), Sebastian Levine (Senior Economist, UNDP Uganda), Fatou Lo (Programme Specialist, United Nations Women), Moazam Mahmood (Director of Economic and Labour Market Analysis Department, ILO), Alberto Minujin (Professor, The New School, USA), David Nabarro (UN Secretary-General's Special Representative for Food Security and Nutrition), Oliver Paddison (Economic Affairs Officer, UN-DESA), Uma Rani (International Institute for Labour Studies, ILO), Shari Spiegel (Senior Economic Affairs Officer, UN-DESA), Raymond Torres (Director of International Institute for Labour Studies, ILO), Oscar Ugarteche (Senior Researcher, National Autonomous University of Mexico), Rolph van der Hoeven (Professor of Employment and Development Economics, Erasmus University), Matías Vernengo

(Associate Professor, University of Utah), Rob Vos (Director of Development Policy and Analysis Division, UN-DESA), Richard Wolff (Professor of Economics Emeritus, University of Massachusetts, Amherst) and Yanchun Zhang (Policy Specialist, UNDP).

Sincere appreciation is also extended to all of the contributors to UNICEF's e-discussion, "A Recovery with a Human Face." While the complete list and and proper professional titles are provided at the end of Chapter II, we would like to specially mention some of the most active members of the network, by alphabetical order: Roberto Bissio (Third World Institute and Social Watch), Aldo Caliari (Center of Concern), Ha-Joon Chang (University of Cambridge), Michael Cichon (ILO), Giovanni Andrea Cornia (University of Florence), Bob Deacon (University of Sheffield), Heiner Flassbeck (UNCTAD), Kevin Gallagher (Boston University), Jayati Ghosh (International Development Economics Associates, IDEAs), Duncan Green (Oxfam GB), Richard Jolly (Institute of Development Studies), Jomo K. Sundaram (UN Assistant Secretary-General for Economic Development), Anita Kelles-Viitanen (Association for the Taxation of Financial Transactions for the Aid of Citizens and former manager at Asian Development Bank), Martin Khor (South Center), Gabriele Koehler (Institute of Development Studies), Paul Krugman (Princeton University), Max Lawson (Oxfam GB), Terry McKinley (SOAS, University of London), Nuria Molina (Save the Children UK), José Antonio Ocampo (Columbia University), Kunibert Raffer (University of Vienna), Dani Rodrik (Harvard University), Rick Rowden (Development consultant), Magdalena Sepúlveda (UN Office of the High Commissioner for Human Rights), Harry Shutt (Development Consultant), Guy Standing (University of Bath), Frances Stewart (University of Oxford), Andy Storey (University College Dublin), Andy Sumner (Institute of Development Studies), Raymond Torres (ILO), Oscar Ugarteche (Universidad Nacional Autónoma de México), John Weeks (SOAS, University of London), Mark Weisbrot (Center for Economic and Policy Research) and Richard Wolff (University of Massachusetts, Amherst).

A very special thanks to Richard Morgan, Director of Policy and Practice, UNICEF, for his guidance and comments.

Contributors

Isabel Ortiz is Associate Director, Policy and Practice, UNICEF.

Matthew Cummins is Social and Economic Policy Specialist, UNICEF.

Jingqing Chai is Chief, Social Policy and Economic Analyses, UNICEF.

Louise Moreira Daniels is Policy Analyst, UNICEF.

List of Acronyms

ADB	Asian Development Bank
ALBA	Bolivarian Alternative for Latin America
CAF	Andean Development Corporation
CBOT	Chicago Board of Trade
CEE/CIS	Central and Eastern Europe and the Commonwealth of Independent States
EAP	East Asia and the Pacific
EU	European Union
FAO	Food and Agriculture Organization
G8	Group of Eight
G20	Group of Twenty
GDP	Gross Domestic Product
GIEWS	FAO's Global Information and Early Warning System
GNI	Gross National Income
HICs	High-income countries
HIPC	Heavily Indebted Poor Countries Initiative
IFF	Illicit Financial Flows
ILO	International Labour Organization
IMF	International Monetary Fund
LAC	Latin America and the Caribbean
LICs	Low-income countries
MDGs	Millennium Development Goals
MENA	Middle East and North Africa
MICs	Middle-income countries
NGO	Non-governmental Organization
ODA	Official Development Assistance
OECD	Organisation for Economic Co-operation and Development
OTC	Over-the-counter trading
SME	Small- and medium-size enterprises
SSA	Sub-Saharan Africa
SWF	Sovereign Wealth Fund
UN	United Nations
UNCTAD	United Nations Conference on Trade and Development
UN-DESA	United Nations Department of Economic and Social Affairs
UNDP	United Nations Development Programme
UNESCO	United Nations Educational, Scientific and Cultural Organization

UNICEF   United Nations Children's Fund
UNRISD   United Nations Research Institute for Social Development
VAT   Value added tax
WHO   World Health Organization
WTO   World Trade Organization

I.   INTRODUCTION

Isabel Ortiz and Matthew Cummins

"We must design recovery from the ground up... High unemployment, rising food and commodity prices and persistent inequalities have contributed to a substantial rise in hunger, poverty and associated social tensions. Now, more than ever, investments for the world's poorest are necessary to recover lost ground in pursuit of development objectives, including the MDGs... Global stabilization and recovery debates must take into consideration the specific needs of vulnerable populations."

"We must act now. We must avoid reverting to the pre-crisis conditions that denied too many of our fellow human beings a fair chance at a decent living... We must work together to establish the basis for a more secure, prosperous and equitable world for all."

UN Secretary-General, Voices of the Vulnerable
and Letter to the G20, June 2010

1.   A Crisis on Top of an Existing Human Crisis

The United Nations (UN) Secretary General's call to action has never been more urgent. The global financial and economic crisis that started in 2008 exacerbated an existing human crisis and structural imbalances in terms of labour markets and inequalities. Prior to 2008, the world was characterized by widespread poverty and hunger, few decent work opportunities and millions of children being denied their rights. Perhaps most telling is that half of the world's children were living below the international $2/day poverty line[1] and suffering from multiple deprivations, such as inadequate nutrition and limited access to health, education, safe drinking water, sanitation and/or housing services.

---

[1] Authors' calculations based on 2008 poverty headcount estimates from the World Bank's *PovcalNet* (2012).

Globally, close to 900 million persons suffered from hunger,[2] with malnutrition affecting approximately one-third of all children under the age of five.[3] In terms of work, the main source of income for households and especially the poor, only 60 percent of the global working-age population had some type of job to support their families, with almost six out of every ten young workers unable to find employment.[4] Income inequality was also on the rise, as evidenced by worsening Gini coefficient trends in more than half of the 132 countries that have available estimates over the 2000-08 period (Ortiz and Cummins 2011).

Those who had experienced earlier global crises, such as the 1997-98 Asian financial crisis, knew that an 'economic tsunami' was looming with potentially devastating consequences for vulnerable populations worldwide. Then, in 2008, the negative impacts of the global financial crisis, along with record-breaking food and fuel prices, began to reverberate across poor households through lower purchasing power, higher unemployment, slower remittance flows, and reduced access to credit and basic social services. In short, millions were pushed into poverty by a crisis that they did not create and could not understand.

In a first phase of the crisis (2008-09), many concerned governments took action and launched fiscal stimulus plans and other measures in order to sustain growth and protect their populations from the adverse effects of the food, fuel and financial shocks—the so-called triple 'F' crisis. While such efforts were generally positive, it quickly became clear that they were insufficient when, in a second phase of the crisis (2010-), governments moved to contract budgets and focus on debt and macroeconomic balances. The fourth 'F' wave of the crisis was thus set in motion: fiscal austerity.

This book argues that children and poor families were left behind before the crisis, that they have been severely affected by the multitude of

---

[2] Refers to population whose food intake is insufficient to meet dietary energy requirements continuously (also referred to as prevalence of undernourishment); based on estimates from the FAO's Statistics Division.

[3] Refers to children whose height for age (stunting) is more than two standard deviations below the median for the international reference population; based on estimates from the WHO's *Global Database on Child Growth and Malnutrition*.

[4] Refers to employment-to-population ratios for adult workers (15 and older) and young adults (15-24 year-old population); authors' calculations based on the ILO's *Key Indicators of the Labour Market database*.

global shocks since 2008, and that, although they were briefly supported during the first phase of the crisis (2008-09), they were again left behind in 2010 despite their significant needs and increasing vulnerability. This book further argues that there are alternatives: there is a range of options to expand fiscal space and support investments for a socially-responsive economic recovery, even in the poorest countries.

Protecting children and their families is not only right in principle— investing in children and poor households is a moral imperative and essential to achieving internationally-agreed development goals—but it is also sound economics—investing in the young and poor is necessary to raise productivity and human capital as well as expand domestic markets and generate inclusive and sustainable growth.

This book also seeks to promote awareness of the distributional impacts of macroeconomic policies. Oftentimes macroeconomic decisions are taken without consideration of their social consequences, with children and poor households arising only as a distant afterthought. It is indispensable, however, that the social impacts of different macroeconomic policies are brought to the attention of Finance Ministers and key decision-makers, and deliberated *before* policies are designed. This book contributes to this debate by encouraging detailed examination of alternative policy options that support children and poor families both during and after the recovery.

These key messages reflect the central mission of the United Nations Children's Fund (UNICEF), which is to reach the most deprived and most vulnerable children everywhere. This approach is founded on the principles of universality, non-discrimination and accountability as described in the Convention on the Rights of the Child, as well as on the recognition that a country's long-term economic growth prospects hinge on investments in children today.

The debt crisis of the 1980s created deep recessions in many developing countries. Adjustment programs forced governments to cut expenditures and led to the collapse of industrial sectors, high unemployment and poverty; these impacts were further aggravated by cost-recovery policies, such as levying user fees for health and education services. UNICEF responded with *Adjustment with a Human Face* (Cornia et al. 1987), which argued that children must be protected during economic crises. It further reasoned that this could be achieved by adopting more expansionary macroeconomic policies, by prioritizing investments in social and economic sectors that serve the poor, and by introducing or scaling up social protection programs.

Today, the world is at a similar crossroads. This time it is a global crisis, and one that affects low- and high-income countries alike. Fortunately, the crisis has opened a space for dialogue and created political momentum to address these challenges. It is fundamental, however, that this policy debate does not simply focus on mitigating the impacts of the crisis and returning to the earlier *status quo*, which deprived millions of people of a decent standard of living, but that it addresses global imbalances and ensures development and prosperity for all persons.

2.   From Global Crisis to Household Crisis

Initiated by the so-called 'subprime mortgage crisis' and the meltdown of the financial sector in advanced economies, a global economic crisis emerged in 2008. The repercussions for households in countries closely integrated in the world economy were immediate and soon spread elsewhere. In an effort to shield their populations from the crisis, most governments adopted counter-cyclical policies during a first phase (2008-09). However, with the freezing of credit markets, the financial crisis turned into a crisis of the real economy, dragging down global aggregate demand and leading to a contraction of trade, output and employment. Countries were generally affected through falling export demand, reversals of capital flows and a slowdown of remittances. The crisis was further accompanied by rampant commodity price volatility, with food and energy prices reaching unprecedented highs in 2008 and 2011, which caused extreme hardships in import-dependent countries.

At the household level, the global economic crisis was transmitted from the domestic economy to the household economy through four main channels, which are summarized below and presented in Figure 1.

-    A first channel was higher costs for basic goods, such as food and energy products, medicines and agricultural inputs, among others. The impact of declining purchasing power was especially marked on the poorest households, who frequently reported eating fewer meals and less nutritious food as well as reducing other essential expenditures, such as on education and healthcare.

- A second channel was fewer jobs, wage cuts, reduced benefits and decreased demand for migrant workers, the latter which decelerated remittance flows. In addition, the reduced supply of decent job opportunities forced many families into the informal sector, often in dangerous and unhealthy conditions and for less pay. The employment shock further led many households to pull their children out of school and send them, along with other family members, to work.

Figure I.1 Macro-Micro Transmission Channels of an Aggregate Shock and Potentially Adverse Outcomes

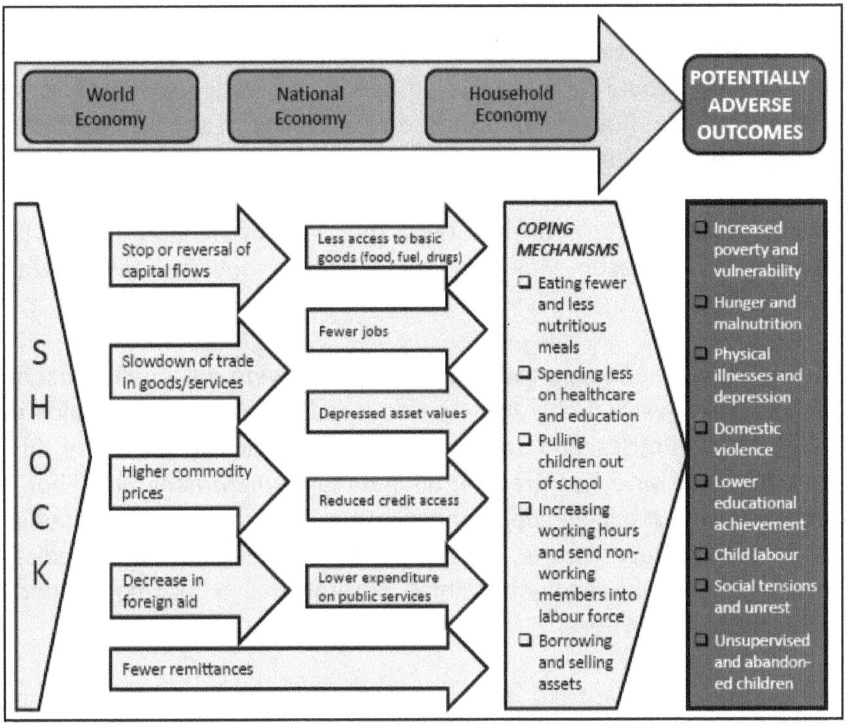

Source: Authors' illustration based on Mendoza (2009), Harper et al. (2011), Ferreira et al. (1999), and Lustig and Walton (1998)
Note: The direction of the arrows does not imply causality.

- A third channel was diminished assets and reduced access to credit. In particular, the crisis led to home foreclosures, lost savings due to bank failures and credit freezes. Moreover, to help make ends meet, households spent their savings, borrowed money or sold available assets, such as livestock.

- A fourth main channel was reduced access to public goods and services, such as education, health, social protection and employment services and programs, which was a delayed effect. While many governments initially bolstered public assistance in an effort to protect their populations from these shocks, there was a dramatic policy reversal beginning in 2010 whereby most governments moved to cut spending through a variety of austerity measures.

It is important to note that the different coping responses were magnified by the multiplicity of shocks. For example, a household would likely adjust its consumption of food when faced with higher food prices, lower income or reduced food subsidies, but a combination of these shocks would increase the probability of inadequate nutritional intake. Similarly, households exposed to a variety of shocks could also be expected to spend even less on healthcare and education as well as dramatically increase the number of working hours of family members, which would, in turn, further raise the risks of hunger, morbidity, depression, domestic violence, child labour, poverty and overall vulnerability.

Moreover, while the negative coping behaviors were observed across all regions, they were clearly most pronounced on poorer households in developing countries, and among children, in particular. On top of this, governments started contracting budgets just when many households had exhausted available coping mechanisms and were in need of public assistance like never before, especially for food, healthcare and medical services, education and job-training programs, and income support, including cash transfers.

The global economic crisis, however, is far from over. In 2012, each of the main global-to-local transmission channels remain wide open and continue to threaten household well-being: food prices remain near all-time highs, with fuel prices also quickly ascending; the jobs crisis continues to deteriorate reflecting the anemic economic growth patterns that characterize much of the globe; and access to quality public goods and services is increasingly being challenged in the worldwide drive toward austerity.

3.   A *'Recovery for All'*

This book is, at its core, a direct response to the Secretary General's call for a *'Recovery for All,'* which includes children and poor households.

Building on a series of analyses and research previously published by UNICEF on the global economic crisis, its objectives are three-fold: (i) to recount the events and chronology of the global economic crisis, highlighting the main thematic issues (Chapter II); (ii) to describe the principal threats facing children and poor households as a result of the crisis, which include unaffordable food, unemployment—both youth and adult—and reduced public assistance (Chapters III, IV and V); and (iii) to address questions related to resources and political will by identifying feasible options that governments can enact to support a *'Recovery for All'* (Chapter VI).

The structure of this book is as follows. Following this introduction, the book opens with Chapter II, "A Recovery with a Human Face? Insights into the global crisis." This chapter is based on an e-discussion that was hosted by UNICEF during 2010-12 and provides a snapshot of the latest thinking on inclusive policies in the context of the economic recovery. Contributors include Nobel Laureate Paul Krugman, former UN Under-Secretary-General José Antonio Ocampo and many other prominent global thinkers from academia and civil society, including Sir Richard Jolly, Dani Rodrik, Nora Lustig, Martin Khor, Duncan Green, Ha-Joon Chang and Nouriel Roubini, among many others. By weaving the main points raised by some of the world's eminent development thought leaders, it offers a chronological narrative of the global economic crisis along with discussion of the key thematic issues of the crisis.

Chapter III, "The Food Price Surge," takes a close look at the first major threat posed by the global economic crisis: unaffordable food. The chapter develops a local food price index for nearly 60 developing countries in order to gauge the micro level impacts of food price changes on children and poor families. It also reviews the possible causes of the food price upswing that began in mid-2010 along with international and domestic policy responses to the 2007-08 price spike through a three-pillar analytical framework (supporting consumption, boosting production and managing food markets). Chapter III ultimately calls for urgent and coordinated policy actions by national governments and the international community to ensure that vulnerable populations have access to affordable and nutritious food at all times.

In Chapter IV, "The Jobs Crisis," the book moves on to discuss unemployment, which is the second major household level threat originating from the global economic crisis. The chapter focuses on the ongoing jobs crisis and the dangers of high unemployment among youth and adult workers. Analysis of recent labour market trends, including the implications of the demographic phenomenon known as the 'youth bulge,' is followed by an in-depth discussion of the household level impacts, with particular attention to the risks posed to children and young workers. The discussion closes by summarizing employment-generating policies and encouraging policymakers to place jobs, especially for youth, at the center of recovery efforts.

Chapter V, "Austerity Measures and the Risks to Children and Poor Households," offers an in-depth examination of the latest household danger that has been proliferating across developing and developed countries since 2010: fiscal austerity. The chapter sets out to understand how fiscal consolidation impacts levels of social assistance and other public spending decisions and ultimately affects the well-being of vulnerable populations. It starts with an empirical analysis of government expenditure projections in 179 countries. By looking at three distinct periods (pre-crisis: 2005-07; crisis phase I, fiscal expansion: 2008-09; and crisis phase II, fiscal contraction: 2010-), it identifies the depth and breadth of ongoing budget cuts along with a series of countries that may be undergoing excessive contraction, defined as cutting expenditures below pre-crisis levels in terms of gross domestic product (GDP). Next, it presents a detailed assessment of the most common adjustment measures being considered by governments during 2010-12 and their potentially adverse impacts on children and poor households. To conclude, Chapter V questions whether the projected fiscal contraction trajectory and the different policy options being discussed worldwide are conducive to adequately protecting vulnerable households and fostering an inclusive recovery.

The book next moves away from analyzing the different shocks of the crisis to address questions related to resources and political will. In Chapter VI, "Fiscal Space: Options for social and economic development for children and poor households," it is argued that expenditure cuts are not inevitable during adjustment periods, and that investments to protect vulnerable populations are possible even in the poorest countries. The chapter reviews all of the available opportunities, which include: (i) re-allocating public expenditures; (ii) increasing tax revenues; (iii) lobbying for increased aid and transfers; (iv) tapping into fiscal and foreign exchange reserves; (v) borrowing and restructuring existing debt; and (vi) adopting a more accommodative macroeconomic framework. Given the significance of public investment in enhancing the prospects for inclusive economic growth and social development, Chapter VI argues that it is critical that governments explore these options to ramp up social and employment-generating investments in support of a '*Recovery for All.*'

The book concludes with Chapter VII, which summarizes the main empirical findings of the persisting threats of the crisis on children and households worldwide, along with policy and resource options to achieve food security, full and decent employment, and a socially-responsive economic recovery.

UNICEF's appeal for a '*Recovery for All*' is in full accordance with calls from the UN Secretary-General and the UN Chief Executives Board for decisive and urgent actions to respond to the global economic crisis. This was expressed through the definition of nine UN Joint Initiatives, which include, *inter alia*, strategies to provide additional financing for the most vulnerable in countries in distress, support for food and nutrition security, a global jobs pact, a social protection floor, and improved monitoring and analysis of crisis impacts (United Nations 2009). Furthermore, progress toward the universal realization of the rights of all children—to which 193 countries have committed by ratifying the Convention on the Rights of the Child—and the achievement of the Millennium Development Goals (MDGs) will be halted if the right developmental policies are not immediately undertaken.

It is only fitting to wrap up this introduction by re-visiting the request laid out in the landmark study *Adjustment with a Human Face*, which remains fully valid and has inspired this book. In particular, *A Recovery for All: Rethinking Socio-Economic Policies for Children and Poor Households* strives to:

> speak to those directly involved in the making of [recovery] policy, whether as policymakers and practitioners or as analysts of the process. It is this group who has the power and influence to make possible a broader approach, and it is this group, nationally and internationally, who must be persuaded if broader policies are to be adopted (Cornia et al. 1987:8).

References

Cornia, G.A., R. Jolly and F. Stewart. 1987. *Adjustment with a Human Face: Protecting the Vulnerable and Promoting Growth*. Oxford: Oxford University Press.

Ferreira, F., G. Prennushi and M. Ravallion. 1999. "Protecting the Poor from Macroeconomic Shocks: An Agenda for Action in a Crisis and Beyond." World Bank Policy Research Working Paper No. 2160, World Bank.

Harper, C., N. Jones, P. Pereznieto and A. McKay. 2011. "Promoting Children's Well-being: Policy Lessons from Past and Present Economic Crises." *Development Policy Review* 29(5): 621-641.

Lustig, N. and M. Walton. 1998. "Crises and the Poor: A Template for Action." World Bank and Inter-American Development Bank Note, processed.

Mendoza, R. 2009. "Aggregate Shocks, Poor Households and Children: Transmission Channels and Policy Responses." *Global Social Policy* 9(1): 55-78.

Ortiz, I. and M. Cummins. 2011. "Global Inequality: Beyond the Bottom Billion – A Rapid Review of Income Distribution in 141 Countries." Social and Economic Policy Working Paper, UNICEF.

United Nations. 2009. "CEB Communiqué," April 05. Paris: Secretariat of the United Nations System Chief Executives Board for Coordination.

II.   A RECOVERY WITH A HUMAN FACE? INSIGHTS INTO THE GLOBAL CRISIS

Isabel Ortiz and Louise Moreira Daniels

"Look around you. Scan the news headlines. Famine in the Horn of Africa. Fighting in Syria, and elsewhere. Protests against growing economic inequality, from Wall Street to Main Street. Rising public anger. Loss of faith in governments and public institutions to do the right thing. Our world is one of terrible contradictions. Plenty of food but one billion people go hungry. Lavish lifestyles for a few, but poverty for too many others. Huge advances in medicine while mothers die everyday in childbirth, and children die every day from drinking dirty water. Billions spent on weapons to kill people instead of keeping them safe. What kind of world has baby seven billion been born into? What kind of world do we want for our children in the future?"

UN Secretary-General's remarks at press event on Day of Seven Billion in New York City on October 31, 2011

1.   Background

In 2010, UNICEF initiated an e-discussion entitled 'A Recovery with a Human Face.'[1] It soon became the largest UNICEF network and one of the most successful e-discussions ever hosted by the UN. Contributors have included Nobel Laureate Paul Krugman, former UN Under-Secretary-General José Antonio Ocampo and many other prominent global thinkers from academia and civil society, including Sir Richard Jolly, Dani Rodrik, Nora Lustig, Martin Khor, Duncan Green, Ha-Joon

---

[1] The e-discussion was moderated by Isabel Ortiz and Louise Moreira Daniels. The findings, interpretations and conclusions expressed in this chapter are those of the contributors to the e-discussion and do not reflect the policies or views of UNICEF or of the UN. The selection of text in this summary was a choice of the moderators and does not necessarily represent core work of the contributors.

Chang and Nouriel Roubini, among many others.[2] Above all, this e-discussion reflects an independent debate that goes beyond orthodox approaches that guide decision making. It further served as an alternative forum for dialogue, offering an important contribution to our understanding of the complex facets of the global economic crisis. As such, this chapter presents a summary of the 'A Recovery with a Human Face' e-discussion that took place between February 2010 and February 2012. It begins by weaving some of the main points in a narrative of the global economic crisis and then discusses the key thematic issues that were raised, both in terms of the overall impacts of the crisis on the most vulnerable populations as well as policy responses.

2.   A Chronology of the Global Economic Crisis

2.1.   The worst crisis since 1929

Largely stemming from reckless lending practices of financial institutions in the United States, the so called 'subprime mortgage crisis,' a financial crisis erupted in 2008. It quickly spread to Europe and then across the rest of the world. This global downturn resulted in a sharp drop in international trade and a steep rise in unemployment and underemployment. As an initial response, most governments in the developed world moved to bail out banks and other financial institutions on the premise of 'too big to fail.' Regular citizens—and in particular the poor, both in high- and low-income countries—became the victims of a crisis that they did not create and bore the costs of a 'recovery' that has largely excluded them.

In April 2009, leaders of high-income economies called for a meeting of the Group of 20 (G20), a relatively unknown group at the time that consisted of the Group of 8 (G8) plus a dozen emerging developing countries. This empowered group took major (and unexpected) decisions on crisis management at the London Summit.[3] There it was decided that US$1 trillion should be allocated to solve the crisis. These funds were primarily given to the International Monetary Fund (IMF) (US$750 billion), with a smaller tranche for the development banks

---

[2] The complete list of contributors is provided at the end of this chapter.
[3] G20. 2009. "London Summit – Leaders' Statement," April 02.

(US$100 billion) and the rest to support trade. Although the UN did not receive any financial support, the G20 tasked it with developing a real-time monitoring system to alert on the possible deterioration of living conditions of the poor (the Global Impact and Vulnerability Alert System [GIVAS], later known as Global Pulse).[4]

These G20 decisions were highly contested. On June 26, 2009, the 192 Member States of the UN ('the G192') met and adopted by consensus a statement on the World Financial and Economic Crisis and its Impact on Development.[5] The analysis and recommendations covered the gamut from short-term mitigation to deep structural change, from crisis response to reform of the global economic and financial architecture. The statement was based on the work of a high-level Panel of Experts led by Nobel Laureate Joseph Stiglitz.[6] Although the outcome document was a minimal consensual synthesis, it remains to date the only legitimate and democratically-supported global agreement on the crisis. Regrettably, corporate global media obscured the compact reached at the UN,[7] and attention turned to the G20 and to the newly-empowered IMF to solve crisis, leaving most countries with no voice.

The opening message in UNICEF's e-discussion 'Recovery with a Human Face' by Sir Richard Jolly, Frances Stewart and Andrea Cornia was heartfelt:

> The debt crisis of the 1980s led to a severe recession in almost all African and Latin American countries. IMF and World Bank adjustment programs required countries to cut back on their expenditures, introduce charges for health and education, and reduce or abolish the minimum wage. Reductions in protection led to the collapse of industrial sectors in many countries and to high unemployment. Poverty rose and income distribution worsened. Most countries had no or very limited programs of social protection. This was what came to be known as the 'lost decade.'

---

[4] United Nations. 2010. *Voices of the Vulnerable: Recovery from the Ground Up.* New York: United Nations Global Pulse.

[5] United Nations. 2009. "Outcome of the Conference of the World Financial and Economic Crisis and Its Impact on Development," June 24-26. New York: United Nations.

[6] United Nations. 2009. *Report of the Commission of Experts of the President of the United Nations General Assembly on Reforms of the International Monetary and Financial System.* New York: United Nations.

[7] As an anecdote, on June 27, 2009 and the following days, the international press focused attention on the death of pop star Michael Jackson rather than the agreement of all world governments to address the global crisis, despite press releases and a press conference by the UN.

UNICEF responded with *Adjustment with a Human Face,* which argued that children must and could be protected during economic crises and explained how this could be done—through more expansionary macro-programs, redirection of meso-policies to protect crucial social and economic sectors serving the poor, and the introduction of social protection programs.

Since then the world has generally acknowledged the critical importance of reducing poverty and of protecting children in difficult circumstances. Worldwide agreement on the MDGs is the outcome of this consensus.

Yet in 2008 a new global recession suddenly developed, the consequence of irresponsible lending by Western banks. The poor in developing countries are again suffering—this time from a crisis that is entirely due to actions taken in the developed world. It is critically important that this does not lead to a new lost decade, and that the poor, and especially children, do not suffer as they did in the 1980s.

Fortunately, the world has moved on since the 1980s and developing countries are more in control of their own destiny. Being less indebted, they do not need to turn to the IMF in large numbers; many have initiated their own macroeconomic stimulus instead of the cuts of the 1980s. More social protection programs are in place, like employment guarantee schemes, cash transfers and micro-finance. Nonetheless, many millions are likely to suffer from the depressed world markets, reduced employment and falling remittances.

It is of crucial importance for the poor of the world that as the global recession recedes there is 'Recovery with a Human Face,' that is, a recovery that is inclusive, expands employment opportunities, sustains health and education services, and provides support for those below the poverty line.

2.2.   The first phase of the crisis (2008-10)

Policy responses to the global economic crisis have varied around the world and over time. In hindsight, however, two distinct phases of the crisis clearly emerge. In a first phase, most governments launched fiscal stimulus plans in order to buffer their populations from the initial shocks. This new type of crisis response was characterized by expansionary policies, which differed significantly from the orthodox reactions of the past. Moreover, the expansionary approach created a general feeling of optimism, especially among those who had been emphasizing the importance of counter-cyclical macroeconomic policies even when the concept had been marginalized from the lexicon of mainstream economics (Ocampo).[8]

In theoretical terms, sound counter-cyclical macroeconomic policy should begin during boom periods to avoid accumulating unsustainable debts—both internal and external. Yet in the years preceding the crisis, support for such instruments was weak: the IMF had a pro-cyclical bias in its monetary policies, emerging and developing countries tended to have pro-cyclical macroeconomic policies that magnified rather than smoothed the effects of strong positive and negative external shocks (Chowdhury). Furthermore, it is now clear that the United States ran massive pro-cyclical policies during the 2003-07 boom, a factor that was a basic major force behind the financial crisis (Ocampo).

It was thus surprising to see the emergence of stimulus plans in the early stages of the crisis. In fact, the term 'counter-cyclical' came back with force during 2008-09: it was strongly endorsed by the G20, frequently heard from the IMF and even supported by some orthodox economists. While the size of fiscal stimuli varied from country to country, in general, the most massive Keynesian macroeconomic packages in history were put in place, including in some emerging markets. According to estimations for 48 countries, the total fiscal stimulus size amounted to US$2.4 trillion, which equaled nearly 4 percent of global GDP in 2008.[9] The data also confirm that some developing countries announced much bigger fiscal stimulus packages than many wealthier economies in terms of national GDP (Zhang, Thelen and Rao).

The size of these stimuli was indeed relevant, but perhaps even more so was their composition. In particular, most countries included significant measures to protect the most vulnerable members of society. On average, about 25 percent of fiscal stimulus funds were spent on social protection (see Chapter III). Cases were presented on Africa,[10] Asia and

---

[8] Ocampo, J.A. 2010. "The Return of Counter-cyclical Policies." *Journal of Globalization and Development* 1(1): 10.

[9] Zhang, Y., N. Thelen and A. Rao. 2010. "Social Protection in Fiscal Stimulus Packages: Some Evidence." UNDP/Office of Development Studies Working Paper, UNDP.

[10] Laryea-Adjei, G. 2010. *The Impact of the International Financial Crisis on Child Poverty in South Africa.* Johannesburg: UNICEF and Financial and Fiscal Commission, South Africa.

Latin America[11] (Jolly, Laryea-Adjei, Mesa-Lago). Such investments were critically important because they could directly help prevent vulnerable populations from losing their income, shedding their assets, or reverting to coping strategies that may be harmful to their current and future well-being (e.g., cutting household spending on health or child education). There are also long-term benefits to strengthening social protection systems. One of the outstanding features of developed welfare states is the existence of a well-functioning social protection system. Such systems are a key ingredient of sustainable economic growth and can provide pivotal help during recessionary periods. Looking at the labour market segment, for example, unemployment benefits coupled with active labour market policies, such as short-term public works programs, are counter-cyclical and act as automatic stabilizers if 'smartly' taking account of the diverse character of the sectors which are most vulnerable to economic contraction (Auer, Molyneux).

The renewed attention to social protection systems became apparent both at global and national levels. One major development at the global level was the agreement of the UN Chief Executive Board in early 2009 to the idea of the Global Social Protection Floor below which no person should fall. This initiative aims to support countries to establish a minimum level of access to essential services and income security for all (Cichon).[12] Generally, the pre-existence of strong social protection policies and institutions prior to the crisis facilitated quick responses, which highlights the need to build social protection systems in all countries. Additionally, at the International Labour Organization's (ILO) Conference in June 2009, governments, delegates of employers and workers from the ILO's Member States, unanimously adopted a 'Global Jobs Pact,' which was a set of job-centered policy measures that countries could adopt to ease the impact of the crisis.

Nevertheless, many argued that some counter-cyclical policies were weak during the global economic crisis, just as in previous crises. In Africa, for example, the experience was diverse, with some countries adopting counter-cyclical policies and others unable to do so (Ocampo). Furthermore, the growing evidence that the employment, human and

---

[11] Mesa-Lago, C. 2010. *World Crisis Effects on Social Security in Latin America and the Caribbean: Lessons and Policies.* London: University of London Institute for the Study of the Americas.
[12] ILO and WHO. 2009. *The Social Protection Floor Initiative.* Geneva: ILO and WHO.

social effects of the financial crisis would be felt well after an economic recovery had taken place called for (immaterialized) corrective actions in fiscal stimuli, with special attention to employment-generating activities and reducing income inequality at both national and international levels (van der Hoeven).

In reality, fiscal stimuli amounts paled in comparison to the elephantine size of funds that were devoted to bailing out the financial sector. While estimates vary widely, the IMF suggests that bank bailouts amounted to over US$9 trillion in the G20 alone, and this does not include the large bailouts in Spain, Ireland, Greece and other non-G20 countries. This should be contrasted to the approximately US$2.4 trillion of announced fiscal stimuli by governments, to the US$1 trillion called by the G20 to solve the global economic crisis or to the total global overseas development assistance (ODA) distributed to developing countries in 2008, which amounted to a meager US$0.1 trillion.

During 2009, the effects of the food, fuel and financial crises were increasingly felt by the poor in developing countries. In terms of declining household income, the number of unemployed persons jumped by 30 million to 210 million worldwide in less than two years (Torres,[13] Espey and Garde[14]). In terms of increasing hunger and malnutrition, UNICEF and the Food and Agriculture Organization (FAO) raised the alarm that persistently high food prices were likely causing irreversible damage to poor children and their families. And in terms of overall poverty rates, the World Bank estimated that on top of the millions already pushed into poverty in 2008-09, an additional 64 million people were likely to fall into extreme poverty during 2010.[15] The Asian Development Bank (ADB) showed the first impacts of this "triple F" crisis on poverty and sustainable development in Asia (Bauer),[16] also identified by Mehrotra.[17] Unfortunately, the adverse human impacts of the global economic crisis were only just beginning to gain momentum.

---

[13] ILO. 2011. *World of Work Report 2011*. Geneva: ILO.
[14] Espey, J. and M. Garde. 2010. "The Global Economic Crisis. Balancing the Books on the Backs of the World's Most Vulnerable Children?" G20 Brief, Save the Children UK.
[15] World Bank. 2010. *Global Monitoring Report 2010: The MDGs after the Crisis*. Washington, D.C.: World Bank.
[16] Bauer, A. and M. Thant (eds.). 2010. *Poverty and Sustainable Development in Asia: Impacts and Responses to the Global Economic Crisis*. Manila: ADB.
[17] Mehrotra, S. 2009. "The Impacts of the Economic Crisis on the Informal Sector and Poverty in East Asia." *Global Social Policy* XX(X): 1-19.

2.3.   The second phase of the crisis (2010-)

It was widely acknowledged that the implementation of counter-cyclical policies during the early stage of the crisis averted an immediate worldwide recession. This policy stance, however, was short-lived. Whereas most governments launched fiscal stimulus plans and policies that resulted in increased public spending during 2008-09, the expansionary trend came to an abrupt end in 2010, when, on top of the 'triple F' food, fuel and financial crises, a fourth 'F' shock began to sweep across developing countries: fiscal austerity. In February 2010, two IMF Board papers called for large-scale fiscal adjustment (e.g., reduction in government deficits) when "the recovery is securely underway" as well as for structural reforms in public finance to be initiated now "even in countries where the recovery is not yet securely underway."[18] While these papers were supposed to be focused on higher-income economies, they were the first signs of a worldwide policy reversal, which had the support of the G20.

The second phase of the crisis saw a sharp shift from fiscal stimulus to fiscal austerity, despite the weakness, unevenness and uncertainty of the economic upturn and the continued impacts on vulnerable populations in many countries (Jomo). Developed countries started to announce and implement severe cuts in government spending along with new taxes, which raised concerns of a double-dip recession. Governments started to argue that austerity was necessary in order to maintain the confidence of financial markets so that they could continue to sell bonds (Herman). The sudden turn to austerity was also driven by fear that if their budget deficits were too large, they may not be able to borrow enough at a reasonable rate of interest, and may be forced to default (Khor).

The rush toward austerity started in Europe, when the near debt default in Greece quickly instigated worries of contagion of sovereign debt crises to Portugal, Ireland and Spain, which were grouped under the derogatory acronym the 'PIGS.' In the periphery of Europe, many countries had been struggling to cope with the inadequate arrangements of the Euro. Moreover, other countries that were thought to be safe from the sovereign debt crisis soon came under question,

---

[18] IMF. 2010. Exiting from Crisis Intervention Policies. Washington, D.C.: IMF; IMF. 2010. Strategies for Fiscal Consolidation in the Post-Crisis World. Washington, D.C.: IMF.

including France and the United Kingdom. Overall, it comes as little surprise that European countries became the breeding ground for such fears since, unlike most governments, countries in the Eurozone do not have the option to print money or devalue their currency due to the loss of monetary policies from having joined a monetary union without other necessary measures such as an adequate fiscal union. As a result, Eurozone countries were forced to rely on private capital markets to meet their borrowing needs (Khor).

In Greece, financial markets began demanding higher returns in order to continue lending to the government. And by mid-2010, bond yields reached double-digits, making a bail out with loans from Europe and the IMF inevitable. With respect to Ireland, Paul Krugman noted that only a satirist could do justice to what was happening there. Once seen as a genuine economic miracle, Ireland's future was hastily transformed into a speculative frenzy driven by runaway banks and real estate developers, and financed with huge borrowing on the part of Irish banks, largely from other European banks. When the bubble burst and those banks faced huge losses, the Irish government stepped in to guarantee the banks' debt, turning private losses into public obligations. Ireland then tried to reassure the markets with a harsh program of spending cuts. The newly-incurred public debts were not used to pay for public programs, but rather to guarantee the profits of private wheeler-dealers who sought nothing but their own profit. Yet ordinary Irish citizens are now bearing the burden of those debts (Krugman).

Other contributors noted that European authorities—especially the European Central Bank (ECB)—seemed to be committed to punishing the weaker economies. In essence, governments were forced to cut spending even if it caused or deepened recession and mass unemployment (over 20 percent in Spain) as a requirement for the so-called 'trillion dollar bailout.' But where is the inflation that the ECB was so worried about? The Eurozone had 1 percent inflation in 2010. These pro-cyclical policies made things worse in the countries that adopted them, and reduced growth in the whole Eurozone (Weisbrot).

Even in the United Kingdom, where the government had the option to continue with fiscal stimulus, policymakers cut spending by £83 billion and raised taxes by £29 billion in 2010. Public outrage erupted when *The Guardian* obtained leaked documents from the Treasury and reported that austerity measures would likely cause 1.3 million job losses by 2015, of which 600,000 would be from the public sector and 700,000 from firms losing government contracts. The government responded by announcing that two million new private sector jobs would be created, which would more than offset the 600,000 lost in the public sector. This prediction, however, was met with skepticism (Khor).[19]

The shift to austerity reached the United States at a later time, but once it did, it arrived in full force. Earlier, the United States had criticized Germany for its focus on reducing the deficit and insisting that Greece and other countries implement austerity measures to qualify for bailout loans. In the second half of 2010, however, the United States began to change its position. The opposition to fiscal stimulus and further deficit growth by the Republicans and some Democrats in Congress ushered in an austerity consensus in policy circles. Since most of the states were already facing deep deficits, which made it increasingly difficult to get new loans, state governments began to scale back their spending. This, in turn, had an immediate effect on employment, aggregate demand, and social and human capital formation. The most adversely impacted, expectedly, were the poorest and most vulnerable in society (Khor, Wolf).

The resurgence of fiscal tightening also took hold in many developing countries, with policy pressure from the financial media and international financial institutions (Jomo; Ortiz, Chai and Cummins). During the first stage of the crisis, the IMF raised expectations about reforms in its fundamental policy approach to crisis response, seemingly abandoning neoliberal prescriptions. As the crisis evolved, however, it became clear that, in practice, there were few changes to its standard recommendations to developing countries on monetary and fiscal policies (McKinley).[20] According to critical voices, the IMF has failed to revise its rigid and traditional approach to macroeconomic policy guidelines, still basing its policy design on low fiscal deficits, low inflation rates, flexible exchange rates, and trade and financial

---

[19] Elliot, L. 2010. "Budget will Cost 1.3m Jobs – Treasury." *The Guardian*, June 29; Elliot, L. 2010. "Where will the Private Sector Jobs Come from?" *The Guardian*, June 30.
[20] McKinley, T. 2010. "Has the IMF Abandoned Neoliberalism?" Development Viewpoint No. 51, Centre for Development Policy and Research (CDPR); Van Waeyenberge, E., H. Bargawi and T. McKinley. 2010. *Standing in the Way of Development? A Critical Survey of the IMF's Crisis Response in Low-income Countries*. Brussels: Eurodad and Third World Network.

liberalization (Molina).[21] As later described in Chapter V, a significant number of developing countries have been contracting aggregate government spending since 2010, with the scope of austerity intensifying and widening quickly (e.g., 94 developing countries are expected to reduce annual expenditures during 2012). Perhaps more alarming, nearly one-quarter of developing countries appear to be undergoing excessive contraction, defined as cutting expenditures below pre-crisis levels in terms of GDP (Ortiz, Chai and Cummins). In other words, austerity is driving the global economy toward recession (Flassbeck).[22]

The disruption of recovery efforts through such premature calls for austerity have exacerbated unemployment and reduced social spending, further impeding progress toward the MDGs and other internationally-agreed development goals (Jomo).[23] Economists such as Robert Pollin, Gerald Epstein[24] and James Heintz[25] showed that alternative approaches to fiscal and monetary policies in low-income countries (LICs) are certainly possible (Hailu, Weeks),[26] but, first, the dominant neoliberal macroeconomic policy framework needs to be replaced with one that better emphasizes the long-neglected demand side (Rowden).

With the G8 struggling, the emerging economies, including China, Brazil, India and South Africa, were expected to lead global recovery in 2011. Yet these emerging market 'darlings' cannot save the world from economic stagnation. Even with three decades of growth and 1.3 billion people, China's economy still only contributes 13 percent of global output (as of 2010), which pales in significance when compared to the combined output of the developed world (55 percent). Brazil, India and South Africa are also relatively small players despite recent growth,

---

[21] Molina, N. 2010. *Bail-out or Blow-out? IMF Policy Advice and Conditions for Low-income Countries at a Time of Crisis.* Brussels: Eurodad.

[22] Flassbeck, H. 2011. "On the Brink: Fiscal Austerity Threatens a Global Recession." UNCTAD Policy Brief 24, UNCTAD.

[23] United Nations. 2011. *World Economic Situation and Prospects 2011.* New York: UN-DESA.

[24] Epstein, G. 2009. "Rethinking Monetary and Financial Policy: Practical Suggestions for Monitoring Financial Stability while Generating Employment and Poverty Reduction." Employment Sector Working Paper 37, ILO.

[25] Pollin, R. , G. Epstein and J. Heintz. 2008. "Pro-Growth Alternatives for Monetary and Financial Policies in Sub-Saharan Africa." IPC Policy Brief 6, UNDP International Policy Center for Inclusive Growth.

[26] Hailu, D. and J. Weeks. 2009. "Can Low-Income Countries Adopt Counter-Cyclical Policies?" One Pager No. 92, UNDP International Policy Centre for Inclusive Growth.

contributing 2.9, 5.5 and 0.7 percent, respectively, of world output (Chang).[27] Furthermore, emerging economies started to lose steam as global demand—led by high-income countries (HICs)—stagnated, questioning their export-oriented development approach and underscoring the need to develop their internal markets by raising domestic living standards. Moreover, while such belated recognition of a changed world economy was welcomed by many, it should be noted that this transformation is still not reflected in the governance structures of major international financial institutions. In sum, the BRICS are unlikely to be able to ensure a strong, protracted global economic 'Recovery for All' on their own (Jomo, Nayyar, Chang).

In this context, the G20 meetings attracted widespread public attention as the hope for decisive and coordinated action on global recovery, to manage global aggregate demand and exchange rates, to regulate the financial sector and to support populations. However, the shift from recovery efforts to fiscal consolidation and to hasty current account rebalancing has undermined the initial G20-led coordination of recovery efforts. Instead, finger-pointing grew in 2010, impeding policy coordination and cooperation—the very bases of the G20's earlier success (Jomo).

Furthermore, the G20 is being selective in the issues that it works on and looks to the private sector to come to the rescue where official cooperation lags (Herman).[28] This is most clearly evidenced in the activities and conclusions of the G20 Development Working Group, which was set up at the Seoul Summit in November 2010 as part of its Multi-Year Action Plan. One year later in Cannes, leaders introduced some discussion of ODA (albeit without meaningful commitments while referring to innovative sources of financing for development); made reference to environmental sustainability and the fight against climate change (alas, no progress here); and implicitly opened up an increasing role for the public sector in infrastructure investment (while mainly seeking ways to attract private investors). Moreover, the international social agenda seems to have been stripped down to nationally defined social protection floors (plural) for the poor (why not some international

---

[27] All GDP estimates based on PPP in current international $ from the World Bank's *World Development Indicators* (2012).
[28] Herman, B. 2011. "G20: Wrong International Forum for Development." The New School Working Paper.

guideline?) and worrying about the creation of decent jobs (without indicating how to do so in the current context of fiscal consolidation). While this may help, much more is needed from the G20 at this critical stage (Herman).

And a critical stage it is. In 2011, the world witnessed a global wave of social and political turmoil and instability: the Arab Spring, riots in the United Kingdom, middle-class protests in Israel, Chilean students taking to the streets, India's anti-corruption movement, mounting discontent with corruption and inequality in China, the *'indignados'* (outraged) in Spain and across Europe, and the 'Occupy Wall Street' movement in the United States. In different ways, these protests express the serious concerns of the world's working and middle classes about their prospects in the face of the growing concentration of power among economic, financial and political elites. The causes of their concern are clear enough: high unemployment and underemployment, resentment against corruption, including legalized forms like lobbying, and a sharp rise in income and wealth inequality (Roubini).

The need for broad-based, socially-inclusive and sustained recovery has never been greater. Some wonder how deep the crisis needs to be before leaders are compelled to act. Yet by then they will have created much unnecessary human suffering and despair (Chang), and for many millions of children around the world, it might simply be too late.

The next section presents a summary of the more detailed discussions of 'Recovery with a Human Face,' including: distributional impacts, employment and wages, food prices, debt and fiscal space for socio-economic recovery, a green new deal, retrogression in human rights, ideology and the crisis, and the need for equitable policies.

3.   Key Topics of the Global Economic Crisis

3.1.   Distributional impacts: Winners and losers

The crisis is having deep impacts on populations all over the world. Yet while the crisis was largely caused by a speculative frenzy driven by reckless bank lending practices in financial markets in the United States and Europe, the highest costs continue to be borne by ordinary citizens, especially by vulnerable populations, making them the real losers of the crisis. As described by Save the Children, the books are being balanced "on the backs of the world's most vulnerable children" (Espey and Garde).[29]

It must be noted that while the world has given top priority to real-time economic and financial data, global leaders have placed little urgency on acquiring time-sensitive social indicators. As a result, while we know today's exchange rates, inflation levels, interest rates, trade volumes and stock market indices, we don't have real-time data on malnourishment, hunger or other deprivations that are affecting children and their families. With the exception of unemployment information, comprehensive data that allow us to evaluate the full aggregate impacts of the crisis are not yet available in 2012. Additionally, many of the human impacts associated with prolonged bouts of malnutrition, such as poor health and rising mortality rates, may only appear in the longer-term.

Still there is significant evidence emerging from ad hoc surveys and studies. For example, the UN Report on the *World Social Situation 2011: The Global Social Crisis*[30] shows a wide range of negative social impacts lingering from the economic downturn, such as increased poverty, unemployment, malnutrition, crime, domestic violence and substance abuse (Lee). As noted earlier, the World Bank estimated that an additional 64 million people could fall into extreme poverty during 2010 due to the combined and lingering effects of the crisis. In addition, the Women in Informal Employment: Globalizing and Organizing (WIEGO) showed the effects of the crisis on the urban working poor: home-based producers, street vendors and waste pickers had to work much longer hours to survive (Chen, Horn).[31] Moreover, Oxfam found that poor families were exhausting available coping strategies in 2008-09, such as eating fewer meals, cutting family expenditures on health and other areas, increasing debt and working longer hours in the informal sector (King).[32]

---

[29] Espey, J. and M. Garde. 2010. "The Global Economic Crisis. Balancing the Books on the Backs of the World's Most Vulnerable Children?" G20 Brief, Save the Children UK.
[30] United Nations. 2011. *World Social Situation 2011: The Global Social Crisis*. New York: UN-DESA.
[31] Horn, Z. 2009. "No Cushion to Fall Back On: The Global Economic Crisis and Informal Workers," Inclusive Cities Study. Cambridge: WIEGO. And Horn, Z. 2011. "Coping with Crises: Lingering Recession, Rising Inflation and the Informal Workforce," Inclusive Cities Study. Cambridge: WIEGO.
[32] Green, D., R. King and M. Miller-Dawkins. 2010. *The Global Economic Crisis and Developing Countries: Impact and Response.* Oxford: Oxfam GB.

Employment data reflect that high unemployment continues to affect much of the globe. ILO labour statistics showed a distressing increase in unemployment—both in terms of the overall rate and number of persons—in 2010 and 2011 in many developing countries. Mass unemployment in higher-income countries precipitated a fall in international remittances since 2009. The World Bank estimated that remittances to LICs declined by almost 7 percent in 2009, to US$317 billion. This posed a huge threat to poor households, who in the face of external shocks, commonly depend on remittances to purchase essential foodstuffs, send children to school and receive healthcare (Espey and Garde). Furthermore, UNICEF reported that reduced remittances were having an impact on children left behind.[33]

Households have also been dealing with unabatedly high food prices since 2008. According to the FAO's Food Price Index, global food prices surpassed the peak levels of the 2007-08 food crisis by January 2011 and continued to set new record highs, adding further hardship to poor families. UNICEF reported increased incidences of hunger and malnutrition in 2008-09, deterioration in acute malnutrition in Afghanistan, the Niger, Sierra Leone and Uganda, and higher acute malnutrition rates among the urban poor of Cambodia, Kenya,[i] the Republic of Congo and Tanzania. More on unemployment and food security can be found in later sections.

In an environment of increasing risks to poor households, levels of public assistance appear to be diminishing. As discussed in Chapter V, 133 countries are expected to reduce public expenditures in 2012, 94 of them developing countries, and 39 countries are undergoing excessive contraction.[34] While aggregate budget cuts are likely affecting social sector allocations, UNICEF analysis further shows that the main austerity measures being considered by governments to achieve expenditure consolidation are posing serious threats to vulnerable children and their families. In particular:

-   *Wage bill cuts or caps* are under consideration in 73 countries. This fiscal consolidation strategy can jeopardize the delivery of essential

---

[33] UNICEF. 2010. "The Children Left Behind: A League Table of Inequality in Child well-being in the World's Rich Countries." Innocenti Research Center Report Card 9. Florence: UNICEF Innocenti Research Centre.

[34] Defined as cutting 2012 spending below pre-crisis levels in terms of GDP (see Chapter V).

services to children and poor families through lower salaries and/or numbers of teachers, medical staff and social workers. Low pay is also a key factor behind absenteeism, informal fees and brain drain, which can further hinder service delivery, especially in rural areas. For example, the real pay of teachers and nurses decreased by 20-30 percent in LICs such as the Democratic Republic of Congo, Madagascar, the Sudan and Yemen in the first years of the crisis.[35]

-   *Reducing or removing subsidies*, such as those supporting food or fuel prices, is being considered in another 73 developing countries, including many LICs. When basic subsidies are withdrawn, food and transport costs increase and become unaffordable for many households; higher energy prices also tend to contract employment-generating economic activities. Given that malnutrition inflicts irreversible physical and mental harm on infants and young children, it is important that food subsidies are maintained unless a well-functioning social protection system is in place that can ensure that vulnerable populations have adequate access to food and nutrition.

-   *Rationalizing social protection schemes* is another common cost-cutting option being considered in 55 countries, including the reform of old-age pensions in another 52 countries. This is expected to be achieved through reducing coverage or benefits, often by further targeting social safety nets. This policy approach runs a high risk of excluding large segments of vulnerable populations—either through timing mismatches or exclusion errors—at a time when they are most in need.

Big spending cuts took place at federal, state and local levels in the United States during 2011. The immediate impact has been lower high school graduation rates, higher child poverty and a high percentage of children without health insurance. The call for austerity also brought steep spending cuts to Medicaid, a public program that is vital to protecting the health of many of the country's most disadvantaged children. In Texas, for example, the proposed funding cuts to Medicaid amounted to a staggering 30 percent, while, in terms of education, school administrators talked about laying off as many as 100,000 public

---

[35] Chai, J., I. Ortiz and X. Sire. 2010. "Protecting Salaries of Frontline Teachers and Health Workers." Social and Economic Policy Working Brief, UNICEF.

employees (Krugman). In response to these drastic cuts, many have called attention to the US$15 billion that Goldman Sachs set aside to compensate its executives at a time when the state of California was slashing its education budget by US$1.5 billion (Wolff).[36]

An analysis of the winners and losers of the crisis must further consider that, particularly in the economies of the Organisation for Economic Co-operation and Development (OECD), a large share of stimulus packages included tax cuts, mainly through reductions in personal income tax for the wealthy. Thus, ironically, while fiscal stimulus packages mainly benefited wealthier income groups—not the poor—during the first phase of the crisis, budget cuts are disproportionately impacting the poor during the second phase. The massive bailouts for the financial industry further indicate that the real problem in addressing this global crisis was not the availability of money, but rather the lack of political will. In fact, the amount of money needed annually to achieve the MDGs is a miniscule fraction of the estimated trillions of public money that was mobilized for bank bailouts (Caliari).[37]

The *Social Watch Report 2012: The Right to a Future*[38] argued that countries like Brazil, China and India, in which fiscal stimulus programs were largely directed to support the poor in different ways, have recovered faster from the crisis than industrialized countries, which, on the contrary, bailed out banks and gave tax breaks to the wealthy. In these major emerging economies, public expenditures were directed to protecting jobs and wages, expanding social services and/or providing income support to the poor through direct cash transfers (Bissio). The alternative approach adopted by many HICs casts doubts over their long-run capabilities, especially when the future labour force is blighted by childhood poverty, bad health and poor education. In response to this reality, Paul Krugman asked, what is supposed to happen when today's neglected children become tomorrow's work force?

---

[36] Wolf, R. 2011. "Bonuses for Bankers, Bankruptcy for Public Services." *The Guardian*, January 20.

[37] ESCR-Net. 2011. *Bringing Human Rights to Bear in Times of Crisis: A human rights analysis of government responses to the economic crisis.* New York: International Network for Economic, Social and Cultural Rights (ESCR-Net).

[38] Social Watch. 2012. *Social Watch Report 2012: The Right to a Future.* Montevideo: Social Watch.

3.2.   Employment and wages

One of the most visible effects of the economic crisis in both developing and developed countries is widespread unemployment and underemployment. It must be noted that unemployment rates are insufficient indicators since they typically only capture those persons claiming unemployment benefits, which are usually confined to a limited number of months, and hide the long-term unemployed. At the global level, trends in the employment-to-population ratio—a more robust indicator—powerfully illustrate that many economies are simply not generating sufficient job opportunities to absorb the growth in working-age populations. As detailed in Chapter IV, more than 120 million potential new young workers are entering the global labour market each year, nearly 90 percent of which are from developing countries.

The ILO's *World of Work Report 2011*[39] warned that the cooling global economy risks pushing the world into a double-dip jobs recession and triggering an outbreak of social strife unless governments take urgent action to stimulate employment growth. The report goes on to paint a grim picture of the future of global employment. While private enterprises are in an even weaker position to retain employees since the start of the crisis, austerity measures are contributing to the growing numbers of unemployed (Torres). The picture is even bleaker when considering the unemployment rate for youth, which jumped to unprecedented levels in many countries (Nayyar); the percent increase in youth unemployment globally was over twice that for the overall working population (Miller).

Yet the crisis merely exacerbated existing labour market vulnerabilities that had developed during the years of jobless growth leading up to it, which brings into question the long-term sustainability of the growth/employment model of development. While generating decent employment is generally acknowledged as a primary development objective, the pattern of job creation in recent years has been the opposite: increased labour insecurity and segmented labour markets characterized by large wage differentials. Moreover, the record of the past 30 years has shown not only that global growth is in long-term

---

[39] ILO. 2011. *World of Work Report 2011*. Geneva: ILO.

decline (excluding the exceptional spike achieved in 2003-07 in a few higher-income countries thanks to unsustainable credit and housing bubbles), but that higher productivity has led to lower employment elasticity, such that even in a high growth economy like China, manufacturing employment has fallen considerably from its peak in 1995 (Shutt).

Furthermore, over the last two decades, rising non-standard and informal employment have become important factors of personal income and factor inequality (van der Hoeven). For example, there has been a continuing shift from protected employees, with high lay-off costs and generous enterprise benefits, to two forms of temporary workers with much lower wages and benefits (no paid holidays, maternity leave, sickness leave, pension benefits, and so on). There has also been a growth of outsourcing to contractors and labour brokers. The discussion further questioned how governments are to support employment by liberalizing their labour laws at a time of declining labour demand (Ugarteche, Rodrik).

Beyond employment, another main issue is labour market liberalization and the erosion of social guarantees. The more urgent reforms being pushed through many legislatures largely aim at reducing the cost of firing workers and making it easier for employers to dismiss them. The assumption is that, at the same level of aggregate demand, employers are more reluctant to hire workers when they expect to be unable to dismiss them during a downturn (or that it will be prohibitively costly to do so). This can then keep unemployment high (Ranis). These reforms are being pursued even in economies, such as Spain, where unemployment has risen to 23 percent—with youth unemployment affecting nearly 50 percent of those aged 16-24—and domestic demand has yet to recover.[40]

However, the experience of several countries suggests that there is not a direct relationship between the liberalization of labour markets and more employment generation or the reduction in informal unemployment. For example, Chile and Colombia liberalized labour legislation and reduced the costs of hiring and firing workers, but

---

[40] Economist Intelligence Unit. 2012. "Spain Economy: Labour Pains." *ViewsWire*, February 07.

unemployment remains high and informal unemployment has grown larger (Puyana).

While the proletariat is being squeezed, a global 'precariat' is emerging and increasing in size. In an open economic system, labour market convergence has been promoted, which inevitably impacts earnings and social benefits (Standing, van Ginneken). With wages in emerging economies one-fiftieth of those in OECD countries, that had to mean sharp falls in the latter, which was politically intolerable. The decline in wages and benefits was offset in ways designed to slow the transfer of industrial jobs to emerging market economies, through subsidies, tax credits and cheap credit. For two decades, center-right and social democratic governments accepted this 'Faustian' bargain (Standing).

This has contributed to the emergence of the 'precariat,' which is a class-in-the-making. In particular, a large and growing number of people across the world are living and working precariously, usually in a series of short-term jobs, without recourse to stable occupational identities or careers, without reliable social protection support and without protective regulations that are relevant to them. The 'precariat'—as this new class has been coined—could potentially produce new instabilities in society. They are increasingly frustrated and dangerous because they have no voice, and hence they are vulnerable to the siren calls of extreme political parties (Standing).[41]

This long-predicted explosive mixture of youth demographics (the 'youth bulge') and high rates of unemployment formed the basis for the Arab Spring that transformed the Middle East and North Africa. It was not only unemployment that drove young people to the streets, but the unfairness of this unemployment (Miller). These developments reflect the fact that adjustment policies in the 1980's, market liberalization policies in the 1990's and, more recently, globalization and anti-poverty policies in the 2000's did not pay sufficient explicit attention to policies for employment and income redistribution (van der Hoeven).

Social and political turmoil and instability was not limited to contexts with this demographic composition, however. Masses of people poured into the real and virtual streets around the world. These various

---

[41] Standing, G. 2011. *The Precariat – The New Dangerous Class*. London: Bloomsbury.

protests and manifestations expressed in different ways the serious concerns of the world's working and middle classes, with high unemployment and underemployment in advanced and emerging economies, and inadequate skills and education for young people and workers to compete in a globalized world (Roubini).[42]

These are some of the imbalances and consequences of globalization that have been exacerbated by the crisis. Dani Rodrik argued that from the mercantile monopolies of seventeenth-century empires to the modern-day authority of the World Trade Organization (WTO), the IMF and the World Bank, nations have struggled to effectively harness globalization's promise.[43] The decrease in productivity differentials between the North and the South led to a 'race to the bottom.' In particular, many companies have shifted their operations to the South seeking cheap labour, lower taxes or tax avoidance, subsidies from governments, and lax social and environmental regulations, among others. The present model of globalization forces Southern countries into global tax and subsidy competition in order to attract investors at a cost to their people (Kelles-Viitanen). India's Ministry of Finance has, for example, been calculating how much tax revenue the country is losing in this manner, money which is direly needed for social programs.

A mechanism proposed to avoid this 'race to the bottom' is a global minimum wage system.[44] That does not mean imposing United States or European minimum wages in developing countries, but rather establishing a global set of rules for setting country minimum wages. Traditionally, minimum wage systems set a fixed wage that is periodically adjusted. Such an approach, however, is fundamentally flawed and inappropriate for the global economy. Instead, countries could set a minimum wage that is a fixed percent (say 50 percent) of their median wage. This design has several advantages, including: (i) the minimum wage will automatically rise with the median wage, creating a true floor that moves with the economy; (ii) the minimum wage is set by reference to local economic conditions and reflects what a country can bear; (iii) countries can still set a higher minimum wage if so desired;

---

[42] Roubini, N. 2011. "The Instability of Inequality." *Project Syndicate*, October 13.

[43] Rodrik, D. 2011. *The Globalization Paradox: Democracy and the Future of the World Economy.* New York: W. W. Norton & Company.

[44] Palley, T. 2012. *From Financial Crisis to Stagnation: The Destruction of Shared Prosperity and the Role of Economic Ideas.* Cambridge: Cambridge University Press.

and (iv) the global minimum wage system would only set a floor, not a ceiling (Palley).

Falling short of purporting a global minimum wage, other contributors discussed how government budgets need to include programs to support employment, not just in terms of regulation, but also through active labour market strategies, such as wage matching schemes or public work schemes that guarantee a minimum level of employment at minimum wage. An increase in the share of wages in GDP would be conducive to growth everywhere, which is possible if wages keep pace with productivity growth and full employment is the primary objective (Nayyar).[45] Corrective actions need to be taken, and fiscal stimuli should give special attention to employment and contribute to reducing income inequality; these types of policies should now become an integral part of national and international economic policymaking (van der Hoeven).[46]

The issue of employment creation has become even more pressing given the demographics in many countries around the world. Policymakers, driven as much by fear as by a desire for social justice, are grappling with how to create employment for young people. The conventional wisdom on youth employment privileges two approaches: (i) vocational education and training; and (ii) entrepreneurship development for self-employment. However, these approaches are not solving the jobs problem. Perhaps rather than telling young people that unemployment is their own fault since they are not ready for the labour market, or that they should create their own job through self-employment, it is time to consider approaches that create new, additional and decent jobs for those entering the labour market, namely young people (Miller).[47]

Decent jobs will require different national development strategies that focus on employment-sensitive macroeconomic and sector policies and

[45] Nayyar, D. 2011. "The Financial Crisis, the Great Recession and the Developing World." *Global Policy* 2(1): 20-32.
[46] van der Hoeven, R. 2010. "Employment, Inequality and Globalization: A Continuous Concern." *Journal of Human Development and Capabilities* 11(1): 1-9.
[47] Lal, R., S. Miller, M. Lieuw-Kie-Song and D. Kostzer. 2010. "Public Works and Employment Programmes: Toward a Long-term Development Approach." Working Paper No. 66, UNDP International Policy Centre for Inclusive Growth.

labour policies and standards.[48] On the one hand, monetary and fiscal policies could aim to boost aggregate demand (e.g., a tight monetary policy focused on containing inflation does not generate jobs), while exchange rate, technology and trade policies could prioritize stimulating output growth, accompanied by gradual and sequential trade opening to support it. On the other hand, given that most poor people work long hours but are unable to bring their families out of poverty, employment policies must not solely focus on creating jobs but also on ensuring adequate wages, labour standards and working conditions (Ortiz).

3.3.   Food prices

The financial crisis exacerbated already high food prices throughout the world, ushering in new spikes. The United Nations Conference on Trade and Development (UNCTAD) shows that commodity price indices displayed record volatility from 2001 through 2010, climbing at an annual average rate of 12.2 percent per year, a sharp change from the two preceding decades when they increased by only 0.5 percent per year (1981 to 1990) and then fell by 1.3 percent per year (1991 to 2000). The price of cereals, an important food staple that accounts for more than two-thirds of dietary calories among populations in many developing countries, jumped a staggering 57 percent from June to December 2010 (Flassbeck).[49] The price of rice, the most important staple food for much of the world's population, showed the sharpest increases between 2001 and 2010, climbing by an average of 15 percent per year. In January 2011, the international food price index surpassed levels reached during the 2007-08 food crisis (Ortiz, Chai and Cummins).[50]

Extreme price movements of agricultural commodities not only threaten the food security of millions of people but also the economic recovery and social stability of developing countries. Soaring global food prices are due to a variety of factors. While some quote weather shocks or the rise of Chinese and Indian food demand, many point to the rapid increase and high volatility of primary commodity prices, which correlate to heightened speculative activity in commodity futures markets in recent years. Interestingly, aggregate food grain

---

[48] United Nations. 2008. *National Development Strategies, Policy Notes*. New York: UN-DESA.

[49] UNCTAD. 2011. *Handbook of Statistics*. Geneva: UNCTAD.

[50] Chapter III.

consumption in both China and India actually decreased when global food prices were rising sharply in 2007-08. Subsequently, food price volatility has not been associated with real demand and supply movements. For example, global wheat prices doubled between June and December 2010 when global wheat output actually increased. This was driven partly by fears generated by the failure of the Ukraine harvest and the Russian ban on wheat exports, but largely powered by financial activity in futures markets (Ghosh).[51][52][53]

A similar story was seen with copper, which accounts for over half of Chile's exports. While the price of copper peaked above US$4.00 per pound in 2007-08, right in the midst of the crisis, at the same time demand was contracting severely and output was still expanding. Within a few days, however, copper prices collapsed to US$1.40 per pound, only to rise again to new record highs (US$4.50 per pound) during 2011. These price movements correlated perfectly, not to the increase of global demand, which has in fact stagnated, or to output, which has continued to increase, but rather to monetary expansion, mainly in the United States (Riesco).

Some contributors questioned whether the recent volatility in commodity markets may precipitate another financial crisis. Akyüz and Pettifor noted that there have been three generalized boom-bust cycles in private capital flows since the end of the Second World War, all with devastating impacts on developing and emerging markets. The first started in the late 1970s and ended with the Latin American debt crisis in the early 1980s. The second began in the early 1990s, which was followed by the East Asian financial crisis of 1997-98 as well as sovereign defaults in Latin America and the Russian Federation. And the third cycle commenced in the early years of the new millennium, ending in the second half of 2008 with the subprime mortgage crisis. However, this was quickly followed by a new boom, a boom of commodity markets which have become like financial markets. This fourth boom in

---

[51] Ghosh, J. 2009. "The Unnatural Coupling: Food and Global Finance." *Journal of Agrarian Change* 10(1): 72-86.
[52] UNCTAD. 2011. *Price Volatility in Food and Agricultural Markets: Policy Responses*. Geneva: UNCTAD.
[53] UNCTAD. 2011. *Price Formation in Financialized Commodity Markets: The Role of Information*. Geneva: UNCTAD.

the post-war era started in the first half of 2009 and continues in full force in 2012 (Pettifor).[54]

The impact of this trend on households at the local level is devastating. While international prices are volatile, an analysis of local food prices in 55 developing countries by UNICEF (Ortiz, Chai and Cummins) found that, on the aggregate, domestic food price levels are sticky and have remained alarmingly high compared to pre-2007-08 crisis levels (about 80 percent higher, on average, in early 2012 compared to May 2007), implying that poor and vulnerable populations in many developing countries have been relentlessly coping with high food costs. Since 2008 poor households have exhausted coping strategies, and their capacity for resilience is very limited in 2012, as reflected in Chapter III.

Living on a Spike, a report by Oxfam and the Institute of Development Studies,[55] provides valuable insights on the impacts of high food prices over time. Using focus groups and other participatory techniques in eight community 'listening posts' in Bangladesh, Indonesia, Kenya and Zambia, the study finds that the recent food price spike has increased inequality, producing a pattern of "weak losers and strong winners." The losers—those already struggling in low-paid, informal sector occupations, such as petty trading, street vending, casual construction work, sex work, laundry, portering and transport—are doing worse. Despite the high price of food, small-scale farmers and small market food traders have also fared poorly. In particular, increased input costs and the squeeze on people's purchasing power have meant that profits from growing and selling food remain low. And this is affecting those persons who have very limited capacity to diversify and spread their risk (Green).

People are adjusting to high food prices in complex ways. While some are eating less and going hungry, the more common pattern is to shift to lower quality and less diverse diets. The effects differ greatly by gender: women come under more pressure to provide good meals with less food, and they also feel the stresses of coping with their children's hunger most directly. Oftentimes, women simply go without eating.

---

[54] Akyüz, Y. 2011. "Coming Soon: Another Global Financial Crash? Capital Mobility and the Commodity Mania." *Debtonation*, May 10.

[55] Hossain, N. and D. Green. 2011. *Living on a Spike: How is the 2011 Food Price Crisis Affecting Poor People?* Oxford: Institute of Development Studies and Oxfam GB.

These stresses push women into poorly paid informal sector work, competing among themselves for increasingly inadequate earnings. Men also feel the effects: the food price rises severely undercut their ability to provide for their families, leading to arguments in the household and fuelling alcohol abuse and domestic violence. Governments have provided some support, but this has generally failed to adequately protect people from the effects of rising prices (Green).

Young urban men appear particularly angry about the failure of governments to act. With revolutions in the Middle East and North Africa and other protests against governments in Europe, the stress and discontent fuelled by high food prices merits close attention by the G20 agriculture ministers (Green). To restore the price stability, which is in the interest of farmers as well as consumers (but not of speculators), a twin-track approach of short- and long-term interventions is needed to support consumers and poverty reduction, boost agricultural production, and reverse much of the deregulation of global markets that has occurred over the past 30 years (see Chapter III).

3.4.   Debt and fiscal space for socio-economic recovery

Public and private debt has been at the center of recovery debates. Massive borrowing led Greece, Ireland, Portugal, Spain, Italy and other countries into massive sovereign debt crises. But how did this borrowing frenzy start? Mediocre income growth for everyone but the rich in the last few decades opened a gap between incomes and spending aspirations. In Anglo-Saxon countries, the response was to democratize credit thereby fueling a rise in private debt, with households borrowing to make up the difference (Fortin, Taylor, Wolff). In Europe, the gap was filled by public services, including free education and healthcare, which were not fully financed by taxes and fueled public deficits and debt. In both cases, debt levels eventually became unsustainable (Roubini).

In the United States, where a deficit ceiling showdown took place, politicians did not explore alternatives to massive deficits and debts because government deficits and debts mean: (i) the government is not taxing corporations and the rich; and (ii) the government is instead borrowing from them and paying them interest. So the two ruling parties quibbled over how much to cut and which government jobs and public services. Yet the tax burdens of corporations and the richest citizens in the United States are significantly lower than in most other advanced industrial economies. Shifting the burden of federal taxation from corporations to individuals and from the richest individuals to the rest of the population contributed to the massive deficits and debts. Instead of correcting and reversing that unjust shift, politicians instead plan to deal with this by cutting social expenditures that help vulnerable populations (Wolff).

In Europe, Greece, Ireland, Portugal, Spain and Italy had been struggling to cope with the inadequate arrangements of the Euro. As previously stated, countries in the Eurozone do not have the option to print money or devalue their currency due to the loss of monetary policies. As a result, they have been forced to rely on private capital markets to lend to them (Khor, Weisbrot, Vernengo).

The focus on debt/deficit reduction ushered in a second phase of the crisis, which saw a great push for austerity. This, combined with an increased pressure for fiscal consolidation, severely limited fiscal and policy space in developed economies. Many developing countries also came under pressure to cut public expenditures, undertake austerity measures, reduce the scope of government action and further liberalize labour markets (Lee).

Austerity led activists and academics around the world to begin questioning the legitimacy of the debt that was provoking such harsh and damaging measures. It was argued that public debt operates like a mask behind which lies a shadowy world of creditors who have entire economies mortgaged to them. The necessity for lifting the mask has been brought up in many countries, and some have indeed achieved this through the mechanism of debt audits. The aim of such initiatives is to untangle the web of secrecy around public debt and to work out who lent what to whom, when and for what purpose. There is typically an expectation that at least a portion of the debt will be found to be 'illegitimate,' and can therefore be repudiated. In Europe, campaigns for debt audits also have an important educational function. People in core countries, including Germany, do not seem to have yet grasped the reality that the loans provided by the European Union (EU) and the IMF are not bailing out Mediterranean and Irish citizens, but rather private banks that engaged in profitable and irresponsible lending throughout the 2000s (Lapavitsas, Storey).[56]

In 2008, Ecuador became the first country to hold an official audit to assess the legitimacy of its sovereign debt.[57] The government-commissioned, two year-long investigation concluded that some of its foreign debts had broken multiple principles of international and domestic law and were therefore deemed 'illegitimate'—these were mostly private sector debts that had been nationalized by former governments. While Ecuador respected all of the debt that had contributed to the country's development—the so-called 'legitimate' debt—it defaulted on its alleged illegitimate debt in November 2008 and bought this back at 35 cents to the dollar just a few weeks later. Based on the experience of Ecuador, as well as Norway, a special UN Commission of Experts on Reforms of the International Monetary and Financial System came out in support of public debt audits as a mechanism for transparent and fair restructuring of debts. Debt audits are ongoing in several other countries, such as Bolivia, Brazil, Greece, Ireland and the Philippines (Lapavitsas, Storey).

In Ireland, a debt audit proved conclusively that the Irish debt crisis is a crisis of private (subsequently socialized) debt and not public debt.[58] In particular, the allegedly 'bloated' nature of public services, or 'generous' welfare entitlements, did not cause the sovereign debt crisis. In fact, the audit found that "the bulk of Irish government debt [arose] directly from the banking crisis, the decision in September 2008 to rescue all of the Irish banks." The lack of transparency means that faceless market actors are exercising enormous influence over Irish government policy, which violates fundamental democratic principles that power should be exercised in an open and accountable manner (Storey).

Similarly, a national referendum was held in Iceland in March 2010 that allowed its citizens to vote on whether and how the country should repay its debts claimed by the Netherlands and the United Kingdom. This was not a sovereign debt issue; a private Icelandic bank held €6.7

---

[56] Lapavitsas, C. and A. Storey. 2011. "Can Europe Escape the Debt Trap? Yes—and Here's How." *The Guardian*, May 04.
[57] Auditing Commission of Public Debt in Ecuador. 2008. *Final Report of the Integral Audit of Ecuador's Debt.* Quito: Government of the Republic of Ecuador, Ministry of Finance; Jubilee Debt Campaign. 2008. "Ecuador Delivers Historic Audit." *Jubilee Debt Campaign News*, October 16.
[58] Killian, S., J. Garvey and F. Shaw. 2011. *An Audit of Irish Debt.* Limerick: University of Limerick.

billion in deposits from British and Dutch savers, and, when it collapsed, the respective governments decided to make this debt public. In the referendum, Icelandic voters delivered a resounding 'no' (more than 90 percent) to reimburse the Dutch and British governments and the orthodox policies that would have accompanied the debt repayment plan. The recent referendum in Iceland and social debt audits, such as in Ecuador, underscore the idea that citizens have concerns about illegitimate sovereign debt and the high social costs.

Legitimate or not, countries need to work out their debt problems. At present, there are no adequate forums to do this. The absence of a restructuring mechanism is both costly, unfair and a glaring gap in international financial architecture. Many countries, if not this time then the next, will need to reschedule, restructure or even default on their debt (Herman). Thus more often than not, debt workouts result in crisis-stricken debtors and disgruntled creditors. This gaping systemic 'hole' has resulted in enormous IMF and national government bailouts, from US$50 billion for Mexico's peso ('tequila') crisis to a staggering US$1,000 billion for Europe's current crisis.[59] These bailouts go the pockets of private creditors and are paid for by taxpayers and citizens across the world.

Every crisis has spawned an effort to create a just system for sovereign debt restructuring. Mexico proposed a mechanism in 1933, Harry Dexter White included such a function in his initial drafts of the IMF articles in the 1940s, UNCTAD saw such a regime as core to a 'New International Economic Order' in the 1970s, and, most recently, the IMF issued a call for a 'Sovereign Debt Restructuring Mechanism' in the wake of Argentina's financial crisis. Each time such attempts have failed, largely because creditors like the upper hand they currently hold and because debtor nations are wary of supporting such an initiative in fear that they might be seen as default-prone. Leadership is thus in order. While up to this point the G20 has been little more than a talk shop, it should take the lead in creating a just, sovereign, debt-restructuring facility (Gallagher).[60] [61]

---

[59] New York Times Editorial. 2011. "Europe's Bailout." *New York Times*, May 10.
[60] Gallagher, K. 2011. "The New Vulture Culture: Sovereign Debt Restructuring and Trade and Investment Treaties." IDEAs Working Paper No. 02/2011, International Development Economics Associates (IDEAS).
[61] UNCTAD. 2011. "Sovereign Debt Restructuring and International Investment Agreements." IIA Issues Note No. 2, UNCTAD.

The capacity to sustain a given level of public debt is a function of investors' perception of the ability of a government to service that debt. This depends on different factors that vary by country. In many countries, there seems to be a belief that stimulus-based policies will ultimately succeed in restoring equilibrium without any need for substantially writing off massive debts crippling the world economy. Yet the reality is more akin to the situation facing Argentina ten years ago, which was only resolved by substantial debt default. At the global level, of course, such a wholesale repudiation of debt—entailing huge capital destruction—would have catastrophic financial, macroeconomic and social consequences, which could only be alleviated by drastic remedial state intervention. Thus any realistic 'Plan B' must entail collective action on a massive scale—at both national and international levels—to support activity and protect the most vulnerable. Global elites, who stand to lose the most from the inevitable wipe-out of so much debt and equity, will of course do anything to avoid recognizing this reality. But if we are serious about averting global disaster and giving hope to the world's poor, there is little choice but to confront large-scale default. In the aftermath, it will be essential to reorder economic priorities, placing less emphasis on growth and more on equitable income distribution (Shutt).

The idea of insolvency protection for member of the EU has been voiced officially. While this is a step in the right direction, there is no logical justification for this solution to be restricted to European countries and not be available to any others. The 'Fair Transparent Arbitration Process' has been suggested by Kunibert Raffer.[62] Unlike the 'Sovereign Debt Restructuring Mechanism,' this proposal treats everybody correctly, does not discriminate against the private sector and does not legalize a preferred creditor status of multilateral institutions, such as the IMF, whose de facto and illegal enforcement makes debt management so much more difficult (Raffer).[63]

Still many efforts toward financial reform can get snared in existing treaties. For example, sovereign debt restructuring could be deemed

[62] Raffer, K. 2011. "Arbitration to Solve the Debt Problem." In B. Herman, F. Pietracci and K. Sharma eds., *Financing for Development, Proposals from Business and Civil Society*. New York: United Nations University Press.

[63] Raffer, K. 2002. "Memorandum, Select Committee on International Development, Appendix 15." United Kingdom Parliament.

illegal under thousands of international trade and investment agreements. In effect, private bondholders can sue a government for reducing the value of the initial bond purchase if a debt restructuring violates clauses of national treatment, expropriation, or fair and equitable treatment. Such treaties thus undermine the ability of nations to recover from financial crises and broaden the impact of such crises. This underscores the importance of reforming trade and investment agreements so that they grant nations and the international community the policy space to prevent and mitigate financial crises (Gallagher).

The e-discussion also called attention to past lessons. In many regards, the situation of Greece, Ireland, Portugal, Spain or Italy today is similar to that of African countries in the mid-1980s, which were crippled by similar debt crises and subjected to external monitoring and interference. Rigorous monetarist discipline not only stopped growth in its tracks, but also undermined human welfare and, in many cases, destroyed the social contract. Progressive economists in the 1980s coalesced around the idea of 'Adjustment with a Human Face,' accepting the need for macroeconomic stabilization and structural reform, but also insisting on protecting the most vulnerable populations and ensuring the delivery of basic social services. In other words, this approach recognized that structural adjustment is a necessary process but that it also has high human costs. Poor people need to be supported as consumers and also as producers, and the international community has to cohere around high-level human development goals. Financing is key, including, if appropriate, through debt relief (Maxwell).

A policy proposal that re-gained momentum in the wake of the crisis was a global financial transaction tax. More commonly known as the 'Tobin tax' after the Nobel Prize economist who first proposed it, a financial transaction tax has been widely considered by the IMF and many countries in Europe, including the EU. And there is a strong chance that it will someday be implemented, in spite of the financial sector's resistance (Kelles-Viitanen). At a global level, such a tax could reduce speculation and inequality, and bring in new money to fund government expenditures (van Ginneken). A Tobin tax could also help balance the distribution of taxes between labour and capital (e.g., labour is taxed much more heavily than capital) and further ensure that the financial sector makes a fair contribution to government budgets to mitigate fiscal consolidation processes.

In current debates, it is often argued that government expenditure cuts are inevitable, and that social and economic investments that benefit poor households are unaffordable. UNICEF, however, has shown that there are a variety of alternatives, even in the poorest countries (see Chapter VI). These include: (i) re-allocating public expenditures; (ii) increasing tax revenues; (iii) lobbying for increased aid and transfers; (iv) fighting illicit financial flows; (v) tapping into fiscal and foreign exchange reserves; (vi) borrowing and restructuring existing debt; and/or (vii) adopting a more accommodative macroeconomic framework (Ortiz, Chai and Cummins).

The need to increase fiscal space for social and economic investments has never been greater. Just at a time when populations are most in need of public assistance, fiscal contraction is intensifying and spreading quickly across the developing world. Given the significance of public investment in enhancing the prospects for equitable, inclusive economic growth and social development, including the achievement of the MDGs, it is critical that governments explore options to ramp up social spending and employment-generating economic investments during— and in support of—the recovery. Only expansionary policies can open a path toward lower fiscal deficits and falling public debt ratios. Moreover, a 'lost decade' for the world economy would risk the development gains achieved during recent years and question the ability of democratic governments to tackle the most urgent challenges of our age (Flassbeck).[64]

3.5.   A Green New Deal?

In order for populations in developing countries to achieve a decent living standard, especially the billions who currently still live in conditions of abject poverty and the additional two billion people who will have been added to the world's population by mid-century, much greater economic progress is needed. Continuation along previously trodden economic growth pathways will further exacerbate the pressures exerted on the world's resources and natural environment, which will approach limits where livelihoods are no longer sustainable. As a result, business as usual is simply not an option (Martinez Alier, Vos).

---

[64] Flassbeck, H. 2011. "On the Brink: Fiscal Austerity Threatens a Global Recession." UNCTAD Policy Brief No. 24. Geneva: UNCTAD.

Thus, in the next three to four decades, humankind must manage a fundamental technological overhaul or risk failure in fulfilling global commitments to end poverty and averting the catastrophic impacts of climate change and environmental degradation. The UN *World Economic and Social Survey 2011* analyzes the options and challenges associated with the shift to more efficient and renewable energy technologies.[65] This also involves transforming agricultural technologies so as to guarantee food security without further degrading land and water resources, as well as applying the technologies to adapt to climate change and reduce the human risks associated with the increasing frequency of natural hazards.

Governments will have to take a leading role through implementing investment and incentive schemes designed to accelerate green technological innovation and structural change directed toward sustainable production and consumption. Strengthened international cooperation and significant adjustments in multilateral trade and financing mechanisms will also be needed if developing countries are to realize the necessary technological transformation without compromising their aspirations in terms of growth and poverty reduction. A *'Recovery for All'* must and can be sustainable (Vos).

3.6.   Retrogression in human rights

Bringing Human Rights to Bear in Times of Crisis: A human rights analysis of government responses to the economic crisis brought civil society voices front and center to the e-discussion.[66] In particular, they reflected a worrisome reality that consisted of deepening unemployment, further disenfranchisement of the most vulnerable, the breakdown of social safety nets and protection systems along with the associated increase in unpaid work done mostly by women, increasing hunger, and limited policy space, especially for developing country governments to take the necessary actions to avoid and prevent economic and social breakdown (Caliari).

---

[65] United Nations. 2011. *World Economic and Social Survey 2011: The Great Green Technological Transformation.* New York: UN-DESA.
[66] ESCR-Net. 2011. *Bringing Human Rights to Bear in Times of Crisis: A Human Rights Analysis of Government Responses to the Economic Crisis.* New York: International Network for Economic, Social and Cultural Rights (ESCR-Net).

The UN Independent Expert on Human Rights and Extreme Poverty reminded us that the challenge of recovering from successive crises must not overshadow the concrete legal obligations that governments have to respect, protect and promote human rights including economic, social and cultural rights. Enshrined in a multitude of human rights treaties at regional and universal levels, these obligations are not expendable during times of economic hardship, but rather must guide the formulation of all government policies and initiatives, including fiscal and economic policies. Even in the context of severe resource constraints, whether caused by budgetary adjustment, recession or other factors, countries are legally required to devote the maximum available resources to ensure the progressive realization of all economic, social and cultural rights as expeditiously and effectively as possible (Sepulveda).

Any deliberately retrogressive measures that have a direct or indirect negative effect on the enjoyment of human rights by individuals will violate human rights standards. This includes unjustified reductions in expenditures that are essential to realizing a number of rights, including those that guarantee basic healthcare, ensure access to primary education, or make food and shelter available to all persons. Other measures that threaten the realization of these rights include cutting funding to social protection and social security systems, reducing minimum wages, large-scale hiring freezes and employment retrenchment, implementing regressive sales taxes and eliminating food subsidies. These and other austerity measures represent significant barriers to the enjoyment of human rights, particularly by people living in poverty who, despite being removed from the origins of the crises, continue to bear the brunt of their impacts. The human rights framework orients recovery discussions away from deficit cutting and debt eradication and toward reducing deprivations and eradicating obstacles to the realization of basic rights. Viewed in this perspective, recovery must start with the poorest and most vulnerable (Sepulveda).[67] The human rights framework should be extended even beyond social security and adequate living standards to the nation, and to its right to have the freedom to adopt and implement macroeconomic policies of its choice to effectively respond to the needs and demands of its

---

[67] United Nations. 2009. Report of the Independent Expert on the question of human rights and extreme poverty, Magdalena Sepúlveda Carmona. Human Rights Council A/HRC/17/34. Geneva: United Nations.

citizens. The ability of a country to implement an economic and fiscal policy regime of its choice is usually conceptualized in the economic literature in terms of 'space' and how organizations like the World Bank and IMF affect this space. But economic policy, when it involves the employment, social security and well-being of individuals, qualifies as part of the new human rights agenda, which the UN has pioneered (Amsden).

The *Social Watch Report 2012*[68] points that policies to meet human rights are, at the same time, sound economic policies. Yet a gap is identified in terms of sustainability. Sustainable development was defined by the Earth Summit in 1992 as the set of policies that meet the needs of the present without compromising the ability of future generations to meet their needs. But in the current national and international governance structure, there is no defender of the rights of future generations. The report concludes that growing inequalities and unregulated finances are expropriating people everywhere from their fair share of the benefits of global prosperity. Our children will inherit the burden of deforestation, desertification, erosion of biodiversity and climate change. To reverse this trend, the promise of universal dignity brought by human rights has to be enforced, and the rights of future generations need to be recognized and properly defended (Bissio).

3.7.   Ideology and the crisis

The crisis has brought into question the neoliberal financial economy that has been operating since the 1980s. In many ways, a mystification of market actors in the world economy, which is widespread in the media coverage of the crisis, makes it easier to ignore a deeper and more relevant issue, mainly that of the weak role of the state and of systemic failure. Contributors have pointed out the imminence of a paradigm shift.

In much of the media coverage, and even—perhaps particularly— among policy circles, a personification of markets took place. For example, the "financial markets wanted Greece, Spain, Portugal and the other currently victimized countries of Europe (Italy and Ireland) to commit" (Weisbrot). This abstraction from the real world of speculators

---

[68] Social Watch. 2012. *Social Watch Report 2012: The Right to a Future.* Montevideo: Social Watch.

and financial fraud ('the markets') is an essential part of the mystification of financial behavior. It facilitates the mythology that the dysfunctional financial system is not the work of people within institutions with socially irrational rules and norms, hiding and disguising those corporations that stand behind and work those markets to pursue their interests; rather this language makes it seem as if the self-interested pursuits of those corporations were the machine-like operations of some unalterable, fixed institution, a manifestation of the inexorable operation of the laws of nature that no government can change (Wolff, Weeks). However, markets are not independent actors; like all other institutions, they are human inventions filled with a mix of positive and negative aspects and open to change.

In this sense, it is not 'markets' that 'wanted' countries to commit themselves to fiscal cuts, but a specific collection of financial speculators that sought to coerce governments to take actions in the immediate economic interests of those speculators (Weeks). In Europe, the chief creditors of governments today are banks, insurance companies, large corporations, pension funds, some other governments (mostly non-European) and wealthy individuals. When politicians and media speak of the need for European governments to 'satisfy the markets,' what they mean is to satisfy those creditors. The chief influences among those creditors are the major banks that represent and/or advise all or most of the rest of them. The major European banks were—and are—the major recipients of the costly bailouts by European governments. Indeed, those bailouts sharply increased the indebtedness of European governments, which were mostly paid for through additional borrowing (Wolff).

This mystification of markets is parallel to a diminished role of the state. Many contributors to this discussion point out the systemic state failure that underpinned this crisis. According to public economics textbooks, in the past few decades, governments have failed to meet the regulatory role expected of them, which includes preventing, and if it occurs, correcting, market failure. States failed and continue to fail in large measure in performing this corrective, market-embedding role. Such pronounced failure facilitated and thus preceded market failure in the 2008 financial crisis (Kaul). In Europe, two democratically-elected governments stepped down in 2011 'to satisfy markets' and were replaced by non-elected technocratic governments to deal with austerity and debt (Greece and Italy). In the earlier experience of Africa, this phenomenon was quickly 'baptized' state fragility. However, in the more developed world, this erosion of state responsibility and responsiveness was initially couched as "the necessary withdrawal of the state from development to allow the more natural agents of the market to adjust and drive change" (Lwanga-Ntale).

This erosion of state responsibility and responsiveness was caused by the dominant ideology since the 1980s (Dominelli). Neoliberal policy orthodoxy has demanded the destruction of the state as an agent of re-equilibration (balanced state/private sector relationships) and social protection, transforming it into a unit that stays out of private business as long as profits accrue, bailing out private business immediately when (rather than if) the private sector produces downturns (Raffer). The absence of appropriate controls and regulations allows private speculators with access to large financial resources to act through markets to undermine the actions of governments. The rules and constraints on financial markets are so weak or inappropriate that speculators can behave recklessly with confidence of never being held accountable (Weeks). What grows in the economy under this model is telling; increasingly it is the financial sector that grows, and money circulates within this sector without really producing a productive role in society (Kelles-Viitanen). The lack of awareness of people is puzzling, and the dismal state of education doubtless bears some responsibility for these views; economics has become like evolution, where what people think is well predicted by their political ideology; it is not fanciful to imagine school boards in Texas legislating against the teaching of Keynesian economics (Deaton).[69]

Still the main locus of legitimate governance remains the nation state. We cannot simultaneously pursue democracy, national self-determination and the 'hyperglobalization' of the last 30 years. We have to moderate our ambitions regarding economic globalization. Recognizing the centrality of nation-states is more likely to contribute to a healthy global economy than trying to eviscerate it (Rodrik).[70]

---

[69] Deaton, A. 2010. "Letter from America—Dispatches from the Gloom: Or the Moon over Texas." Royal Economic Society's Newsletter, Issue No. 151.
[70] Rodrik, D. 2011. *The Globalization Paradox: Democracy and the Future of the World Economy.* New York: W. W. Norton & Company.

3.8.   The need for equitable policies

The global economic crisis intensified existing problems and brought new challenges. Still as a transformation crisis, in the Polanyian sense, it presents an opportunity to reframe and rethink development and the path of the global economy. Contributors to this discussion agreed that a new progressive vision must be based on a massive strategy for equitable policies to reverse the growth of unsustainable insecurities and inequalities.

Although inequality has been on the radar of some of the major international organizations for quite some time, notably the United Nations Department of Economic and Social Affairs (UN-DESA), UNICEF, the United Nations Development Programme (UNDP) and the World Bank, the crisis led to its emergence as a major issue in the media and amongst the general public around the world. Inequality matters because high levels can inhibit growth, discourage the development of accountability among governments, and undermine civic and social life, ultimately leading to conflict, especially in multi-ethnic settings. Inequality reproduces itself across generations as a result of 'inequality traps' or persistent differences in power, wealth and status between socio-economic groups that are sustained over time by economic, political and socio-cultural mechanisms and institutions. Several studies have discussed the adverse impact of inequalities, be it in gender, income or health, on economic growth, or fragility and conflict (Sumner).

UNICEF's comprehensive look at income distribution in 141 countries showed that global asymmetries are staggering. Using different estimation models, "Global Inequality: Beyond the Bottom Billion" describes a world in which the top 20 percent of the population enjoys more than 70 percent of total income, contrasted by 2 paltry percentage points for those in the bottom quintile (as of 2007 under PPP-adjusted exchange rates). Using market exchange rates, the richest population quintile gets 83 percent of global income with just a single percentage point for those in the poorest quintile. While there is evidence of progress, it is too slow; it is estimated that it would take more than 800 years for the bottom billion to achieve 10 percent of global income under the current rate of change (Ortiz and Cummins).[71]

Yet trends in inequality vary among different countries and regions. The experience in many countries highlights the fact that social and redistributive policies can, in fact, reduce inequalities. In the case of Latin America, historically the most unequal region in the world, inequality declined in 16 out of 21 countries in the new millennium (Ortiz and Cummins). Interestingly, in many countries the decline continued during the global economic crisis (Lustig).[72] Brazil, for example, has managed to grow, become more equal and reduce poverty over the last decade (Lawson). The changes in inequality seen in the recent years in Latin America can be attributed to external shocks and changes in domestic policies, particularly macroeconomic and social policies introduced in recent years, since the 'left-of-center wave' hit the region.

While the average regional decline in the Gini coefficient was two-to-three points, in countries ruled for most of the 2002-2007 period by left-of-center governments, the drop was more pronounced. An important factor in the reduction of inequality was the rise in public social expenditure in such countries, including targeted transfers to the poor, which reduced inequality by about one-tenth of the total (Cornia).[73] In Brazil, success did not come by accident, but by design, with strong government action to implement policies that redistribute wealth and help the poorest. Investment in progressive taxation and in social policies, like education for all and healthcare, are huge assets to its population and to the fight against inequality. Overall, it is estimated that Brazil lifted nearly 12 million people out of poverty between 1999 and 2009—that brings the proportion of those living in poverty from around one in nine to fewer than one in 25 (Lawson).[74] For the region as a whole, a continuation of fiscally prudent distributive and redistributive

---

[71] Ortiz, I. and M. Cummins. 2011. "Global Inequality: Beyond the Bottom Billion – A Rapid Review of Income Distribution in 141 Countries." Social and Economic Policy Working Paper, UNICEF.

[72] Lopez-Calva, L. and N. Lustig. 2010. *Declining Inequality in Latin America: A Decade of Progress?* Washington, D.C. and New York: Brookings Institution Press and UNDP.

[73] Cornia, G.A. and B. Martorano. 2010. "Policies for Reducing Income Inequality: Latin America During the Last Decade." Social and Economic Policy Working Paper, UNICEF.

[74] Gower, R., C. Pearce and R. Kate. 2012. "Left Behind by the G20? How Inequality and Environmental Degradation Threaten to Exclude Poor People from the Benefits of Economic Growth." Oxfam Briefing Paper No. 157, Oxfam GB.

policies, which emerged in the 2000s, should preserve most of the income inequality gains recorded in recent years (Cornia).

The reduction of inequality in many other parts of the world can also be attributed to redistributive policies. At least 20 developing countries have reduced inequalities in recent years, including Thailand, Malaysia, and a few in Africa. The expansion of social protection, minimum wages and the purposeful use of public finance to reduce inequalities has started to make a difference (Jolly). What all these experiences show is that rising inequality is in no way a given, but a clear result of political choice (Lawson).

At the global level, several policies have been discussed as tools for reducing poverty and inequality. Included in the global social policy response to the crisis was a significant development called the 'Global Social Floor' or minimum social protection package.[75] This initiative supports countries to establish a minimum level of access to essential services along with income security for all. Grounded in the Universal Declaration of Human Rights, the Convention on the Rights of the Child and the ILO's campaign, 'Extending Social Security to All,' it focuses on two critical components: (i) *services*: ensuring the availability, continuity, geographical and financial access to essential services, such as water and sanitation, adequate nutrition, health and education, housing and other services; and (ii) *transfers*: realizing access to services and providing a minimum income and livelihood security through a set of essential social transfers, in cash and in kind throughout the life cycle (children, working life, older persons), paying particular attention to vulnerable groups (Cichon).[76]

The idea of a global social protection floor has gained momentum with the crisis. It is not only supported by all UN agencies, donors and non-governmental organizations (NGOs), but was also recommended by the G20. This is certainly a great advance. However, some commented that adequate social policies and social development responses to the crisis must go beyond the concept of the global social floor. In particular, what is needed is a more universal and inclusive approach to state-led development with which the welfare needs of the middle class and

---

[75] ILO and WHO. 2009. *The Social Protection Floor Initiative*. Geneva: ILO and WHO.
[76] ILO and WHO. 2011. *Social Protection Floor for a Fair and Inclusive Globalization*. Report of the Advisory Group chaired by Michelle Bachelet. Geneva: ILO and WHO.

state builders are met along with those of the poor. If the professional and middle class of many developing countries are to be weaned away from a self-serving attachment to a global market in private welfare (overseas universities, private pensions, consumption of health service abroad), then developing countries need good universities, good hospital provision and adequate remuneration for the state builders. Otherwise, there will be no chance of rebuilding bonds of solidarity between the poor and the non-poor within countries, which are needed to (re)build universal and high quality social provision for all. This is the lesson of effective European welfare state building (Deacon, Gross).[77]

Furthermore, we should not lose sight of the fact that government social spending in most developing countries continues to be highly regressive, especially when subsidies for private health and education are included. This continues to be the case in most of Latin America. Despite the extension of cash transfer schemes and other interventions targeting poorer groups, there remain grave inequities in terms of contributory pension and health insurance schemes. Hopefully the current crisis can create openings for public debate and the reform of these inequitable programs (Lloyd-Sherlock).[78]

Another approach proposed is 'basic income,' which was put forth by a network of economists, the Basic Income Earth Network (BIEN), in 1986. A basic income is an income unconditionally granted to all persons on an individual basis, without means testing or work requirements. It is a form of minimum income guarantee that differs from those that now exist in various European countries. In particular, it is being paid to individuals rather than households, irrespective of any income from other sources, and without requiring the performance of any work or the willingness to accept a job. The inability to tackle unemployment with conventional means has led to the idea being taken seriously by a growing number of scholars and organizations. This further underscores how social and economic policy can no longer be conceived separately, and basic income is increasingly viewed as the only viable way of

---

[77] Deacon, B. 2009. "Shifting Social Policy Discourse: The Impact of the Crisis on Ideas about Social Protection and Global Social Governance." Paper presented at the UNRISD Conference, 'Social and Political Dimensions of the Global Crisis: Implications for Developing Countries,' November 12-13.

[78] Lloyd-Sherlock, P. 2009. "Social Policy and Inequality in Latin America: A Review of Recent Trends." *Social Policy and Administration* 43(4): 347-363.

reconciling two of their respective central objectives: poverty relief and full employment (Standing).

Yet equity will not be achieved by social policies alone. While social policies will alleviate poverty and make a difference to many individuals, they cannot substitute development (Aroche). Most contributors agreed on the urgency to promote robust social and economic policies in parallel, in a complementary and mutually reinforcing manner. Further, the disconnect between economic policies and their social consequences can create a vicious circle of slow growth and poor social progress. As an alternative, the UN development agenda has been proposing the combination of social, economic and environmental policies (Ortiz and Cummins, Lee, Vos). Any equity approach would be quite incompatible with anything resembling the current pattern of globalized 'free' markets. In particular, it will require a rebalancing of the world economy that extends beyond current market manipulation, account deficits and surpluses, and managed flows of trade and capital to income-expenditure gaps and income distribution within countries (Shutt). The current series of crises therefore need to be instrumentalized to rethink the notion of growth, to reinsert employment and income distribution into discussions on productivity and value-added, and to revisit growth and recovery discussions bearing in mind human needs and rights (Koehler).

Equitable development policies are difficult to implement because they are deeply political. The creation of the welfare states in OECD countries have been and continue to be political projects, be it of nation building, restoration after civil wars (Scandinavia), after international wars (United Kingdom) or responses to threats to stability (of the left, as for Bismarck). They are deeply intertwined with democratic structures (e.g., the 'polder model' in the Netherlands, which is now challenged by populism). Recent progressive politics in the South are equally political projects: in Brazil, former President Lula managed to redistribute while reassuring investors; the Mahatma Gandhi National Rural Employment Guarantee Act (NREGA) in India was part of a Congress-led response to perceived failures of the conservative Bharatiya Janata Party; and, in China, its leaders' idea of harmonious society is as much a reaction to rising unrest as it is to growing inequalities (de Haan).

This is why initiatives like a broad coalition of NGOs, social movements, academics, UN agencies, governments and others are being established to advocate for these approaches, as well as the prioritization of equity and social justice in development agendas, are extremely important. To cite one example, a coalition started by Sir Richard Jolly and others after an 'Inequality and Social Justice Consultation' in 2011 calls on governments and development agencies to place the reduction of inequality at the heart of their recovery and development agendas (Jolly).[79]

The extreme inequality in the distribution of the world's income should make us question the current development model (development for whom?), which has accrued mostly to the wealthiest. Despite the political and difficult nature of equitable policies, addressing and adopting them is an essential task. The policy choice might be different for different countries, but some of the key elements appear to be employment-generating macroeconomic policies, progressive taxes and redistributive transfers, universal public services, particularly education and health, and social pensions (Van der Hoeven, Deacon, Justino, Beales). An inclusive development agenda promoting jobs growth and universal social policies was a key ingredient to legitimizing governments and nation-building in the past. This differs radically from today's standard development formula that is based on growth that benefits the highest income quintile with a few targeted safety nets for the poorest.

Against a backdrop of greater unrest from the 99 percent, whether in Lagos or London, this is an issue that will be harder and harder for leaders to ignore (Lawson). The ILO created a social unrest index, highlighting global levels of discontent related to perceived economic inequality. Marking an uptick in popular anger in advanced economies, such as those of the EU, the *World of Work Report 2011* warns of a significant aggravation of social unrest in over 45 of the 118 countries surveyed. As the recovery derails, social discontent is becoming more widespread; public dissatisfaction is also simmering in the Middle East and North Africa, and, albeit to a much lesser extent, in Asia (Torres). Any economic model that does not properly address inequality will eventually face a crisis of legitimacy. And unless the relative economic

---

[79] IDS. 2011. "Summary: Inequality and Social Justice Roundtable Consultation." Sussex: Institute of Development Studies (IDS).

roles of the market and the state are rebalanced, the protests of 2011 will become more severe, with social and political instability eventually harming long-term economic growth and welfare (Roubini).

List of Contributors

Amsden, Alice—Professor of Development Economics, Massachusetts Institute of Technology (MIT), USA

Aroche, Fidel—Lecturer, Universidad Nacional Autónoma de México (UNAM)

Auer, Peter—Fellow, International Institute for Labour Studies, ILO

Bauer, Armin—Senior Economist, ADB

Beales, Sylvia—Head of Strategic Alliances, HelpAge International, UK

Bissio, Roberto—Executive Director, Third World Institute, and Coordinator, Social Watch

Breman, Jan—Professor Emeritus, University of Amsterdam

Caliari, Aldo—Director, Rethinking Bretton Woods Project, Center of Concern

Campbell, Duncan—Director for Policy Planning in Employment, ILO

Cantillo, Marco V. Sanchez—Economic Affairs Officer, UN-DESA

Chai, Jingqing—Chief, Social Policy and Economic Analysis Unit, UNICEF HQ

Chang, Ha-Joon—Reader in Economics, University of Cambridge, UK

Chen, Martha—Lecturer in Public Policy, Harvard Kennedy School and WIEGO Network

Chowdhury, Anisuzzaman—Senior Economic Affairs Officer, UN-DESA

Cichon, Michael—Director, Social Security Department, ILO

Cornia, Giovanni Andrea—Professor of Development Economics, University of Florence, Italy

Cummins, Matthew—Social and Economic Policy Specialist, UNICEF HQ

de Haan, Arjan—Program Leader, Supporting Inclusive Growth, International Development Research Centre, Canada

de Rooy, Carel—Representative, UNICEF Bangladesh

Deacon, Bob—Professor of International Social Policy, University of Sheffield, UK and UNUCRIS; founder of the journal Global Social Policy

Deaton, Angus S.—Professor of Economics and International Affairs, Princeton University, USA

Dominelli, Lena—Professor, School of Applied Social Sciences, Durham University, UK

Edwards, Chris—Senior Fellow, University of East Anglia, UK

Elkjaer, Morten—Danish Embassy, Bolivia

Flassbeck, Heiner—Director, Division on Globalization and Development Strategies, UNCTAD

Fortin, Carlos—Research Associate, Institute of Development Studies, UK, and Chile 21 Foundation; former Deputy Secretary-General of UNCTAD

Gallagher, Kevin—Associate Professor of International Relations, Boston University, USA, and Research Fellow, Global Development and Environment Institute

Garde, Rica—Economic Policy Officer, Save the Children UK

Ghosh, Jayati—Professor, Centre for Economic Studies and Planning, Jawaharlal Nehru University, India, and Executive Secretary, International Development Economics Associates (IDEAs)

Green, Duncan—Head of Research, Oxfam GB

Gross, Peter Beat—Social Policy Specialist, UNICEF Botswana

Gulbrandsen, Hakon Arald—Senior Adviser, Multilateral Bank and Finance Section, Ministry of Foreign Affairs, Norway

Hailu, Degol—Economic Policy Advisor, UNDP

Harland, Charlotte—Chief of Social Policy and Economic Analysis, UNICEF Zambia

Herman, Barry —Visiting Senior Fellow, The New School, USA

Horn, Zoe Elena—Project Co-ordinator, Global Economic Crisis Study, WIEGO Network

Jolly, Richard—Honorary Professor, Institute of Development Studies, UK; former UN Assistant Secretary-General, UNICEF

Jomo Kwame Sundaram—UN Assistant-Secretary-General for Economic Development, UN-DESA

Justino, Patricia—Fellow, Institute of Development Studies, UK, and Director, MICROCON, and Co-director, Households in Conflict Network

Kaplinsky, Raphael—Professor of International Development, The Open University, UK

Kaul, Inge—Professor, Hertie School of Governance, Berlin, Germany; former Director, Office of Development Studies, UNDP

Kelles-Viitanen, Anita—Chair, Association for the Taxation of Financial Transactions for the Aid of Citizens (ATTAC) Finland; former manager, ADB

Khor, Martin—Executive Director, South Center

King, Richard—Policy Researcher, Oxfam GB

Koehler, Gabriele—Development Economist; former senior official UNCTAD and UNICEF

Krugman, Paul—Nobel Laureate, Professor of Economics and International Affairs, Princeton University, USA

Lapavitsas, Costas—Reader in Economics and Associate Dean in Research, School of Oriental and African Studies (SOAS), University of London, UK

Laryea-Adjei, George—Chief of Social Policy, UNICEF South Africa

Lawson, Max—Head of Advocacy and Public Policy, Oxfam GB

Lee, Donald—Chief, Social Perspective on Development Branch, UN-DESA

Leigh, Kirk—Lead Consultant, Financial Market Intelligence, Nigeria

Levy, Noemi—Professor of Economics, UNAM

Lloyd-Sherlock, Peter—Professor of Social Policy and International Development, University of East Anglia, UK

Lustig, Nora—Professor of Latin American Economics, Tulane University, USA; former Director of Poverty Group, UNDP, and Chief of Poverty and Inequality Unit, Inter-American Development Bank

Lwanga-Ntale, Charles—Head of Social Protection for Africa, HelpAge International, and Founder Director, Development Research and Training, Uganda

Martinez-Alier, Joan—Professor Professor of Economics and Economic History, Autonomous University of Barcelona, Spain

Maxwell, Simon—Development Economist, former Director of Overseas Development Institute, UK

McKinley, Terry—Director, Centre for Development Policy and Research, SOAS, University of London, UK

Mehrotra, Santosh—Director, Institute of Applied Manpower Research, Planning Commission, Government of India

Mesa-Lago, Carmelo—Distinguished Service Professor Emeritus of Economics, University of Pittsburgh, USA

Miller, Steve—Visiting Professor, The New School, USA

Miller-Dawkins, May—Research Manager, Oxfam Australia

Molina, Nuria—Director, European Network on Debt and Development (Eurodad)

Molyneux, Maxine—Director, Institute for the Study of the Americas, University of London, UK

Monastiriotis, Vassilis—Senior Lecturer in the Political Economy of South, European Institute, London School of Economics, UK

Murniningtyas, Endah—Director for Poverty Alleviation, Ministry of National Development, Indonesia

Nayyar, Deepak—Professor of Economics, The New School, USA, and Jawaharlal Nehru University, India

Nwuke, Kasirim—Senior Economic Affairs Officer and Chief of MDGs/Poverty Analysis and Monitoring, United Nations Economic Commission for Africa (UNECA)

Ocampo, José Antonio—Professor, School of International and Public Affairs, Columbia University, USA; former UN Under-Secretary-General for Economic and Social Affairs and former Minister of Finance of Colombia

Oncu, Sabri—Head of Research, Centre for Advanced Financial Research and Learning, Reserve Bank of India; formerly at Stern School of Business, New York University, USA

Ortiz, Isabel—Associate Director, Policy and Practice, UNICEF HQ

Palley, Thomas—Associate, Economic Growth Program, New America Foundation, USA

Patel, Mahesh—Regional Advisor, UNICEF East Asia and Pacific

Pettifor, Ann—Fellow, New Economics Foundation, and Director of Advocacy, International Ltd and PRIME (Policy Research in Macroeconomics)

Puyana, Alicia—Professor, Government and Public Affairs, FLACSO, Mexico

Raffer, Kunibert—Associate Professor at the Department of Economics, University of Vienna, Austria

Ranis, Gustav—Professor Emeritus of International Economics, Yale University, USA

Riesco, Manuel—Director, Centro de Estudios Nacionales de Desarrollo Alternativo (CENDA), Chile

Rodrik, Dani—Professor of International Political Economy, Harvard University, USA

Roubini, Nouriel—Chairman, Roubini Global Economics, and Professor of Economics, Stern School of Business, New York University, USA

Rowden, Rick—Independent consultant and author

Ryan, Elaine—Secretariat, Office of the High Commissioner for Human Rights

Sepúlveda, Magdalena—Special Rapporteur on extreme poverty and human rights, United Nations Office of the High Commissioner for Human Rights

Shrestha, Ava—Development consultant

Shutt, Harry—Economic consultant and author

Sire, Xavier R.—Knowledge Management Officer, UNICEF HQ

Standing, Guy—Professor of Economic Security, University of Bath, UK, and Founder and Co-chair, Basic Income Earth Network

Stewart, Frances—Director, Centre for Research on Inequality, Human Security and Ethnicity, University of Oxford, UK

Storey, Andy—Lecturer, School of Politics and International Relations, University College Dublin, Ireland

Sumner, Andy—Research Fellow, Institute of Development Studies, UK, and Visiting Fellow, Center for Global Development, USA

Taylor, Lance—Professor of International Cooperation and Development, The New School, USA

Tiberti, Luca—Post-doc Research Fellow, University of Laval, Canada

Torres, Raymond—Director, International Institute for Labour Studies, ILO

Ugarteche, Oscar—Researcher, Economic Research Institute, UNAM

van der Hoeven, Rolph—Professor of Employment and Development Economics, Institute of Social Studies, Erasmus University, the Netherlands

van Ginneken, Wouter—ISSA Consultant on the Extension of Social Security Coverage

Vernengo, Matías—Associate Professor, University of Utah, USA

Vos, Rob—Director, Development Policy and Analysis Division, UN-DESA

Weeks, John—Professor Emeritus of Development Economics, SOAS, University of London, UK

Weisbrot, Mark—Co-Director, Center for Economic and Policy Research, USA

Wolf, Richard—Professor of Economics Emeritus, University of Massachusetts, Amherst, USA

III.   THE FOOD PRICE SURGE

Isabel Ortiz, Jingqing Chai and Matthew Cummins

"There is more than enough food on the planet to feed everyone. Yet, almost one billion people are hungry... When food prices surge, poor families suddenly find themselves unable to afford enough nutritious food. If this happens during the first thousand days of a child's life, the damage to his or her body and mind can be permanent. When food prices rise, families send their children to work instead of school, they sell their hard-earned assets or livestock... or they go into debt... Recovery can take years. In some cases, the losses are passed from one generation to the next. We have the resources and the knowledge to end hunger. We know how to protect the poorest from the impact of rising prices. We know how to tame volatile prices. Every child, woman and man has a right to enough nutritious food for an active and healthy life. Let us act—now."

UN Secretary-General's remarks at World Food Day Commemoration in New York City on October 27, 2011

1.   Introduction

In early 2012, the international price index for basic foodstuffs remained far above the peak levels reached during the 2007-08 food crisis. The alarming spike in prices that began in mid-2010 is led by sugar commodities as well as cereals (e.g., maize, rice and wheat), the latter which are important food staples for many developing country populations, especially among the poor. While the full picture of the drivers behind the food price increases continues to develop, there is a growing consensus that high prices are likely to persist into the foreseeable future (FAO 2011a).

The 2007-08 food crisis clearly demonstrated that soaring international food prices have serious consequences for developing countries, especially those that are dependent on food imports. To the extent that the recent increases in global food prices impact local prices, they further threaten the survival, nutritional status and livelihood of vulnerable populations, especially children, who are still reeling from the income shocks resulting from the cumulative, lingering impacts of the previous food, fuel and financial crises. Poor households all over the world are in an increasingly weak and vulnerable situation in 2012, oftentimes having already exhausted available coping strategies, such as eating fewer and less nutritious meals, reducing limited expenditures on basic health services and essential medicine, selling or pawning assets, racking up household debt and working longer hours in informal activities. As discussed in Chapters IV and V, such adverse impacts are further compounded by the jobs crisis and austerity measures, including reduced levels of social assistance. Moreover, extreme price movements of agricultural commodities not only threaten the food security of millions of people but also the economic recovery and social stability of developing countries.[1]

Yet unlike the previous crisis, when most developing country governments expanded spending and adopted other measures to mitigate the negative social impacts, the risk of an inadequate response seems particularly high in the current run-up of food prices. For one thing, as many developing country governments began to consolidate public expenditures beginning in 2010, food subsidies are being phased out or removed; governments are also further targeting and scaling down their already meager social protection schemes rather than scaling up social protection floors (see Chapter V). This adds to the concern that, having endured the blows of the previous global shocks, many developing countries are in a weakened position to respond to the ongoing rise in food prices. For instance, just as current account balances have deteriorated and strained the ability of many governments to pay for more expensive food import bills, food stock inventories for key staples are forecasted to be depleting in many countries during 2012, such as cereal stocks in Algeria, Ethiopia, Iran, Pakistan, the Philippines, South Africa and Syria (FAO 2011b). Even more worrisome, the cereal import bill for the group of low-income, food-deficit countries is expected to reach US$33 billion during 2012, which is a record level (FAO 2011b). These challenges cast doubt on the

---

[1] Given that food insecurity mainly threatens the well-being of populations in developing countries, this chapter does not focus on the impacts of high food prices among HICs.

appropriateness of fiscal tightening expenditure when the need for prompt food responses has been significant since mid-2010.

As the degree of urgency for a given developing country depends, in part, on the global-to-local price transmission process—the scope and pace of which can vary widely both across and within countries—it is critically important to timely monitor the development of local food prices in order to enable speedy and effective policy responses. Indeed, a principle objective of this chapter is to ascertain where local food price increases have been associated with the ongoing rise of international food market indices.

This chapter begins by briefly reviewing the possible causes of the food price spike that began in mid-2010 (Section 2). The global-level assessment is followed by an examination of local food price movements in a sample of 55 developing countries between 2007 and 2011 (Section 3). In addition to identifying where local food price increases have been associated with increases on international food markets, Chapter III also looks at observed food price differences across regions and income groups as well as intra-country disparities. The chapter then describes the adverse impacts of rising food prices on households, which include hunger and malnutrition, poverty and inequality and poorer provision of public services along with inflation and weaker economic growth (Section 4). Next, a desk review of international and domestic policy responses in 98 developing countries is presented (Section 5), which is followed by a discussion of a three-pillar policy framework to address short and longer-term food security needs (Section 6). The chapter concludes by calling for prompt and coordinated policy actions by national governments and the international community to ensure a *'Recovery for All'* (Section 7).

2.   The Recent Surge of International Food Prices

After a year-and-a-half of relative price stability following a steep decline from the 2008 peak, the FAO Food Price Index—which measures monthly (spot) price changes for an international traded food commodity basket composed of dairy, meat, sugar, cereals and oilseeds—increased by nearly 60 percent between June 2010 and February 2011 (Figure 1). In particular, the price of cereals, which account for more than two-thirds of dietary caloric intake among populations in many developing countries, jumped by a staggering 76 percent over the same time period. Despite somewhat subsiding, in early 2012 global food prices remained significantly above the apogee of the earlier 2007-08 food crisis, and 35 percent higher than prices in June 2010. Understanding the main drivers behind the recent increases is essential to identifying appropriate policy responses aimed at reducing price volatility and steep price increases in international food markets.

Figure III.1. International Price Indices, Jan. 2007 to Jan. 2012
(Jan. 2007=100)

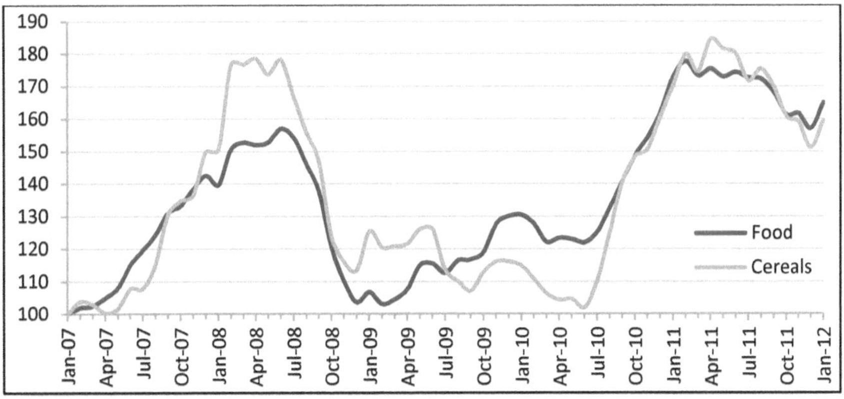

Source: Authors' calculations based on FAO (2012a)

The earlier 2007-08 food crisis is attributed to a variety of causes: expansion of biofuel production (e.g., higher demand for corn and sugar), high oil prices, exogenous supply shocks (e.g., bad weather and droughts), government policies (e.g., export bans and prohibitive taxes), high transportation costs, increasing prices for agricultural inputs, exchange rate fluctuations and the use of commodities by financial investors (the so-called 'financialization of commodities'). As research continues to generate more evidence, some of these factors appear to play a bigger role in the recent price increases of essential staple foodstuffs, including corn, rice, soybeans and wheat.

-   *Weather shocks.* Droughts in Eastern Europe and Argentina, and heavy rains in North America and Australia, led to production shortfalls in cereals (e.g., wheat), starchy roots (e.g., cassava) and oilseeds (e.g., soybeans). This may have had an unusually unnerving impact on international food markets where the memory of the 2007-08 precipitous price climb remains fresh. For instance, on August 05, 2010, the Russian Federation announced a ban on the country's grain exports, which sent European wheat futures prices up by more than 12 percent in a single day. Coupled with news of bad weather in several key exporting countries, the price of wheat soared nearly 90 percent between June and December 2010.[2]

- *Exchange rate fluctuations.* In the latter half of 2010, the US dollar depreciated nearly 10 percent against major currencies (United States Federal Reserve 2012). As internationally traded food commodities are often quoted in US dollars, the weakening currency led to higher commodity prices (FAO 2010a). In fact, the recent increases are less dramatic, albeit still substantial, when adjusted by a basket of currencies. This implies that when the US dollar weakens, consumers in a dollar-pegged economy pay even higher domestic prices for imported food items compared to consumers in a flexible exchange rate economy, all else being equal.

- *Pressure from financial speculation.* Financial flows into food commodity markets since mid-2000 have been massive compared to the amount of underlying physical commodity stocks (Box 1). While indicative data on recent activities in food commodity derivatives are slow to emerge, recent evidence from the Chicago Board of Trade (CBOT) markets seems to show increased speculative trades in some food commodity groups, such as maize and soybeans (Figure 2), which have also been associated with increased price volatility. Over-the-counter (OTC) activities, which are substantial and outside of regulated markets such as the CBOT, are also adding pressure on food prices.

Figure III.2. Non-Commercial Trading Interest of Selected CBOT Markets
(in percentage of total open interest)

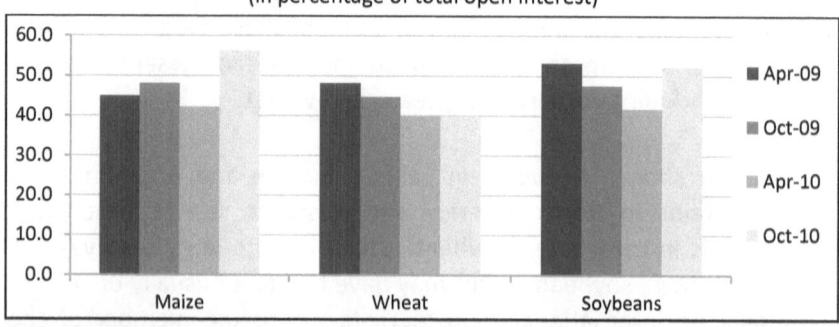

Source: FAO (2010a)

---

[2] Belton, C. et al. 2010. "Russia Grain Export Ban Sparks Price Fears." *Financial Times*, August 05.

Box III.1 Financial Speculation, Food Prices and the Need for Better Regulation

There has been a significant increase of financial flows into commodities over the past five years. Between 2005-10, the number of futures and options traded globally on commodity exchanges nearly quadrupled reaching more than 66 million contracts in late 2010—not including OTC trades—of which trading in food commodities accounts for a small but fast-growing share (Figure 3). Unregulated OTC activities also exploded during this period, reaching a nominal outstanding amount of US$12 trillion in non-gold commodity contracts in 2008 (BIS 2010). Excess liquidity in financial markets played a significant role in this rapid increase, as major institutional investors, which were generally unconcerned with agricultural market fundamentals but rather in gaining short-term returns, moved into commodity derivatives markets, generating a commodity bubble (Baffes and Haniotis 2010).

Commodity futures are instruments that, in principle, should be useful to producers and consumers as they 'hedge' against price risks. However, only 2 percent of futures contracts end in the actual delivery of the physical commodity, while 98 percent are traded before their expiration date by investors who are purely seeking speculative gains (FAO 2010b). Such activities have contributed to excessive fluctuations in food commodity futures prices and distorted signals for expected prices (Figure 4). By doing so, speculation impedes practical hedging strategies and imposes significant unanticipated costs and undue burden on food farmers, processors and distributors, potentially contributing to unwarranted changes in local food costs (United States Senate 2009). Given that speculative activity can potentially yield life and death consequences for millions of people across the developing world, the UN and the G20 have called for urgent regulatory actions to improve the functioning and transparency of financial commodity markets to address excessive price volatility (United Nations 2009, UNCTAD 2009a and 2009b, G20 Summit Leaders' Statements from 2009-11).

Figure III.3. Outstanding Contracts on Commodity Exchanges, 2000-10
(in millions of futures and options)

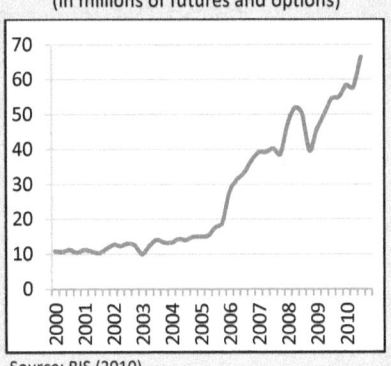

Source: BIS (2010)

Figure III.4. Implied Price Volatility of Selected Staple Foods
(in percentage)

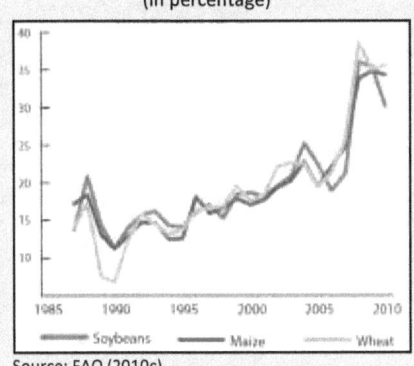

Source: FAO (2010c)

3.   Recent Developments in Local Food Prices

Using data from the FAO's *Global Information and Early Warning System* (GIEWS), this section examines local food price trends in 55 developing countries between 2007 and 2011. It does not attempt to establish causality from international prices to local prices, but rather aims to assess the extent to which increases in local food prices have been associated with those in international food prices among a sample of developing countries that have available data. To do so, a local (staple) food price index is constructed by taking price data for different food products included in the FAO's *GIEWS* and weighting the values by the corresponding percentage of dietary energy supply (DES) for each country.[1] The average local food price index for a given country represents three or more food items and covers roughly half (46.6 percent) of the DES of the respective populations in the sample (see Annex 1 for complete details). While data limitations preclude the construction of representative food baskets for each country, the local food price indices present a general depiction of how changes in domestic prices may be impacting consumption behavior—and hence the nutritional intake—of populations in developing countries.

3.1.   Local food prices remain at historic highs at the start of 2012

The widespread global attention given to the 2007-08 food crisis was clearly warranted. Between mid-2007 and the end of 2008, local food prices soared by 83 percent, on average (Figure 5). Once reaching the peak in December 2008, prices steadily declined by about 16 percent over the following six months, and vacillated little during the second-half of 2009 and most of 2010. Even though talk of the food crisis waned during this period, local prices remained 54 percent higher, on average, than before the start of the crisis.

Then, in October 2010, local food prices began a renewed climb, which lasted into mid-2011. After increasing by 20 percent between October 2010 and July 2011, prices slightly leveled off but remained constant through the end of the year. Alarmingly, recent trends in local food prices reveal that, at the start of 2012, prices were as high as the levels

---

[1] A food price shock can also be examined through the food component of consumer price index inflation. However, due to the lag time in reporting such data, this analysis could not be carried out at the time of writing.

reached during the 2007-08 food crisis and more than 80 percent higher, on average, than before the onset of the previous crisis, in June 2007. These findings suggest that many developing countries were confronting food crises during 2011, which are likely to continue during 2012.

Figure III.5. Local Food Price Index for 55 Developing Countries, 2007-11
(unweighted average index values; Jan. 2007=100)

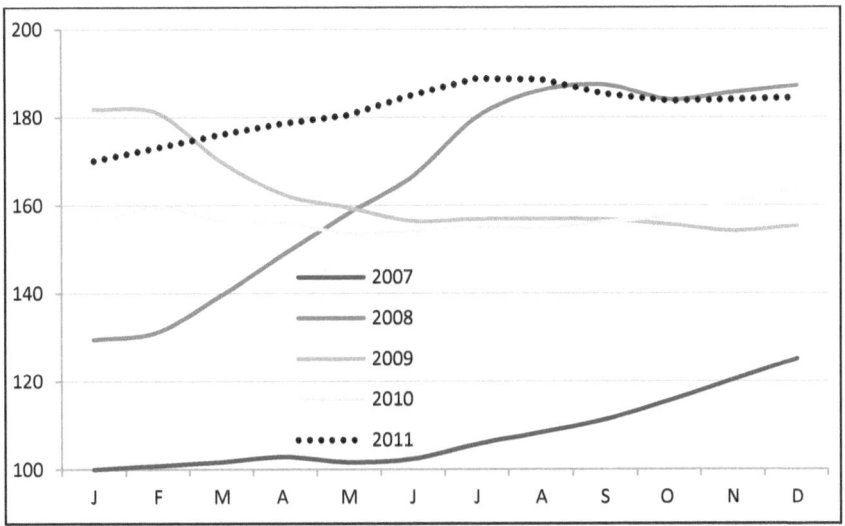

Source: Authors' calculations based on FAO's *GIEWS* (2012)

Analysis of country-level data shows that the latest food price shock has impacted a number of developing countries severely. For example, local food price indices leaped by more than 20 percent between August 2010 and December 2011 in 22 of the 55 countries in the sample (Figure 6). Moreover, to highlight the scale of overall changes over the recent past, vulnerable populations in 12 developing countries were paying more than double for basic foodstuffs in December 2011 than before the start of the 2007-08 food crisis, including Belarus, Cambodia, the Democratic Republic of Congo, Ethiopia, Kenya, Malawi, Pakistan, Somalia, the Sudan, Tajikistan, Uganda and Zimbabwe.

Figure III.6. Local Food Price Index Changes in Selected Countries, Aug. 2010 to Dec. 2011

(as a percent)

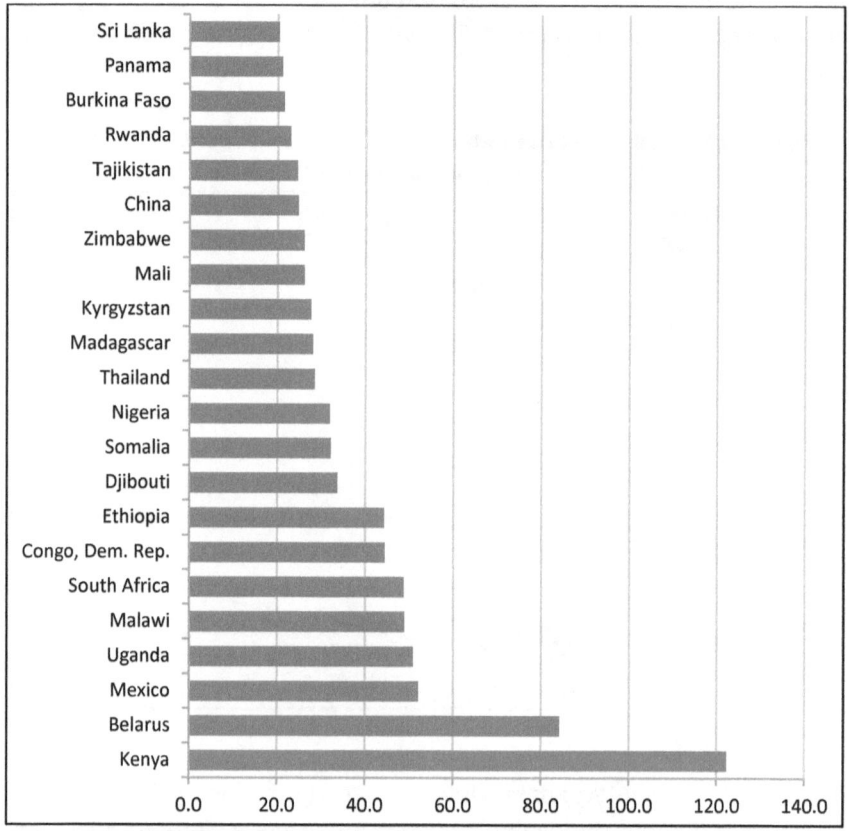

Source: Authors' calculations based on FAO's *GIEWS* (2012)

3.2.   Local food prices react quickly to global upticks, and they rise more and decline less

In theory, if a country is linked to the world market in a free-trade environment, domestic prices move with international prices. If domestic prices are higher than global prices, imports will occur until national and international prices are equalized, less transport costs. The same equilibrating role is fulfilled by increased exports if local prices are below global prices. As a result, under perfect competition, the transport cost should be the only difference between the price of a commodity sold on international and domestic markets. In the real world, however, various factors impact the price transmission process, including public policies (e.g., subsidies, price controls and border measures, including tariffs, quotas and bans), exchange rates, consumer preferences and intermediation costs (Rapsomanikis, Hallam and Conforti 2006). As a result, the global-to-local price transmission process—both the reactionary time and the magnitude of change—can be expected to fluctuate widely across countries.

Causal observation of local and global food price indices between 2007 and 2011 suggests that local prices react quickly to upticks in international markets; their increase also tends to be more prolonged, with the subsequent decline occurring at a slower pace and at a smaller margin (Figure 7). In terms of price run-ups, the global-to-local price delay appeared to be approximately three months during 2007-08, a finding that generally corroborates transmission time estimates of other studies on the earlier food crisis (Compton et al. 2010 and Keats et al. 2010). Moreover, the lag time seems to have shortened considerably in the more recent price spike that began in mid-2010, as local food price increases seemed to trail global rises by a single month.

Despite the increasingly speedy reaction to rises in global food prices, domestic food prices appear to continue climbing long after prices retract on international markets. For instance, in both 2007-08 and 2010-11, local food prices surged an additional six months, on average, after the global index descended. Perhaps more important, however, is the apparent 'stickiness' of local food prices once reaching new highs. During the six-month price decline following their respective crests in 2008, the global food index dropped by more than 50 percent while the local food index fell by less than 20 percent. Moreover, after the 2011 price peaks, global food prices dropped by 13 percent, but local food prices appear to have only retracted by 2 percent.[2]

---

[2] This is only a preliminary finding. Given the lack of more recent local price data, it is not possible to know whether local food prices had reached a new bottom in late 2011, although the steep ascent in the global food index at that time suggests that this is probable.

Figure III.7. Local and Global Food Price Indices, Jan. 2007 to Jan. 2012[3]
(local food prices in unweighted average index values; Jan. 2007=100 for both metrics)

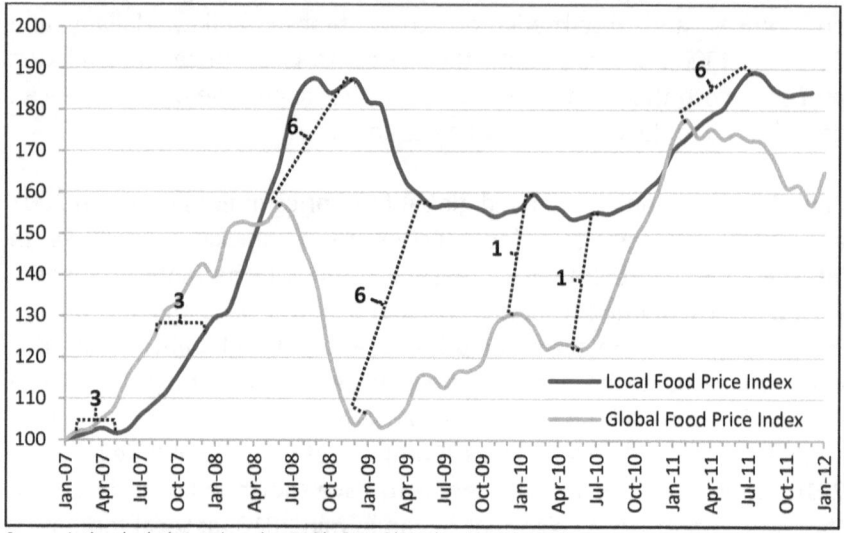

Source: Authors' calculations based on FAO's *GIEWS* (2012) and FAO (2012a)
Note: The black lines connect corresponding local and global food price crests and nadirs, with the corresponding number representing the estimated global-to-local price transmission time in number of months.

The relatively moderate pace of increases in local food prices during 2011, on the aggregate, suggests two possible scenarios moving forward. On the one hand, the global-to-local price transmission process could remain relatively muted, with local food prices slowly descending during 2012. On the other hand, local food prices, which at the end of 2011 equaled the peak levels reached during the 2007-08 crisis, could further accelerate due to the cumulative pressure of the private and public sectors' inability to pay for essential food imports. A renewed upturn in global commodity prices, which increased in January 2012 following six months of gradual decline, could also be a foreboding signal; the strong positive correlation observed between local and global food price indices gives support to the hypothesis that many

---

[3] The findings presented in Figure 7 show some slight dissimilarities from those in an earlier analysis by Ortiz, Chai and Cummins (February 2011). Overall, the main observed differences can be attributed to three factors. First, given that backward price revisions are carried out each month when the FAO's Food Price Index and the FAO's *GIEWS* are updated, the price datasets are slightly different. Second, the sample size was reduced from 58 to 55 countries because three countries did not have price information during 2011. Third, while there was missing price data for most of 2008 for Somalia when the earlier analysis was undertaken, data for those months has since become available, and the substantial price rises during that period pulled up the overall sample average.

developing countries may undergo even further price increases.[4] In either case, close monitoring of local food price movements is critical both across and within countries.

3.3.   Developing countries in Sub-Saharan Africa and the CEE/CIS and are under greatest risk

It is important to highlight that aggregate findings hide significant regional variance in terms of the price transmission process and the magnitude of impact (Figure 8). In the latest price spike, for example, local food prices in developing countries in Central and Eastern Europe and the Commonwealth of Independent States (CEE/CIS) increased in near perfect harmony with global prices beginning in mid-2010, while prices in Sub-Saharan Africa started to ascend roughly three months later. Food prices in many countries in Asia and Latin America, on the other hand, reacted only minimally and did not mirror the steep rise in international prices. The overall rates of change were also quite diverse. Again focusing on the most recent price uptick, food prices soared by nearly 50 percent in the CEE/CIS between June 2010 and July 2011, but increased by only 7 percent in Asia.

In sum, causal observation reveals several noteworthy regional trends. First is the high vulnerability of local prices in Sub-Saharan Africa to both of the recent upsurges in global food prices. Second is the relative resilience of local prices in Latin America against high international prices, as well as for many developing countries in Asia during the latest uptick. And third is the severe and steady upswing of food prices in the CEE/CIS during the 2010-11 shock, which appears to be the region hardest hit by the latest spike. Perhaps most important, however, are the recent prices being paid by populations in developing countries. When compared to the average prices before the 2007-08 food crisis, the cost of basic foodstuffs at the start of 2012 had increased by 107 percent in the CEE/CIS, by 108 percent in Sub-Saharan Africa, by 66 percent in Asia and by 38 percent in Latin America.

---

[4] Simple statistical analysis confirms the observed positive relationship between global and local food prices. Local food price indices in 95 percent of the countries in the sample are positively correlated with the FAO's Food Price Index (overall unweighted average correlation value of 0.43), with the top 25 percent showing a strong correlation of 0.73.

Figure III.8. Local Food Price Indices by Region, 2007-11
(unweighted average index values; Jan. 2007=100)

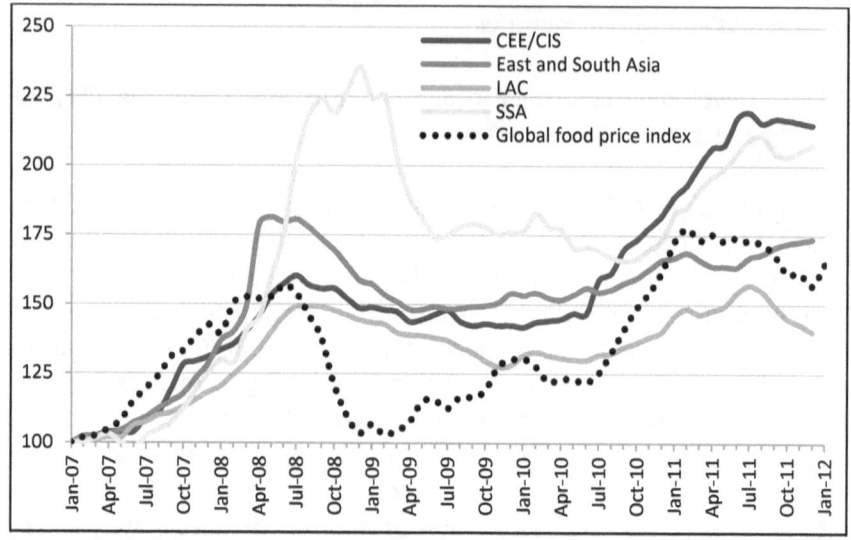

Source: Authors' calculations based on FAO's *GIEWS* (2012)
Note: Sample includes 6 countries from CEE/CIS, 10 from East and South Asia, 14 from Latin America and 24 from Sub-Saharan Africa; the Middle East and North Africa is not included since there is data for only one developing country in the region (Djibouti).

While local food price trends among regions are clear, the causes are not. Just as the Russian Federation's trade restriction may help to explain part of the disproportionate rise in food prices in the CEE/CIS region during the most recent price surge, good agricultural harvests in many Sub-Saharan African countries may have helped account for the region's early resilience to the international price spike through 2010 and helped prevent an even higher rise during 2011 as happened during 2008. However, additional research is needed to better understand the differing local price behaviors observed during the 2007-08 and the latest global food price spike.

3.4.   Food price increases are most acute in poor countries

When analyzing the price data by different income levels, LICs appear to have experienced much larger food price increases than richer, middle-income countries (MICs) (Figure 9). Price rises in both groups of countries appeared to be closely aligned during the early phase of the 2007-08 food crisis, but price differences became pronounced in mid-2008 as they receded in MICs and continued to ascend in LICs. Since then a significant food price premium has persisted in LICs. In particular, between August 2008 and December 2011, populations in developing countries appear to be paying about 30 percent more, on average, for basic foodstuffs than those in MICs.[5]

Figure III.9. Local Food Price Indices by Income Group, 2007-11
(unweighted average index values; Jan. 2007=100)

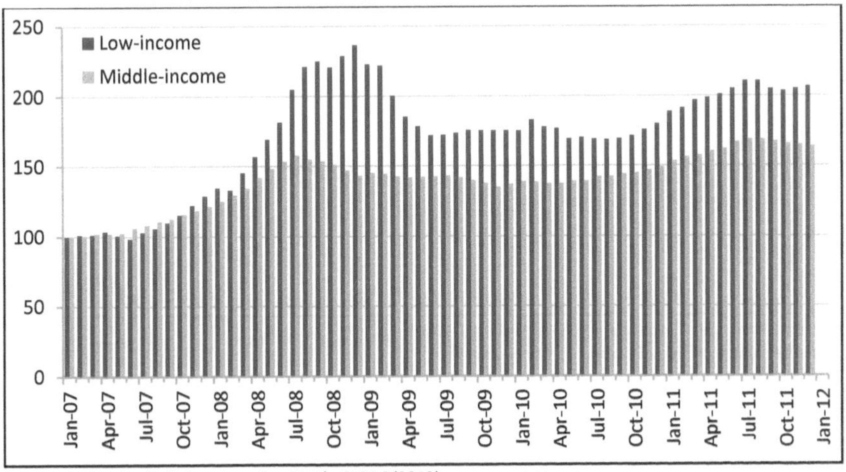

Source: Authors' calculations based on FAO's *GIEWS* (2012)
Note: The sample includes 26 LICs and 29 MICs.

3.5.   Vulnerable geographic areas fare worse than urban centers

The aggregate pictures, which are primarily based on major urban centers or national averages, also mask noteworthy variations within countries. The *GIEWS* database offers price data for multiple locations in a number of countries, which allows for comparison of price movements between major urban centers and food insufficient or vulnerable areas. As expected, food price increases can be considerably larger in specific locations within countries (Figure 10). Looking at the entire time series, populations in vulnerable geographic areas appear to pay a 3.2 percent premium, on average, for the same foodstuffs as their compatriots in urban centers. Interestingly, the spread between local food prices in vulnerable areas and major urban centers increased sizably during the major price upswings in 2007-08 and 2010-11, signaling that populations in food insufficient locations suffer disproportionately during global food price shocks.

---

[5] Nearly identical results are also achieved when examining the data by levels of food security (secure versus insecure) using FAO's (2011c) classification of countries that require external assistance to meet basic food needs.

**Figure III.10. Food Price Differences between Vulnerable Areas
and Major Urban Centers, 2007-11**
(unweighted average percent difference of index values)

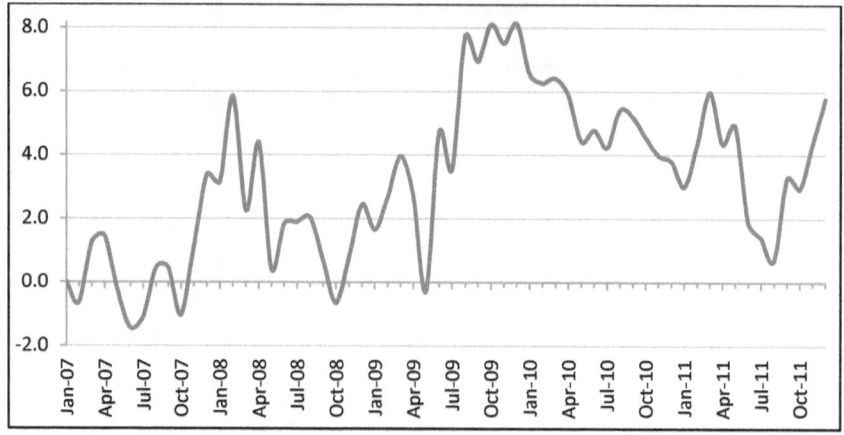

Source: Authors' calculations based on FAO's *GIEWS* (2012)
Note: The sample includes 24 intra-country observations.

4.   Impacts of Rising Food Prices on Households[6]

Higher local food prices have serious consequences for households and
economies. At the household level, dietary modifications can lead to
hunger and malnutrition, especially among children, while losses in
purchasing power can increase poverty and inequality. At the state
level, higher import bills add further pressure on scarce public resources
and reduce the availability and quality of key public goods; governments
must also keep a close watch on the impact of higher food prices on
overall levels of inflation. When combined, the adverse impacts of
soaring food prices can wreak devastating havoc on societies. Indeed,
2011 was blanketed with strident reminders, as food protests erupted
in Algeria, Bangladesh, Burkina Faso, Egypt, India, Iraq, Jordan,
Morocco, Mozambique, Nigeria, Senegal, Syria, Tunisia, Uganda and
Yemen.

Moreover, in 2012 rising local food prices pose additional challenges to
poor households that have been coping with the income shocks

---

[6] This section focuses exclusively on the negative impacts of higher food prices. It should be noted,
however, that high commodity prices can also create opportunities for developing agricultural
production and rural development. Unlike the 2007-08 food crisis, increases in almost all
agricultural prices (e.g., sugar and cotton) may benefit farmers in some low-income countries
through commodity exports, although the net impact of higher costs for basic food staples is likely
to be far worse for the majority of smallholders, landless labourers and the urban poor.

associated with the previous price spikes, including food and fuel, as well as the jobs crisis (Chapter IV). In upper-MICs, such as Turkey, 73 percent of households had earlier substituted into cheaper food items while 53 percent had decreased their amount of food consumption (TEPAV, UNICEF and World Bank 2009). In lower-MICs, like the Philippines, 85 percent of households had lowered food consumption, 55 percent had reduced essential medical expenditures and 40 percent had borrowed money (Reyes et al. 2010). And in LICs, ActionAid, the Overseas Development Institute, Oxfam, Save the Children, UNICEF, the World Bank and others have provided ample evidence of more severe coping strategies, such as eating fewer meals, cutting back sharply on health and medical expenditures, increasing informal labour market activities, especially among mothers (e.g., working longer hours as street vendors or waste pickers), or forcing children to leave school in order to beg or work in the fields or at home (see, for example, Mendoza 2010). In sum, poor households have been adjusting to high food costs for years, and their capacity for resilience is limited in 2012.

4.1.   Hunger and malnutrition

One of the main coping mechanisms to counter rising food costs at the household level is alternative consumption patterns. In response to higher food prices since 2008, families across the globe have reported eating fewer meals (sometimes skipping whole days), smaller quantities (usually mothers and elder sisters among adults, but also infants and young children) and less nutritious foods. These behaviors have been widely reported, such as in India, Pakistan, Nigeria, Peru and Bangladesh (Save the Children 2012), in Bangladesh, Cambodia, the Central African Republic, Ghana, Kazakhstan, Kenya, Mongolia, the Philippines, Serbia, Thailand, Ukraine, Vietnam and Zambia (Heltberg et al. 2012), in Bangladesh, Indonesia, Jamaica, Kenya, Yemen and Zambia (Hossain and Green 2011, and Hossain and McGregor 2011), in Nigeria (Samuels et al. 2011), in Bangladesh, Cambodia, Guinea, Kenya, Lesotho Swaziland (Compton et al. 2010), in Cambodia (Green et al. 2010), in the Philippines (Reyes et al. 2010) and in Ukraine (UNDP 2010).

Such behavior changes cause micronutrient and caloric deficiencies in the body and ultimately lead to weight loss and severe malnutrition. Altogether, the 2008 food price spike is estimated to have increased undernourishment by nearly 7 percent worldwide, or 63 million people

(Tiwari and Zaman 2010). Moreover, many countries that were most vulnerable to rising food prices during the previous crisis were those that were already facing high pre-existing levels of malnutrition (e.g., Burundi, Madagascar, the Niger, Timor-Leste and Yemen), a trend which appears to remain consistent during the latest food price shock (see Section 3.4).

The harmful outcomes of malnourishment and hunger are most pronounced on infants and young children. In particular, children who suffer from malnutrition while in the womb to 24 months of age can experience irreversible effects later in life in terms of health, cognitive development, productivity and earning potential. Undernourished children also tend to develop their physical and mental capabilities more slowly than healthy children since constant hunger weakens their immune systems and makes them more susceptible to diseases (Victora et al. 2008). Perhaps most worrisome is the finding that malnutrition contributes to more than one-third of all under-five deaths (Black et al. 2008). This reflects the fact that food-deprived children are physically weak and oftentimes unable to fight off common illnesses. The link between maternal nutrition and children's health is also critical. For example, poorly nourished women—including those that suffer from low weight-for-height or anemia during pregnancy—are likely to give birth to underweight babies, thus perpetuating the cycle of under-nutrition; they are also more likely to die during childbirth (UNICEF 2009).

It is also imperative that nutritional trends are viewed within both the context of reduced household income due to the jobs crisis (detailed in Chapter IV). Given that the income and price shocks have simultaneously reverberated across many countries unabatedly since 2008, the danger of hunger and malnutrition remains severe and serious in 2012, especially among infants and young children.

Rising local food costs also pose serious threats to the MDGs. For instance, achieving MDG1 by 2015 is at stake (reducing half the proportion of people who suffer from hunger). While the proportion of malnourished and hungry people has slightly decreased since 1990, the trend is increasing in terms of absolute numbers. The latest FAO estimates put the number of hungry and malnourished persons at 925 million in 2010 (about 16 percent of the total population of developing countries); that figure, however, does not reflect the impact of the recent food price spike that began in mid-2010, which has likely increased the risk of malnourishment (Figure 11). Moreover, given that local food prices have remained at historic highs in many of the developing countries studied earlier in Section 3, the estimated fall of hungry and malnourished people in 2010 is questionable; other projections place the number of hungry persons in 2010—before the most recent price surge—potentially as high as 1.3 billion (Brinkman et al. 2010).

Figure III.11. Undernourishment in Developing Countries, 1970-2015

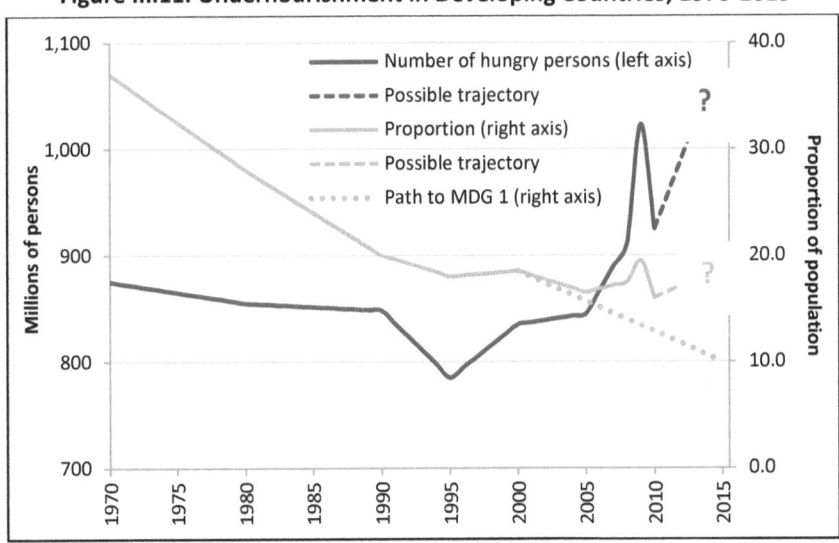

Source: FAO (2011e)

The potential setback to MDG1 may be especially severe in countries that are undergoing protracted food emergencies (Figure 12). Given the negative impacts of rising food prices on child and maternal mortality rates, MDG targets 4A and 5A are also in grave danger as a result of high food prices coupled with the other impacts associated with the global economic crisis.

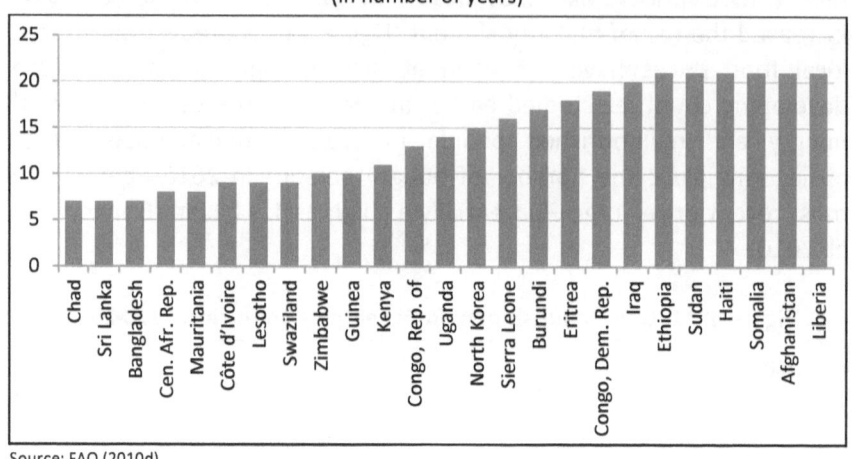

Figure III.12. Duration of Current Food Emergencies (as of 2010)
(in number of years)

Source: FAO (2010d)

4.2.   Exacerbated poverty and inequality

Rising local food prices can aggravate both poverty and inequality. Given that poor and vulnerable households spend up to 80 percent of their total expenditures on basic foodstuffs, higher food prices erode their disposable income. In aggregate terms, estimates from the 2007-08 food crisis suggest that higher food prices increased global poverty 3-5 percent (Dessus et al. 2008, Ivanic and Martin 2008, and Wodon et al. 2008). Food price increases also impact the degree of poverty by pushing those already below the poverty line farther down. Evidence shows that the price shock increased the depth of poverty among the existing poor in rural areas, while the 'new poor'—a trend that was less common—were largely concentrated in urban areas (Compton et al. 2010).

Given the disproportionate negative impact on poor and vulnerable populations, higher local food prices can also increase levels of inequality. In particular, studies of Bangladesh, Vietnam and Latin America show that inequality rates rose as a result of the 2007-08 food price shocks (Save the Children 2009 and World Bank 2008a). These findings support estimates by the ADB (2008) that a 20 percent nominal food price increase leads to a 1 percent increase in the Gini coefficient (actual prices were often quadruple that level during 2008).

4.3.   Poorer provision of public services

Due to the climb in world food prices, FAO (2011a) estimates that food import bills for least developed countries jumped by more than one-third during 2011, which far exceeded the record increase of the 2007-08 high-price episode. For governments, high food prices increase the cost of food assistance and subsidy programs as well as decrease revenue from lower taxes and tariffs (in food import-dependent countries). The overall fiscal impact was clearly evidenced during the 2007-08 crisis where many developing country governments faced the daunting challenge of financing social protection activities, subsidies and food. Importantly, lower fiscal space for social expenditures, including education and health, further shift these burdens on households and communities, just at a time when their need for public assistance is high and rising. Higher food costs can also adversely impact ongoing social protection programs as a result of real losses in the value of any cash or income transfers (Overseas Development Institute 2008).

4.4.   Inflation and weaker employment-generating growth

Inflation is a key concern to governments since it typically requires a monetary policy to increase interest rates which, in turn, stymies economic activity and threatens employment-generating growth. This was clearly evident during the 2007-08 food crisis. While developing countries as a whole saw an average inflation rate of 5.9 percent from 2003-06, inflation jumped to 7.6 percent in 2007 and 8.1 percent in 2008 before tapering off (IMF 2011); the IMF (2008a) estimated that food price increases accounted for about 70 percent of total inflation among emerging economies. Developing countries in Sub-Saharan Africa and the Middle East and North Africa were hardest hit, with the former peaking at 13.4 percent and the latter at 12.1 percent, on average. During 2011, many developing country governments began to voice headline inflation concerns as a result of rising domestic food prices. In Indonesia, for example, President Yudhoyono urged households to plant food in their gardens to help ease price pressures.[7]

---

[7] Fullick, N. and P. Apps. 2011."Record High Food Prices Stoke Fears for Economy." *Reuters*, January 06.

5.   Policy Responses through 2011

The above evidence makes an unequivocal case for prompt and adequate policy responses in the face of the renewed threat of high food prices. General policy responses to counter unaffordable food can be understood through the following three-part analytical framework: (i) *supporting consumers* to promote household food security; (ii) *supporting producers* to enhance the food supply; and (iii) *managing and regulating food markets* to reduce domestic food price volatility.

- *Consumers:* In much of the world, the ultimate reason why many local foods remain unaffordable is low living standards and high levels of poverty. Nobel Laureate Amartya Sen transformed the understanding of this issue by focusing on the importance of increasing food access. According to Sen, the main problem associated with hunger is distribution and access; his work subsequently raised awareness on the need to address inequity and social justice in order to reduce household poverty and raise incomes, mainly through social protection.

- *Producers:* Agriculture has been neglected in recent decades and is a sector in massive need of public and private investment, as shown by many UN organizations and the World Bank.

- *Managing and regulating food markets*: Like any other market, food is regulated. Sanitary regulations protect consumers across developed countries, and governments have been regulating commodities in physical and financial markets for nearly a century. Given the life and death consequences of price fluctuations in food markets, there is a clear role for more effective government involvement.

Through this analytical framework, a review of the various international and national responses to the 2007-08 food crisis and, where available, of their effects and adequacy, can provide useful insights as to what may be most needed to address current food security challenges. An update of what has happened to some of the responses through 2011 also offers an initial assessment of the extent of the policy actions that are required moving forward.

5.1.   International responses

The UN has been calling for the eradication of world hunger for decades, such as through the right to food and the MDGs (Box 2). When the 2008 food crisis erupted, initial responses focused on supporting consumption and agricultural production. The UN Secretary-General formed the High-Level Task Force on the Global Food Security Crisis, which proposed a *Comprehensive Framework for Action* to overcome the food crisis. This was updated in September 2010 and recommended a twin-track approach based on short-term emergency support and long-term development interventions (United Nations 2010). It also called for US$25 to US$40 billion annually for food aid, agricultural development, and social protection and nutrition programs. A *Road Map for Scaling Up Nutrition (SUN)* and a *Framework for Action* were also prepared in 2010-11 to ensure sustained improvements in nutrition and the achievement of MDG1 by 2015.

At the G8 meeting in L'Aquila, Italy in July 2009, the G8 countries plus the European Commission, Australia, the Netherlands, Spain and Sweden supported the need for a comprehensive and coordinated international response for food security. Donors pledged US$20 billion under the so-called *L'Aquila Food Security Initiative*, which supports country-owned plans and is largely focused on increasing agriculture productivity (see G20 L'Aquila Statement 2009).[8]

In 2009, calls for regulation were added to the need to support consumption and production. The UN Conference on the World Financial and Economic Crisis urged countries to coordinate a global response to address the financial and economic causes of food insecurity. Several UN reports have noted that higher food prices are not only a result of underinvestment in agriculture, but also of speculative activities in commodity derivatives markets (United Nations 2009 and 2011, UNCTAD 2009a). The G20 group of leading economies has also acknowledged the need for regulation. At the Pittsburgh Summit in September 2009, G20 leaders agreed "to improve the

---

[8] Double-counting has been reported, and some donors have not provided additional resources but instead included funds already committed for climate change and other development priorities (Oxfam 2010). The G8's 2010 *Muskoka Accountability Report* pointed that, while the decline in investment was reversing, the need to monitor financial disbursements was important for transparency and accountability.

regulation, functioning, and transparency of financial and commodity markets to address excessive commodity price volatility."[9] And at the G20 Seoul Summit in November 2010, leaders further vowed to "work on the regulation and supervision of commodity derivatives markets."[10]

Box III.2. The Right to Food

Food is one of the most basic human needs, and people are entitled to adequate food that is sufficient, safe, nutritious and culturally acceptable. The right to food was first recognized in 1948 in Article 25 of the Universal Declaration of Human Rights. Since then it has been repeatedly recognized by other international instruments, including Article 11 of the International Covenant on Economic, Social and Cultural Rights (1976), Article 12 of the Convention on the Elimination of All Forms of Discrimination against Women (1979), and Articles 24 and 27 of the Convention on the Rights of the Child (1989). In September 2000, 189 states further expressed their commitment to the eradication of hunger and poverty by endorsing the Millennium Declaration, which was translated into eight time-bound, measurable goals to be reached by 2015, known as the MDGs.

A number of countries have recently revised their constitutions or passed new legal frameworks to give greater effect to the right to food. Since the mid-1990s new constitutions, including bills of rights, have been adopted in a slew of countries in the CEE/CIS, Africa, Latin America and, more recently, Asia. In India, for example, in addition to passing the Food Security Act in 2010, the government has adopted a number of policy innovations based on the right to food, including acts on universal school meals, employment, social security for the informal sector and the right to information, which, combined, can lead to better food security outcomes (Bonnerjee and Koehler 2010). People and citizenry organizations can demand that governments respect, protect and fulfill appropriate access to, and acceptable quality of, food.

In 2011, France, as host of the G20, pushed for the first ever meeting of G20 agriculture ministers to deal with food price volatility. In Paris, the ministers met and agreed to an *Action Plan on Food Price Volatility and Agriculture*, which addressed a variety of issues, including financial market speculation, biofuels, an early warning agricultural market information system (Amis), food productivity, export restrictions and food reserves. The *Action Plan* was discussed at the Cannes Summit in

---

[9] G20 Pittsburgh Leaders' Statement (2009).
[10] G20 Seoul Summit Leaders' Declaration (2010).

November 2011, and led to the agreement of the G20 leaders to act on five objectives: (i) improving agricultural production and productivity; (ii) increasing market information and transparency; (iii) reducing the effects of price volatility for the most vulnerable; (iv) strengthening international policy coordination; and (v) improving the functioning of agricultural commodity derivatives' markets.[11] This argument has been further echoed by the G20 Ministries of Finance and by the EU in 2011, who acknowledged the need for regulation of commodity markets to ensure better functioning and more transparent agricultural financial markets (including OTC trading) to prevent and to address market abuses, cross-market manipulations and price volatility. Critics point that these efforts fall short of tackling excessive financial speculation.[12]

One notable area where the international community has yet to make substantial progress on food security issues is agricultural subsidies. In 2010, while the EU paid out €39 billion on direct agriculture subsidies,[13] the United States government spent US$21.3 billion to subsidize mainly large-scale farmers.[14] The use of domestic subsidies in developing countries is discussed in the next section; these are small in magnitude and do not impact international prices. Subsidies in higher-income economies, however, can drive international commodities prices down. While proponents of subsidies claim that they provide cheap food for consumers in developing countries, opponents argue that subsidies in higher-income economies hinder the development of agriculture elsewhere since they cannot compete and are often advised against minor subsidy use in favor of market forces to boost crop production (the comparative advantage argument purported by wealthier countries). Moreover, lower international food prices due to subsidies have encouraged developing countries to be buyers of food from developed countries, which has hindered agricultural self-sufficiency and local farm production. Resistance to lower agricultural subsidies from the developed world was one of the main issues that led to the collapse of negotiations of the Doha Round of the WTO.

---

[11] G20 Cannes Summit Final Declaration (2011).
[12] World Development Movement. 2011. "450 Economists Tell the G20: Regulate Speculation on Food Prices." *World Development Movement*, October 11.
[13] EU 2010 General Budget: Agriculture and Rural Development.
[14] Budget of the United States Government: Fiscal Year 2011, Historical Tables, Table 3.2 (budget function 351).

5.2.   National policy approaches

Most developing countries responded to the 2007-08 food crisis—and some to the price run-up that began in 2010—by implementing a mix of polices aimed at consumers, producers and food markets. These different approaches are broadly summarized below.

- *Supporting consumption*: Policy responses included food assistance (e.g., direct food transfers, food stamps/vouchers and school feeding programs), price subsidies and controls, cash transfers, reduced consumption taxes and food-for-work schemes.

- *Boosting agricultural production*: This mainly focused on providing subsidies and reducing taxes on grain producers, although some countries also offered other types of incentives to spur agricultural output, such as credit programs for small farmers.

- *Managing and regulating food markets*: Many developing countries tried to lower domestic food prices by encouraging imports and discouraging exports, most commonly by reducing import tariffs and/or introducing different export restrictions. Building up and releasing strategic food reserves was another frequently employed strategy to stabilize local food prices. A number of governments also intervened in food markets by restricting stockholding by private traders, imposing anti-hoarding measures and restricting futures trading of basic foods.

A review of various sources from the FAO and the IMF shows that out of 98 developing country governments, 75 supported consumers, 57 promoted agricultural production and 76 intervened in food markets (Table 1). While the adoption of these general policy approaches appears balanced on the aggregate, interesting patterns emerge when examining responses across regions and income levels. For example, on average, developing countries in Asia appear the most proactive in terms of supporting consumers and managing/regulating food markets when facing higher food prices, while countries in Sub-Saharan Africa are most inclined to foster agricultural production. Using an income lens, poorer countries are, on average, more reactive to higher food prices across all policy categories when compared to wealthier, upper-MICs.

Table III.1 General Policy Responses to Rising Commodity Prices in 98 Developing Countries, 2008-10
(in number of developing countries)

Region/Income group	Sample Size	General Policy Area		
		Consumption	Production	Managing Food Markets
Sub-Saharan Africa	39	30	29	29
Middle East and North Africa	13	10	5	12
Latin America and Caribbean	22	17	11	16
CEE/CIS	6	4	3	4
Asia	18	14	9	15
Low	33	25	25	28
Lower-middle	39	32	22	30
Upper-middle	26	18	10	18
Total	98	75	57	76

Sources: Demeke et al. (2009), FAO (2009a, 2010e-g) and IMF country reports (2009-10)

Analysis of specific responses to rising commodity prices suggests that food assistance, production subsidies and lower tariffs are the most commonly adopted policies by developing countries (Figure 13).[15] On the demand side, about 40 percent of developing countries in the sample implemented some form of food assistance program; about one-third of the countries also used price subsidies and price controls to support consumers. On the supply side, production or input subsidies appeared to be the preferred policy choice among developing country governments to encourage domestic production (about 40 percent), although a large number (22 percent) have also reduced taxes on grain producers. Regarding the management and regulation of food markets, more than half of developing countries have reduced tariffs to encourage cheaper imports while nearly one-quarter have introduced export bans or other controls to discourage food exports. A large proportion of developing countries have also focused on stocking strategic food reserves in order to stabilize domestic market prices (43 percent).

---

[15] These findings largely corroborate other meta reviews of policy responses to higher food prices (e.g., Wiggins et al. 2010, and Wodon and Zaman 2010).

Figure III.13. Specific Policy Responses to Rising Commodity Prices in 98 Developing Countries, 2008-10

(in number of countries)

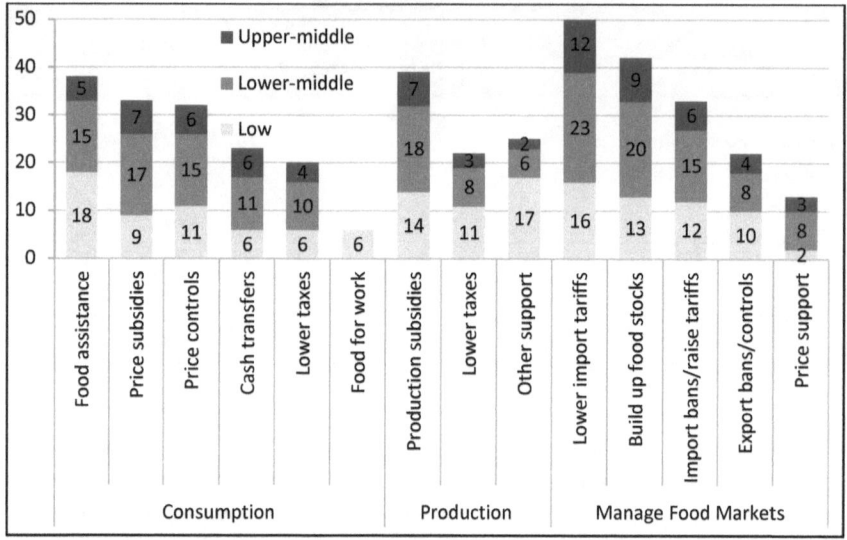

Sources: Demeke et al. (2009), FAO (2009a, 2010e-g) and IMF country reports (2009-10)

5.3.   Policy impact

The impact of the unique national policies adopted to fight rising food prices is less clear than the overall approaches taken. In general, there is limited quantitative information available regarding the extent and coverage of policies and programs. For instance, while many countries in the different samples reported to have 'lowered import tariffs,' the scope and values vary widely (e.g., a single commodity versus a large basket, or a 100 percent reduction versus a 5 percent reduction). Similarly, a country classified as having a food assistance or a cash transfer program could be referring to a national program or a small pilot project in a remote province. Despite the information shortcomings, preliminary analyses of the responses adopted during the 2007-08 crisis do offer some insights into which strategies may be most effective moving forward. The impacts of selected consumption, production and food market management-related policies are discussed below.

5.3.1. Supporting consumption

Food and nutrition assistance: Developing country governments adopted various food and nutrition initiatives in response to the 2007-08 food crisis. Distributing emergency food aid was a common strategy in poorer countries, such as Afghanistan, Angola, Bangladesh and Cambodia (FAO 2009b). While emergency programs may effectively meet the short-term food security needs among vulnerable groups, food aid can also act as a disincentive for local producers if continued beyond the initial emergency or if not linked to specific requirements, such as work.

In MICs, conversely, school feeding programs (e.g., in-school meals, fortified biscuits, take-home rations) emerged as one of the preferred options to deliver food assistance. This reflected the existence of comprehensive programs in many countries prior to the crisis (e.g., Brazil, China, Honduras and Mexico), as well as the numerous benefits associated with school feeding programs: easy scalability on short notice, provides a benefit per household that is often more than 10 percent of household expenditures, and increases school attendance, cognition and educational achievement among children, especially when complemented by deworming and micronutrient initiatives (Bundy et al. 2009). For example, after high food prices increased dropout rates and reduced enrolment rates in the Philippines, the government launched an 'enhanced' feeding program to give porridge to public elementary students from pre-selected areas when they attended classes;[16] in South Africa, the government expanded allocations of its school nutrition program to keep pace with the rate of food inflation (World Bank 2008b).

While school feeding programs generally served as an effective short-term mitigation measure, they are costly to maintain and do not support infants and toddlers—in other words, those children that are at greatest risk of mortality due to malnutrition—nor children that are too poor to attend school—typically the hungriest and most undernourished. These drawbacks are pronounced in poorer countries that are characterized by overall low school enrollment rates (Bundy et al. 2009). As a result, school feeding programs should not be viewed as

---

[16] Mailo, R. 2008. "GMA Launches the 'Enhanced' Food for School Feeding Program." *Philippine Information Agency*, July 31.

a standalone panacea, but rather as an effective response to be complemented by other social protection measures. School feeding initiatives may also serve as a good intervention to combat rising food prices in the absence of a cash transfer program (Lustig 2009).

Price subsidies: Universal price subsidies to basic foods tended to provide quick results and were most effective in countries with high levels of poverty where targeting is less relevant. Haiti is one effective example. The government subsidized rice to all households, where more than three-fourths of the population—the poorest segment—consumes about 70 percent of total rice in the country (Demeke et al. 2009). Many countries, however, used targeted price subsidies, with mixed results. In Egypt, the targeted rationing-card of subsidized basic foodstuffs for eligible poor households led to significant leakages to the non-poor and under coverage in rural areas (Korayem 2010). In Bangladesh, on the other hand, the government launched a self-targeted subsidy program that allowed consumers to purchase rice at below market prices and succeeded in reaching vulnerable populations, especially in urban areas (World Bank 2008b).

Price controls: Many developing country governments experimented with various types of controls. For example, Malawi empowered a public agricultural corporation to conduct all maize transactions and set prices, Malaysia imposed a price ceiling on rice sold to consumers, and Sri Lanka fixed maximum retail and wholesale prices for different grades of rice (Demeke et al. 2009). While such measures can be effective in controlling prices in the short run, it is important to note that fixing prices at low levels tends to discourage domestic production (FAO 2009a). Enforcement was also shown to be complex, since it often requires police or armed forces to monitor retail prices and/or enforce a system of fines. In addition, some governments built partnerships with the private sector, which can be an effective strategy to achieve price controls. Mexico, for example, announced a price freeze on 150 basic food items as part of a pact with the National Confederation of Chambers of Industry, which agreed not to pass on higher prices to consumers over a fixed period of time.[17] And in Jordan, the government reached an agreement with the private sector to print the prices of rice and sugar on all packages to avoid retail mark-ups (Janjua 2008).

---

[17] Dickerson, M. 2008. "Mexico is Freezing Prices on Scores of Food Staples." *Los Angeles Times*, June 19.

Cash transfers: Cash transfers can be most effective in addressing hunger where social protection systems with wide coverage exist, given that they can provide an adequate income supplement to households. However, social protection coverage tends to be low in most developing countries, and, in general, national administrations were not flexible or well-financed enough and unable to quickly adjust coverage and/or benefits in response to rapidly rising local food prices. In many national programs, high prices led to a dramatic drop in the purchasing power among beneficiaries. Ethiopia, for example, which has the largest safety net in Africa, increased the transfer value by 33 percent, but the food basket rose in excess of 300 percent (Mousseau 2010). Following the 2007-08 experience, many have recommended that transfer amounts be indexed to inflation and that existing programs be complemented by food transfers in order to provide the right support at the right time. Many countries are also building a social protection floor—which nobody should fall below—to protect the most vulnerable both during and after the crisis.[18] Where a social protection system does not exist, establishing a new cash transfer program requires extensive start-up time and should not be viewed as an appropriate emergency short-term food security response, unless complemented with other faster instruments to support households.

Lower taxes: Reducing consumption taxes, especially on grain, was another widely used policy intervention in both LICs and MICs. For example, Brazil eliminated taxes (from 9.25 percent) on wheat products,[19] Ethiopia removed value added taxes (VATs) and turnover taxes (15 percent) on food grains and flour (IMF 2008b), Kenya removed a VAT (16 percent) on rice and bread,[20] and Madagascar reduced its VAT on rice from 20 to 5 percent (IMF 2008b). While such measures did soften the price shocks, they are not without fiscal costs. In the case of Brazil, abolishing wheat-based taxes was projected to cost the government $300 million in lost revenue from May to December 2008.[21]

---

[18] The Social Protection Floor Initiative is one of the UN's crisis response initiatives that promotes universal access to essential social transfers and services.

[19] Versiani, I. and E. Barreto. 2008. "Brazil Cuts Wheat Sector Taxes to Ease Inflation." *Reuters*, May 15.

[20] Bi Mingxin. 2008. "Kenya's Food Crisis to Persist despite Budget Proposals." *Xinhua News*, June 14.

[21] Versiani, I. and E. Barreto. 2008. "Brazil Cuts Wheat Sector Taxes to Ease Inflation." *Reuters*, 15 May 15.

5.3.2. Boosting agricultural production

In general, the effectiveness of individual measures to support food production during the 2007-08 crisis is difficult to estimate because they were generally taken as part of a package that combined different interventions (Demeke et al. 2009). It must be noted that these measures require time to deliver results (e.g., the next crop) and, therefore, should be complemented with other short-term food security policies to protect vulnerable households.

Production or input subsidies: Subsidies, especially on grain production and on inputs, such as fertilizer and seeds, were commonly used to reinforce production incentives. In India and Bangladesh, the governments provided subsidies to poor and marginal farmers to mitigate higher costs of production for irrigation and fertilizer (Mousseau 2010). Similarly, the governments of Kenya, Madagascar, Malawi, Tanzania and Zambia introduced or expanded input (mainly fertilizer) subsidy programs, between 30 and 70 percent (Demeke et al. 2009 and International Food Policy Research Institute 2008). Adequate subsidies and distribution of productive inputs can bolster short-term production. However, subsidies alone are insufficient to sustainably transform agricultural systems, especially without other forms of support, such as credit programs, marketing infrastructure and national agricultural development strategies that also address land and labour issues.

Other production measures: Other measures used to support producers during the 2007-08 crisis included improved access to funds and credit facilities, tax exemptions on fertilizer and farm machinery, and increased state investment in the agriculture sector. India stands as a remarkable example, as the government cancelled the entire debt of small farmers in 2008 to encourage production among smallholders—a policy that cost around US$15 billion.[22] And in China, the central government increased financial support for agricultural production by 30 percent in its 2008 budget compared to 2007, mainly to support farmers.[23]

---

[22] BBC News. 2008. "India Cancels Small Farmers' Debt." *BBC News*, February 29.
[23] Xinhua News. 2008. "China Giving Greater Support to Agriculture to Cool Inflation," *Xinhua News*, March 26.

Acquisition of agricultural land abroad: A number of countries responded to higher food prices by buying or leasing land in developing countries as a strategy to secure basic food supplies or simply for profit. This behavior was observed in Asia (e.g., China and India), in Europe (e.g., Germany, the Netherlands and the United Kingdom) and in the Middle East (e.g., Kuwait, Saudi Arabia and Qatar). These transactions— popularly known as 'land grabbing'—are highly controversial. According to the World Bank, over 46 million hectares of large-scale farmland acquisitions or negotiations were announced between October 2008 and August 2009 alone, with 70 percent of the demanded land concentrated in Sub-Saharan Africa; of these, 37 percent involved food crops, 21 percent cash crops and 21 percent biofuels (Deininger et al. 2010). The stakes are high for displaced small farmers, women and children where land is being leased in large amounts. In particular, small-scale family agriculture, which is vital to supporting most of the world's rural poor, is being threatened by large-scale plantations, export-led agriculture and the production of commodities rather than food. It is imperative that governments and communities negotiate or renegotiate land deals with extreme caution (UN Special Rapporteur on the Right to Food 2009).

5.3.3. Management and regulation of food markets

Lower tariffs: Tariff reductions did not lead to significant food price declines in most developing countries. This largely reflects the reality that the price impact depends on the extent of the reduction, and, in general, there was little room to lower tariffs following years of pressure to liberalize trade. For instance, Bangladesh removed tariffs on rice and wheat, but they were a meager 5 percent to begin with, and Sierra Leone decreased its import tariffs from 15 to 10 percent (Wiggins et al. 2010). However, in countries where this policy was still feasible, reducing tariffs was shown to be easy to implement. For example, Morocco sliced tariffs on wheat imports from 130 to 2.5 percent, and Nigeria dropped duties on rice imports from 100 to 2.7 percent (Demeke et al. 2009). While lowering import tariffs can be an attractive option when feasible, it is important to gauge the fiscal cost of lost revenue, which can be significant.

Export bans/restrictions: Export control measures were a fast and effective way to protect consumers in the short term during the 2007-

08 food crisis. Not only are these trade measures cheap and easy to implement, introducing export taxes also raises government revenue. A host of developing countries were wooed by these benefits and restricted food exports, including Argentina, Cambodia, China, Egypt, India, Kazakhstan, Pakistan, the Russian Federation, Ukraine and Vietnam (Demeke et al. 2009). Unfortunately, such policies are not without downside. On the one hand, export restrictions led to higher prices for food staples on international markets. On the other hand, they also created disincentives for farmers, and a number of major exporting countries experienced a decrease in cereal planting due to lower output prices coupled with higher input prices (FAO 2009b).

Food stocks: The degree to which prices are influenced on the open market depends on the amount of food stock released or made available for release on the market. While the nature and size of domestic food stocks varied greatly between developing countries during 2007-08, the poorest countries had trivial reserves and, hence, little impact on prices in general (Mousseau 2010). However, in countries where food stocks are managed by government agencies that annually purchase grain—such as Bangladesh, India and Indonesia— public reserves can serve as an effective price buffer, limit inflation and provide resources for food distribution or subsidized sales to the poor. The Food Corporation of India (the government's grain procurement and distribution agency), for example, purchased a record amount of rice and wheat prior to the 2007-08 food crisis, which enabled the government to release enough reserves to stabilize prices (Demeke et al. 2009).

Restricting or banning futures markets: Some governments, including India, Pakistan and Thailand, took measures against speculation and enacted harsh penalties for those who were caught hoarding grain. The Philippines even went as far as establishing an Anti-Rice-Hoarding Task Force to find and punish offenders with life sentences in prison for 'economic sabotage' (Mousseau 2010).

6.   Policy Responses for 2012 and Beyond

Analysis of the responses to the earlier food crisis suggests that several improvements may be desirable in the renewed charge against the threat of higher food prices. First, a better balance between short-term and long-term policy responses is needed to improve the effectiveness and adequacy of the policy responses to counter rising food prices. Second, as food insecurity facing children poses particularly serious harms to both individual households and the economic future of a country, a more child-sensitive policy framework is necessary. Finally, there is a timely need to reprioritize expenditure policy toward enabling prompt and adequate interventions that can strengthen food security among the most vulnerable populations.

6.1.   A sound mix of short- and long-term interventions

A review of the policies into 2011 shows that responses to rising food prices have overwhelmingly focused on short-term mitigation measures, which is worrisome because temporary strategies are incapable of protecting populations from future food price increases. The limitations of many of these shorter-term strategies are further underscored by their general failure to combat domestic food inflation, which continued to hover at historic highs in early 2012 (Section 3). Moving forward, provisional measures are still warranted to protect poor and vulnerable populations from the immediate, adverse impacts of higher food costs—albeit more effectively. But just as important, countries must also adopt a longer-term policy framework aimed at *reducing poverty, securing sustainable food production* and *adequately regulating food markets* (Box 3).

6.2.   A renewed focus on protecting the next generation... today

While some governments have continued to introduce measures to address rising local food prices, Chapter V shows that many developing countries are phasing out or eliminating subsidies, including on food items. The removal of public support for food is also most commonly found in Sub-Saharan Africa and the Middle and North Africa as part of fiscal consolidation efforts.

Additionally, fiscal adjustment is being pursued by measures such as further targeting already meager social protection systems. The overall timing and scope of the projected spending contraction raise concern in light of the still fragile and uneven economic recovery and the continued crisis impacts on vulnerable populations, which are being exacerbated by the current run-up in local food prices. Not responding

Box III.3. A Long-term Policy Framework

Poverty reduction is an effective policy objective to anchor the fight against hunger. The ultimate reason why many local foods remain unaffordable is because of low living standards. A main problem associated with hunger is distribution and access rather than insufficient food production (Dreze and Sen 1989). As a result, it is necessary to address inequity and social justice in order to reduce household poverty and raise incomes. This may be effectively achieved through introducing or scaling up social protection programs to ensure that vulnerable households have access to affordable and nutritious foods—moving toward a universal social protection floor. Over the longer term, reducing poverty requires comprehensive national policy planning, such as equitable national development and/or poverty reduction strategies that are aimed at both employment-generating growth and inclusive, equitable social development (United Nations 2008).

Sustainable food production is another important channel. Transforming the role of agriculture in national development strategies requires supporting investment and productivity growth in agriculture, livestock and fisheries. Given that women produce between 60 and 80 percent of food in most developing countries (80 to 90 percent in some Sub-Saharan African countries), a gender focus is warranted. Ultimately, effective interventions should support small-scale farming that lifts populations out of poverty by addressing land redistribution, credit access, rural extension services, etc. (see, for example, World Bank 2008c, ActionAid International 2010 and FAO 2011e). Moreover, in a context of climate change, floods and droughts need to be addressed by better irrigation and water management.

Markets matter importantly in ensuring affordable living standards. And regulation can and should play a key role in ensuring that food markets— as well as other markets that affect food prices—are well-functioning and provide sufficient price signals to aid in supply responses and smooth international and interstate food commerce. Some long-term measures aimed at improving national food markets distribution are discussed in recent FAO publications, but higher food prices were not only a result of underinvestment in agriculture or ineffective food market functioning, but also financial speculation that contributed to commodity price volatility (United Nations 2009). Thus, there is an equally important need to improve the regulation, functioning and transparency of financial and commodity markets to address excessive commodity price volatility and enhance consumer protection (see G20 Summit Leaders' Statements from 2009-11). Collective action at the international level is also needed to ensure global trade policies that favor the poor.

quickly and sufficiently is a risk not only to the survival and security of millions of poor and vulnerable persons, but also to a sustained and inclusive economic recovery.

Children must be a priority when designing both short- and long-term responses to rising food prices. While households in every country will adapt uniquely to food price shocks, the potential harm to infants and young children, as well as other highly vulnerable groups, is significant (Section 4.1). Policymakers have a series of rapid responses at their disposal—which often have large, positive spillover effects—such as school feeding programs, support to childcare services, cash transfers, nutritional supplements and community healthcare services, among others. Regarding longer-term approaches to achieve food security, children must be at the center of any such strategy, whether it be promoting rural development or employment or strengthening social protection, education or health systems. Table 2 summarizes possible interventions as they correspond to household coping mechanisms and the potential detrimental impacts on children.

Table III.2. National Policy Responses to Protect Children from Rising Food Prices

(A) Household Response	(B) Impact on Children	(C) Policy Options	
		Short term	Longer term
Increase household income through child labor	Children have less time to attend school or study, or even drop out	- Consumption subsidies - Cash or food transfers or workfare programs to support income - School feeding programs - Programs to prevent school dropouts (flexible school hours, attendance incentive funds, awareness campaigns for parents, mentoring programs)	- Increase income through employment-generating growth and ensure a social protection floor - Invest in agriculture / rural development programs - Adequately manage / regulate food markets
Increase household income through additional female employment	Mother's spend less time supervising children, breastfeeding, cultivating crops, preparing healthy food	- Cash or food transfers or workfare programs to support income - Community childcare services - Nutritional supplements for pregnant and lactating mothers - Food subsidies	- Points above plus: - Support provision of public childcare - Promote gender-sensitive extension services to recognize women's unpaid work in the home and role in food production

(A) Household Response	(B) Impact on Children	(C) Policy Options	
		Short term	Longer term
Change consumption patterns	Mothers and children eat less nutritious foods and/or fewer meals	- Nutrition programs, including school and hospital feeding - Cash/food transfers or work-based programs to support income - Nutritional supplements to vulnerable groups - Awareness campaigns regarding healthy substitute foodstuffs	- Increase family income through job-creating growth and a social protection floor - Invest in agriculture / rural development programs - Adequately manage / regulate food markets - Support diversification of staple consumption and production
Households reduce spending in areas such as health, education or water	Children are pulled out of school and/or have less access to healthcare, vaccinations, medicines, water supply, etc.	- Increase social spending in local budgets - Consumption subsidies - Cash/food transfers or work-based programs to support income - Conditional cash transfers (education and health-based)	- Finance free education and healthcare services for children - Ensure access to drinking water - Ensure adequacy of social protection benefits and coverage

Source: Authors' adaptation of Overseas Development Institute (2008)

Responding to children in countries where prices have been escalating requires coordinated action on two twin tracks: short and medium/longer term. This may be carried out in the context of the UN's *Updated Comprehensive Framework for Action* and other initiatives, such as *Scaling Up Nutrition* and the *Initiative on Soaring Food Prices*.[24] A series of rapid assessments are needed to design appropriate policy decisions, both in the short and long term. These may include, but not be limited to:

-   Understanding food security risks facing children and households, such as changes in food consumption patterns (eating less meals or less nutritious foods), increasing child and mothers' labour to supplement household income, decreasing access to education and health services due to increased household expenditure on food, etc.;
-   Assessing the coverage and adequacy of current food assistance programs (e.g., food distribution, school meals and nutrition supplements), existing social protection systems (including all forms of child support), food subsidies/vouchers, etc.;

---

[24] See http://www.scalingupnutrition.org/ and http://www.fao.org/isfp/isfp-home/en/.

- Reviewing current policies (e.g., fiscal, trade and agriculture) and their impact on food prices to identify possible changes in the short and longer term to support consumption, boost production and regulate/manage food markets;
- Examining potential fiscal space to scale up interventions, including food aid flows;
- For shorter-term responses, identifying farmers that are best positioned to rapidly respond to price increases, as well as existing capacities for transport and distribution of food, nutrition supplements, agricultural inputs, etc.;
- For medium/longer-term responses, identifying obstacles for enhanced agricultural production, with particular attention to small-scale farming, fishing and livestock, along with effective poverty reduction.

Each country is unique and requires tailored policy interventions. If evaluations of the cost-effectiveness of earlier policies and interventions are available, this is clearly a good starting point of analysis. It is also important to emphasize open and participatory processes in policy design, especially since policy decisions are rarely only technocratic, and powerful groups may resist change and/or induce policy failure. As a result, public consultations and dissemination of alternatives that are best for children and poor households—who do not have a strong voice—are necessary to address socially-responsible priorities to combat soaring food prices and ensure a '*Recovery for All.*'

International coordinated action is also fundamental to ensure food security for children, both in the short- and long-term. In the short term, it is critically important that donors support adequate food aid and agricultural development, as well as social protection and nutrition programs. Yet the world needs to move beyond managing crisis; high food prices and volatility will continue unless their structural causes are addressed.

Box III.4. Hunger and Malnutrition in the Horn of Africa

In the early months of 2012, more than 13 million people required emergency food and nutrition assistance in Djibouti, Eritrea, Ethiopia, Kenya and Somalia, of which an estimated 2.3 million were malnourished children, many of which may have died or suffered long-lasting mental or physical damage (Oxfam and Save the Children 2012 and UNICEF 2011). The degree of human suffering is nothing short of a global tragedy, above all, because it was preventable.

The effects of the famine conditions received widespread global attention, but the untold story was that vulnerable populations across the Horn of Africa had been coping with rampant food inflation long before the onset of the unprecedented drought. In fact, local food prices had been rapidly ascending since mid-2010 and nearly doubled, on average, between August 2010 and May 2011 (Figure 14). This then, is the real tragedy: price information and early warning systems detected the looming disaster but policymakers did not react soon enough.

Figure III.14. Local Food Price Indices in the Horn of Africa, Jan. 2007 to Jan. 2012 (Jan. 2007=100)

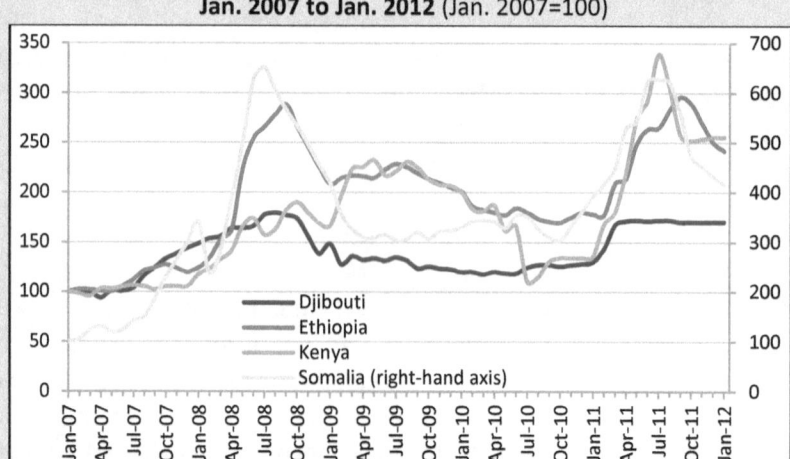

Source: Authors' calculations based on FAO's *GIEWS* (2012)

Bringing food security to the populations in the Horn of Africa is feasible and must become a policy priority. It does, however, require concerted efforts by both governments and donors to address both short- and long-term challenges in parallel. Given the likely persistence of drought conditions coupled with the inability of governments to protect vulnerable populations, the immediate term calls for emergency food and nutrition interventions to avert hunger and starvation. Here, governments and the international community must unite and act swiftly.

Over the medium-term, however, it is clear that government policies must prioritize sustainable access to affordable food. This requires addressing several major challenges. First is poverty. The Horn of Africa is one of the least developed regions in the world in terms of the Human Development Index (HDI), with Djibouti, Eritrea, Ethiopia and Somalia ranking in the bottom 10 percent of all countries and Kenya scoring only slightly better.[25] Second is a lack of water. Driven by severe droughts, the 2011-12 famine is the fourth to affect the Horn of Africa since 2006; hence, recurring water shortages will constantly threaten future harvests. And third is demographics. With more than 40 percent of the national populations under 15 years of age, on average, children stand to lose the most from food insecurity.[26] Achieving food security is therefore predicated on reducing poverty, investing in food production and water management, and building effective social protection systems.

Donor resources are, indeed, important to provide emergency support and help scale up longer-term solutions. However, governments in the Horn of Africa also have a variety of options to expand fiscal space and invest in food security solutions. For example, Djibouti ran a budget surplus in 2011 and spent nearly 4 percent of its GDP on the military; Eritrea has ample scope to increase its tax base and to lobby for increased ODA flows; Ethiopia could potentially capture more than 7 percent of its GDP, which is lost to illicit financial flows, and channel those resources into food security programs, and further shows space to increase public debt; and Kenya could re-direct a portion of its military expenditures (2 percent of GDP) as well as invest some of its excess foreign exchange reserves into food security measures, as explained in Chapter VI. Additionally, given that vast extensions of productive land are being leased to foreign firms in the area, the proceeds could be used to ensure food security.

Short-term humanitarian interventions are imperative to preventing widespread hunger and malnutrition. Over the medium term, however, governments and their development partners must plan and invest effectively to ensure that food security is the principal guiding force of national policy frameworks, which includes accessing all possible sources to boost fiscal space and invest in poverty reduction and sustainable food production.

---

[25] http://hdr.undp.org/en/statistics/hdi/.
[26] Authors' calculations based on United Nation's *World Population Prospects: The 2010 Revision* (2011), medium variant projections.

7.   Conclusion

This chapter has reviewed the possible causes of the renewed food price spike that began in mid-2010, which can be attributed to the combined impacts of weather shocks, exchange rate fluctuations and pressures from speculation on commodity markets. Motivated by the detrimental consequences of higher local food prices, including hunger and malnutrition, poverty and inequality, poorer delivery of social services and inflationary pressures, it further looked at recent local food price movements in a sample of 55 developing countries from 2007 to 2011, identifying where local food price increases have been associated with the recent surge in international food prices.

Following the second major price spike that begin in mid-2010, the chapter found that, on the aggregate, local food prices remained at historic highs heading into 2012. In particular, populations in developing countries were paying 80 percent more, on average, for basic foodstuffs in December 2011 when compared to pre-2007-08 crisis levels. Regionally, Sub-Saharan Africa and the CEE/CIS appear to be facing the most significant price rises, where, at the start of 2012, food costs had more than doubled, on average, when compared to early 2007. Country-level data further verify that the latest food price shock has impacted a large number of developing countries severely, with local food price indices soaring by more than 20 percent between August 2010 and December 2011 in 23 of the 55 countries examined. In terms of distributional impacts, food price increases emerge most acutely in LICs, with vulnerable geographic areas faring worse than urban centers among intra-country observations. Not only do these findings mean that vulnerable populations had been relentlessly coping with high food costs even prior to the latest price spike, but they also suggest that many developing countries were confronting food crises during 2011, which could possibly intensify during 2012. Appropriate and urgent policy actions are therefore imperative.

Drawing from the experiences of the 2007-08 food crisis, this chapter also presented a desk review of policy responses in 98 developing countries. While many governments adopted complex policy approaches, most interventions, in general, were short term with little focus on reducing poverty or improving long-term food security. This is a clear signal that the world needs to move beyond crisis management;

high food prices and volatility will continue unless their structural causes are addressed. As a result, a twin-track approach that addresses food insecurity in the short term and development solutions in the long term must be pursued in parallel.

To address both immediate and longer-term needs, the chapter concluded by offering a policy framework focused on supporting consumers, boosting agricultural production and managing food markets. Given that children face the greatest risk of suffering from unaffordable food, as well as the overall importance of children's health to long-term economic vitality, the chapter further purported a 'child lens' as a guiding principle for designing interventions to fight high food prices and achieve food security. Moreover, as many developing country governments are undertaking fiscal consolidation and scaling back or altogether cutting social protection services, including food subsidies, in the process (see detailed discussion in Chapter V), this chapter calls for a turn from austerity-based fiscal policies to inclusive, food security responses in those countries that are threatened by escalating food prices.

Global and local food price trends over the past five years serve as a somber reminder that high food prices are likely to persist into the foreseeable future and that economic recovery alone will not be soon or strong enough to avert this persistent threat and protect vulnerable populations, including children and poor households. Furthermore, rising food prices jeopardize the global recovery as consumers continue to lose purchasing power and more people are pushed into poverty—or deeper. It is now time to act coherently and decisively to enact comprehensive policy frameworks at national and international levels to ensure a '*Recovery for All.*'

At the national level, policymakers should consider:

- Protecting poor and vulnerable populations from higher food costs as part of the national strategy for socio-economic recovery;
- Guaranteeing the basic right to food to all persons, which helps maintain the legitimacy of governments;
- Considering the long-term social and economic costs of leaving vulnerable populations and children unassisted in the face of higher food costs;

- Planning and implementing longer-term policies to support consumers and producers, as well as manage and regulate food markets, to achieve food security.

At the global level, some of the initiatives that could support and complement the efforts of national governments include:

- Ramping up real-time monitoring and tracking of local food prices (and local supply/demand forecasts) in order to mobilize timely interventions (UN);
- Fulfilling funding and food assistance commitments, especially to food deficit countries (G8, donors);
- Providing technical and financial assistance to agriculture sector investments(UN, development banks, South-South cooperation);
- Promoting a universal social protection floor to support adequate food consumption and essential social services (UN, development banks);
- Improving the regulation, functioning and transparency of financial and commodity markets to address excessive commodity price volatility (G8/G20, UN);
- Addressing the international impacts of agricultural subsidies in developed economies (G8/G20, UN);
- Fostering South-South cooperation on food management and security issues (UN, development banks).

References

ActionAid International. 2010. *HungerFREE Scorecard 2010: Who's Really Fighting Hunger?* ActionAid International.

ADB. 2008. *Food Prices and Inflation in Developing Asia: Is Poverty Reduction Coming to an End?* Manila: ADB.

Baffes, J. and T. Haniotis. 2010. "Placing the 2006/08 Commodity Price Boom into Perspective." World Bank Policy Research Working Paper No. 5371, World Bank.

BIS. 2010. *BIS Quarterly Review: International Banking and Financial Market Developments, December 2010.* Basel: Bank for International Settlements (BIS).

Black, R., et al. 2008. "Maternal and Child Undernutrition: Global and Regional Exposures and Health Consequences." *The Lancet* 371(9608): 243-260.

Bonnerjee, A. and G. Koehler. 2010. "Hunger: The True Growth Story in India." Featured Article, International Development Economics Associates (IDEAs).

Brinkman, H., S. de Pee, I. Sanogo, L. Subran and M. Bloem. 2010. "High Food Prices and the Global Financial Crisis Have Reduced Access to Nutritious Food and Worsened Nutritional Status and Health." *Journal of Nutrition* 140(1): 153S-161S.

Bundy, D., C. Burbano, M. Grosh, A. Gelli, M. Jukes and L. Drake. 2009. *Rethinking School Feeding: Social Safety Nets, Child Development and the Education Sector*. Washington, D.C.: World Bank.

Compton, J., S. Wiggins and S. Keats. 2010. *Impact of the Global Food Crisis on the Poor: What is the Evidence?* London: Overseas Development Institute.

Deininger, K., D. Byerlee, J. Lindsay, A. Norton, H. Selod and M. Stickler. 2010. *Rising Global Interest in Farmland: Can it Yield Sustainable and Equitable Benefits?* Washington D.C.: World Bank.

Demeke, M., G. Pangrazio and M. Maetz. 2009. *Country Responses to the Food Security Crisis: Nature and Preliminary Implications of the Policies Pursued*. Rome: FAO.

Dessus, S., S. Herrera and R. de Hoyos 2008. "The Impact of Food Inflation on Urban Poverty and its Monetary Cost: Some Back-of-the-Envelope Calculations." *Agricultural Economics* 39(1): 417-429.

Dreze, J. and A. Sen (1989). *Hunger and Public Action.* Oxford: Clarendon Press.

FAO. 2012a. "World Food Situation: Food Price Indices, January 2012." FAO. http://www.fao.org/worldfood situation/wfs-home/foodpricesindex/en/ (accessed February 2012).

_____. 2012b. *Global Information and Early Warning System (GIEWS), National Basic Food Prices Data and Analysis Tool.* FAO. http://www.fao.org/giews/pricetool2/ (accessed February 2012).

_____. 2011a. *Food Outlook: Global Market Analysis, November 2011.* Rome: FAO.

_____. 2011b. *Crop Prospects and Food Situation, No. 4, December 2011.* Rome: FAO.

_____. 2011c. "Countries Requiring External Assistance for Food." GIEWS, FAO. http://www.fao.org/giews/english/hotspots/index.htm (accessed February 2012).

_____. 2011e. *The State of Food Insecurity in the World: How oes International Price Volatility Affect Domestic Economies and Food Security?* Rome: FAO.

_____. 2010a. *Food Outlook: Global Market Analysis, November 2010.* Rome: FAO.

_____. 2010b. "Price Surges in Food Markets: How should Organized Futures Markets be Regulated?" Economic and Social Perspectives Policy Brief 9, FAO.

_____. 2010c. "Price Volatility in Agricultural Markets." Economic and Social Perspectives Policy Brief 12, FAO.

_____. 2010d. "When Emergencies Last for Decades: How to Improve Food Security in Protracted Crises." Economic and Social Perspectives Policy Brief 7, FAO.

_____. 2010e. "World Food Situation: Food Price Indices, December 2010." FAO.

_____. 2010f. "Country Policy Monitoring: Main Food-related Policy Measures." GIEWS, FAO. http://www.fao.org/giews/countrybrief/policy_index.jsp (accessed February 2012).

_____. 2010g. "Country Briefs." GIEWS, FAO. http://www.fao.org/giews/countrybrief/index.jsp (accessed February 2012).

_____. 2009a. *The State of Agricultural Commodity Markets: High Food Prices and the Food Crisis – Experiences and Lessons Learned*. Rome: FAO.

_____. 2009b. *The State of Food and Agriculture: Livestock in the Balance*. Rome: FAO.

Green, D., R. King and M. Miller-Dawkins. 2010. *The Global Economic Crisis and Developing Countries: Impact and Response*. Oxford: Oxfam GB.

Heltberg, R., N. Hossain, A. Reva and C. Turk. 2012. "Anatomy of Coping: Evidence from People Living through the Crises of 2008-11." Policy Research Working Paper No. 5957, World Bank.

Hossain, N. and D. Green. 2011. *Living on a Spike: How is the 2011 Food Price Crisis Affecting Poor People?* London: Institute of Development Studies and Oxfam GB.

Hossain, N. and J. McGregor. 2011. "A 'Lost Generation'? Impacts of Complex Compound Crises on Children and Young People." *Development Policy Review* 29(5): 565-84.

IMF. 2011. *World Economic Outlook: Slowing Growth, Rising Risks, September 2011*. Washington, D.C.: IMF. http://www.imf.org/external/pubs/ft/weo/2011/02/weodata/index.aspx (accessed December 2011).

_____. 2008a. *World Economic Outlook, April 2008: Housing and the Business Cycle*. Washington D.C.: IMF.

_____. 2008b. "The Balance of Payments Impact of the Food and Fuel Price Shocks on Low-income African Countries: A Country-by-Country Assessment." African Department Note, IMF.

International Food Policy Research Institute. 2008. *Responding to the World Food Crisis: Three Perspectives*. Washington, D.C.: International Food Policy Research Institute (IFPRI).

Ivanic, M. and W. Martin. 2008. "Implications of Higher Global Food Prices for Poverty in Low-income Countries." Policy Research Working Paper Series No. 4594, World Bank.

Janjua, K. 2008. "Food Security and Poverty in Jordan." Report prepared for the Office of the United Nations Resident Coordinator, Jordan.

Keats, S., S. Wiggins, J. Compton and M. Vigneri. 2010. "Food Price Transmission: Rising International Cereals Prices and Domestic Markets." Project Briefing No. 48, Overseas Development Institute.

Korayem, K. 2010. "Food Subsidy and Social Assistance Programme in Egypt: Assessment and Policy Options." Report prepared for the Ministry of Social Solidarity of Egypt and the World Food Programme, Cairo.

Lustig, N. 2009. "Coping with Rising Food Prices: Policy Dilemmas in the Developing World." Working Paper Number 164, Center for Global Development (CGD).

Mendoza, R. 2010. "Inclusive Crisis, Exclusive Recoveries, and Policies to Prevent a Double Whammy for the Poor." Social and Economic Policy Working Paper, UNICEF.

Mousseau, F. 2010. *The High Food Price Challenge: A Review of Responses to Combat Hunger*. Oakland: The Oakland Institute.

Ortiz, I., J. Chai and M. Cummins. 2011. "Escalating Food Prices: The Threat to Poor Households and Policies to Safeguard a Recovery for All." Social and Economic Policy Working Paper, UNICEF.

Oxfam. 2010: *Halving Hunger: Still Possible? Building a Rescue Package to Set the MDGs Back on Track*. London: Oxfam GB.

Overseas Development Institute. 2008. *Understanding the Impact of Food Prices on Children*. London: Plan United Kingdom.

Rapsomanikis, G., D. Hallam and P. Conforti. 2006. "Market Integration and Price Transmission Paper in Selected Food and Cash Crop Markets of Developing Countries: Review and Applications." In A. Sarris and D. Hallam (eds.), *Agricultural Commodity Markets and Trade: New Approaches to Analyzing Market Structure and Instability*. Rome: FAO.

Reyes, C., A. Sorbrevinas and J. Jesus. 2010. "Impacts of the Global Financial Crisis on Poverty in the Philippines." Paper presented at 8th Poverty and Economic Policy (PEP) Research Network General Meeting, June 2010, Dakar, Senegal.

Samuels, F., M. Gavrilovic, C. Harper and M. Niño-Zarazúa. 2011. *Food, Finance and Fuel: The Impacts of the Triple F Crisis in Nigeria, with a Particular Focus on Women and Children – Adamawa State Focus*. London: Overseas Development Institute.

Save the Children. 2012. *Multi-Country Nutrition Poll 2011 Topline Report*. London: GlobeScan Incorporated.

_____. 2009. *How the Global Food Crisis is Hurting Children: The Impact of the Food Price Hike on a Rural Community in Northern Bangladesh*. London: Save the Children United Kingdom.

TEPAV, UNICEF and World Bank. 2009. "Economic Crisis Affecting the Welfare of Families in Turkey." Social and Economic Policy Working Paper, UNICEF and World Bank.

Tiwari, S. and H. Zaman. 2010. "The Impact of Economic Shocks on Global Undernourishment." Policy Research Working Paper No. 5215, World Bank.

United Nations. 2011. *World Economic and Social Prospects*. New York: UN-DESA.

_____. 2010. "Updated Comprehensive Framework for Action, September 2010." United Nations High-Level Task Force on the Global Food Security Crisis, United Nations.

_____. 2009. *Report of the Commission of Experts of the President of the United Nations General Assembly on Reforms of the International Monetary and Financial System*. New York: United Nations.

_____. 2008. *National Development Strategies, Policy Notes*. New York: UN-DESA.

United Nations Special Rapporteur on the Right to Food. 2009. *Large-scale Land Acquisitions and Leases: A Set of Minimum Principles and Measures to Address the Human Rights Challenge*. Report of the Special Rapporteur on the Right to Food, Human Rights Council, Thirteenth Session, December 28, United Nations.

UNCTAD. 2009a. *The Global Economic Crisis: Systemic Failures and Multilateral Remedies*. Geneva: UNCTAD.

_____. 2009b. *Trade and Development Report, 2009*. Geneva: UNCTAD.

UNDP. 2010. *Poverty and Social Impact Analysis of the Global Economic Crisis: Synthesis Report of 18 Country Studies*. New York: UNDP.

UNICEF. 2009. *Tracking Progress on Child and Maternal Nutrition: A Survival and Development Priority*. New York: UNICEF.

USAID. 2011. "Central America Executive Brief." Famine Early Warning Systems Network, United States Agency for International Development (USAID).

United States Federal Reserve. 2012. *Nominal Major Currencies Dollar Index Database*.   http://www.federalreserve.gov/Releases/h10/Summary/ (accessed February 2012).

United States Senate. 2009. *Excessive Speculation in the Wheat Market*. Majority and Minority Staff Report, Permanent Subcommittee on Investigations. Washington, D.C.: United States Government.

Victora C., L. Adai, C. Fall, P. Hallal, R. Martorell, L. Richter and H. Sachdev. 2008. "Maternal and Child Undernutrition: Consequences for Adult Health and Human Capital." *Lancet* 371(9609): 340-357.

Wiggins, S., J. Compton, S. Keats and M. Davies. 2010. "Country Responses to the Food Price Crisis 2007/08: Case Studies from Bangladesh, Nicaragua and Sierra Leone." London: Overseas Development Institute.

Wodon, Q. and H. Zaman. 2010. "Higher Food Prices in Sub-Saharan Africa: Poverty Impact and Policy Responses." *World Bank Res Obs* 25(1): 157-176.

Wodon, Q., C. Tsimpo, P. Backiny-Yetna, G. Joseph, F. Adoho and H. Coulombe. 2008. "Potential Impact of Higher Food Prices on Poverty: Summary Estimates for a Dozen West and Central African Countries." World Bank Policy Research Working Paper Series No. 4745, World Bank.

World Bank. 2008a. "Rising Food and Fuel Prices: Addressing the Risks to Future Generations." Human Development and Poverty Reduction and Economic Management Networks, World Bank.

_____. 2008b. "Rising Food Prices: Policy Options and World Bank Response." Background Note, World Bank.

_____. 2008c. *World Development Report 2008: Agriculture for Development*. Washington, D.C.: World Bank.

Annex 1. Detailed Information on the Local Food Price Index in 55 Developing Countries[27]

Country	Geographic Area	Foodstuffs included in the local food price index (LFPI)	DES[28]	LFPI Changes (%)	
				5/2007- 12/2011	5/2009- 12/2011
Afghanistan	Jalalabad	bread, wheat, wheat flour	...	47.9	10.7
	Kabul			54.4	19.3
Armenia	National avg.	bread, potatos, wheat flour	54	29.5	13.1
Azerbaijan	National avg.	beef meat, bread, mutton/ goat, potatos, wheat flour	59	71.6	19.7
Bangladesh	National avg.	rice, wheat	79	46.6	9.4
	Dhaka			32.4	-2.6
Belarus	Minsk	bread, potatos	29	281.2	126.6
Benin	Natitingou	maize, manioc, rice	48	59.1	9.7
	Cotonou			61.4	-0.7
Bolivia	Cochabamba	maize, potatos, rice (estaquilla and grano de oro), wheat	44	43.7	1.0
	La Paz			46.7	9.3
Brazil	National avg.	maize, rice (1st and 2nd quality), wheat, wheat flour	33	18.0	-2.4
	São Paulo			13.9	-2.6
Burkina Faso	Dori	millet, rice, sorghum	55	58.9	18.6
	Ouagadougou			65.1	33.4
Burundi	Bujumbura	beans, cassava, maize, rice, wheat	50	57.1	26.2
Cambodia	Banteay Mea.	rice, soya beans	71	71.4	-3.3
	Phnom Penh			94.6	14.2
Cameroon	Bamenda	bananas, beans, maize, potatos, rice	33	44.3	23.4
	Yaundé			42.5	8.7
Cape Verde	S.Vincente	manioc, rice (short and long grain), wheat flour	40	32.7	1.5
	Santiago			39.9	2.8
Chad	Moussoro	maize, millet rice	37	51.1	0.0
	N'Djamena			39.8	-4.2
China	Hubei and Hunan	rice	27	52.8	25.2
Colombia	Barranquilla	maize, rice (1st and 2nd quality), flour, white sugar	45	41.9	6.3
	Bogotá			35.8	11.0
Costa Rica	National avg.	beans (black/red), maize, flour	17	72.8	12.3
Congo, Dem. Rep. of	Bunia	beans, cassava, rice	61	209.9	41.7
	Kinshasa			121.6	32.5
Djibouti	Djibouti	rice (belem/american), flour	51	68.5	43.4
Dom. Rep.	Santo Domingo	maize, beans, chicken, rice	25	37.7	1.1
Ecuador	National avg.	beans, maize, potatos, rice, wheat flour	36	2.7	-24.4
El Salvador	San Salvador	beans (red/red seda), maize, rice, sorghum, wheat flour	55	41.6	24.1
Ethiopia	Addis Ababa	maize, sorghum (red and white), teff, wheat	57	149.1	36.0

[27] Note: The aggregate LFPI reflects the average price values for each country. As a result, if a country has two price observations, a single country value was obtained by taking the average of the two points, unless one of the two points is the national value.
[28] Total dietary energy supply (DES) represented in each respective LFPI.

Country	Geographic Area	Foodstuffs included in the local food price index (LFPI)	DES[28]	LFPI Changes (%)	
				5/2007-12/2011	5/2009-12/2011
Guatemala	Guatemala City	beans, maize, rice	46	21.0	6.5
Haiti	Hinche	maize, rice, sorghum	41	34.8	-1.8
	Port-au-Prince			6.2	-3.5
Honduras	San Pedro Sula	beans, maize, rice	39	3.0	1.0
	Tegucigalpa			9.5	3.9
India	Patna	rice, wheat	51	90.1	33.4
	Delhi			47.7	9.4
Kenya	Eldoret	beans, maize	41	146.8	43.9
	Nairobi			148.7	68.2
Kyrgyzstan	Osh	beef, bread, mutton, potatos, wheat flour	63	98.8	42.7
	Bishkek			72.5	29.8
Madagascar	National avg.	rice (local and imported)	49	29.1	30.4
Malawi	Mzuzu	maize, rice	53	153.3	35.4
	Lilongwe			133.3	49.3
Mali	Kayes	millet, rice, sorghum	45	39.5	30.4
	Bamako			62.6	21.7
Mauritania	Nouakchott	beef meat, camel meat, couscous, rice, wheat flour	43	21.9	-3.9
Mexico	Guadalajara	beans, maize, rice	38	75.1	45.4
	Mexico City			81.0	53.0
Mongolia	Ulaanbaatar	beef meat, bread, mutton meat, potatos, rice, flour	63	62.7	-11.5
Mozambique	Nampula	maize, rice	30	94.0	14.6
	Maputo			95.2	-3.8
Nicaragua	National avg.	beans, rice, maize	50	45.0	3.8
	Managua			48.7	3.2
Niger	Maradi	millet, rice, sorghum	62	76.3	10.5
	Niamey			52.1	5.7
Nigeria	Kano	maize, sorghum	20	152.8	20.0
Pakistan	Multan	rice (irri and basmati), wheat, wheat flour	44	123.1	17.7
	Karachi			113.3	17.7
Panama	Panama City	beans (poroto and red), lentils, maize, rice	38	70.2	21.4
Peru	Lima	bread, chicken, maize, potatos, wheat flour	45	26.1	6.3
Philippines	MetroManila	rice (regular and well milled)	46	44.6	0.0
Russia	National avg.	beef meat, bread, pork meat, potatos, rice, wheat flour	48	60.9	13.2
Rwanda	Kigali	beans, maize, rice	17	44.9	24.4
Senegal	Matam	millet, rice, sorghum	43	35.6	2.5
	Dakar			32.8	-6.4
Somalia	Bossaso	maize, rice, sorghum	67	385.2	52.3
	Modadishu			193.3	3.5
South Africa	Randfontein	maize (yellow and white), wheat	48	36.7	71.8
Sri Lanka	Colombo	rice, wheat flour	54	73.4	19.0
Sudan	Al-Fashir	millet, sorghum, wheat	46	286.0	-0.7
	Khartoum			270.3	23.1

Country	Geographic Area	Foodstuffs included in the local food price index (LFPI)	DES[28]	LFPI Changes (%)	
				5/2007-12/2011	5/2009-12/2011
Tajikistan	National avg.	potatos, wheat flour	61	103.0	43.0
	Dushanbe			221.5	42.5
Thailand	Bangkok	cassava, maize, rice (5% and 25% broken)	45	61.8	29.1
Uganda	Kampala	beans, maize, rice	18	90.9	68.1
Zambia	National avg.	maize (breakfast meal, roller meal and white), rice	53	33.6	-13.9
Zimbabwe	Harare	maize	43	625.0	26.1
Averages		**3.3 food items per country**	**46.6**	**83.4**	**19.0**

Source: Authors' calculations based on FAO's *GIEWS* (2012)

IV. THE JOBS CRISIS

Isabel Ortiz and Matthew Cummins

"The time has come to write a new social contract for the 21st century. That contract must include a global jobs pact. We all know that growth is essential. But we also know that growth does not automatically mean jobs. We need a job-rich recovery. Policymakers must make employment a priority, not an afterthought. The new social contract must also include a social protection floor with stronger safeguards for the poorest and most vulnerable... Investing in people will generate decent jobs and decent incomes. Sharing productivity gains more fairly will, in turn, boost purchasing power and global demand. That virtuous circle is key to building healthy local markets and a healthy world economy. It is good for business and it is good for people... [However] in recent decades, labour's share of income has fallen. And the gap between those who work hard and those who reap the greatest rewards continues to grow. At this time of crisis and confusion, discord and division, inequality and injustice, we are all called to moral battle once again. Let us write a fair and just social contract for the 21st century... For Unity. For Solidarity. For Social Justice. For All."

> UN Secretary-General's remarks to the G20 Labour
> Summit in Cannes, France on November 03, 2011

1.   Introduction

Just as higher food costs associated with the first major shock of the global economic crisis have a direct impact on the ability of poor households to meet basic consumption needs and improve their well-being, so too does the second major shock: fewer opportunities to obtain decent work. The global economic crisis has only exacerbated pre-existing trends, including a lack of sufficient jobs, rising vulnerable employment and widespread working poverty. And in 2012, the jobs outlook is increasingly daunting. Overall, the crisis has increased the backlog of unemployment by 27 million worldwide, with an unprecedented 200 million persons without work (ILO 2012a). The number of unemployed young persons, aged 15-24 years, has also reached 75 million, up by more than four million since 2007.

Importantly, these aggregate estimates understate the magnitude of the jobs crisis. Given that unemployment rates tend to reflect people claiming unemployment benefits and actively seeking work, they overlook the long-term unemployed and underemployed. A more robust indicator is the employment-to-population ratio, which shows the proportion of the working-age population that has some form of employment. Under this metric, the jobs crisis appears much more acute, with two out of every five workers in the world without employment; this is 40 percent of the potential global labour force, many of which are youth. This further shows that employment opportunities have grown at a slower rate than the increase in world population.

The deteriorating jobs outlook provides little solace. Through 2016, global unemployment is expected to remain unchanged (ILO 2012a). This largely reflects weakened economic growth since mid-2011. In particular, sovereign debt concerns in many developed countries have reverberated across financial sectors worldwide, reducing access to credit and lowering consumer confidence, both of which have negatively impacted aggregate demand and new job opportunities (United Nations 2012a). Fiscal tightening in both developed and developing countries is further dragging down economic growth prospects and casting increasing doubts on the ability of markets to generate new and decent jobs (see Chapter V). Even more alarming, more than 120 million potential new young workers are entering the global labour market each year, nearly 90 percent of which are from developing countries. Millions of jobs need to be created over the next ten years just to meet this growing supply of young job seekers—nearly 1.1 billion are expected between 2012 and 2020—and to evade further unemployment woes.

In this context, Chapter IV sets out to examine the scope of the jobs crisis, its varied impacts on poor families and young populations, and options for policymakers to generate decent work opportunities. It starts by describing recent labour market trends, which include fewer jobs and lower pay along with a higher incidence of vulnerable employment and working poverty in many countries (Section 2). The chapter then turns to youth by analyzing how young people are experiencing a double employment crisis as a result of the demographic phenomenon known as the 'youth bulge,' which aggravates the negative employment impacts of the economic downturn (Section 3). The jobs crisis is next scrutinized in terms of household level impacts, with particular attention to the severe risks posed to children and young workers, as well as the overall heightened risks of 'wage scars,' domestic violence and social unrest more generally (Section 4). The impact assessment is followed by a discussion of employment-generating policies, which covers macroeconomic and sector options along with labour-specific strategies to ensure decent jobs for the world's workforce (Section 5). To conclude, Chapter IV challenges policymakers to place jobs, especially for youth, at the center of recovery efforts in support of a *'Recovery for All'* (Section 6).

2.   Labour Market Trends

This section examines recent developments in labour markets. It begins by describing the effects of the global economic crisis on levels of employment across global, regional and country levels. It then discusses the evolution of wages and earnings inequality in an environment of increasingly volatile employment opportunities. The section closes by assessing recent trends in jobs vulnerability and informal employment, as well as the incidence of working poverty worldwide.

2.1.   Fewer jobs

Since the onset of the global economic crisis, unemployment figures have continued to deteriorate and reached unprecedented levels. According to the ILO (2012a), the number of unemployed persons worldwide rose by 5.8 million in 2008 and by an additional 21 million in 2009, where it reached roughly 195 million, or about 6.1 percent of global working population, and held steady through 2011. In 2012, however, the number of unemployed persons is expected to further increase to around 200 million persons, or about 6.2 percent of the global labour force.

From a regional perspective, the highest unemployment rates are found in the Middle East and North Africa, which are projected to be above 10 percent during 2012 (Figure 1). In terms of the overall magnitude of the initial unemployment shock, HICs and countries in the CEE/CIS experienced an increase of more than 2 percent between 2008 and 2009, on average, while unemployment rates in Latin America and the Caribbean rose by more than 1 percent. Also noteworthy is the relative resilience of jobs in Sub-Saharan Africa to the global shock, where unemployment rates have hovered between 8.1 and 8.2 percent since 2005.

Figure IV.1. Total Unemployment Rates by Regions and World, 2005-12

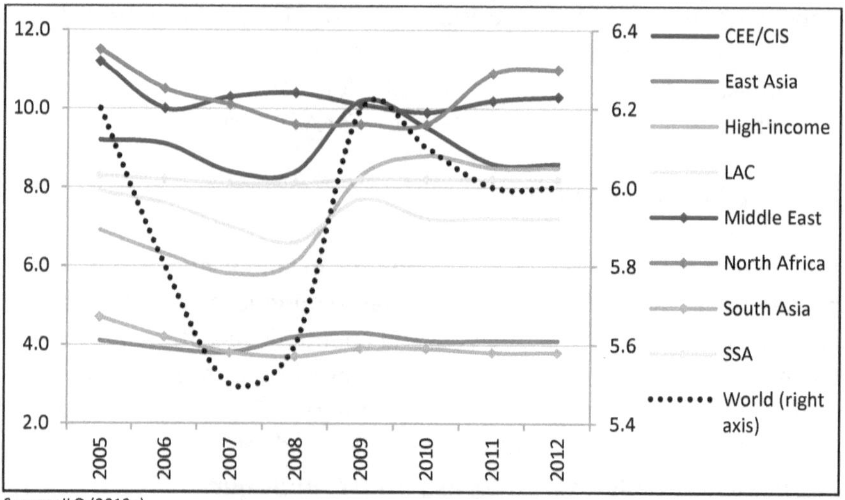

Source: ILO (2012a)

Regional aggregates, of course, hide important country-level differences. When analyzing overall unemployment trends throughout the global economic crisis, three unique country typologies emerge. First, there is a large set of countries whose total unemployment rates rose significantly in response to the initial global shock and have either continued to increase or remained elevated (Figure 2A—Hard Hit and Still High). In a second group of countries, unemployment rates were hard hit by the early shock during 2008-09 but have since started to recover (Figure 2B—Hard Hit, but Recovering). And in a third set of countries, the global economic crisis had little-to-no impact on overall employment rates (Figure 2C—Muted Impact).

Figure IV.2. Unemployment Rates by Country Typologies, 2005-11

2A. Hard Hit and Still High

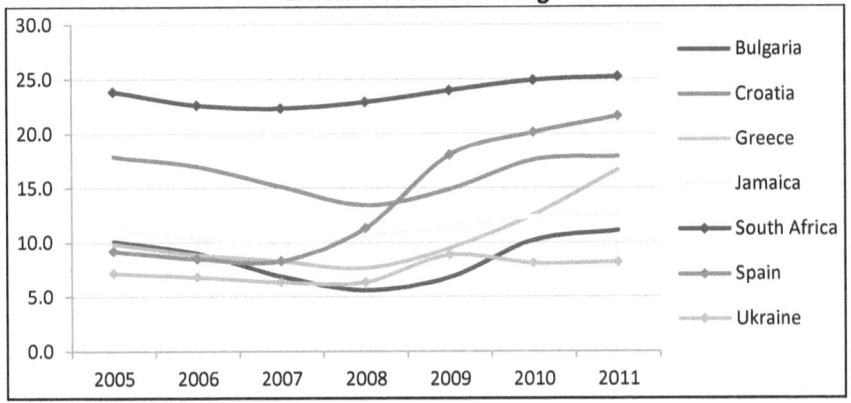

2B. Hard Hit, but Recovering

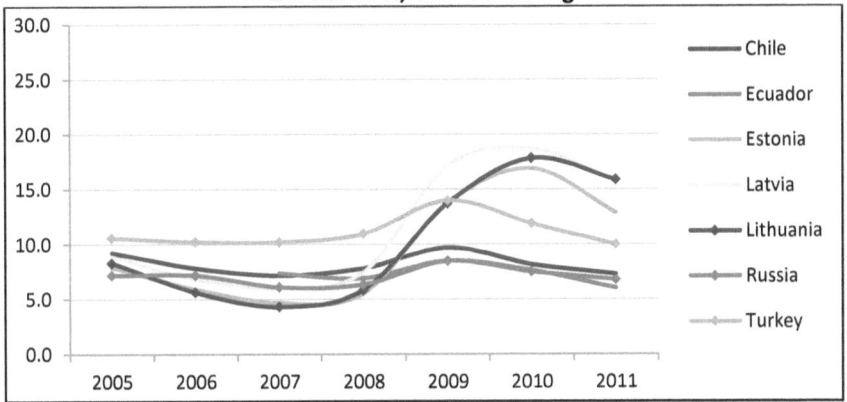

2C. Muted Impact

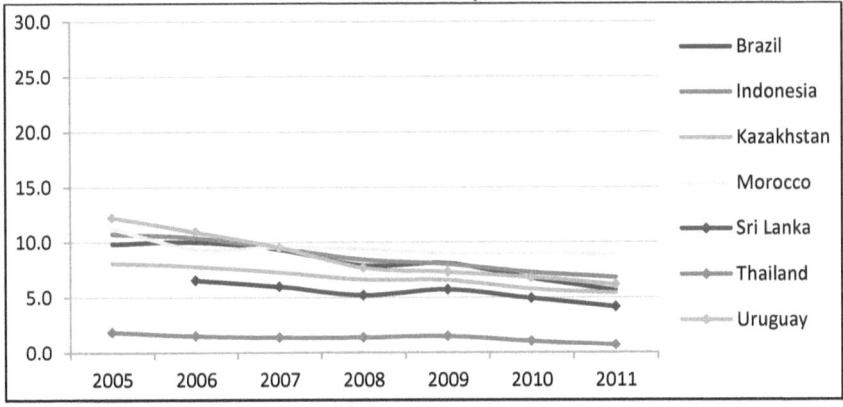

Source: ILO's *LABOURSTA* (2012)

While the global economic crisis has clearly hurt employment growth in a large number of developed and developing countries, many countries are also struggling with dangerously high jobless rates. Analysis of IMF estimates shows that 35 of 102 countries with available data are expected to have unemployment rates in excess of 9 percent during 2012 (Figure 3 presents the double-digit countries). Five countries, in particular, are dealing with unemployment rates near or above 20 percent, including Bosnia and Herzegovina, Macedonia, Serbia, South Africa and Spain.

Figure IV.3. Projected Unemployment Rates in Selected Countries, 2012

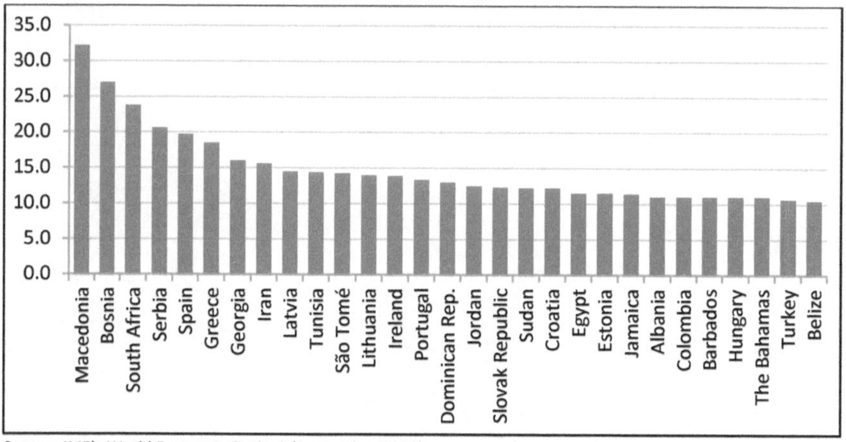

Source: IMF's *World Economic Outlook* (September 2011)

As mentioned in the introduction, aggregate unemployment estimates significantly understate the severity of the world's employment crisis. Since unemployment rates tend to reflect people who are claiming unemployment benefits and actively seeking work, they commonly exclude persons who have stopped job hunting through official channels due to demoralization, as well as those who are underemployed. To highlight the vast size of these populations, the ILO (2010d) estimated that nearly 40 percent of jobseekers had been unemployed for more than one year in a sample of 35 countries, and that more than four million had stopped searching altogether by the end of 2009, all of who would not be counted in official unemployment rates.

Turning to a broader measure of employment, the employment-to-population ratio shows that only 60 percent of the world's labour force has some type of job. In terms of the actual number of unemployed persons worldwide, this amounted to more than 225 million in 2011, or 7 percent of the total global labour force (ILO 2012a).

More importantly, the employment-to-population ratio verifies that the capacity of the world economy to create jobs has been steadily declining since the early 1990s (Figure 4). Over the past two decades, the ratio has fallen by 2 percentage points, with the East and South Asian regions both dropping by more than 3 percentage points.

Figure IV.4. Employment-to-Population Ratios by Regions and World, 2005-11

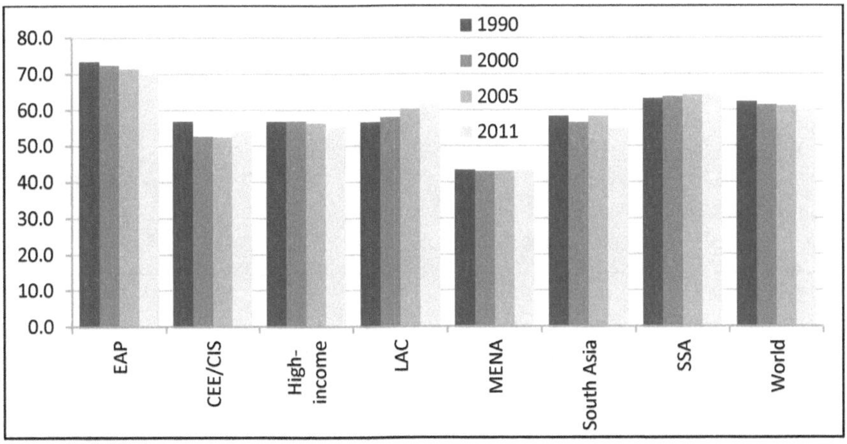

Source: ILO (2012a)

The global economic crisis appears to have exacerbated the longer-term declining trends. When contrasting the employment-to-population ratio before the start of the crisis, in 2007, with the latest available, in 2011, the worldwide ratio dropped by nearly 1 percentage point. Moreover, over this time period the global pace of decline was two-and-a-half times greater than in the five years leading up to the crisis. Regionally, the crisis has most severely impacted employment-to-population ratios in South Asia and in HICs, where they fell by 2.3 and 1.9 percentage points, respectively. Employment-to-population ratios have also been shrinking in East Asia and the Middle East and North Africa since the start of the crisis, with slight improvements recorded elsewhere.

Country-level data further show that employment-to-population ratios have been waning rapidly since the start of the crisis. Between 2007 and 2010, the ratios fell or stayed the same in 86 of 169 countries with available estimates.[1] Moreover, employment-to-population ratios dropped by more than 2 percentage points in some 20 countries since the start of the crisis, several of which are illustrated in Figure 5.

Figure IV.5. Employment-to-Population Ratios in Selected Countries, 2005-10

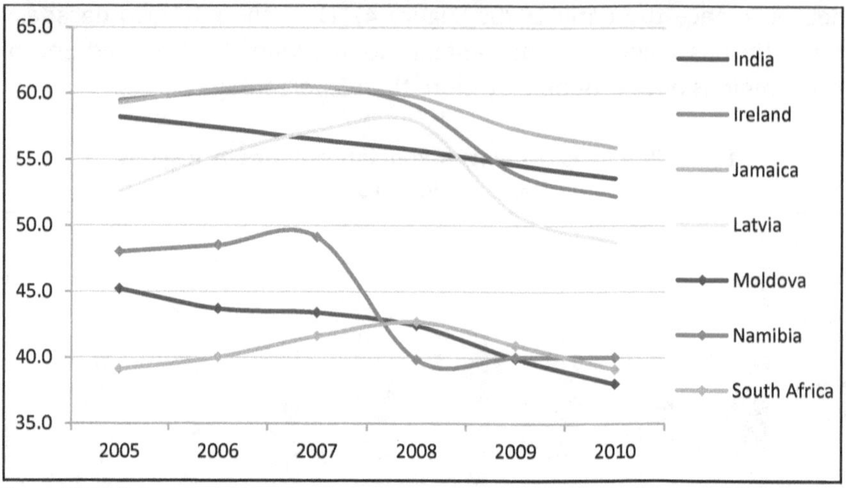

Source: ILO (2012a)

2.2.   Lower wages and higher wage inequality

In addition to fewer jobs, labour markets have also recently been characterized by negative wage growth and increasing wage inequality, at least for those who are fortunate enough to have salaried work in the formal sector. The initial shock of the global economic crisis had a particularly strong, negative effect on average wages during 2008-09. When looking at regions, wage growth turned negative in the CEE/CIS, Central Asia and HICs (ILO 2010a). The sharpest declines were observed in the CEE/CIS, where real wage growth plummeted from about 17 percent in 2007 to 10.6 percent in 2008 and to -2.2 percent in 2009. Real wage growth also turned negative in the CEE/CIS, from 6.6 percent in 2007 to 4.6 percent in 2008 to -0.1 percent in 2009, as well as in HICs—from 0.8 percent in 2007 to -0.5 percent in 2008. Data from advanced economies shows that a large part of the decline in wage growth was due to shorter work weeks achieved either through company-level arrangements, such as lower wages and shorter working

---

[1] Authors' calculation based on ILO's *LABOURSTA* (2012).

hours in the United States, or through 'work sharing' schemes to reduce working time and avoid lay-offs, such as in Germany.

Other recent analyses offer further evidence of the negative impacts of the global economic crisis on wages. The ILO (2011b) found that seven countries in South-East Europe experienced slowing but still positive real wage growth in 2008, which then turned negative in 2009. For example, between 2008 and 2009 real wage growth dropped by 3 percent in Hungary and by more than 5 percent in Romania; these downward trends continued during 2010-11. The World Bank (2011) also found that real wages declined sharply in a number of countries in the CEE/CIS. Of the six countries that reported negative growth during 2009, real wages plummeted by more than 5 percent in Estonia, Latvia and Lithuania. Much of this was attributed to lower pay, reduced hours of work, increased mandatory administrative leave and higher wage arrears. Negative real wage impacts were witnessed in other places, too, such as in South Africa (Verick 2010).

Although timely wage data are invariably difficult to obtain, the ILO's *LABOURSTA* database does collect recent information on manufacturing and non-agricultural activities for selected countries. In terms of manufacturing, when comparing the average wage growth during 2006-07, before the crisis hit, and the most recent period, 2010-11, it is clear that wage growth declined considerably (Figure 6). Overall, 22 of the 32 countries with available data over the 2006-11 time period show a strong downward decline in the growth of manufacturing wages, which appears to be intensifying over time. When applying this same analysis to non-agricultural activities, 7 of the 12 countries that have data show a slowdown of wage growth when comparing the 2010-11 and 2006-07 time periods (Table 1).

Figure IV.6. Manufacturing Wage Growth in Selected Countries, 2006-11
(period averages)

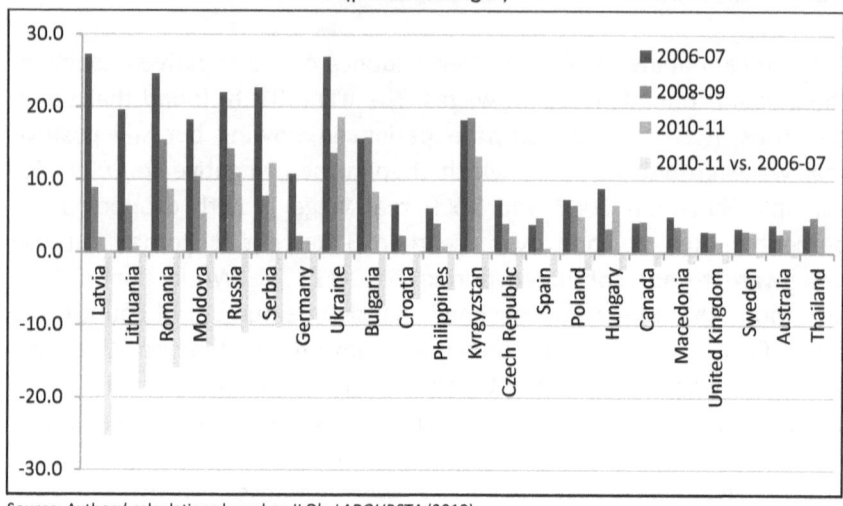

Source: Authors' calculations based on ILO's *LABOURSTA* (2012)

Table IV.1. Non-Agricultural Activity Wage Growth in Selected Countries, 2006-11
(period averages)

Country	Average Wage Growth			2010-11 vs. 2006-07
	2006-07	2008-09	2010-11	
Romania	21.8	17.0	3.3	-18.6
Spain	4.3	6.4	0.4	-4.0
Japan	-0.3	-3.0	-2.6	-2.3
New Zealand	4.5	4.4	2.8	-1.8
Philippines	4.5	4.2	3.3	-1.2
Canada	3.4	2.2	3.0	-0.4
Australia	4.5	3.9	4.4	-0.1
Thailand	3.8	4.8	4.0	0.2
South Africa	8.8	11.2	9.3	0.5
Singapore	4.7	1.4	6.1	1.5

Source: Authors' calculations based on ILO's *LABOURSTA* (2012)

It is imperative that recent wage trends are viewed in the context of rising wage inequality, which is characterized by rapidly increasing wages at the top end of the income distribution and stagnating wages at the median and bottom end. Further, wage inequality should be considered as an important contributing factor to the world's severe income distribution asymmetries (Ortiz and Cummins 2011, Van der Hoeven 2010). When comparing the lowest and highest paid deciles of workers in 30 countries over the 1995-2000 and 2007-09 time periods, the ILO (2010b) found that the distance had increased in 17 of the countries, including Argentina, Australia, Azerbaijan, Belgium, Canada, Czech Republic, Denmark, Finland, Honduras, Ireland, Norway, Poland, the Republic of Korea, Switzerland, the United Kingdom, the United States and Uruguay. While the rise in wage inequality was primarily attributed to significant increases among the top earners, it was also determined that wages at the bottom were dropping.

And wage inequality has likely increased during the global economic crisis. For instance, Heathcote et al. (2010) find that the bottom of the earnings distribution falls off relative to the median during recessionary periods, which has largely characterized many economies worldwide since 2008. It is also probable that the jobs crisis will intensify longer-term earnings trends. On the one hand, a large number of countries have been experiencing dramatic increases in wage inequality since the 1970s, which could easily be accelerated in an environment of decreasing decent employment opportunities (Machin and van Reenen 2007, OECD 2008). The United States offers an egregious example: while CEOs were paid 51 times as much as a minimum wage earner in 1965, this skyrocketed to 821 times as much in 2005 (Howell 2005). On the other hand, the near-record bonuses provided to executives and financial sector workers in advanced economies during 2010-11 can also be expected to have boosted the income share of the top earners.[2]

Importantly, low wages are strongly associated with income instability. For example, in developed countries, such as those in the EU, the risk of being unemployed or inactive can be two or three times higher among low-wage workers than higher-wage workers (European Commission 2005). And since earnings volatility is relatively higher among low-wage workers, this group can be expected to be suffering disproportionately from the impacts of the ongoing economic recessions in both developed and developing countries.

Who is most likely to be affected by wage inequality? A series of case studies on Brazil, Chile, China, Indonesia, the Philippines and South Africa indicate that the incidence of low-wage employment is strongly

---

[2] Lucchetti, A. and S. Grocer. 2011. "On Street, Pay Vaults to Record Altitude." *Wall Street Journal*, February 02.

Lublin, J. 2011. "Executive Bonuses Bounce Back." *Wall Street Journal*, March 17.

associated with personal characteristics, including level of education, age, gender, race and migrant status, as well as geographical issues and employment type (ILO 2010b). Overall, the highest wage inequality can be expected to occur to somebody who is uneducated, young (15-24), female, an ethnic minority and a migrant, who lives in a rural area and has a temporary or informal job in one of the following sectors: agriculture, retail trade, hotels and restaurants, transport, social services, including household activities, and certain areas of manufacturing (e.g., food processing and textiles).

2.3.   Precarization: Increasing vulnerable employment

Global labour markets have also been increasingly characterized by vulnerable employment, which is strongly related to low-paying jobs and difficult working conditions where wage inequality is high and fundamental worker's rights are likely to be in jeopardy.[3] Since a high and rising share of vulnerable jobs indicates that informal work is likely to be widespread, this metric offers important insights about the supply of quality jobs. As displayed in Figure 7, globally more than 1.5 billion persons were estimated to be in conditions of vulnerable employment in 2011. Compared to the longer-term trend, the latest data reveal that the number of vulnerable workers increased by nearly 150 million between 2000 and 2011. In terms of the impacts of the crisis, the absolute number of persons in vulnerable employment is estimated to have increased by 34 million between 2009 and 2011, if excluding East Asia.

In terms of precarious and vulnerable work, there is an important gender dimension. Although female labour force participation rates have risen in most countries, the majority of working women are paid less than their male counterparts—even for the same level of productivity in the same job—and they are also concentrated in jobs that are undervalued, such as domestic work. These trends are well-documented in the literature, which attributes lower pay and undervaluation of female work to a variety of factors, including: (i) the unique patterns of women's economic lives (e.g., low valuation of skills and status, perception as second income-earners, high concentration in low-paying firms in secondary labour markets, frequency of part-time

---

[3] Vulnerable employment is defined by the ILO (2012a) as the sum of own-account workers and unpaid family workers.

work); (ii) lower reservation wages (e.g., gender biases in eligibility rules for unemployment benefits and social protection, limited maternity protection); (iii) gender biases in wage-setting institutions (e.g., female-dominated sectors and occupations are less likely to be covered by national wage legislation); and (iv) independent workplace effects (e.g., willingness of employers to pay wages according to the gender composition of workplace, mobility barriers, cost minimization in female-dominated private services) (Grimshaw 2010 and ILO 2010a).

Figure IV.7. Global Vulnerable Employment Trends, 2000-11

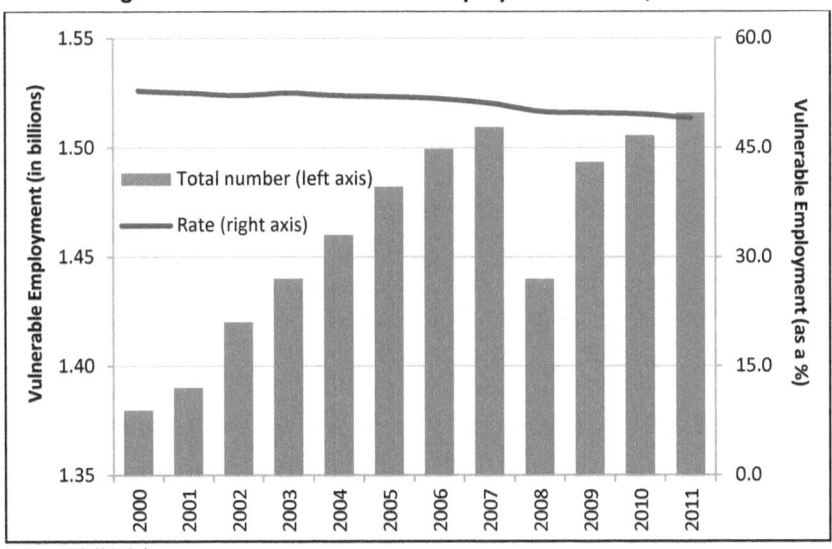

Source: ILO (2012a)

Looking across regions, the incidence of vulnerable employment is very high in South Asia (77 percent), Sub-Saharan Africa (76 percent) and South-East Asia and the Pacific (61 percent), reflecting the predominance of the agricultural sector in those economies. While East Asia has made substantial progress toward reducing the prevalence of vulnerable employment since 2007, trends are worsening elsewhere. For example, vulnerable employment increased by 22 million in Sub-Saharan Africa between 2007 and 2011, by 12 million in South Asia, by about 6 million in South-East Asia and the Pacific, by 5 million in Latin America and the Caribbean, and by more than 1 million in the Middle East (ILO 2012a).

Aside from the rising trend in absolute numbers worldwide and across most regions, a further cause for alarm is the high proportion of recent employment growth that can be attributed to vulnerable employment. Since 2007 vulnerable employment has accounted for nearly 70 percent of all jobs growth in Sub-Saharan Africa, more than 50 percent of all jobs growth in South-East Asia and the Pacific, and more than 25 percent of all jobs growth in Latin America and the Caribbean (ILO 2012a).

In addition to aggregate vulnerable employment trends, country-level informal employment information sheds further light on the degree to which the global economic crisis has impacted the availability of quality jobs (Figure 8). Only ten countries have comparable informal employment data that cover a recent time period. Given that they are mostly from Latin America, which is the lone region that has significantly increased employment-to-population ratios in recent years, they fall short of offering a representative global picture; they do, however, offer some insights into how the crisis has affected informal activity. When comparing the percentage change of persons employed in the informal sector between 2007 and 2009, six of the 10 countries experienced a 3 percent increase, on average.

Figure IV.8. Informal Employment Rates in Selected Countries, 2005-09
(as a percent of non-agricultural employment)

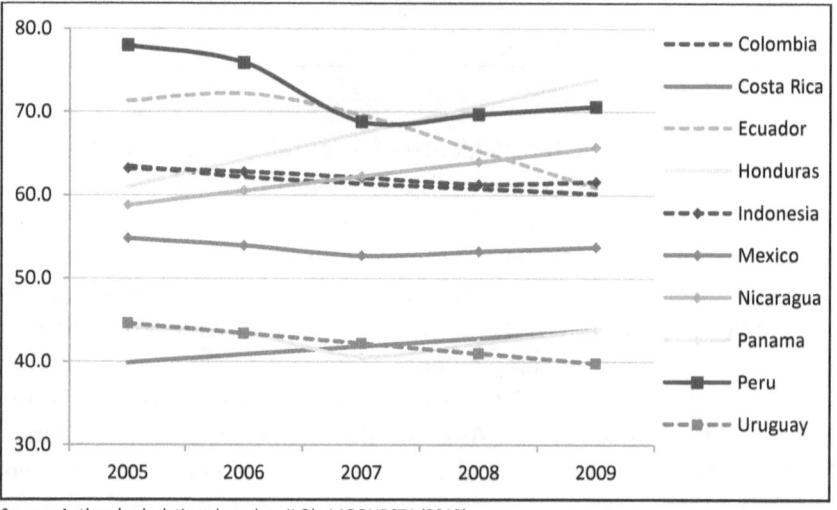

Source: Authors' calculations based on ILO's *LABOURSTA* (2012)
Note: The dotted lines represent countries that experienced a decline in informal employment from 2007-09.

Other studies have also documented a significant expansion of employment in the informal economy. This includes Colombia, India, Indonesia, Kenya, Malawi, Pakistan, Peru, South Africa and Thailand (Horn 2011), Albania and Serbia (ILO 2011b), and Cambodia, Chile, Colombia, Ecuador, Indonesia, Nicaragua, the Philippines and Vietnam (Green 2010). These findings support the rising trends in vulnerable employment, such as street vendors, waste pickers and home-based work, and suggest that informal jobs have likely increased considerably in a number of developing countries since the start of the crisis.

It is also important to recognize that informal employment remains a pervasive characteristic of many developing countries (Figure 9). Of the 33 countries that have recent estimates, the share of persons employed in the informal sector exceeds 30 percent of the total non-agricultural labour force in 29 countries. Even more alarming, 20 countries have informal employment rates near or above 50 percent, including Argentina, Armenia, Colombia, the Dominican Republic, Ecuador, Egypt, El Salvador, Honduras, Indonesia, Liberia, Mexico, Nicaragua, Palestine (OPT), Paraguay, Peru, Sri Lanka, Uganda, Venezuela, Vietnam and Zambia. This verifies that many developing countries were already facing a crisis of informal employment and low quality jobs even prior to the onset of the global economic crisis.

Figure IV.9. Estimated Informal Employment Rates in Selected Countries, 2010 or latest available*
(as a percent of non-agricultural employment)

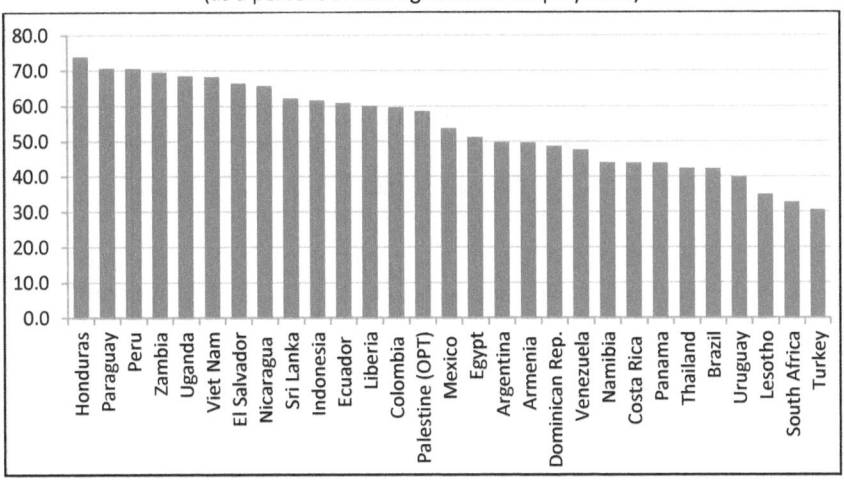

Source: ILO's *LABOURSTA* (2012)
* All estimates are from 2008 to 2010.

The phenomenon of increasing 'labour precarization' has been noted by many with concern. Standing (2011) describes the 'precariat' as a class in the making, a growing number of people across the world living and working precariously, usually in a series of short-term jobs, without recourse to stable occupational identities, social protection or protective regulations relevant to them. While they include migrant workers, most are locals. Standing argues that this class of people could produce new instabilities in societies worldwide. They are increasingly frustrated and dangerous because they have no voice, and, hence, they are vulnerable to the siren calls of extreme political parties. Standing further contends that getting the 'precariat' to re-engage positively into societies requires more equitable policies with universal social protection, which includes an unconditional basic income or wage for everyone that is publicly financed and can be topped up through employment.

2.4.   Working poverty

The culmination of widespread unemployment, lower pay and fewer decent work opportunities has also enhanced the risk of working poverty worldwide. If defined as living below the poverty line and working out of economic necessity, the ILO (2012a) estimates more than 912 million persons and their families were affected by working poverty in 2011, which equals about 30 percent of the global workforce. Put differently, one in every three workers in the world live with their families below the US$2/day poverty line. If applying the US$1.25/day international benchmark, then half of the working poor are in conditions of extreme poverty. Regionally, nearly three-quarters of the world's working poor are concentrated in Asia, with about half in South Asia (Figure 10). Sub-Saharan Africa is also home to close to 200 million working poor persons (just over 20 percent of the global total).

The world has recorded significant inroads against working poverty since 2000 (Figure 11). As an aggregate, the number of working poor was reduced from nearly 1.2 billion in 2000 to just over 900 million in 2011, which represents a decline in the overall global incidence from 33.1 to 29.5 percent over the time period (ILO 2012a). However, most of this progress is attributed to rapid poverty reduction in China. The number of working poor has actually increased in other regions since

2000, including in the Middle East and North Africa, South Asia and Sub-Saharan Africa.

Figure IV.10. Global Working Poverty by Regions, 2011 (US$2/day)
(as a percent of global total)

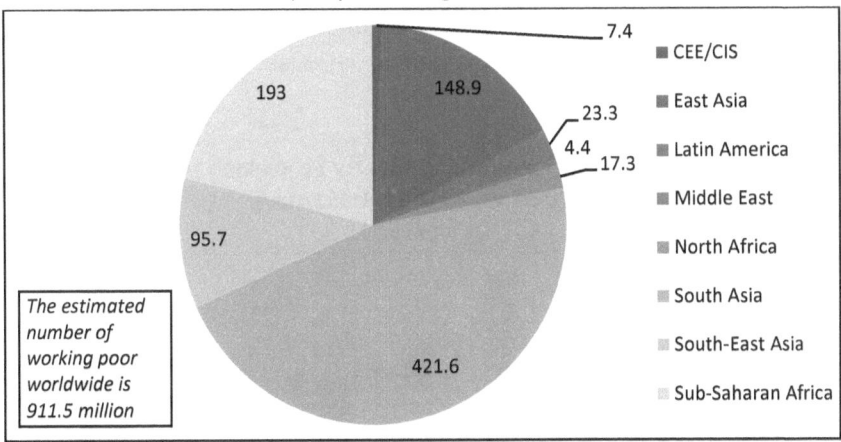

The estimated number of working poor worldwide is 911.5 million

Source: ILO (2012a)

Figure IV.11. Global Working Poverty Trends by Regions and World, 2000-11 (US$2/day)
(in millions of persons)

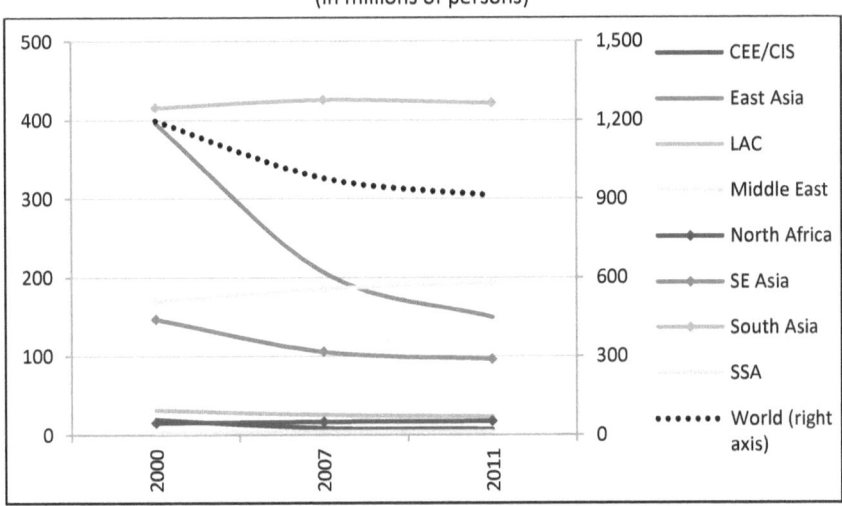

Source: ILO (2012a)

Even more important than the uneven trajectory of progress, the impacts of the global economic crisis, including the jobs crisis, are estimated to have either increased the number of working poor or slowed or reversed earlier gains. The ILO projects that the number of working poor had increased by 55 million through 2011 relative to the pre-crisis trend using the US$2/day poverty metric (ILO 2012a). Comparison of pre-crisis (2000-07) and crisis (2007-11) phases further shows how progress has either been significantly slowed or reversed across all regions (Figure 12). Above all, these trends demonstrate that current efforts to fight poverty and address the global jobs challenge are simply insufficient. As explained in later sections, much more is needed.

Figure IV.12. Growth in Working Poverty by Regions and World, 2000-07 vs. 2007-11 (US$2/day)

(as a percent)

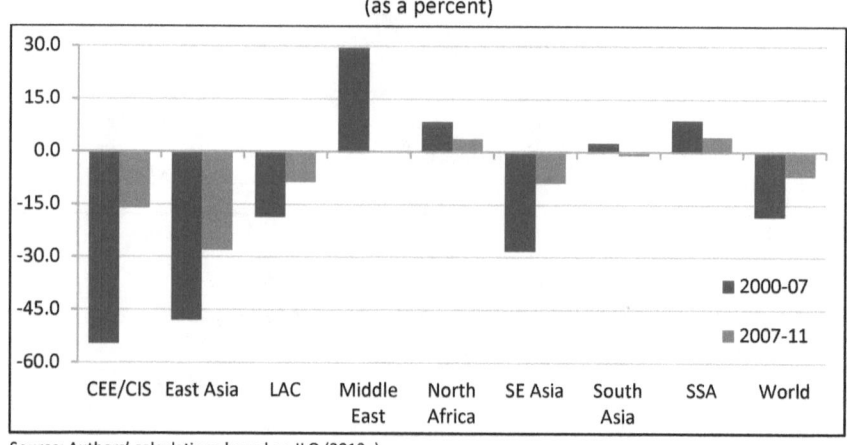

Source: Authors' calculations based on ILO (2012a)

Additionally, while working poverty affects workers of all ages, vulnerability increases at different stages of the life cycle. Youth, in particular, have a higher likelihood of being among the working poor than adults. Based on the latest estimates for 52 countries with available data, youth accounted for 23.5 percent of the total working poor but accounted for only 18.6 percent of non-poor workers (ILO 2011d). In Bhutan, for example, the working poverty rate among youth appears to exceed the adult rate by more than 10 percentage points, and youth working poverty rates were 5 or more percentage points higher than adult rates in Bolivia, Ghana, Guinea, Mali, the Republic of Congo, Sierra Leone, Togo and Vietnam (ILO 2010c).

Given their higher labour force participation rates, poor youth workers forego educational opportunities that could raise their future earnings potential. In Colombia, for example, 60 percent of the young working poor lacked a primary education compared to the 20 percent of youth who lived above the US$2/day poverty line. And in the Philippines, 35 percent of poor youth workers did not possess a basic education, versus only 6 percent of the non-poor youth population (ILO 2010c—based on data for 2003 for both countries). Such illustrations underscore how large cohorts of poor youth remain trapped in low-productivity jobs, principally in subsistence agriculture. Out of economic necessity, their offspring are, in turn, likely to enter the labour force at an early age, perpetuating the vicious circle of poverty from one generation to the next. Having looked at recent developments in labour markets more broadly, the chapter next turns to youth.

3.   Youth Labour Market Trends

This section examines youth labour markets in the context of the global economic crisis. Adopting international standards, youth are defined as those persons aged 15-24 (ILO 2010c). Looking at this age cohort, it first explores the demographic phenomenon known as the 'youth bulge,' which has been affecting a large number of developing countries since the start of the crisis. It then assesses the ability of labour markets to absorb the increasing numbers of young workers.

Overall, this section argues that the youth bulge should be a primary concern for many governments. Every year, approximately 121 million adolescents turn 16 years old—89 percent of which are located in developing regions—and can enter the world's labour market.[4] But many of those who want to work are unable to find jobs. Moreover, with nearly 1.1 billion new potential workers expected between 2012 and 2020, demographic forces will only exacerbate youth unemployment over time. While many young persons will hopefully continue their education and enhance their careers with a technical or university degree, many may not have this opportunity, especially in developing countries. In short, it is imperative that economies promote employment growth and active labour programs for youth, as explained in Section 5.

---

[4] Authors' calculations based on United Nations' *World Population Prospects: The 2010 Revision* (2011), medium variant projections.

3.1.   Increasing demand for new jobs and the 'youth bulge'

The global economic crisis hit many countries just as they were experiencing a 'youth bulge.' If a youth bulge is defined as a peak in the share of persons aged 15-24 in the population, then the world as a whole passed through this demographic milestone around 1985 (Figure 13). However, when looking at the group of least developed countries, the youth bulge appears more recently, around 2005, where the total share of youth in the population in these countries is expected to remain above 20 percent through 2015.

**Figure IV.13. Share of Youth in World Population and
Least Developed Countries, 1950-2050**

(as a percent)

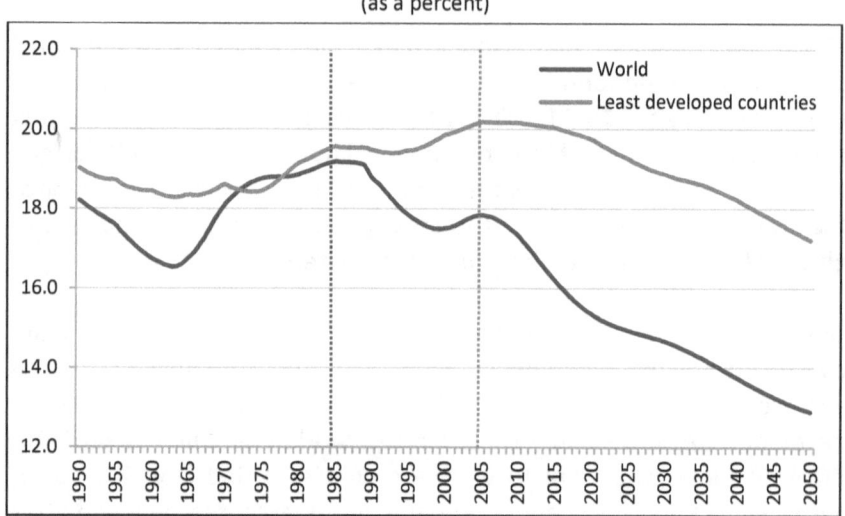

Source: Authors' calculations based on United Nation's *World Population Prospects: The 2010 Revision* (2011)
Note: Least developed countries are based on the UN classification.

While this demographic trend reflects declining fertility rates coupled with the inertia in population growth as a result of large child-bearing populations, the youth bulge has severe implications for labour markets worldwide. Just as many developing countries are dealing with pervasive levels of high youth unemployment, so too are their youth populations quickly growing, with increasing numbers entering the labour force each year. For countries affected by this double whammy— a youth jobs crisis and an expanding supply of young labourers in need of work—the risk of even higher levels of unemployed youth and a 'lost' generation remains great. Such countries also jeopardize missing the one-time opportunity to boost economic growth through a rising share of working-age persons in their population.

Which countries have been impacted by the youth bulge during the global economic crisis? When examining population projections for 180 countries from 1950-2050, 140 countries have experienced their youth bulge prior to 2008, while 18 have an imminent youth bulge during the crisis period between 2008 and 2012 (Figure 14). Population projections further reveal that an additional 22 countries can expect a youth bulge after 2012. Annex 1 provides the complete list of estimated youth bulge peak years for all 180 countries, along with a brief note on the methodology.

Figure IV.14. Youth Bulge Peaks in 18 Countries between 2008 and 2012
(as a percent)

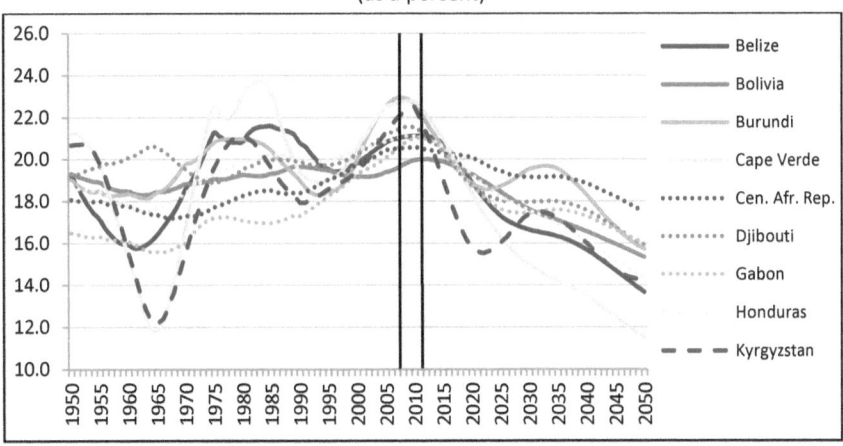

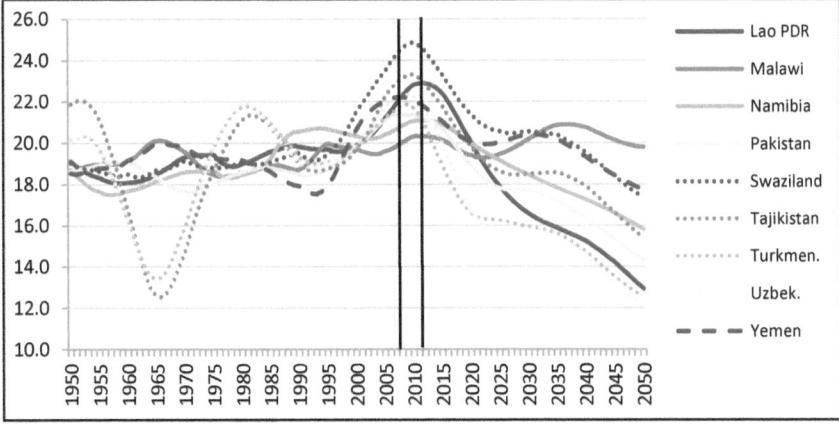

Source: Authors' calculations based on United Nation's *World Population Prospects: The 2010 Revision* (2011), medium variant projections

To more accurately understand the interplay between the youth bulge and the global economic crisis, however, other considerations are warranted. Foremost, it is important to recognize that the actual peak year of a youth bulge is only symbolic insomuch that a given country experiences an abnormally high share of youth in its national population immediately before and after the peak point. Causal observation of population data suggests that this affects the preceding and succeeding four years, on average, from the actual high point. It is also important to note that the length of the recovery period of the global economic crisis is not yet clear, but is likely to last at least into 2014. Under these parameters, some 53 countries have been—or are expected to be—impacted by both the combined effects of the youth bulge and the global economic crisis (see Annex 1).

Focusing on the year 2012, the top 10 countries with the largest youth share in their respective populations are presented in Figure 15. With the exception of the Maldives, which recently became an upper-middle-income country according to World Bank classifications, all of these countries are low-income or lower-middle-income. Interestingly, this trend characterizes the list of the top 80 countries, all of which have 16-24 year old populations that equal 19 percent or more of their national population (Table 2).

**Figure IV.15. Top 10 Countries with Largest Share of Youth in
Total National Population, 2012**
(as a percent)

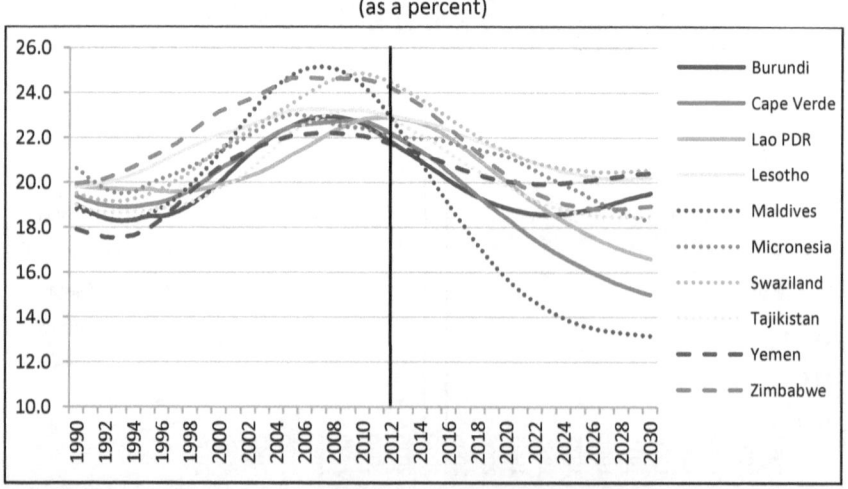

Source: Authors' calculations based on United Nation's *World Population Prospects: The 2010 Revision* (2011), medium variant projections

Table IV.2. Top 80 Countries with Largest Share of Youth in
Total National Population, 2012

#	Country	%	#	Country	%
1	Swaziland	24.4	41	Côte d'Ivoire	20.3
2	Zimbabwe	24.2	42	Cameroon	20.3
3	Lesotho	23.0	43	Guatemala	20.2
4	Lao PDR	22.9	44	Kenya	20.1
5	Maldives	22.8	45	Madagascar	20.1
6	Tajikistan	22.8	46	Uganda	20.0
7	Cape Verde	22.2	47	Bolivia	20.0
8	Micronesia	22.1	48	Burkina Faso	20.0
9	Burundi	21.8	49	Angola	19.9
10	Yemen	21.7	50	Bangladesh	19.9
11	Cambodia	21.7	51	Guinea-Bissau	19.8
12	Palestine (OPT)	21.6	52	Vanuatu	19.8
13	Uzbekistan	21.6	53	Mauritania	19.8
14	Ethiopia	21.5	54	Mongolia	19.8
15	El Salvador	21.5	55	Mozambique	19.8
16	Botswana	21.4	56	Guinea	19.7
17	Kyrgyzstan	21.3	57	Paraguay	19.7
18	Timor-Leste	21.2	58	Zambia	19.7
19	Djibouti	21.2	59	Philippines	19.7
20	Pakistan	21.1	60	Chad	19.7
21	Namibia	21.1	61	Benin	19.7
22	Belize	21.1	62	Sudan	19.6
23	Honduras	21.0	63	Rwanda	19.6
24	Gabon	21.0	64	Mali	19.6
25	Nicaragua	21.0	65	Ghana	19.6
26	São Tomé and Príncipe	20.9	66	Iraq	19.5
27	Nepal	20.8	67	Eritrea	19.5
28	Turkmenistan	20.8	68	Samoa	19.5
29	Haiti	20.7	69	Sierra Leone	19.5
30	Jordan	20.7	70	Guyana	19.4
31	Grenada	20.6	71	Tanzania	19.4
32	Togo	20.6	72	Solomon Islands	19.4
33	Syria	20.6	73	Iran	19.3
34	Afghanistan	20.5	74	Equatorial Guinea	19.3
35	Senegal	20.5	75	Nigeria	19.2
36	Bhutan	20.5	76	Papua New Guinea	19.2
37	Gambia	20.5	77	Liberia	19.2
38	Central African Republic	20.5	78	Congo, Republic of	19.1
39	Malawi	20.3	79	Algeria	19.1
40	Congo, Dem. Republic of	20.3	80	Vietnam	19.0

Source: Authors' calculations based on United Nation's *World Population Prospects: The 2010 Revision* (2011), medium variant projections

When looking at the data over time, it is further evident that many of these countries reached their youth bulge peaks either just before or during the global economic crisis. In such places, the youth bulge represents a potential opportunity to spur social and economic development. At the same time, however, it also represents a significant challenge in terms of creating jobs and other opportunities for advancement, which, in the current environment remains increasingly worrisome.

3.2.   Limited employment opportunities

As demonstrated in the previous section, a growing number of young workers are in need of jobs. But are labour markets generating opportunities for the world's youth? Even before the global economic crisis, the answer was a resounding no. Over the 2005-07 period, the global youth unemployment rate was 12.3 percent, on average, with all regions, less Asia, experiencing double-digit rates (Figure 16). And when the global economic crisis struck, the worldwide youth unemployment rate jumped to nearly 13 percent where it remained through 2011. In aggregate numbers, approximately 75 million youth worldwide were without work in 2011, which represents an increase of more than four million since 2007 (ILO 2011a).

Figure IV.16. Youth Unemployment Rates by Regions and World, 2005-11

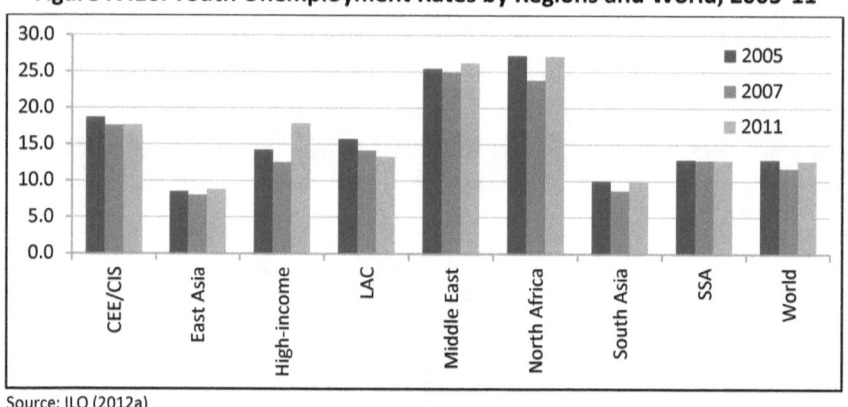

Source: ILO (2012a)

As was the case with overall employment trends, official unemployment rates also mask the actual severity of the jobs crisis confronting youth. Turning to an alternative gauge, the youth employment-to-population ratio suggests that more than one out of every two potential young workers was not in the labour force in 2011 (a global ratio of 44.3), which is a truly staggering figure (Figure 17).

Figure IV.17. Youth Employment-to-Population Ratios by Regions and World, 2005-11

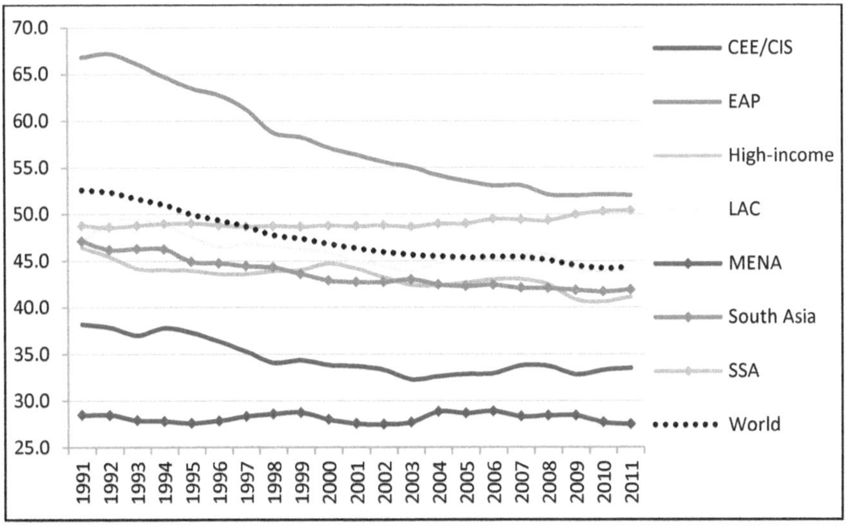

Source: ILO (2010c)

Perhaps more alarming, however, is the longer-term trend. Over the past two decades, the youth employment-to-population ratio has plunged by nearly 10 percentage points globally (Figure 18). At the same time, the number of youth in the world population has increased by about 200 million. When combined, these factors indicate that the world economy has failed impressively to create enough jobs for youth. As described earlier in Section 3.1, much of this can be explained by the demographic forces driving the youth bulge, especially in East Asia and the Pacific where the youth employment-to-population ratio plummeted by nearly 15 percentage points between 1991 and 2011.

The global economic crisis has further weakened the capacity of economies to create jobs for youth. Globally, the youth employment-to-population ratio dropped by more than a percentage point between 2007 and 2011, with all regions outside of Sub-Saharan Africa recording declines. Latin America and the Caribbean and HICs were most affected, as their ratios fell by nearly 2 percentage points. The more negative outlook painted by employment-to-population ratios when compared to unemployment rates is partly reflected by the estimated 6.4 million youth who have given up hope of finding a job and dropped out of the labour market altogether (ILO 2012a).

Figure IV.18. Global Youth Employment-to-Population Ratio and Share of Youth in World Population, 1991-2011

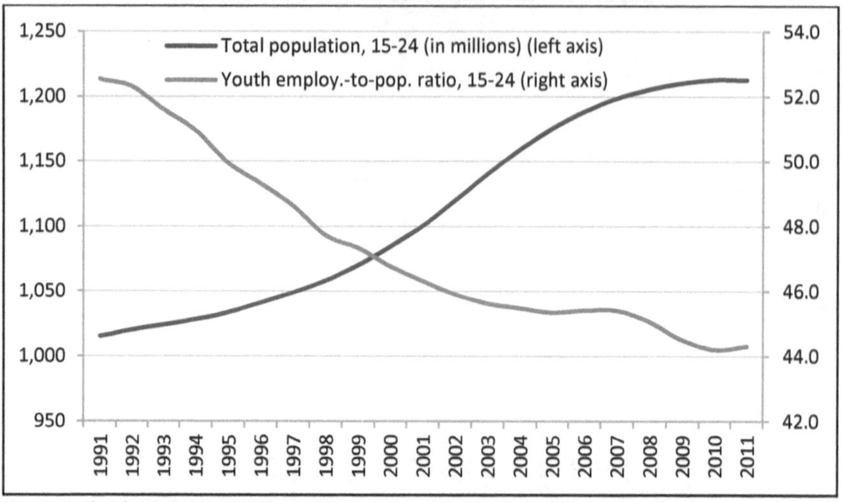

Source: Authors' calculations based on ILO (2010c) and United Nation's *World Population Prospects: The 2010 Revision* (2011), medium variant projections

Job quality is another important consideration when assessing employment opportunities for youth. And, regrettably, youth who do have jobs are increasingly likely to be in situations of part-time work, often on temporary contracts. Projections for 2012 further indicate that the number and share of unemployed young persons is unlikely to change over the near term, which is coupled with a rising share of youth withdrawing from the labour market (ILO 2012a). As a result, the near-term outlook for increasing job opportunities for youth remains dismal.

Importantly, youth have been disproportionately affected by jobs losses since the start of the global economic crisis (Figure 19). Overall, young persons are about three times as likely as adults to be unemployed; the ratio of the youth-to-adult unemployment rate stood at 2.8 in 2011, up from 2.6 in 1998.[5] This confirms the heightened vulnerability of young persons to shocks and supports the common notion that youth are 'first out' and 'last in' during economic downturns.

---

[5] Authors' calculations based on ILO (2010c).

Figure IV.19. Global Youth and Adult Unemployment Trends, 2005-11

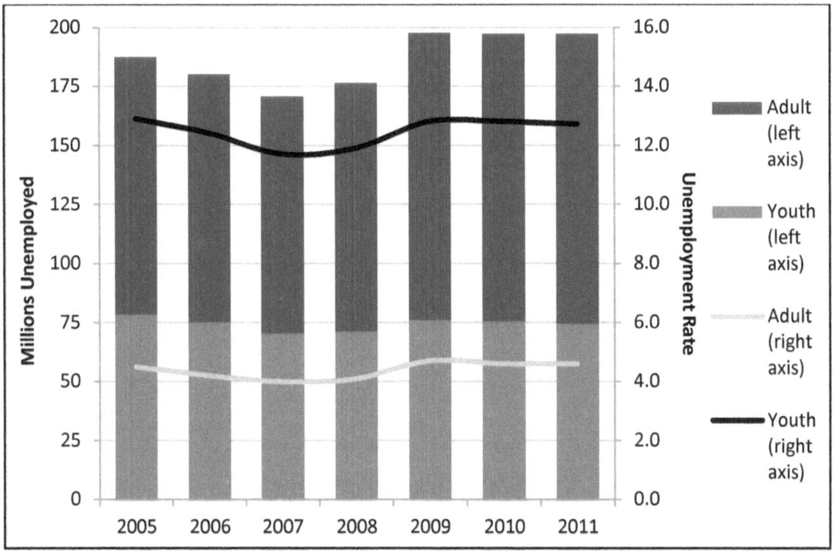

Source: ILO (2012a)

Turning to country-level data, youth unemployment rates mirror those observed in the total population since the start of the crisis. Similar to the findings presented earlier, three unique country typologies emerge when looking at the impact of the crisis on unemployed young persons in a limited sample of countries for which data are comparable over the recent time period. On the one hand, in a large set of countries youth unemployment rates rose quickly beginning in 2008 and continued to steadily increase through 2010 (Figure 20A—Hard Hit and Still High). This trend characterizes 11 of the 43 countries that have available data, but it is likely to be much more widespread in light of the small sample size that is mainly restricted to HICs and the CEE/CIS region. On the other hand, another group of countries suffered high spikes in youth employment in the early phase of the crisis, but quickly reversed this trend during 2010 (Figure 20B—Hard Hit, but Recovering). In yet a third set of countries, the global economic crisis appeared to have little-to-no impact on youth unemployment (Figure 20C—Muted Impact). It is worth noting that these countries tended to have a low incidence of youth unemployment prior to the crisis.

Figure IV.20. Youth Unemployment Rates by Country Typologies, 2005-10

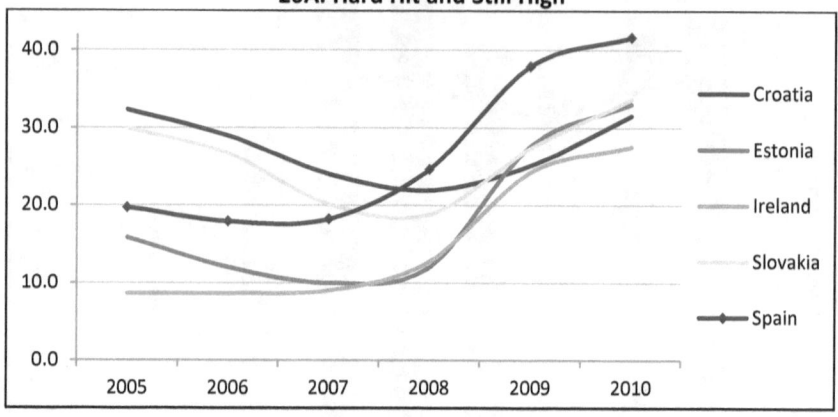

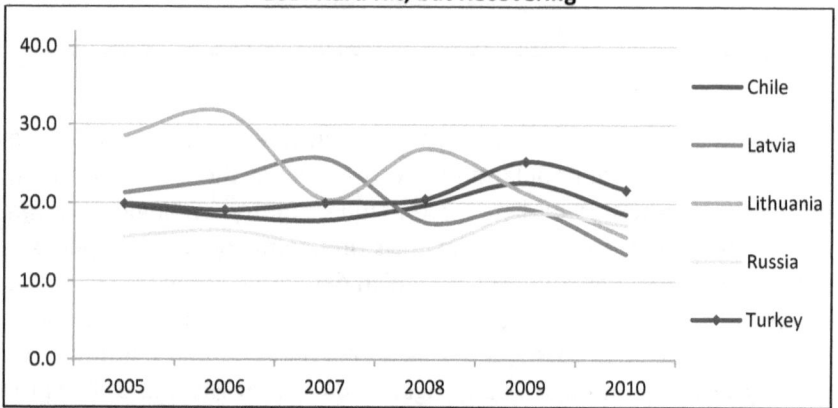

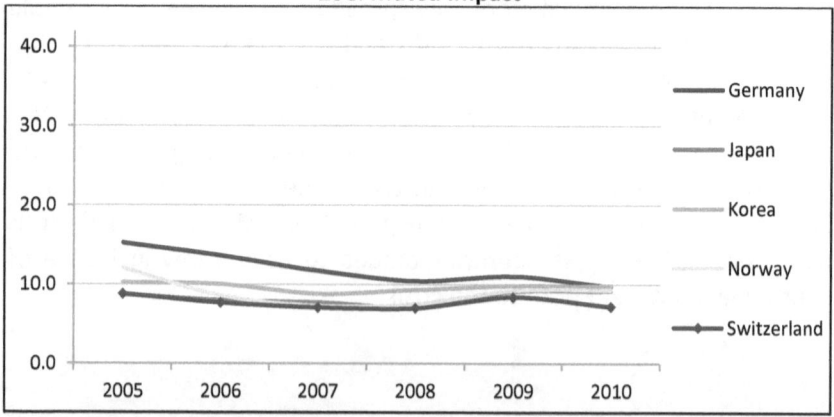

Source: ILO's *LABOURSTA* (2012)

Still youth unemployment rates remain alarmingly high in a large number of countries. ILO estimates show that 28 of the 43 countries with available data had youth unemployment rates above 15 percent in 2010 (Figure 21). Six countries, in particular, boasted youth unemployment rates in excess of 30 percent, including Croatia, Estonia, Greece, Macedonia, Slovakia and Spain.

Figure IV.21. Youth Unemployment Rates in Selected Countries, 2010

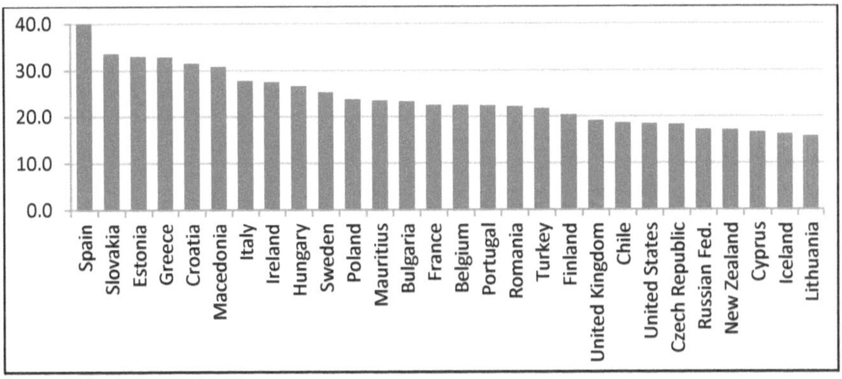

Source: ILO's *LABOURSTA* (2012)

Country-level youth employment-to-population ratios further evince rapid declines in job opportunities for young workers since the start of the crisis. Between 2007 and 2010, the ratio fell or stayed the same in 127 of 169 countries with available data.[6] In 51 of those countries, the ratio plummeted by more than 2 percentage points since the start of the crisis, and by more than 5 percentage points in 19 countries, several of which are illustrated in Figure 22.

The latest estimates also reveal that youth employment-to-population ratios are dangerously low in a significant number of countries (Table 3). Overall, ratios are under 50 percent in 125 countries and below 30 percent in 47 countries. In the case of the latter group of countries, seven out of every ten potential young workers is unable to find a job, and in places such as Namibia, Saudi Arabia and South Africa, nearly nine out of every ten young persons is outside of the labour force. Annex 2 provides the youth and adult employment-to-population ratios for 169 countries. Having outlined recent labour market trends among adult and youth populations, the chapter next looks at the household-level implications.

---

[6] Authors' calculation based on ILO's *LABOURSTA* (2012).

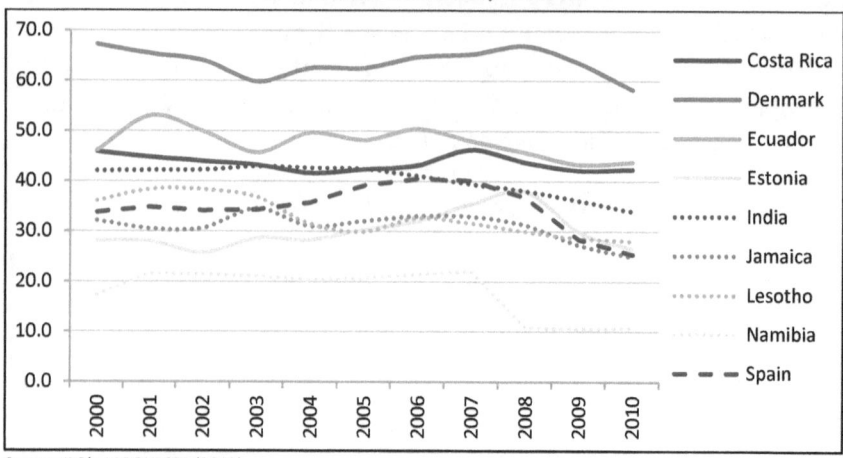

Figure IV.22. Youth Employment-to-Population Ratios in Selected Countries, 2005-10

Source: ILO's *LABOURSTA* (2012)

Table IV.3. Top 50 Countries with Lowest Youth Employment-to-Population Ratios, 2010

#	Country	Ratio, 2010	Change, 2007-10	#	Country	Ratio, 2010	Change, 2007-10
1	Namibia	10.7	-11.3	26	Syria	24.1	-2.7
2	Saudi Arabia	11.5	-0.9	27	Bulgaria	24.2	-2.9
3	South Africa	13.0	-3.1	28	Romania	24.4	-0.1
4	Gabon	14.7	-0.1	29	Czech Republic	24.6	-3.6
5	Macedonia, FYR	15.4	0.1	30	Egypt	24.8	0.1
6	Palestine (OPT)	15.9	-1.7	31	Jamaica	24.9	-8.0
7	Mauritania	16.3	0.3	32	Croatia	25.1	-2.0
8	Bosnia and Herz.	16.6	2.8	33	Belgium	25.2	-2.8
9	Iraq	16.9	-1.3	34	Taiwan	25.3	-3.0
10	Moldova	18.0	-0.4	35	Spain	25.4	-14.7
11	Armenia	18.0	1.6	36	Swaziland	25.8	0.0
12	Hungary	18.4	-2.6	37	Estonia	26.5	-8.9
13	Suriname	19.4	0.0	38	Yemen	26.5	0.7
14	Jordan	19.5	-0.6	39	Sudan	27.0	-0.6
15	Lithuania	19.6	-5.6	40	Poland	27.0	0.6
16	Georgia	20.1	-1.5	41	Latvia	27.3	-11.4
17	Italy	20.3	-4.5	42	Israel	27.3	-0.3
18	Slovakia	20.7	-6.7	43	Lesotho	28.0	-3.6
19	Greece	21.2	-4.1	44	Portugal	28.7	-6.4
20	Luxembourg	21.5	-0.9	45	Libya	28.9	-0.9
21	Algeria	21.8	-0.4	46	Haiti	29.3	-0.7
22	Tunisia	22.7	-0.1	47	Morocco	29.9	-2.8
23	Lebanon	22.8	-0.5	48	Sri Lanka	30.1	-4.3
24	Korea, DPR	23.8	-3.8	49	Belarus	30.5	-0.1
25	Iran	24.0	-1.5	50	Afghanistan	30.7	0.7

Source: Authors' calculations based on ILO's *LABOURSTA* (2012)

4.   **The Impacts of the Jobs Crisis on Children and Poor Households**

The global economic crisis has squeezed the incomes of workers across the globe through job losses, pay cuts and wage arrears, and further reduced the availability of decent work opportunities. In response to the worsening conditions of labour markets, many households are adopting a series of coping mechanisms that have potentially severe and irreversible consequences, especially for infants and young children, which include hunger and malnutrition, illness, lower educational outcomes, children being left alone and even abandoned, and increased poverty and vulnerability of families to ongoing and future shocks. The jobs crisis has also heightened the risk that workers, especially young adults, are being permanently 'scarred' in terms of future employability and earnings potential. Moreover, households stand to lose even further from rising levels of domestic violence, as well as social unrest and political instability, linked to the jobs crisis. Each of these is discussed in the following.

4.1.   Hunger and malnutrition

Income shocks resulting from the jobs crisis have led to lower household spending on food, which risks inflicting nutritional damage on poor households. These risks have been widely reported across the globe, as families purchase smaller quantities and cheaper food items and subsequently consume fewer meals—sometimes reducing food intake to just once a day instead of three times—and smaller, less nutritious portions (see Chapter III).

Importantly, households whose nutritional status was at risk even prior to the jobs crisis appear most likely to further reduce their dietary intake. In particular, a series of crisis response surveys carried out in Armenia, Bulgaria, Latvia, Montenegro and Romania show that job losses or lower pay reduced the quality and quantity of food consumed disproportionately among households in the poorest quintile relative to non-poor households (World Bank 2011). This trend was similarly observed in crisis impact studies conducted in Kiribati (UNDP 2010) and Turkey (TEPAV, UNICEF and World Bank 2009).

Evidence also suggests that children and women bear the brunt of dietary cutbacks related to unemployment and income shortfalls. For instance, focus groups of recently unemployed women in Nicaragua show that 70 percent of mothers and their children had severely reduced their nutritional intake, while Indonesian women who had been out of work for more than a year reported eating fewer and smaller size meals as well as watering down baby formula and feeding their children less (Green et al. 2010). And in Nigeria, focus group discussants identified that children and women from poor families were most likely to suffer the most from reduced food expenditures (Samuels et al. 2011).

Relatedly, the most severe outcomes, including acute malnutrition, were also found to be among vulnerable women. For instance, female beggars reported experiencing dizziness and fainting in rural Bangladesh due to nutritional shortfalls, and women workers in rural areas of Zambia identified themselves as being too weak to work because of inadequate food intake (Institute of Development Studies 2009).

Lastly, it is imperative that nutritional trends are viewed within both the context of reduced household income due to the jobs crisis as well as the rising costs of basic food items as described in Chapter III. Given that the income and price shocks have simultaneously affected many countries since 2008, the danger of hunger and malnutrition remains severe and serious in 2012, especially among infants, young children and female-headed households.

4.2.   Poor health

Another common coping mechanism related to the jobs crisis is reduced expenditure on healthcare. In a number of developing countries, in particular, households have consistently reported lower healthcare spending and service utilization, which has exposed many people to a higher risk of sickness, disability or even death. For instance, crisis-affected households in Armenia, Bulgaria, and Montenegro significantly reduced doctor visits, medical care and prescription drug use, with the poorest households most commonly adopting these risky behaviors (World Bank 2011). In Nigeria, reduced household income was widely cited as a key barrier to healthcare access, which made many drug and treatment costs unaffordable, increased the incidence of self-diagnosis and self-medication, and prevented many pregnant women from accessing antenatal care (Samuels et al. 2011). Self-diagnosis and resorting to folk remedies were also observed in Bangladesh and Jamaica (Institute of Development Studies 2009). Moreover, while 55 percent of Filipino households reported reducing essential medical expenditures (Reyes et al. 2010), more than one-quarter of Turkish households decreased their use of health services, with another 20 percent avoiding preventive care doctor visits (TEPAV, UNICEF and World Bank 2009).

Aside from the short-term health risks linked to coping strategies, there is also ample evidence that unemployment can cause serious physical and mental impacts. In general, unemployment has been shown to increase susceptibility to physical illness, mental stress and loss of self-esteem, and ultimately lead to severe depression (Banks and Jackson 1982, Brenner and Mooney 1983, Linn et al. 1985, Frese and Mohr 1987, Jackson and Warr 1987, Darity and Goldsmith 1996, Goldsmith et al. 1996 and 1997, and Brand et al. 2008). And indeed, surveys have indicated a growing prevalence of depression in India, Pakistan, South Africa and Thailand since the onset of the crisis, in addition to a rise in demand for mental health services offered by clinics and hotlines in China, India, Japan, Latvia and countries throughout Europe (United Nations 2011b). Worsening economic conditions have also led to higher stress levels in Indonesia and Kenya (Institute of Development Studies 2009).

Many studies further show that unemployed persons have a higher propensity to take their own lives (Platt 1984 and Blakely et al. 2003). This trend appears evident in the current crisis through increased suicide rates in Egypt, Japan, Latvia, South Africa and the United States (United Nations 2011b). Joblessness has been further connected to a series of deadly health outcomes later in life, including heart attacks and strokes (Beale and Nethercott 1987, Iverson and Sabroe 1988, Mattiasson et al. 1990, Gallo et al. 2006 and Strully 2009), as well as reducing the life expectancy of workers (Moser et al. 1987 and 1990).

4.3.   Lower school attendance and higher child labour rates

The jobs crisis has also forced many families to pull their children out of school and put them to work. This trend has been mainly driven by the increasing need to supplement household income coupled with the inability to cover the costs of school attendance, as observed in Bangladesh, Cambodia, Kenya, Thailand and Zambia (Heltberg et al. 2012), in Bangladesh, Kenya and Zambia (Raihan 2009), as well as in India (Self-Employed Women's Association 2009). Qualitative evidence in rural areas of Nigeria further show that children as young as five years old were increasingly involved in supporting family farms, selling produce in markets and working as apprentices to traders; rises in school dropout rates and absenteeism were also attributed to increased difficulties in paying school costs and transport fees, especially in rural areas (Samuels et al. 2011). In Nicaragua, while many girls were found to be helping their mothers earn additional income in towns and cities, boys increasingly appeared to be working on family farms and serving as substitutes for waged farm employees who were no longer affordable (Green et al. 2010). Decreased school attendance and increased employment among Salvadoran girls and boys aged 10-16 were also shown to be linked to the income shock at the household level resulting from the employment crisis (Duryea and Morales 2011).

4.4.   Unsupervised and abandoned children

Another negative consequence of the job crisis is that higher unemployment and lower pay have forced many parents to increase their working hours and/or send non-working members of the household into the labour market, especially mothers. As a result, the jobs crisis has increased the prevalence of children being left at home unattended and unsupervised. This increasingly common manifestation has been well documented in both LICs and MICs, including in Armenia, Bulgaria, Latvia, Montenegro and Romania (World Bank 2011), in Botswana, Brazil, Mexico and Vietnam (Sigurdsen et al. 2011), in Nigeria (Samuels et al. 2011) and in Malawi (Green et al. 2010). In extreme cases, there have been reports of children being abandoned in orphanages and care centers in both low- and high-income countries as a result of the jobs crisis, including Greece, Somalia and Zimbabwe.[7]

---

[7] Smith, H. 2011. "Greek Economic Crisis Turns Tragic for Children Abandoned by their Families." *The Guardian*, December 28. And Australia Network News. 2011. "Children Abandoned in Somali crisis." *Australia Network News*, July 26. And Caritas International. 2009. "Children Abandoned in Zimbabwe's Economic Crisis." *Caritas International*, 2009.

4.5. Increased vulnerability to future shocks

A final widespread coping strategy linked to the jobs crisis has been selling household assets and borrowing money. In order to maintain consumption needs during periods of unemployment or reduced or erratic wages, many households have drawn down savings and sold possessions, as well as turned to friends, relatives, membership-based clubs, community groups and banks, where possible, for financial help. This behavior has been observed in a wide range of countries since 2008, including Bangladesh, Cambodia, the Central African Republic, Ghana, Kazakhstan, Kenya, Mongolia, the Philippines, Serbia and Thailand (Heltberg et al. 2012), Armenia, Bulgaria, Latvia, Montenegro and Romania (World Bank 2011), Nigeria (Samuels et al. 2011), Armenia (UNDP 2010), the Philippines (Reyes et al. 2010) and Tonga (Patel and Thapa 2010).

To cite some specific examples, a survey in India found that the limited availability of services at government hospitals had forced them to borrow money at high interest rates and increase indebtedness in order to seek treatment at private facilities (Self-Employed Women's Association 2009). Furthermore, as livelihood opportunities declined, many Indian households were observed taking out loans to meet minimum needs, especially for food, rent, electricity and education, as well as selling small valuables, including eating utensils. Elsewhere, Zambians sold their livestock, including goats, HIV/AIDS victims in Kenya resorted to selling food donations that they had received, and Indonesians were found to be selling livestock, poultry and gold (Institute of Development Studies 2009).

While selling assets and borrowing are, indeed, important safety nets for the poor, they are also easily exhaustible: personal items cannot be sold twice, different sources of formal or informal lending quickly evaporate in prolonged crises, such as the current situation, and existing debt prevents additional borrowing and must be repaid. All in all, having been forced to confront an array of shocks since 2007, virtually unabatedly, poor households in many parts of the world increasingly find themselves in situations of extreme vulnerability to any prolonged shock—including ongoing high unemployment, high food prices (Chapter III) and reduced social assistance (Chapter V)—as well as any renewed shock, such as the current rise in fuel prices.

4.6.   Wage scars

Aside from the dangerous coping mechanisms linked to the jobs crisis, recent employment trends have also heightened the risk that workers, especially young adults, are being permanently 'scarred' in regards to their future employability and earnings potential. In particular, workers who experience unemployment, especially of long duration, have an increased likelihood of being jobless in later years and earning lower wages. These effects, which are known as 'wage scars,' are observed in both young and adult populations, but the evidence overwhelmingly shows that the impacts are much more acute on youth workers.

There is a plethora of evidence from developed countries that verifies the existence of wage scars over time. For instance, when studying labour markets in the United Studies, Ellwood (1982) concluded that lost work experience while a teenager was reflected in considerably lower wages and a higher probability of being unemployed later on in life; Kletzer and Fairlie (1999) estimated that being unemployed while young results in lower future earnings by a magnitude of 8.4 and 13 percent for males and females, respectively; and Wachter et al. (2009) found that laid-off adult workers experience an immediate 30 percent drop in annual earnings when compared to workers who keep their jobs, with a 20 percent income difference persisting even 20 years after the fact.

A host of studies from the United Kingdom further document that unemployment produces permanent scars rather than temporary blemishes, especially on youth populations: Burgess et al. (1999) showed that youth unemployment raises the probability of unemployment later on; Arulampalam (2001) observed that a shorter spell of unemployment carries a wage penalty of 6 percent on re-entry into the labour market, and after three years results in a 14 percent earnings loss when compared to the counterfactual; Gregg and Tominey (2005) estimated an earnings loss of up to 21 percent at age 41 for workers who experience unemployment in early adulthood; and Bell and Blanchflower (2009) concluded that unemployment in a person's early twenties negatively affects employment and earnings prospects, as well as health and job satisfaction, up to two decades later.

In sum, the evidence is clear that unemployment, even if temporary, can have a lasting impact. And there is little reason to assume that this phenomenon is restricted to developed countries. This means that unemployment today is likely leaving permanent scars on workers worldwide, especially among youth.

4.7.   Domestic violence

In addition to the heightened risks already discussed, preliminary evidence further suggests that the jobs crisis has increased domestic violence at the household level. Data sources are scarce, but higher incidences of violence have been documented in several countries. For example, the number of requests for support from domestic violence centers in the United States jumped by 75 percent among 630 surveyed shelters during the early part of the crisis, with jobs losses and financial concerns cited as the main contributing factors.[8] And phone calls received by the National Domestic Violence Hotline, also in the United States, rose by 21 percent between 2007 and 2008, with more than half of violence related to declining household income.[9] Increased rates of domestic violence linked to the crisis have also been reported in Curaçao, India, the Lao People's Democratic Republic and the United Kingdom (United Nations 2011b). Domestic violence has even been connected to alcohol and substance abuse (Self-Employed Women's Association 2009).

4.8.   Social instability

In addition to the heightened risks already discussed, the jobs crisis further threatens to harm household well-being through rising levels of social discontent and instability. The ILO (2011e) recently produced a social unrest index, which found that global levels of discontent are related to unemployment, worsening living standards, a lack of confidence in governments and the perception that the burden of the crisis is not being fairly shared. The ILO (2011e) further warned of a significant aggravation of social unrest in 45 of the 118 countries surveyed. The regions under greatest threat include the Middle East and

---

[8] Mary Kay. 2011. "Domestic Violence Rises Nationwide for Third Year While Economy Struggles; Government Budget Cuts Take Toll on Survivors and Shelters." *Mary Kay Press Release*, April 26.
[9] National Domestic Violence Hotline. 2009. "Increased Financial Stress Affects Domestic Violence Victims." *Hotline News*, January 30.

North Africa, parts of Asia and the group of developed countries. One of the most obvious manifestations of these findings is the increasing number of street demonstrations and protests observed worldwide since 2010, which have been closely linked to the Arab Spring and European sovereign debt crises. The income shock is also connected to higher incidences of crime and theft, which have been observed as common coping mechanisms in Bangladesh, Cambodia, the Central African Republic, Kenya, Mongolia, the Philippines, Thailand, Ukraine, Vietnam and Zambia (Heltberg et al. 2012) as well as in Dominica (UNDP 2010).

In terms of root causes, the short supply of decent employment opportunities emerges as a main driving force behind rising social unrest. Across virtually all regions, the majority of people report being frustrated by the lack of quality jobs in their labour markets (Figure 23). In the CEE/CIS and Sub-Saharan Africa regions, for example, general dissatisfaction is expressed by more than 70 percent of the populaces, on average. And outside of East Asia and the Pacific, job discontentment appears to affect more than half of regional populations, on average. There are, of course, significant country-wide variances. Despite lower regional aggregates, more than 70 percent of people expressed unhappiness with available job opportunities in Egypt, Jordan and Lebanon from the Middle East, as well as in Greece, Italy, Portugal and Spain from the EU (ILO 2011e).

It is obvious that unemployment is not the sole determinant of rising worldwide social unrest. Other factors include perceptions of rising inequalities, higher food prices, austerity measures and low confidence in governments. However, ILO (2011e) econometric analysis verifies that unemployment is the indicator that is most strongly associated with heightened risk of social unrest. In other words, there is a clear connect between the jobs crisis and rising social instability, which has subsequently led to political regime changes—both peacefully and forcefully—across many parts of Europe and the Middle East and North Africa. While political change can ultimately improve household-level well-being over the longer-term (see, for example, McLeod and Lustig 2011), increased social instability is unlikely to benefit poor households in the immediate term, especially when accompanied by unaffordable food, pervasive unemployment and reduced safety nets. Having outlined the different negative impacts of the job crisis, the chapter next focuses on appropriate policy responses to protect the most vulnerable and foster a robust, employment-generating economic recovery.

**Figure IV.23. Dissatisfaction with the Availability of
Good Jobs by Regions, 2010**
(percentage dissatisfied)

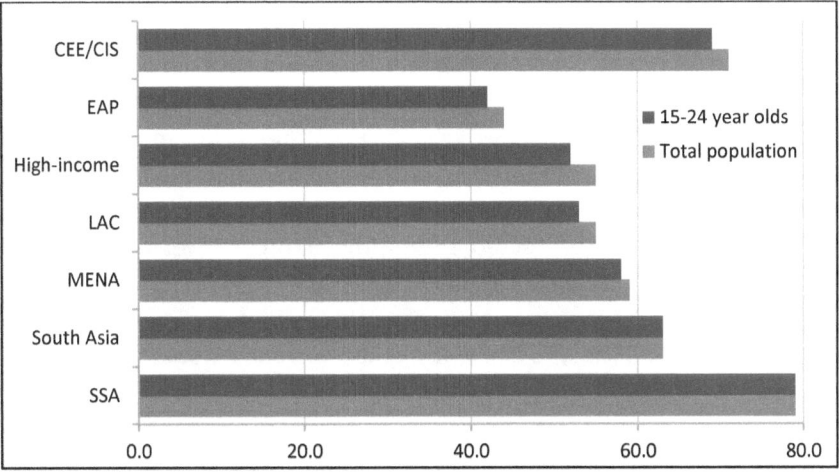

Source: ILO (2011e)

5.   Responding to the Jobs Crisis

This section discusses employment policies. It starts by recounting recent policy trends, first summarizing how governments responded to the early impacts of the global economic crisis and then describing the dramatic change in policy stances that began to take hold in 2010. The section next offers a decent jobs agenda by outlining the main areas that must be considered in order to generate decent employment.

5.1.   Recent employment policy trends

5.1.1.   Initial reaction to the crisis (2008-09): Promoting employment

During the first phase of the global economic crisis (2008-09), many governments launched fiscal stimulus plans, which generally included measures to promote employment; these were in line with ILO recommendations for a Global Jobs Pact (ILO 2009a) and endorsed by the UN and G20. An ILO survey of 54 developing and developed countries indicated that many governments initially responded to the jobs crisis by: (i) increasing spending on infrastructure and offering subsidies and tax reductions for small- and medium-size enterprises (SMEs) to stimulate labour demand; (ii) expanding public employment services, training programs and labour market intermediation facilities to support unemployed persons and jobseekers; (iii) bolstering unemployment, health and/or old-age retirement benefits, as well as cash transfers and social assistance programs, to provide income support to workers and their families; and/or (iv) consulting with employer and worker organizations to foster greater social dialogue and workers' rights. The frequency of the different measures adopted by the surveyed countries is presented in Table 4. While unemployment figures worsened globally, the ILO estimates that between seven and 11 million jobs were created or protected among the G20 countries alone during 2009 as a result of fiscal stimulus packages (ILO 2009b).

Table IV.4. Incidence of Employment-Generating Measures in Fiscal Stimulus Plans in 54 Countries, 2008-09

1. Stimulating Labour Demand	(%)
Additional fiscal spending on infrastructure	87.0
with employment criteria	*33.3*
with green criteria	*29.6*
Public employment	24.1
New/expanded targeted employment programs	51.9
Access to credit for SMEs	74.1
Access to public tenders for SMEs	9.3
Subsidies and tax reductions for SMEs	77.8
2. Expanding Social Protection and Food Security	**(%)**
Social security tax reductions	29.6
Additional cash transfers	53.7
Increased access to health benefits	37.0
Changes in old-age pensions	44.4
Changes to minimum wages	33.3
New protection measures for migrant workers	14.8
Introduction of food subsidies	16.7
New support for agriculture	22.2

Table IV.4 (cont).

3. Supporting Jobseekers, Jobs and Unemployed	(%)
Additional training measures	63.0
Increased capacity of public employment services	46.3
New measures for migrant workers	27.8
Working time reductions	27.8
Partial unemployment with training and part-time work	27.8
Wage reductions	14.8
Extension of unemployment benefits	31.5
Additional social assistance and protection measures	33.3
4. Social Dialogue and Rights at Work	**(%)**
Consultations on crisis responses	59.3
Agreements at national level	35.2
Agreements at sectoral levels	11.1
Additional measures to fight labour trafficking	3.7
Additional measures to fight child labour	3.7
Changes in labour legislation	22.2
Increased capacity of labour administration/inspection	13.0

Source: ILO (2009a)

5.1.2. Second phase of the crisis (2010-): Abandoning labour

These Keynesian measures, however, were short-lived. In a second phase of the crisis (2010-), rising concerns over sovereign debt levels and fiscal deficits led most governments to abandon fiscal stimuli and introduce a series of austerity measures in order to curtail public spending. As detailed in Chapter V, analysis of public expenditure estimates shows that 106 of the 179 countries with available data moved to contract spending in 2010, which is projected to expand to 133 countries during 2012 (or about three-quarters of the sample). It is important to note that this trend is observed quite evenly across all country income typologies. Specifically, during 2012 spending contractions are projected to affect 24 LICs, 40 lower-MICs, 30 upper-MICs and 39 HICs.

In terms of cutting public expenditures with important social impacts, a review of recent IMF country reports indicates that a combination of four main policy options is being discussed in 138 of the 158 countries surveyed (see Chapter V for details). Overall, 73 countries are considering wage bill cuts/caps, 73 countries are eliminating or phasing out subsidies, including food and fuel subsidies, 55 countries are targeting social protection to the poorest, which is a *de facto* reduction in social protection coverage, and 52 countries are reforming pension systems by expanding retirement age and/or limiting benefits. A global summary of austerity trends is presented in Table 5.

Table IV.5. Incidence of Austerity Measures in 158 Countries, 2010-12

Austerity Measures	# of Countries	% of Countries
Contracting public expenditures in 2012*	133	74.3
Cutting or capping the wage bill	73	46.2
Phasing-out or removing food and fuel subsidies	73	46.2
Targeting or further rationalizing social safety nets	55	34.8
Reforming pensions	52	32.9

Source: Authors' analysis of 158 IMF country reports published from January 2010 to February 2012 (see Chpt. V)
* Authors' calculations based on IMF's *World Economic Outlook* (September 2011); Contractions are based on changes in total expenditure as a percent of GDP, and the sample covers 179 countries.

It is striking that all of the different fiscal consolidation measures that are being discussed by governments worldwide will reduce the quantity and quality of decent jobs as well as social protection. When viewing the crisis recovery in this context, there has been an enormous imbalance between the treatment of labour and finance. While government efforts since 2010 have mainly centered on servicing debt (mostly to private banks) and achieving fiscal balances, employment and social protection have become a secondary—and seemingly forgotten— priority. In other words, finance has benefited enormously at the cost of labour during the recovery. Moreover, governments have acted as a banker of last resort to avoid the collapse of the financial system, but, despite stimulus plans and some labour market policies in the earlier phase of the crisis, governments have generally failed to serve as an employer of last resort (van der Hoeven 2010). Moving forward, the delayed labour market recovery is only going to further exacerbate the tremendous human costs of the crisis.

Given that austerity measures and job creation are incompatible objectives, many have questioned whether the tendency of policymakers to highlight employment in speeches and official statements is merely lip service. Criticism of austerity measures has been widespread, including, among many, Nobel Laureates Joseph Stiglitz—"Austerity measures 'don't work' and prevent countries from creating jobs needed to generate economic growth"[10]—and Paul Krugman—"Jobs now, deficits later was and is the right strategy.

---

[10] Schwartzkopff, F. 2011. "Nobel Winner Stiglitz Warns Job-Killing Austerity Measures Hurt Economies." *Bloomberg*, May 13.

Unfortunately, it's a strategy that has been abandoned in the face of phantom risks and delusional hopes."[11]

Generating high levels of decent employment was and is a critical priority, yet now faces even more obstacles than before. A key component of the solution to the current crisis is massive expansionary fiscal actions, preferably in a coordinated fashion, which are complemented by more and better aid to support the world's most vulnerable (Epstein 2009).

Defenders of fiscal consolidation often reference a dated IMF study of 74 episodes in 20 industrialized countries during 1970-95, which found that sharp government spending contractions can lower interest rates and encourage consumption and investment (Dermott and Wescott 1996). Historical evidence, however, shows that fiscal consolidation is much more likely to contract economic activity, lower aggregate demand and ultimately lead to higher unemployment (Islam and Chowdhury 2012, 2010a, 2010b). Employment creation is associated with investment in productive capacities and growth of aggregate demand, which also requires adequate social programs (Ocampo and Jomo 2007).

Over the short term, there is limited support to validate that fiscal austerity can stimulate economic activity, especially among developing countries and in the context of a global crisis. In LICs in Sub-Saharan Africa, for example, an effective employment-generating strategy should be based on: (i) an expansionary fiscal policy that fosters public investment and increases domestic revenues; (ii) a managed exchange-rate regime that promotes export competitiveness and currency stability; and (iii) a monetary policy that supports fiscal expansion and export promotion by achieving low real interest rates to encourage private investment and alleviate public sector debts (Weeks and McKinley 2007, and Pollin, Epstein and Heintz 2008). Such policies must further be complemented by social development programs as well as a social protection floor to foster human development, boost labour market productivity, increase incomes and expand domestic markets (Ortiz 2008, ILO 2011f). There is additionally a large body of evidence that shows the negative impacts of austerity measures on employment

---

[11] Krugman, P. 2011. "The Austerity Delusion." *The New York Times*, March 24.

and social outcomes, including UNICEF's earlier work on *Adjustment with a Human Face* (Cornia et al. 1987).

To reiterate, an appropriate jobs-creating policy framework requires significant expansion of public investments, which is wholly incongruent with fiscal tightening. Given the ongoing fragile state of the recovery coupled with the pervasive jobs crisis, the UN has repeatedly warned that austerity is likely to tip the global economy back into recession and called on governments to avoid premature fiscal adjustment (United Nations 2012a and UNCTAD 2011).

In addition to the main austerity measures earlier outlined, a number of governments—especially in Europe—have been adopting labour flexibilization reforms since 2011. All in all, many countries are viewing labour reforms as an easier strategy to support businesses rather than introducing financial sector reforms to supply credit to companies. However, there is limited evidence that labour market flexibilization can generate jobs (Palley 1999, Rodgers 2007, Standing 2011). In fact, evidence suggests that, in a context of economic contraction, labour market flexibility is more likely to generate labour market 'precarization' and vulnerable employment, as well as depress domestic incomes and, therefore, aggregate demand, ultimately hindering crisis recovery efforts (van der Hoeven 2010).

5.2.   How to generate decent employment

As earlier described, economic growth has been unable to absorb growing labour market populations, indicating that there was a serious jobs crisis even prior to the onset of the global economic crisis.

The current generalized pattern of 'jobless growth' is recent, a result of policy choices since the 1980s. It is important to notice that from the late 1940s until the mid-1970s, many governments focused on employment-generating economic development that combined with labour market policies, which fostered real wage and employment growth. At the end of World War II, politicians from advanced economies were determined that unemployment and economic crisis, which had provoked political crisis and fueled the rise of fascism, should never be repeated. They accepted that full employment, political stability and social cohesion should be primary national policy objectives, and, as a result, governments became more involved in education, medical care, and social and housing assistance, as well as in employment policies, which included introducing minimum retirement benefits and enforcing different labour laws and regulations. Such programs were not new; they were an essential part of modernization programs in these societies during the early stages of their development. Historically, these governments progressively formalized their labour forces as a way to expand the tax base, build social protection systems, raise social standards and develop domestic markets (United Nations 2008, UNRISD 2010). This approach was highly successful: postwar policies achieved high productivity gains in the workforce, expanded internal markets and increased economic growth, with the populations of Europe, North America, Japan, Australia and New Zealand experiencing unprecedented prosperity. A similar policy push is needed today.

Since the 1980s, however, economic policy frameworks have been largely designed with a narrow focus on growth and macroeconomic stability—employment, equity and social cohesion being only afterthoughts—and failed to maximize synergies between macroeconomic and sectoral policies. As a result, a return to these earlier orthodox policies will only continue the recent patterns of 'jobless growth,' vulnerable employment and highly-segmented labour markets that are characterized by large wage differentials and rising inequality. Rethinking policies for a socially-responsive recovery is thus imperative.

Employment growth, especially for youth, must be a top priority for socio-economic recovery. The UN, particularly the ILO, has consolidated a policy agenda to achieve decent jobs for all (ILO 1999 and 2012a, United Nations 2008 and 2010). This is based on a combination of macroeconomic and sectoral policies, active labour market policies and programs, enforcement of labour standards, social protection measures and social dialogue, each of which is briefly summarized in the following. It is important to highlight that this agenda was endorsed by all governments at the UN Summit in September 2010:

> We acknowledge that much more needs to be done in achieving the MDGs as progress has been uneven among regions and between and within countries... There has been slow progress in reaching full and productive

employment and decent work for all.../... We stress the need to create full and productive employment and decent work for all and further resolve to promote the Global Jobs Pact as a general framework within which each country can formulate policy packages specific to its situation and national priorities in order to promote a job intensive recovery and sustainable development. We call on Member States to take effective measures for promoting social inclusion and integration and incorporate these into their national development strategies.

Macroeconomic and sector policies: At the macroeconomic level, economic and sector policies must be geared toward fostering aggregate demand, investment and new jobs. This means that they must steer away from an orthodox focus on containing inflation and budget deficits, as well as liberalizing product/factor markets and trade. Ultimately, new employment will only be generated if a country's economic activities are able to absorb the existing labour supply.

To create new and decent jobs, policymakers should therefore analyze the labour-absorbing patterns of their economies. This requires a detailed understanding of, *inter alia*: (i) the composition of economic growth and the relative labour intensities; (ii) the leading sectors and sub-sectors of the economy; (iii) the size of the informal sector; (iv) domestic and foreign investment prospects; and (v) medium- and longer-term growth and population projections. Such timely assessment can provide a sound basis for evaluating options to overcome any supply and demand mismatches in labour markets, as well as determine which growth, investment and labour market policies may best promote widespread employment with good working conditions. This, above all, requires that macroeconomic policies are designed and implemented by means of coordinated actions of all development-related ministries, and be informed by the inter-linkages between economic and social policies. Of particular importance are the following:

-   Monetary and fiscal policies that boost aggregate demand (e.g., tight monetary and fiscal policies focused on containing inflation and/or deficits do not generate jobs; rather than targeting inflation, national development plans could, alternatively, target employment)—in other words, a key solution to the current jobs crisis is, in fact, expansionary fiscal policies, not austerity;
-   Adopting incentives to increase investment and employment in both the private and public sectors;

- Ensuring that sector policies promote real economic activities (e.g., an inclusive financial sector that supports the broad-based needs of agriculture, industry and services, not just in main cities but also small-scale economic activities in remote locations, including through branching out private banking services and expanding national development banks); and
- Exchange rate and technology policies that stimulate output growth, which are further complemented by the gradual and sequential opening of trade.

Active labour market policies and programs: A series of different active labour market programs and policies can be considered: (i) direct employment generation (promoting SMEs, cooperatives, wage subsidies, public works, guaranteed job schemes, etc.); (ii) labour exchanges or employment services (e.g., job brokerage and counseling offices); (iii) skills development programs (e.g., training and retraining of labour to enhance employability and productivity); and (iv) special programs for youth and persons with disabilities (Box 1).

Box IV.1. Employment Programs for Youth

There is often a lack of understanding of the interaction between economic and social policies. For example, education does not result in employment; education raises productivity and fosters innovation, but promoting education will not generate jobs. The current young generation is much more educated than their parents, but they have fewer employment opportunities. In addition to the right mix of employment-generating macroeconomic and labour policies, young people need programs that are tailored to helping them enter the labour market. Examples of innovative programs abound, such as the 'Jobstart' programs for youth in Australia and the United Kingdom, as well as special programs to help youth start their own businesses in Thailand, which were devised as part of the crisis stimulus plan.

Source: Ortiz (2008)

Labour standards: Decent employment is not only about generating jobs. As earlier discussed in Section 2.4, nearly one billion poor persons are employed, but they work long hours, often in unsafe conditions, and, ultimately, they are unable to bring their families out of poverty. As a result, employment policies must not solely focus on creating jobs but also on ensuring adequate wages and working conditions.

Wage policies, for instance, are important from both an economic and a human rights perspective. On the one hand, a decent remuneration can enable workers to provide for themselves and their families and help fulfill the basic human right to a decent standard of living, which includes food, clothing, housing and medical care. On the other hand, raising the incomes of workers increases domestic demand, which, in turn, encourages economic growth and recovery.

In situations of excess supply of labour, however, employers find themselves in a very strong bargaining position. In developing countries, for example, it is not unusual for an employer to be able to offer a wage equal to the value of a daily meal—even if productivity criteria allow for higher wages—simply because many poor persons may not have any other employment alternatives. Properly enforced minimum wage legislation can and should prevent such abuses. It benefits employers in the longer term, as higher incomes in the labour force ensure demand for their products and services.

In terms of specific labour regulations, there is a wide range that should be adopted nationally and enforced. To name just a few of the broad categories: (i) wage policies (minimum salaries, wage indexation, equal pay for work of equal value); (ii) working conditions (minimum age, maximum working hours and overtime, leave provisions, occupational health and safety); (iii) job security provisions (recruitment/dismissal of employees); and (iv) industrial relations. Of special importance to UNICEF is avoiding child labour and anti-discrimination provisions to protect women, young people, persons with disabilities and minority groups. Countries should aim for an appropriate legislative framework that strikes a balance between economic efficiency and labour protection.

Social protection: Given that not everybody can or should work, policies to promote employment should be accompanied by adequate social protection measures. In particular, social protection must aim to prevent child labour and provide adequate income support for the unemployed, older persons, women on maternity leave and persons with disabilities. Social protection should not be regarded as a cost to society, but rather as an investment (Cichon et al. 2006); investing in children has large impacts on human development and productivity, and raising the incomes of the poor expands domestic markets.

Social dialogue: Now, more than ever in recent history, it is essential that employers, unions and governments dialogue together about how to achieve socio-economic recovery. Social pacts can be an effective strategy to articulate labour market policies that have positive synergies between economic and social development; they are especially well-suited to arrive at optimal solutions in macroeconomic policy, in strengthening productivity, job and income security, and in supporting employment-generating enterprises. However, to foster social dialogue, governments must first repair and regulate their financial systems in the interests of the public. To this end, it is absolutely critical that policymakers reduce the fear and uncertainty that is hindering private investments so that the private sector can re-start the main engine of global job creation (ILO 2012). While the level of labour protection, benefits and flexibility will vary from country to country, the key is to identify a balance to ensure sustained economic activity and positive social outcomes, where employers benefit from productivity gains and workers benefit from job and income security (Box 2).

Box IV.2. Arguments for the Decent Work Agenda

In the 1980s and 1990s, the conventional free-market argument was that a flexible labour market with limited regulation was better for development. This was based on a belief that greater flexibility reduced costs and made firms more competitive, thus expanding entrepreneurial activities and leading to more jobs. Recent evidence, however, points otherwise:

- *Employment:* Labour flexibility has not been accompanied by increased employment in economies where the demand for labour is low, which characterizes most countries. Instead, it leads to informalization and job precariousness. For example, before the crisis, many European countries substantially reduced unemployment without labour market reforms while maintaining generous unemployment schemes. This shows that employment is not related to labour market flexibility, but rather to macroeconomic policies that are effectively coordinated with social policies. The strong welfare states in northern Europe offer further evidence. Given that countries such as Denmark, the Netherlands, Norway and Sweden maintained employment rates as high as those in the

United States and the United Kingdom, they show that employment is fully compatible with 'rigid' labour markets, high social protection and collective bargaining.

- *Productivity:* It is fully demonstrated that decent work raises productivity; it improves workers' health, skills and motivation, and reduces wasteful labour turnover.
- *Labour costs:* There is more controversy regarding the effects of labour market flexibility on costs. While raising employment standards clearly correlates with increasing labour expenses, there are several trends worth noting that are likely to minimize some of the perceived rise in costs. First, higher labour standards, unless very high, do not reduce foreign direct investment (FDI); evidence shows that FDI in developing countries has far more concern for non-labour issues, such as access to domestic markets, ease of doing business, levels of corruption or quality of infrastructure. Second, while higher labour standards impact local labour-intensive firms that use unskilled labour at very low wages with no protection, it is important to note that the competitiveness that a country gains by exploiting cheap labour is short-lived since 'race-to-the-bottom' situations do not develop domestic markets. Third, investor and consumer activism in developed countries is increasingly demanding higher labour standards for both imported goods as well as for multinational companies, and local firms can build on these norms.
- *Poverty reduction:* Impacts on poverty reduction are large. Work-related injuries can plunge families into poverty, outcomes which are avoidable with adequate occupational health, safety and social protection measures. Moreover, better earnings can improve the health and education of poor households, as well as help to reduce child labour.
- *Domestic demand:* By raising incomes, the decent work agenda contributes to boosting domestic demand and expanding national markets.
- *Equity:* Labour standards address discrimination in employment and are key to supporting inclusive policies for women, youth, or ethnic and minority groups. Freedom of association may even allow informal workers to negotiate better prices for their work.
- *Political Stability:* Social dialogue may help to foster national coalitions for development; citizens living with more dignity and income tend to support their governments.

All governments committed to support full employment and decent work for all as a central objective of national development strategies at the 2005 and 2010 World Summits, and the decent work agenda is officially supported by UN agencies and by major financiers like the EU.

Sources: DFID 2004, Commission of the EU 2006, Howell 2005, ILO 1999 and 2009b, OECD 2000, United Nations 2008 and 2010.

6.   Conclusion

The employment crisis is severe. Labour markets worldwide are characterized by fewer, lower-paying jobs that are increasingly vulnerable and proliferating the incidence of working poverty that had trapped nearly one billion workers and their families through 2011. Many developing countries are further facing unsettling high youth unemployment rates and a quickly expanding supply of young labourers in need of work—a result of the youth bulge. These are dangerous conditions indeed. For poor households, smaller and erratic incomes are leading to hunger and malnutrition, worse health, lower educational outcomes, child labour, unsupervised and even abandoned children, escalating vulnerabilities to ongoing or future shocks, and rising rates of domestic violence. For societies at large, labour market frustrations are catalyzing civil unrest unseen in decades.

The youth bulge should be a primary concern for many governments. Every year, there are more than 120 million new potential workers entering the world's labour market, nearly 90 percent of which are from developing countries, with nearly 1.1 billion expected between 2012 and 2020. A majority of countries experiencing this demographic trend are among the most vulnerable in terms of political and social instability, and are already severely limited by the lack of employment opportunities. High rates of youth unemployment are perpetuating 'wage scars;' they are further eroding prior investments in education and health, as well as limiting tax contributions and savings among younger generations, all of which limit aggregate demand and hinder socio-economic recovery.

Given that work is the main source of income for households and particularly the poor, a job-creating labour market strategy is essential to reducing poverty, developing human capital, addressing youth development and gender discrimination, and enhancing overall welfare and productivity. An employment-based recovery is further vital to protecting and supporting the most vulnerable populations, especially children. On the one hand, ensuring that parents have access to stable, quality jobs and income streams is one of the most important factors that contribute to the overall well-being of infants and young children. On the other hand, addressing youth unemployment is critical to fostering stable and inclusive societies, safeguarding earlier investments in human development, and tapping into the productive and innovative capacity of national labour markets.

Some potential questions for policymakers to consider in this regard may include:

- What were the characteristics of growth, employment and poverty in the country prior to the crisis? Has there been a strong, negative correlation between lower poverty rates and higher growth rates? Has growth generated sufficient and remunerative employment?
- What are the most dynamic sectors of the economy? Are they labour-intensive? What is their contribution to public revenue? What is the size of the informal economy? What can be done to promote the dynamic, employment-generating sectors of the economy and create more revenue that can be directed toward social development?
- What is the percentage of youth in the national population? Will the economy be able to absorb all new entrants into the labour market? Which policies should be prioritized to create good job opportunities for youth?
- Is the government undertaking austerity measures? Is there any assessment of the potential negative impacts of fiscal contraction on employment?
- What can be done to accelerate employment-generating growth? Which macroeconomic policies and sector interventions should be promoted over the short and longer term to secure employment, including for youth?
- Is the financial sector serving the needs of small-scale agriculture, industry and services in remote locations? If not, what should be done?
- Has the government engaged in a social dialogue with employers and workers to target job growth in the real economy? What specific labour market interventions should be prioritized to promote labour demand and good working conditions to ensure a *'Recovery for All'*?

References

Arulampalam, W. 2001. "Is Unemployment Really Scarring? Effects of Unemployment Experiences on Wages." *Economic Journal* 111(475): F585-F606.

Banks, M. and P. Jackson. 1982. "Unemployment and the Risk of Minor Psychiatric Disorder in Young People: Cross-sectional and Longitudinal Evidence." *Psychological Medicine* 12: 789-798.

Beale, N. and S. Nethercott. 1987. "The Health of Industrial Employees Four Years after Compulsory Redundancy." *Journal of the Royal College of General Practitioners* 37: 390-394.

Bell, D. and D. Blanchflower. 2010. "Youth Unemployment: Déjà Vu?" IZA Discussion Paper No. 4705, Institute for the Study of Labour (IZA).

Blakely, T., S. Collings and J. Atkinson. 2003. "Unemployment and Suicide. Evidence for a Causal Association?" *Journal of Epidemiological Community Health* 57: 594-600.

Brand, J., B. Levy and W. Gallo. 2008. "Effects of Layoffs and Plant Closings on Depression among Older Workers." *Res Aging* 30(6): 701-721.

Brenner, M. and A. Mooney. 1983. "Unemployment and Health in the Context of Economic Change." *Social Science and Medicine* 17(16): 1125-1138.

Burgess, S., C. Propper, H. Rees and A. Shearer. 2003. "The Class of 1981: The Effects of Early Career Unemployment on Subsequent Unemployment Experiences." *Labour Economics* 10(3): 291-309.

Cichon, M., K. Hagemejer and J. Woodall. 2006. *Changing the Paradigm in Social Security: From Fiscal Burden to Investing in People*. Geneva: ILO.

Commission of the EU. 2006. *Promoting Decent Work for All: The European Union Contribution to the Implementation of the Decent Work Agenda in the World*. Brussels: EU.

Cornia, G.A., R. Jolly and F. Stewart. 1987. *Adjustment with a Human Face: Protecting the Vulnerable and Promoting Growth*. Oxford: Oxford University Press.

Darity, W. and A. Goldsmith. 1996. "Social Psychology, Unemployment and Macroeconomics." *Journal of Economic Perspectives* 10(1): 121-140.

Dermott, C.J. and R.F. Wescott. 1996. "Fiscal Reforms that Work." Economic Issues, No. 4, IMF.

DFID. 2004. "Labour Standards and Poverty Reduction," Issues, United Kingdom Department for International Development (DFID).

Duryea, S. and M. Morales. 2011. "Effects of the Global Financial Crisis on Children's School and Employment Outcomes in El Salvador." *Development Policy Review* 29(5): 527-46.

Ellwood, D. 1982. "Teenage Unemployment: Permanent Scars or Temporary Blemishes?" In B. Freeman and D. Wise (eds.), *The Youth Labour Market Problem: Its Nature, Causes and Consequences*. Chicago: University of Chicago Press.

Epstein, G. 2009. "Rethinking Monetary and Financial Policy: Practical Suggestions for Monitoring Financial Stability while Generating Employment and Poverty Reduction." Employment Working Paper No. 37, ILO.

European Commission. 2005. *Employment in Europe 2005*. Brussels: European Commission.

Fairlie, R. and L.G. Kletzer. 2003. "The Long-term Costs of Job Displacement among Young Workers." *Industrial and Labour Relations Review* 56(4): 682-698.

Frese, M. and G. Mohr. 1987. "Prolonged Unemployment and Depression in Older Workers: A Longitudinal Study of Intervening Variables." *Social Science and Medicine* 25: 173-178.

Gallo, W., T. Hsun-Mei, T. Falba, S. Kasl, H. Krumholz and E. Bradley. 2006. "The Impact of Late-career Job Loss on Myocardial Infarction and Stroke: A 10-Year Follow-up Using the Health and Retirement Survey." *Occupational and Environmental Medicine* 63(10): 683-7.

Goldsmith, A., J. Veum and W. Darity. 1997. "Unemployment, Joblessness, Psychological Well-being and Self-esteem: Theory and Evidence." *Journal of Socio-Economics* 26(2): 133-158.

_____. 1996. "The Psychological Impact of Unemployment and Joblessness." *Journal of Socio*-Economics 25(3): 333-358.

Green, D., R. King and M. Miller-Dawkins. 2010. *The Global Economic Crisis and Developing Countries: Impact and Response*. Oxfam Research Report, Oxfam GB.

Gregg, P. and E. Tominey. 2005. "The Wage Scar from Youth Unemployment." *Labour Economics* 12(2005): 487-509.

Grimshaw, D. 2010. "What do we Know about Low Wage Work and Low Wage Workers? Analysing the Definitions, Patterns, Causes and Consequences in International Perspective." Technical Background Report prepared for the Global Wage Report, ILO.

Heathcoate, J., F. Perri and G. Violante. 2010. "Inequality in Times of Crisis: Lessons from the Past and a First Look at the Current Recession." *VoxEU.org*, February 02.

Heltberg, R., N. Hossain, A. Reva and C. Turk. 2012. "Anatomy of Coping: Evidence from People Living through the Crises of 2008-11." Policy Research Working Paper No. 5957, World Bank.

Horn, Z.E. 2011. *Coping with Crises: Lingering Recession, Rising Inflation and the Informal Workforce*. Manchester: Women in Informal Employment: Globalizing and Organizing (WIEGO).

Howell, D. 2005. "Fighting Unemployment: Why Labor Market 'Reforms' are Not the Answer." CEPA Working Papers, The New School.

Institute of Development Studies. 2009. *Accounts of Crisis: Poor People's Experiences of the Food, Fuel and Financial Crises in Five Countries*. Brighton: Institute of Development Studies (IDS).

Machin, S. and J. van Reenen. 2007. "Changes in Wage Inequality." London School of Economics Special Paper No. 18.

McLeod, D. and N. Lustig. 2011. "Inequality and Poverty under Latin America's New Left Regimes." Tulane Economics Working Paper Series No. 1117.

ILO. 2012a. *Global Employment Trends 2012: Preventing a Deeper Jobs Crisis.* Geneva: ILO.

_____. 2011a. *Global Employment Trends for Youth: 2011 Update.* Geneva: ILO.

_____. 2011b. *The Impact of the Crisis on Wages in South-East Europe.* Budapest: ILO.

_____. 2011c. *Global Employment Trends 2011: The Challenge of a Jobs Recovery.* Geneva: ILO.

_____. 2011d. *Key Indicators of the Labour Market, 7th Edition.* Geneva: ILO.

_____. 2011e. *World of Work Report 2011: Making Markets Work for Jobs.* Geneva: ILO.

_____. 2011f. *Social Protection Floor for a Fair and Inclusive Globalization.* Report of the Social Protection Floor Advisory Group chaired by Michelle Bachelet. Geneva: ILO.

_____. 2010a. *Global Wage Report 2010/11: Wage Policies in Times of Crises.* Geneva: ILO.

_____. 2010b. *Accelerating a Job-Rich Recovery in G20 Countries: Building on Experience.* Geneva: ILO.

_____. 2010c. *Global Employment Trends for Youth: Special Issue on the Impact of the Global Economic Crisis on Youth.* Geneva: ILO.

_____. 2010d. *World of Work Report 2010: From One Crisis to the Next?* Geneva: ILO.

_____. 2009a. *Recovering from the Crisis: A Global Jobs Pact.* Geneva: ILO.

_____. 2009b. *Protecting People, Promoting Jobs: A Survey of Country Employment and Social Protection Policy Responses to the Global Economic Crisis in 54 Countries.* An ILO report to the G20 Leaders' Summit, Pittsburgh, September 24-25. Geneva: ILO.

_____. 1999. *Decent Work.* Geneva: ILO.

Islam, I. and A. Chowdhury. 2012. "Full Employment and the Global Development Agenda: Going Beyond Lip Service." *VoxEU.org,* January 19.

_____. 2010a. "Fiscal Consolidation, Growth and Employment: What do we Know?" G-24 Policy Brief No. 57.

_____. 2010b. "The Fallacy of Austerity-based Fiscal Consolidation." G-24 Policy Brief No. 58.

Iverson, L. and S. Sabroe. 1988. "Participation in a Follow-up Study of Health among Unemployed and Employed People after a Company Closedown: Drop Outs and Selection Bias." *Journal of Epidemiology and Community Health* 42: 396-401.

Jackson, P. and P. Warr. 1987. "Mental Health of Unemployed Men in Different Parts of England and Wales." *British Medical Journal* 295: 525.

Linn, M., R. Sandifer and S. Stein. 1985. "Effects of Unemployment on Mental and Physical Health." *American Journal of Public Health* 75: 502-506.

Machin, S. and J. van Reenen. 2007. "Changes in Wage Inequality." Special Paper No. 18, London School of Economics.

Mattiasson, I., F. Lindgarde, J. Nilsson and T. Theorell. 1990. "Threats of Unemployment and Cardiovascular Risk Factors: Longitudinal Study of Quality of Sleep and Serum Cholesterol Concentrations in Men Threatened with Redundancy." *British Medical Journal* 301: 461-466.

Moser, K., P. Goldblatt, A. Fox and D. Jones. 1990. "Unemployment and Mortality." In P. Goldblatt (ed.), *Longitudinal Study: Mortality and Social Organisation*. London: OPCS.

_____. 1987. "Unemployment and Mortality: Comparison of the 1971 and 1981 Longitudinal Study Census Samples." *British Medical Journal* 1: 86-90.

Ocampo, J.A. and K.S. Jomo (eds.). 2007. *Toward Full and Decent Employment*. London and New York: Zed Books.

OECD. 2008. *Growing Unequal? Income Distribution and Poverty in OECD Countries*. Paris: OECD.

_____. 2000. "International Trade and Core Labour Standards." Policy Brief, OECD.

Ortiz, I. 2008. "Social Policy." In *National Development Strategies, Policy Notes*. New York: United Nations.

Ortiz, I., G. Fajth, J. Yablonski and A. Rabi. 2010. "Social Protection: Accelerating the MDGs with Equity." UNICEF Social and Economic Policy Brief, UNICEF.

Ortiz, I. and M. Cummins. 2011. "Global Inequality: Beyond the Bottom Billion – A Rapid Review of Income Distribution in 141 Countries." Social and Economic Policy Working Paper, UNICEF.

Palley, T. 1999. "The Myth of Labor Market Flexibility and the Costs of Bad Macroeconomic Policy: U.S. and European Unemployment Explained." In S. Lang, M. Mayer, and C. Scherr (eds.), *Jobswunder U.S.A.*. Munster: Westfalisches Dampfboot.

Patel, M. and S. Thapa. 2010. *Impact of the Global Economic Crisis on Children: UNICEF Update on Real-time Monitoring Efforts in East Asia and the Pacific Islands*. Bangkok: UNICEF.

Platt, S. 1984. "Unemployment and Suicidal Behaviour: A Review of the Literature." *Social Science and Medicine* 19(2): 93-115.

Pollin, R., G. Epstein and J. Heintz. 2008. "Pro-Growth Alternatives for Monetary and Financial Policies in Sub-Saharan Africa." Policy Research Brief No. 6, UNDP International Poverty Centre.

Raihan, S. 2009. *Impact of Food Price Rise on School Enrolment and Dropout in the Poor and Vulnerable Households in Selected Areas of Bangladesh*. Dhaka: United Kingdom Department for International Development (DFID).

Reyes, C., A. Sorbrevinas and J. Jesus. 2010. "Impacts of the Global Financial Crisis on Poverty in the Philippines." Paper presented at 8th Poverty and

Economic Policy (PEP) Research Network General Meeting in Dakar, Senegal.

Rodgers, G. 2007. "Labour Market Flexibility and Decent Work." UN-DESA Working Paper No. 47, UN-DESA.

Samuels, F., M. Gavrilovic, C. Harper and M. Niño-Zarazúa. 2011. *Food, Finance and Fuel: The Impacts of the Triple F Crisis in Nigeria, with a Particular Focus on Women and Children – Adamawa State Focus*. London: Overseas Development Institute.

Self-Employed Women's Association. 2009. *Financial Crisis Based on Experiences of SEWA*. Gujarat: Self-Employed Women's Association (SEWA).

Sigurdsen, P., S. Berger and J. Heymann. 2011. "The Effects of Economic Crises on Families Caring for Children: Understanding and Reducing Long-term Consequences." *Development Policy Review* 29(5): 547-64.

Standing, G. 2011. *The Precariat: The New Dangerous Class*. London: Bloomsbury.

Strully, K. 2009. "Job Loss and Health in the U.S. Labour Market." *Demography* 46(2): 221-246.

UNCTAD. 2011. "On the Brink: Fiscal Austerity Threatens a Global Recession." Policy Brief No. 24, UNCTAD.

UNDP. 2010. *Poverty and Social Impact Analysis of the Global Economic Crisis: Synthesis Report of 18 Country Studies*. New York: UNDP.

United Nations. 2012a. *World Economic Situation and Prospects 2012*. New York: United Nations.

_____. 2011a. *World Population Prospects: The 2010 Revision*. New York: United Nations.

_____. 2011b. *The Global Social Crisis: Report on the World Social Situation 2011*. New York: United Nations.

_____. 2010. *Keeping the Promise: United to Achieve the Millennium Development Goals*. New York: United Nations.

_____. 2008. *National Development Strategies, Policy Notes*. New York: United Nations.

UNRISD. 2010. *Combating Poverty and Inequality: Structural Change, Social Policy and Politics*. Geneva: UNRISD.

Van der Hoeven, R. 2010. "Labour Markets Trends, Financial Globalization and the Current Crisis in Developing Countries." UN-DESA Working Paper No. 99, UN-DESA.

Verick, S. 2010. "Unravelling the Impact of the Global Financial Crisis on the South African Labour Market." Employment Working Paper No. 48, ILO.

Wachter, T., J. Song and J. Manchester. 2009. "Long-term Earnings Losses due to Job Separation during the 1982 Recession: An Analysis Using Longitudinal Administrative Data from 1974 to 2004." Department of Economics Discussion Paper No. 0708-16, Columbia University.

Weeks, J. and T. McKinley. 2007. "The Macroeconomic Implications of MDG-Based Strategies in Sub-Saharan Africa." Policy Research Brief No. 4, UNDP International Poverty Centre.

World Bank. 2011. *The Jobs Crisis: Household and Government Responses to the Great Recession in Eastern Europe and Central Asia*. Washington, D.C.: World Bank.

Annex 1. Youth Bulge Peak Years in 180 Countries

Methodology Note: A number of countries have experienced—or are expected to experience—more than one youth bulge between 1950 and 2050. To cite some examples, this list includes Armenia, Bahrain, Bangladesh, Belarus, the Gambia, Jamaica, Russian Federation, Spain, Timor-Leste, Tonga, Turkey, Vietnam and Zambia, among others. In these special cases, the year reported in the table below reflects the most recent occurrence, or the next expected occurrence, of the youth bulge, and not the prior youth bulge.

Country	Year	Country	Year
Zambia	2036	Jordan	1993
Uganda	2029	Myanmar	1992
Benin	2028	Mexico	1991
Tonga	2025	Spain	1989
Chad	2025	Ecuador	1989
Guinea	2025	Indonesia	1989
Sierra Leone	2025	China	1988
Mozambique	2023	Panama	1987
Angola	2022	Peru	1986
Gambia	2020	Cuba	1985
Congo, Dem. Rep. of	2020	Lebanon	1985
Afghanistan	2019	St. Vincent and Grenadines	1985
Sudan	2019	Thailand	1985
Guyana	2018	Austria	1984
Timor-Leste	2016	Colombia	1984
Madagascar	2016	Germany	1984
Jamaica	2015	Mauritius	1984
Ethiopia	2015	United Kingdom	1984
Guatemala	2015	Equatorial Guinea	1983
Nepal	2015	French Guiana	1983
Palestine (OPT)	2014	Grenada	1983
El Salvador	2013	Samoa	1983
Bolivia	2012	Venezuela	1983
Namibia	2012	Saint Lucia	1982
Lao PDR	2011	Suriname	1982
Malawi	2011	Bahamas	1981
Belize	2010	Belgium	1981
Central African Republic	2010	Chile	1981
Gabon	2010	Dominican Republic	1981
Honduras	2010	Ireland	1981
Kyrgyzstan	2010	Malaysia	1981
Swaziland	2010	New Zealand	1981
Tajikistan	2010	Albania	1980
Cape Verde	2009	Aruba	1980

Country	Year	Country	Year
Djibouti	2009	Brazil	1980
Turkmenistan	2009	Costa Rica	1980
Uzbekistan	2009	Trinidad and Tobago	1980
Burundi	2008	Tunisia	1980
Pakistan	2008	Australia	1979
Yemen	2008	Barbados	1979
Bahrain	2007	Brunei Darussalam	1979
Azerbaijan	2007	Canada	1979
Lesotho	2007	Cyprus	1979
Maldives	2007	Korea, Republic of	1979
Oman	2007	Sri Lanka	1979
Cambodia	2006	Iceland	1978
Mongolia	2006	Singapore	1978
Russian Federation	2005	United States	1978
Belarus	2005	Bosnia and Herzegovina	1976
Armenia	2005	India	1976
Vietnam	2005	Philippines	1976
Bhutan	2005	Moldova	1976
Botswana	2005	Fiji	1975
Cameroon	2005	Slovakia	1974
Haiti	2005	Poland	1973
Iran	2005	Hungary	1972
Micronesia (Fed. States of)	2005	Macedonia, FYR	1972
Paraguay	2005	United Arab Emirates	1972
Rwanda	2005	France	1971
Senegal	2005	Guinea-Bissau	1971
Togo	2005	Israel	1971
Vanuatu	2005	Czech Republic	1969
Zimbabwe	2005	Finland	1969
Egypt	2004	Norway	1969
Kenya	2004	Netherlands	1968
South Africa	2004	Qatar	1967
Bangladesh	2003	Denmark	1966
Algeria	2002	Japan	1966
Nicaragua	2002	Sweden	1966
Tanzania	2002	Switzerland	1965
Ghana	2001	Niger	1960
Morocco	2001	Korea, DPR	1957
Burkina Faso	2000	Kuwait	1956
Comoros	2000	Kazakhstan	1954
Côte d'Ivoire	2000	Montenegro	1954
Liberia	2000	Ukraine	1954
Libya	2000	Estonia	1953
Nigeria	2000	Latvia	1953
São Tomé and Príncipe	2000	Georgia	1952
Syria	2000	Greece	1951
Turkey	1999	Lithuania	1951

Country	Year	Country	Year
Mali	1999	Argentina	1950
Saudi Arabia	1999	Bulgaria	1950
Congo, Republic of	1998	Croatia	1950
Eritrea	1997	Italy	1950
Mauritania	1997	Luxembourg	1950
Solomon Islands	1996	Portugal	1950
Somalia	1995	Serbia	1950
Iraq	1994	Slovenia	1950
Papua New Guinea	1994	Uruguay	1950

Source: Authors' calculations based on United Nation's *World Population Prospects: The 2010 Revision* (2011), medium variant projections

Annex 2. Adult and Youth Employment-to-Population Ratios in 169 Countries, 2010

Country	Adult (15+)	Youth (15-24)	Country	Adult (15+)	Youth (15-24)
Afghanistan	45.1	30.7	Kuwait	66.2	31.1
Albania	51.8	36.3	Kyrgyzstan	60.5	40.1
Algeria	38.6	21.8	Lao PDR	77.0	62.0
Angola	64.4	45.7	Latvia	48.7	27.3
Argentina	56.1	33.8	Lebanon	41.7	22.8
Armenia	41.2	18.0	Lesotho	47.2	28.0
Australia	62.1	60.7	Liberia	58.6	33.3
Austria	57.9	53.7	Libya	49.2	28.9
Azerbaijan	60.3	30.8	Lithuania	47.9	19.6
Bahamas	64.2	39.5	Luxembourg	54.6	21.5
Bahrain	64.9	32.3	Macedonia, FYR	37.9	15.4
Bangladesh	67.9	53.3	Madagascar	83.9	71.1
Barbados	64.7	45.8	Malawi	76.8	51.4
Belarus	50.1	30.5	Malaysia	58.5	35.1
Belgium	49.5	25.2	Maldives	57.2	43.0
Belize	59.3	44.7	Mali	48.3	35.7
Benin	72.1	56.5	Martinique	37.4	10.2
Bhutan	68.4	41.9	Mauritius	54.9	31.4
Bolivia	68.5	49.4	Mexico	58.4	43.1
Bosnia	35.1	16.6	Moldova	38.0	18.0
Botswana	63.4	41.4	Mongolia	56.9	31.7
Brazil	64.8	53.1	Morocco	45.0	29.9
Brunei Darussalam	63.3	41.0	Mozambique	78.3	57.3
Bulgaria	48.5	24.2	Myanmar	75.7	52.5
Burkina Faso	81.1	73.0	Namibia	40.0	10.7
Burundi	76.5	56.4	Nepal	82.2	73.3
Cambodia	81.4	70.2	Netherlands	61.9	62.8
Cameroon	67.5	43.4	New Zealand	63.2	50.1
Canada	61.3	54.8	Nicaragua	59.7	45.9
Cape Verde	61.2	51.8	Niger	61.3	52.8
Central Afr. Rep	72.7	54.3	Nigeria	51.4	32.4
Chad	66.7	49.1	Norway	63.5	51.6
Chile	55.4	31.0	Palestine (OPT)	30.7	15.9
China	71.1	56.5	Oman	54.9	31.6
Colombia	59.2	34.5	Pakistan	50.5	40.9
Comoros	53.4	34.3	Panama	61.7	42.1
Congo, Dem. Rep. of	66.1	39.4	Papua New Guinea	70.5	54.4
Congo, Republic of	65.5	39.0	Paraguay	68.5	57.3
Costa Rica	59.7	42.4	Peru	71.1	55.1
Côte d'Ivoire	64.2	47.9	Philippines	59.6	39.1
Croatia	46.3	25.1	Poland	50.5	27
Cuba	55.7	40.2	Portugal	55.3	28.7
Cyprus	60.4	34.3	Qatar	85.8	65.9
Czech Republic	54.2	24.6	Romania	51.9	24.4
Denmark	59.8	58.2	Russian Fed.	58.0	36.4

Country	Adult (15+)	Youth (15-24)	Country	Adult (15+)	Youth (15-24)
Dominican Republic	55.5	37.3	Rwanda	85.3	73.0
East Timor	54.4	40.5	Saudi Arabia	47.3	11.5
Ecuador	63.8	43.8	Senegal	69.2	57.1
Egypt	44.2	24.8	Sierra Leone	65.3	41.9
El Salvador	57.4	42.3	Singapore	63.1	34.0
Equatorial Guinea	80.1	65.7	Slovakia	50.6	20.7
Eritrea	77.9	66.9	Slovenia	54.7	33.5
Estonia	51.1	26.5	Solomon Islands	64.4	45.0
Ethiopia	79.5	71.2	Somalia	52.6	39.0
Fiji	57.0	40.1	South Africa	39.1	13.0
Finland	55.2	40.4	Spain	47.4	25.4
France	51.2	31.1	Sri Lanka	52.2	30.1
Gabon	50.3	14.7	Sudan	48.6	27.0
Gambia	71.5	55.8	Suriname	47.2	19.4
Georgia	53.5	20.1	Swaziland	43.7	25.8
Germany	55.4	47.2	Sweden	58.4	38.4
Ghana	66.8	36.2	Switzerland	64.9	61.4
Greece	47.7	21.2	Syria	38.8	24.1
Guatemala	65.3	57.5	Taiwan	55.0	25.3
Guinea	69.5	51.7	Tajikistan	58.1	37.7
Guinea-Bissau	67.5	47.8	Tanzania	78.9	69.1
Guyana	53.4	34.8	Thailand	71.0	45.9
Haiti	59.7	29.3	Togo	74.6	57.3
Honduras	60.3	46.5	Trinidad & Tobago	62.8	48.0
Hungary	45.0	18.4	Tunisia	40.7	22.7
Iceland	68.8	56.5	Turkey	43.6	31.6
India	53.6	33.9	Turkmenistan	54.0	35.2
Indonesia	62.6	39.9	Uganda	74.6	55.4
Iran	39.8	24.0	Ukraine	54.1	33.5
Iraq	33.5	16.9	United Arab Emir.	75.9	43.1
Ireland	52.2	31.3	United Kingdom	57.1	47.6
Israel	53.5	27.3	United States	57.5	41.6
Italy	44.3	20.3	Uruguay	61.1	44.1
Jamaica	55.9	24.9	Uzbekistan	54.0	35.4
Japan	57.3	38.9	Venezuela	61.0	39.7
Jordan	36.0	19.5	Vietnam	75.2	58.2
Kazakhstan	67.2	44.3	Yemen	41.5	26.5
Kenya	60.1	32.5	Zambia	66.9	51.2
Korea, Dem. Rep.	74.0	56.5	Zimbabwe	82.6	73.2
Korea, Rep. of	58.0	23.8			

Source: ILO's *LABOURSTA* (2012)

V. AUSTERITY MEASURES AND THE RISKS TO CHILDREN AND POOR HOUSEHOLDS

Isabel Ortiz, Jingqing Chai and Matthew Cummins

"We must not allow the new atmosphere of global austerity to undermine progress."

UN Secretary-General's statement at Least Developed Countries Leaders Summit in Istanbul, Turkey on May, 08 2011

"Think about our children. Think about the future, with vision and foresight. Yes, we face a serious economic crisis. For much of the world, fiscal austerity is the new order of the day. Yet even in these difficult times, we cannot afford to cut loose those who are hardest hit... the world's poor."

UN Secretary-General's remarks at press event on Day of Seven Billion in New York City on October 31, 2011

1.   Introduction

In the wake of the food, fuel and financial shocks, a fourth wave of the global economic crisis began to sweep across countries in 2010: fiscal austerity. This chapter first examines how fiscal consolidation can impact levels of social assistance and other public spending decisions and then describes how different austerity measures threaten children and poor families. Moreover, while fiscal austerity has received a significant amount of attention in high-income economies, this chapter presents evidence of its widespread prevalence among developing countries.

Using fiscal estimates from the IMF, Chapter V begins by analyzing the extent to which public expenditure consolidation has occurred among 179 countries since the start of the global economic crisis (Section 2). In addition to looking at total government spending trends across the three unique phases of the crisis, which include 2005-07 (pre-crisis), 2008-09 (crisis phase I: fiscal expansion) and 2010 onward (crisis phase II: fiscal contraction), the later phases of the crisis are contrasted to better understand the scope and magnitude of aggregate budget cuts during 2012. This section also identifies a number of countries that may be at risk of excessive contraction.

Following the assessment of fiscal consolidation, Section 3 gauges how social expenditures have evolved since 2008. This includes a review of evidence to see how social spending has historically fared in environments of general budget cuts, as well as an examination of country surveys and expenditure estimates from the World Bank to determine whether governments boosted social assistance during 2008-09. Based on a series of preliminary studies, Section 3 then offers an assessment of the likely trajectory of social spending since 2010.

To gain additional insights into social spending trends during 2010-12, Chapter V next turns to policy discussions and other information contained in IMF country reports. After identifying the five most common policy options that governments are considering or implementing to achieve cost savings (Section 4), it then describes how reduced social assistance and specific austerity measures can detrimentally impact children and poor households (Section 5). The chapter concludes by summarizing the main empirical findings and questioning whether the projected trajectory of fiscal contraction, in terms of timing, scope and magnitude, as well as the specific austerity measures being considered to achieve expenditure consolidation, are conducive to adequately protecting vulnerable populations (Section 6).

2.   Total Expenditure Trends during the Global Economic Crisis

2.1.   Data and methodology

The assessment of public expenditure trends is based on IMF projections contained in the September 2011 *World Economic Outlook*, which is the only source of comparable, cross-national fiscal data. In terms of methodology, changes in total government spending are analyzed using two unique measures: (i) public expenditure as a percent of GDP; and (ii) the real value of public expenditure (or, in other words, the value of nominal expenditure adjusted by the consumer price index). Regarding the former, this is the most commonly used metric for cross-national comparisons of public expenditures and the most useful for assessing a government's fiscal position. In terms of the latter, absolute spending changes offer a better indication of the possible impact on the real welfare of populations. Both of these measures are applied to the 130 developing countries and 49 developed countries that have fiscal estimates across the three unique time periods of the crisis: 2005-07 (pre-crisis), 2008-09 (crisis phase I: fiscal expansion) and 2010 onward (crisis phase II: fiscal contraction). The projected changes in total government expenditures for all countries during 2005-12 are provided in Annex 1.

2.2.   Results

Analysis of fiscal projection data verifies two distinct phases of government spending patterns since the onset of the global economic crisis. During the first phase, most countries—in both the developing and developed world—moved swiftly to introduce fiscal stimulus packages and boost spending, which largely characterizes 2008-09. Beginning in 2010, however, a majority of governments started to scale back stimulus programs and slash budgets, a trend that appears to be gaining momentum in 2012 and 2013. The detailed results of each of these phases are presented and then contrasted, which is followed by an assessment of countries that may be under risk of excessive contraction.

2.2.1.   Crisis phase I, 2008-09: Expansion

The vast majority of governments boosted public expenditures significantly during 2008-09 to buffer the impact of the different global shocks on their populations in what could be described as the expansionary phase of the global economic crisis (Table 1). When comparing pre-crisis spending levels to those during this first phase of the crisis, nearly three-fourths of developing countries (95 out of 130) and 86 percent of HICs (42 out of 49) ramped up public expenditures, with the average expansion amounting to a robust 3.9 percent of GDP worldwide. At 5 percent of GDP, developing countries in the Middle East and North Africa undertook the largest spending increases, on average. Also noteworthy, nearly all countries in the CEE/CIS (20 of 22) raised spending by 4.2 percent of GDP, on average, and 29 of the 43 countries in Sub-Saharan Africa increased total expenditure by an average of 4.5 percent of GDP.

Table V.1. Changes in Total Government Spending,
2008-09 avg. over 2005-07 avg.[1]
(in percent of GDP)

Developing Region / Income Group	Total Sample		Expanded		Contracted	
	# of countries	Average spending Δ	# of countries	Average spending Δ	# of countries	Average spending Δ
CEE/CIS	22	3.6	20	4.2	2	-2.0
EAP	17	2.6	14	3.2	3	-0.5
LAC	29	1.7	20	3.0	9	-1.2
MENA	11	2.0	6	5.0	5	-1.6
South Asia	8	1.2	6	2.0	2	-1.2
SSA	43	1.9	29	4.5	14	-3.4
All developing	**130**	**2.2**	**95**	**3.8**	**35**	**-2.1**
Low	36	2.4	26	4.3	10	-2.5
Lower-middle	51	2.0	36	3.7	15	-2.1
Upper-middle	43	2.4	33	3.6	10	-1.8
High	**49**	**3.2**	**42**	**3.9**	**7**	**-0.9**
All countries	179	2.5	137	3.9	42	-1.9

Source: Authors' calculations based on IMF's *World Economic Outlook* (September 2011)

Positive trends are also evidenced in terms of real government spending (Table 2). More than 90 percent of developing countries increased real expenditures, with average growth equaling 23 percent when comparing the average levels of public spending between 2008-09 and 2005-07. Expansions were largest in the CEE/CIS Asia along with East Asia and the Pacific, with real expenditure growth amounting to roughly 30 percent, on average, in both of these regions. Interestingly, at 17 percent, on average, HICs show the lowest total spending growth when compared to other regions and income groups, suggesting that fiscal stimulus programs were larger in developing countries.

---

[1] All empirical analyses in this section exclude Libya, Mauritania, Timor-Leste, Tuvalu and Zimbabwe due to lack of data and/or peculiar fiscal circumstances. Also, median values were obtained for all analyses but show similar patterns and are, therefore, not reported in any tables.

Table V.2. Growth of Real Government Spending,
2008-09 avg. over 2005-07 avg.
(as a percent)

Developing Region / Income Group	Total Sample		Expanded		Contracted	
	# of countries	Average spending Δ	# of countries	Average spending Δ	# of countries	Average spending Δ
CEE/CIS	22	33.9	22	33.9	0	Na
EAP	17	24.0	15	28.2	2	-7.7
LAC	29	16.5	25	19.5	4	-2.5
MENA	11	18.1	10	20.0	1	-0.9
South Asia	8	25.2	8	25.2	0	Na
SSA	43	21.7	40	24.8	3	-19.9
All developing	130	22.8	120	25.4	10	-8.6
Low	36	27.2	34	30.0	2	-20.3
Lower-middle	51	21.7	48	23.3	3	-3.3
Upper-middle	43	20.4	38	24.0	5	-7.2
High	49	15.4	46	16.7	3	-3.8
All countries	179	20.8	166	23.0	13	-7.5

Source: Authors' calculations based on IMF's *World Economic Outlook* (September 2011)

2.2.2. Crisis phase II, 2010- : Contraction

Beginning in 2010, however, in a second phase of the crisis, most governments started to withdraw fiscal stimulus programs and scale back public spending (Table 3). Overall, 68 developing country governments (or more than half of this sample) reduced total expenditures by 2.7 percent of GDP, on average, between 2009 and 2010, and 38 HICs (or nearly 80 percent of this sample) cut spending by an average of 1.6 percent of GDP. This shift was most acute in the Middle East and North Africa, both in terms of breadth—about three-quarters of countries in the region contracted—as well as depth—5.3 percent of GDP, on average.

The outlook for 2011 and 2012 is equally troubling. In 2011, 62 developing countries contracted government expenditures by an average of 1.8 percent of GDP, while 94 (nearly 75 percent of the sample) are forecasted to adopt further austerity measures during 2012 by 1.8 percent of GDP, on average. For both years, the CEE/CIS had the largest percentage of countries expected to reduce aggregate spending—14 and 18 of 22 countries in 2011 and 2012, respectively. Sub-Saharan Africa, on the other hand, is the region with the biggest anticipated expenditure contractions—2.7 percent, on average, for 15 countries in 2011, and 34 countries reducing spending by about 2.8

percent, on average, in 2012. HICs are also expected undergo significant contractions, with 37 of 49 countries cutting total expenditure by 2 percent, on average, during 2011, and 39 further slashing budgets by an average of 1 percent during 2012.

Two key trends emerge from the fiscal projections. First, for the cohort of developing countries, the growing number of governments that are projected to cut spending in 2012 is alarming. Overall, an additional 32 countries are forecasted to undergo expenditure cuts between 2011 and 2012, with the largest changes occurring in the poorest region: Sub-Saharan Africa (from 15 to 34 countries). Second, for HICs, total budget contractions in terms of magnitude and number of countries affected have remained relatively stable during the second phase of the global economic crisis. However, while increasing fiscal austerity does not appear to be a major concern, the absolute number of countries that continues to be impacted is (about 80 percent). Perhaps even more worrisome, spending projections for 2013 suggest that these trends will continue into the foreseeable future among both developing and developed countries.

Although less severe, expenditure contraction is also evidenced in terms of changes in real spending. Fiscal estimates indicate that about 30 percent of developing countries are anticipated to experience negative growth in real government spending, which amounts to roughly 6 percent, on average, during 2010-12, with the total number of countries affected steadily increasingly from 32 to 40 over the time period. While expenditure growth is forecasted to remain positive for the developing country sample as a whole, there is a downward trend from around 6 percent in 2010-11 to 1.7 percent in 2012, on average. Regionally, Sub-Saharan Africa appears to be the hardest hit, as 19 countries are expected to decrease real spending by an average of 8.6 percent in 2012. In terms of HICs, roughly 40 percent of governments are projected to undergo negative real spending growth during 2010-12, by 3.9 percent, on average. While projections for 2013 indicate that real spending trends will improve slightly for both developing and developed countries, still 40 countries are estimated to experience negative growth, by an average decline of 3.2 percent.

Table V.3. Projected Total Government Spending Trends, 2010-13

Region / Income Group (n=)	Indicator	(A) Change in Spending (year on year, in % of GDP)				(B) Growth of Real Spending (year on year, as a %)			
		2010	2011	2012	2013	2010	2011	2012	2013
CEE/CIS (22)	Overall avg.	-1.3	-0.4	-0.8	-0.4	2.8	5.5	2.0	3.3
	Avg. contraction	-2.2	-1.6	-1.1	-0.6	-2.9	-2.4	-1.2	Na
	# of countries	16	14	18	19	8	8	5	0
EAP (17)	Overall avg.	0.5	-0.7	-0.8	-1.1	7.7	2.9	2.4	2.6
	Avg. contraction	-1.4	-1.8	-1.5	-1.3	-5.9	-5.1	-7.3	-3.1
	# of countries	9	12	11	14	2	7	3	4
LAC (29)	Overall avg.	-0.7	0.0	0.0	-0.5	3.6	4.1	3.9	2.4
	Avg. contraction	-2.7	-1.4	-0.9	-0.7	-9.5	-4.5	-3.4	-2.4
	# of countries	16	15	19	24	9	10	6	6
MENA (11)	Overall avg.	-3.8	2.0	-1.0	-1.8	0.0	13.0	-0.3	0.7
	Avg. contraction	-5.3	-1.5	-1.6	-2.6	-7.8	-9.2	-4.7	-7.0
	# of countries	8	3	9	8	3	1	5	3
South Asia (8)	Overall avg.	-0.3	1.4	-0.4	-0.3	5.4	10.7	5.2	6.2
	Avg. contraction	-1.6	-0.7	-2.9	-2.1	-6.1	na	-5.8	-1.6
	# of countries	5	3	3	2	1	0	2	1
SSA (43)	Overall avg.	0.2	0.4	-2.1	-0.6	9.0	7.2	-0.3	3.1
	Avg. contraction	-3.2	-2.7	-2.8	-1.5	-6.9	-7.1	-8.6	-3.0
	# of countries	14	15	34	25	9	10	19	12
All developing (130)	**Overall avg.**	**-0.6**	**0.2**	**-1.0**	**-0.7**	**5.6**	**6.4**	**1.7**	**2.9**
	Avg. contraction	**-2.7**	**-1.8**	**-1.8**	**-1.2**	**-6.7**	**-5.0**	**-6.2**	**-3.3**
	# of countries	**68**	**62**	**94**	**92**	**32**	**36**	**40**	**26**
Low (36)	Overall avg.	1.0	0.4	-1.0	-0.4	10.3	8.0	4.2	4.5
	Avg. contraction	-1.8	-2.7	-2.5	-1.3	-9.3	-6.9	-7.1	-2.1
	# of countries	11	13	24	20	5	9	12	8
Lower-middle (51)	Overall avg.	-1.1	0.5	-1.3	-1.1	4.8	7.0	0.4	2.2
	Avg. contraction	-3.3	-2.0	-1.9	-1.5	-4.5	-6.5	-6.8	-4.1
	# of countries	28	21	40	38	12	12	17	12
Upper-middle (43)	Overall avg.	-1.3	-0.2	-0.7	-0.5	2.6	4.2	1.2	2.4
	Avg. contraction	-2.5	-1.2	-1.2	-0.7	-7.5	-2.7	-4.2	-3.1
	# of countries	29	28	30	34	15	15	11	6
High (49)	**Overall avg.**	**-0.7**	**-1.2**	**-0.6**	**-0.7**	**1.8**	**1.6**	**0.2**	**0.6**
	Avg. contraction	**-1.6**	**-2.0**	**-1.0**	**-1.0**	**-4.4**	**-4.7**	**-2.5**	**-3.0**
	# of countries	**38**	**37**	**39**	**39**	**18**	**18**	**20**	**14**
All countries (179)	Overall avg.	-0.6	-0.2	-0.9	-0.7	4.5	5.1	1.3	2.3
	Avg. contraction	-2.3	-1.9	-1.6	-1.1	-5.8	-4.9	-4.9	-3.2
	# of countries	106	99	133	131	50	54	60	40

Source: Authors' calculations based on IMF's *World Economic Outlook* (September 2011)

2.2.3.   Contrasting the phases

To better appraise the breadth and depth of ongoing contractions in government spending, it is also useful to compare the expansionary and contractionary phases of the crisis. When taking the average spending values of the stimulus phase (2008-09) and contrasting those against the projected expenditures of the ongoing austerity phase (2010-12), 60 out of 130 developing countries (or 46 percent of this sample) and 19 out of 49 HICs (or nearly 40 percent of this sample) are expected to contract total government expenditure by an average of 2.6 and 1.6 percent of GDP, respectively (Table 4). In real terms, 20 percent of governments are predicted to have negative spending growth when comparing the time periods, by 7.5 percent, on average (Table 5).

Table V.4. Changes in Total Government Spending,
2010-12 avg. over 2008-09 avg.
(in percent of GDP)

Developing Region / Income Group	Total Sample		Expanded		Contracted	
	# of countries	Average spending Δ	# of countries	Average spending Δ	# of countries	Average spending Δ
CEE/CIS	22	-0.5	7	3.1	15	-2.1
EAP	17	1.2	9	2.9	8	-0.7
LAC	29	0.4	20	2.0	9	-3.2
MENA	11	-2.2	4	2.4	7	-4.8
South Asia	8	0.5	4	2.9	4	-1.9
SSA	43	0.6	26	2.9	17	-3.0
All developing	**130**	**0.2**	**70**	**2.6**	**60**	**-2.6**
Low	36	1.6	23	3.7	13	-2.0
Lower-middle	51	-0.2	25	2.6	26	-3.0
Upper-middle	43	-0.5	22	1.6	21	-2.6
High	**49**	**0.5**	**30**	**1.8**	**19**	**-1.6**
All countries	179	0.3	100	2.4	79	-2.4

Source: Authors' calculations based on IMF's *World Economic Outlook* (September 2011)

Table V.5. Growth of Real Government Spending,
2010-12 avg. over 2008-09 avg.

(as a percent)

Developing Region / Income Group	Total Sample		Expanded		Contracted	
	# of countries	Average spending Δ	# of countries	Average spending Δ	# of countries	Average spending Δ
CEE/CIS	22	9.9	13	19.2	9	-3.5
EAP	17	15.7	15	17.9	2	-0.5
LAC	29	11.1	23	17.4	6	-13.3
MENA	11	8.0	9	11.7	2	-8.4
South Asia	8	20.0	8	20.0	0	Na
SSA	43	16.6	37	20.8	6	-9.8
All developing	**130**	**13.6**	**105**	**18.6**	**25**	**-7.5**
Low	36	22.7	34	24.6	2	-10.6
Lower-middle	51	12.2	41	16.6	10	-6.0
Upper-middle	43	7.7	30	14.6	13	-8.2
High	**49**	**4.8**	**38**	**8.4**	**11**	**-7.6**
All countries	179	11.2	143	15.9	36	-7.5

Source: Authors' calculations based on IMF's *World Economic Outlook* (September 2011)

At the country level, a number of governments are projected to undergo steep spending cuts in terms of GDP when comparing the expansionary and contractionary phases of the crisis (Figure 1A). In particular, significant contractions (4-12 percent of GDP) are expected in 15 countries, including Angola, Antigua and Barbuda, Barbados, Belarus, Botswana, Burundi, Djibouti, Iraq, Jamaica, Kuwait, Liberia, Moldova, the Sudan, Swaziland and Yemen. In terms of real spending growth, 18 countries are anticipated to reduce total expenditure by more than 5 percent when comparing the average spending values over the two time periods (Antigua and Barbuda, Barbados, Botswana, Dominica, Greece, Grenada, Honduras, Iceland, Jamaica, Latvia, Lithuania, Madagascar, Montenegro, Romania, the Sudan, Swaziland, Trinidad and Tobago, and Yemen) (Figure 1B).

Figure V.1. Projected Change in Government Spending, 2010-12 avg. over 2008-09 avg.

A. Total Spending (in percent of GDP)

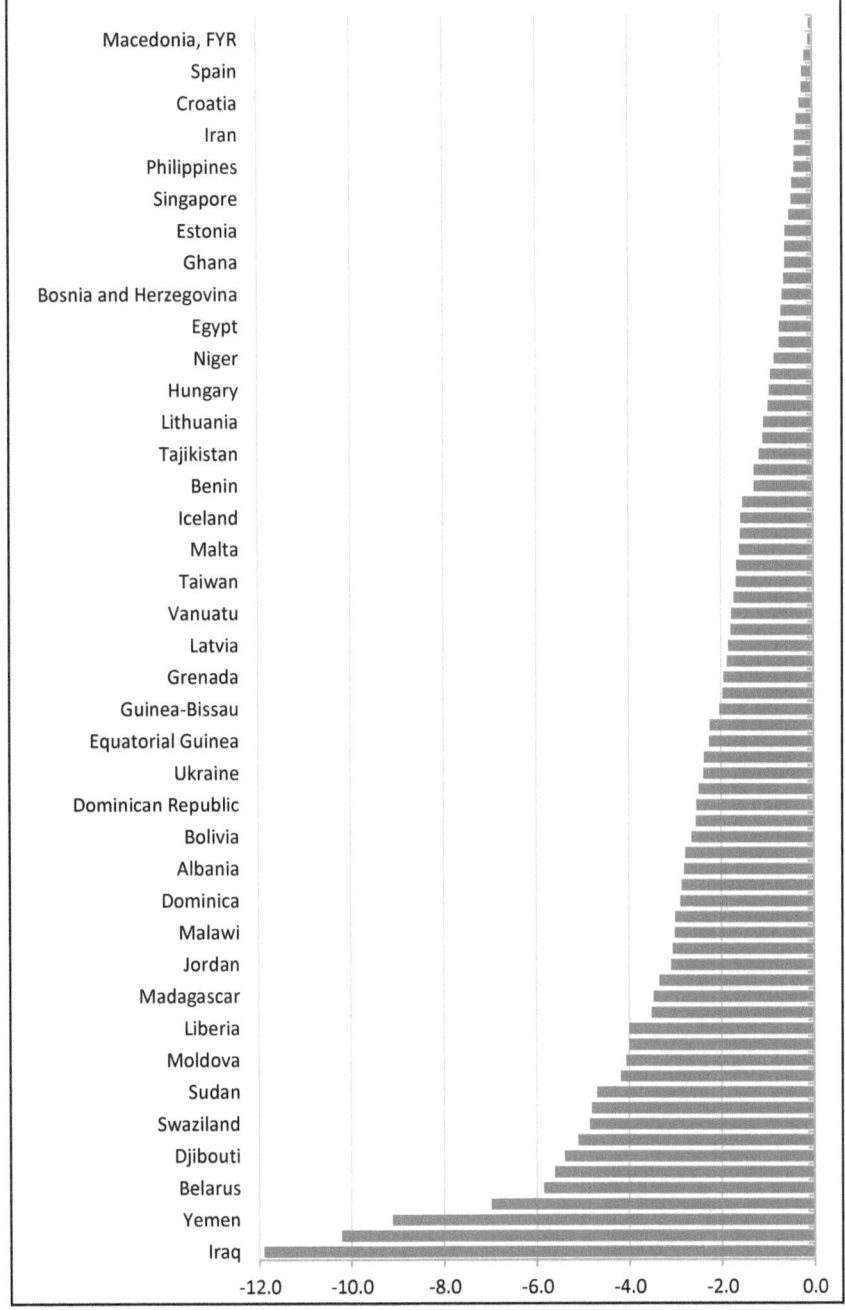

Source: Authors' calculations based on IMF's *World Economic Outlook* (September 2011)

Figure V.1. (cont). Projected Change in Government Spending, 2010-12 avg. over 2008-09 avg.

B. Growth of Real Spending (as a percent)

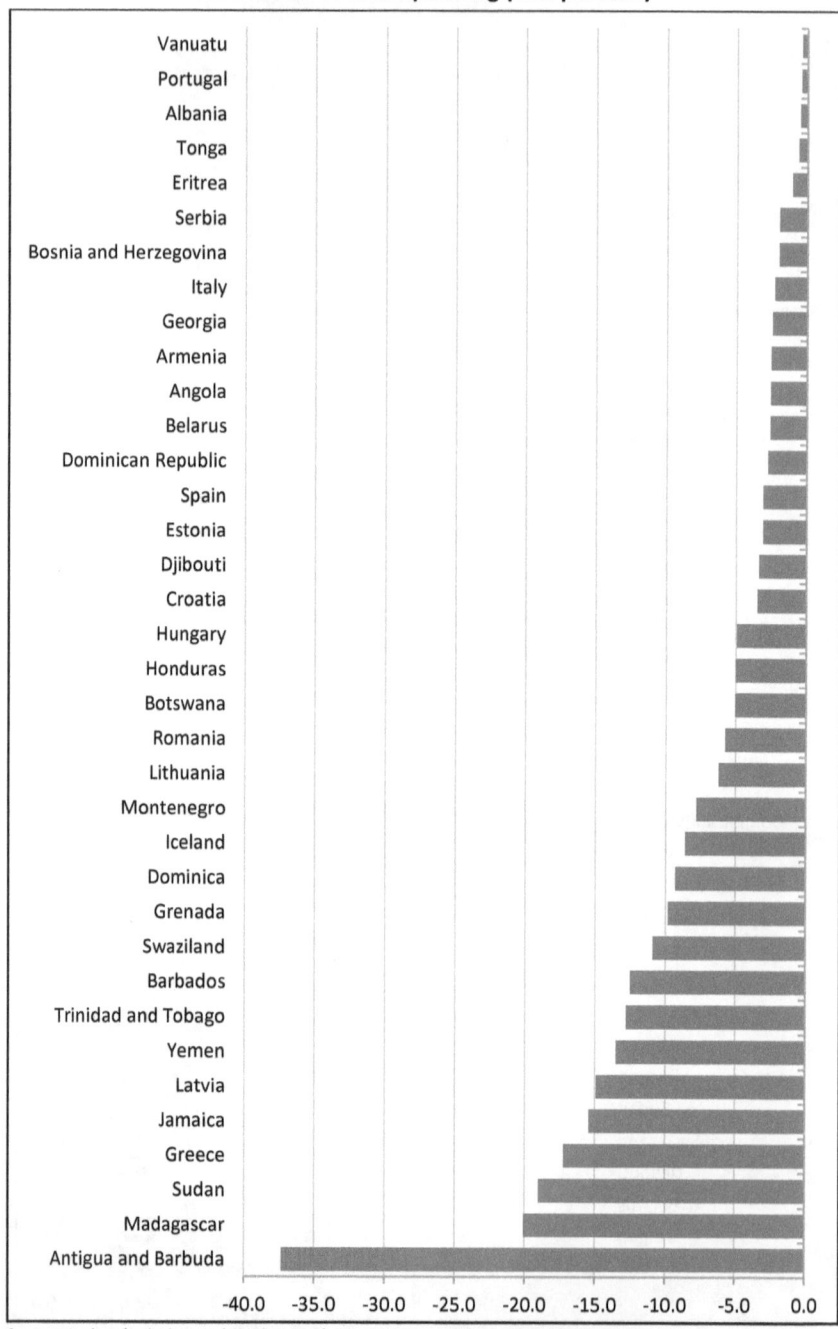

Source: Authors' calculations based on IMF's *World Economic Outlook* (September 2011)

2.2.4.   Excessive fiscal contraction

As discussed later in Section 5, there are significant risks associated with premature as well as excessive consolidation. In this context, a government can be defined as undergoing excessive fiscal austerity if it spends less during the second phase of the crisis (2010-12) than during the pre-crisis phase (2005-07) in terms of GDP.

Comparing the 2010-12 and 2005-07 periods suggests that, globally, nearly 80 percent of all countries have maintained total expenditures far above pre-crisis levels (Table 6). Overall, average spending levels in the contractionary phase of the crisis are about 4.3 percent higher in terms of GDP than those in the pre-crisis. This includes average increases of 4 percent of GDP among 102 developing countries and 5.2 percent of GDP among 38 HICs. In real terms, more than 90 percent of all countries have increased expenditure, with average growth amounting to nearly 40 percent, on average, when comparing the two phases (Table 7). These findings indicate that most governments have maintained considerably higher levels of public assistance since the start of the global economic crisis.

Table V.6. Changes in Total Government Spending,
2010-12 avg. over 2005-07 avg.
(in percent of GDP)

Developing Region / Income Group	Total Sample		Expanded		Contracted	
	# of countries	Average spending Δ	# of countries	Average spending Δ	# of countries	Average spending Δ
CEE/CIS	22	3.2	19	4.1	3	-2.5
EAP	17	3.8	15	4.4	2	-0.6
LAC	29	2.1	25	3.0	4	-3.3
MENA	11	-0.1	5	4.4	6	-3.9
South Asia	8	1.7	6	3.0	2	-2.3
SSA	43	2.5	32	4.8	11	-4.1
All developing	130	2.4	102	4.0	28	-3.4
Low	36	4.0	30	5.7	6	-4.3
Lower-middle	51	1.7	37	3.5	14	-2.9
Upper-middle	43	1.9	35	3.2	8	-3.6
High	49	3.7	38	5.2	11	-1.3
All countries	179	2.8	140	4.3	39	-2.8

Source: Authors' calculations based on IMF's *World Economic Outlook* (September 2011)

Table V.7. Growth of Real Government Spending,
2010-12 avg. over 2005-07 avg.
(as a percent)

Developing Region / Income Group	Total Sample		Expanded		Contracted	
	# of countries	Average spending Δ	# of countries	Average spending Δ	# of countries	Average spending Δ
CEE/CIS	22	48.8	22	48.8	0	Na
EAP	17	44.0	15	50.4	2	-3.8
LAC	29	30.0	26	35.2	3	-14.4
MENA	11	28.0	10	31.5	1	-7.7
South Asia	8	50.6	8	50.6	0	Na
SSA	43	41.5	39	47.8	4	-20.1
All developing	**130**	**39.9**	**120**	**44.4**	**10**	**-13.9**
Low	36	55.8	34	60.9	2	-29.8
Lower-middle	51	37.2	48	40.1	3	-8.7
Upper-middle	43	29.8	38	35.1	5	-10.6
High	**49**	**21.3**	**45**	**23.9**	**4**	**-7.7**
All countries	179	34.8	165	38.8	14	-12.1

Source: Authors' calculations based on IMF's *World Economic Outlook* (September 2011)

Although these are, indeed, positive signs on the aggregate, a large number of countries can be characterized as undergoing excessive contraction. In terms of GDP, fiscal projections reveal that 39 countries worldwide (or 30 percent of the sample) are adopting excessive reductions in government spending (Figure 2). Particularly alarming, eight of those countries are projected to be spending more than 5 percent of GDP less, on average, during the second phase of the crisis when compared to the pre-crisis period, including Antigua and Barbuda, Belarus, Eritrea, Jordan, Madagascar, Seychelles, the Sudan and Yemen. In terms of real spending, 14 countries are estimated to be spending less in 2010-12 than during 2005-07, seven of which have undergone real negative expenditure declines greater than 10 percent, including Antigua and Barbuda, Barbados, Eritrea, Grenada, Hungary, Madagascar and the Sudan.

Figure V.2. Projected Change in Government Spending, 2010-12 avg. over 2005-07 avg.
(in percent of GDP)

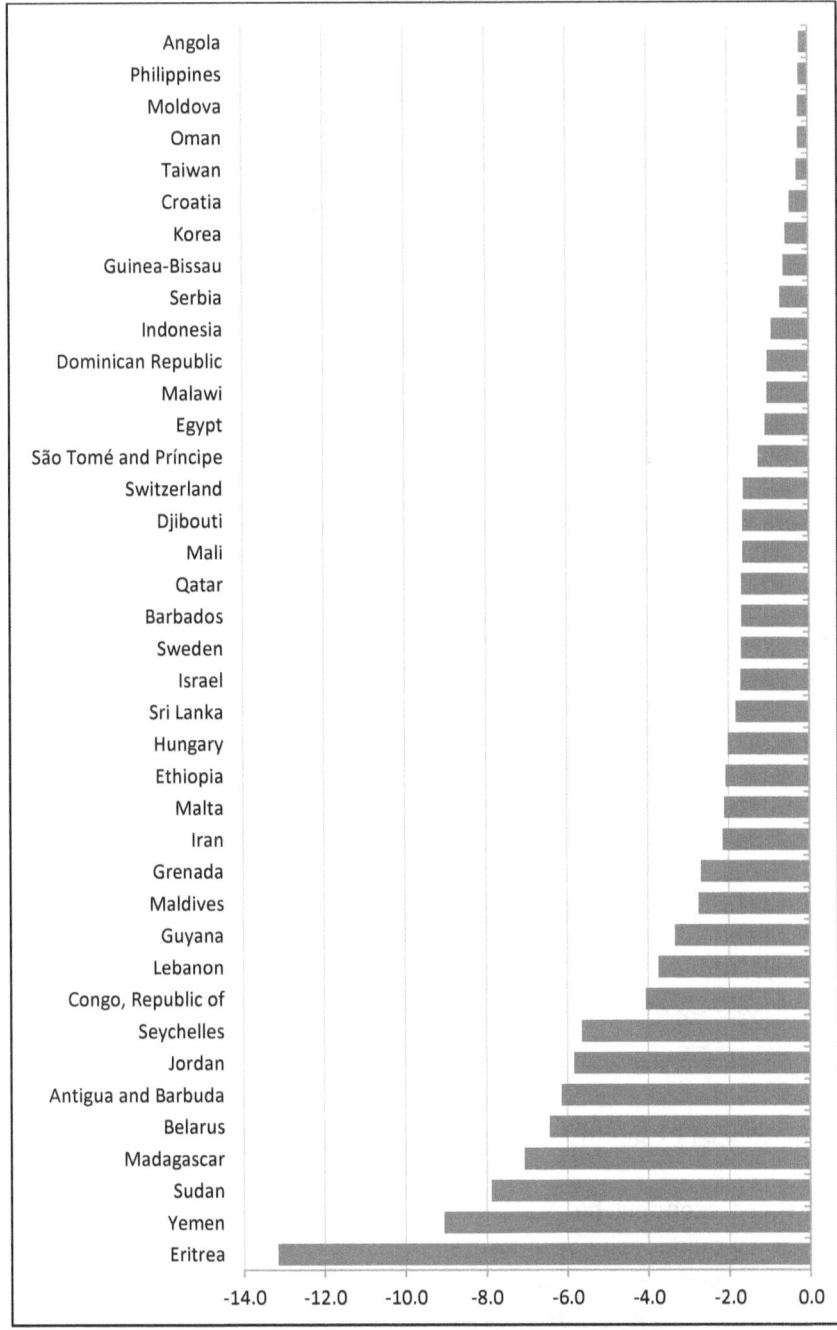

Source: Authors' calculations based on IMF's *World Economic Outlook* (September 2011)

Excessive contraction is perhaps best illustrated by several country examples. Figure 3 presents cases from different regions. It is clear that each of these countries moved to bolster expenditures in the face of the global shocks during the 2008-09 period, but have since undergone steep spending cuts, so much that projected levels are far below pre-crisis levels. Some argue that limiting government spending to below pre-crisis levels may well be justified in those instances where public finances were previously viewed as unsustainable. This book, however, questions such logic, as governments—even in the poorest countries— have a variety of feasible options to expand fiscal space to ensure the well-being of vulnerable populations, especially those who depend on public assistance to meet basic needs (Chapter VI). The implications of these trends, both in terms of the overall impact on levels of social assistance, as well as the potentially adverse impacts associated with policy choices taken to achieve steep fiscal consolidation, are discussed in the following sections.

Figure V.3. Total Government Expenditures in Selected Countries, 2005-13
(in percent of GDP)

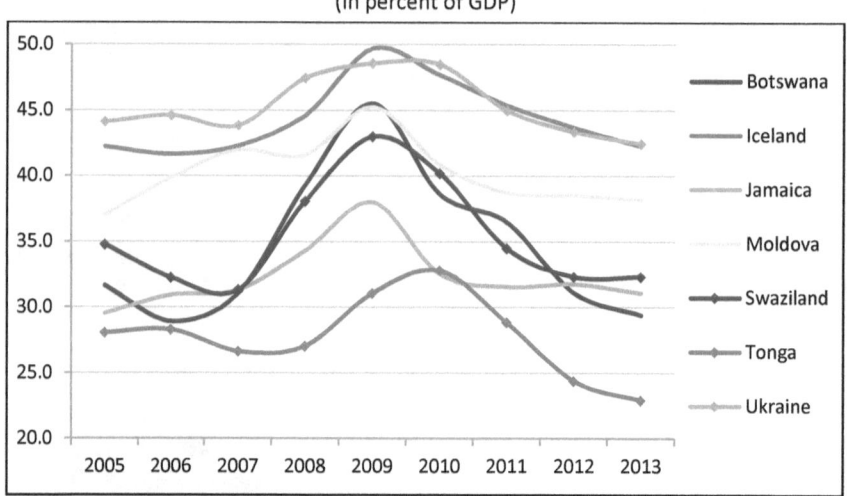

Source: IMF's *World Economic Outlook* (September 2011)

3.   Social Expenditure Trends during the Global Economic Crisis

Will social spending be preserved in a contracting environment? This question would ideally be answered by using real-time expenditure data based on ministerial, sectoral and economic classifications, as well as across different levels of government, in order to measure actual changes in pro-poor spending allocations, both nationally and locally. However, comparable, cross-national and disaggregated social expenditure data are not available for a large sample of countries during 2008-12 at the time of writing.

Despite data shortcomings, this section examines all available information sources to infer social assistance trends since the start of the global economic crisis. It begins with a review of evidence from the 1980s and 1990s to see how social expenditures have historically fared in environments of aggregate budget cuts. It then looks at surveys along with health and education spending estimates from the World Bank to see whether the fiscal stimulus programs that were widely adopted during 2008-09 included social components to buffer populations from the initial shocks of the crisis. Based on studies conducted during 2010, this section concludes by assessing the likely trajectory of social spending during the second phase of the crisis (2010-).

3.1.   Aggregate budget cuts and social expenditures: Historical evidence

Evaluation of historical experiences shows that social spending is typically unprotected during budget crises. Research on the 1980s confirms that a significant share of countries experienced disproportionately large cuts in social spending areas (e.g., health, education and social security) when compared to aggregate budget contractions (Table 8). Even more importantly, vulnerable populations were found to have suffered the largest cutbacks, both within social and other spending categories, like economic services and defense. Hicks (1991) also finds that when a sample of 24 developing reduced expenditures during 1970-84, social sectors experienced smaller cuts, on average, than the total expenditure, but still received the third highest cuts; defense budgets, in contrast, were found to be the most protected.

Table V.8. Government Expenditure Cuts by Sector, 1979-83
(percentage of cases in each category)

Spending Category	All countries (n=51)	Africa (n=16)	Asia (n=8)	Latin (n=20)	Middle (n=7)
General Public					
Vulnerable	40	38	25	45	43
Protected	23	25	25	25	14
Highly Protected	37	31	50	30	43
Defense					
Vulnerable	25	44	38	32	29
Protected	36	19	25	26	29
Highly Protected	39	38	38	42	43
Education					
Vulnerable	46	38	25	65	29
Protected	22	25	50	5	29
Highly Protected	33	38	25	30	43
Health					
Vulnerable	40	56	63	26	33
Protected	25	25	13	32	17
Highly Protected	36	19	25	42	50
Economic Services*					
Vulnerable	66	53	70	58	70
Protected	13	20	0	21	0
Highly Protected	22	27	25	21	29

Source: Cornia et al. (1987)
Note: 'vulnerable' = percentage decline more than aggregate expenditure; 'protected' = percentage decline less than aggregate expenditure; 'highly protected' = percentage increase during cuts in aggregate expenditure.
* Includes expenditure on agriculture and forestry, fishing, mining, manufacturing, construction, utilities and transport.

Country-level analyses further support the findings of these larger studies. For example, Ravallion (2002) shows that general budget cuts in Argentina during the 1980s and 1990s typically resulted in proportionately greater reductions in social spending, and that spending on targeted social assistance and employment programs was more vulnerable to aggregate spending cuts than that on more universal social services. Research by Paxson and Schady (2005) on Peru also indicates that public spending on health contracted sharply during the crisis in the late 1980s, which partly explains the rise in infant mortality.

Historical evidence thus highlights the urgent need to protect pro-poor spending at times of aggregate fiscal contraction. And while the food and fuel price increases and global economic slowdown that began in 2008 differ in nature and magnitude from previous crises, they have caused significant revenue shortfalls among most governments. In the current context, what has been the experience in social spending essential to the well-being of vulnerable populations?

3.2.   Crisis phase I, 2008-09: Increased public support

General increases in social spending during 2008-09 were largely facilitated by an overall expansionary fiscal stance and reflected a greater policy emphasis on protecting vulnerable populations from the negative shocks of the crisis (Zhang et al. 2010). For example, in a sample of 16 developing countries, nearly one-quarter of the total announced fiscal stimulus amounts, on average, was directed at social protection programs; among 19 HICs surveyed, the proportion of funds allocated to social protection was even higher, at 27 percent, on average (Figure 4). When looking for evidence among the cohort of developing countries, Yang et al. (2010) show that 16 of 19 low-income governments budgeted higher social spending in 2009 compared to the previous year. And available spending outturn data from the IMF (2010) indicate that the median value of social spending increased by 0.5 percent of GDP between 2008 and 2009 among countries in Sub-Saharan Africa, with real social expenditure growth accelerating from 4.8 to 6.8 percent.

Figure V.4. Size of Social Protection Component of Stimulus Packages
(in percent of total announced amount)

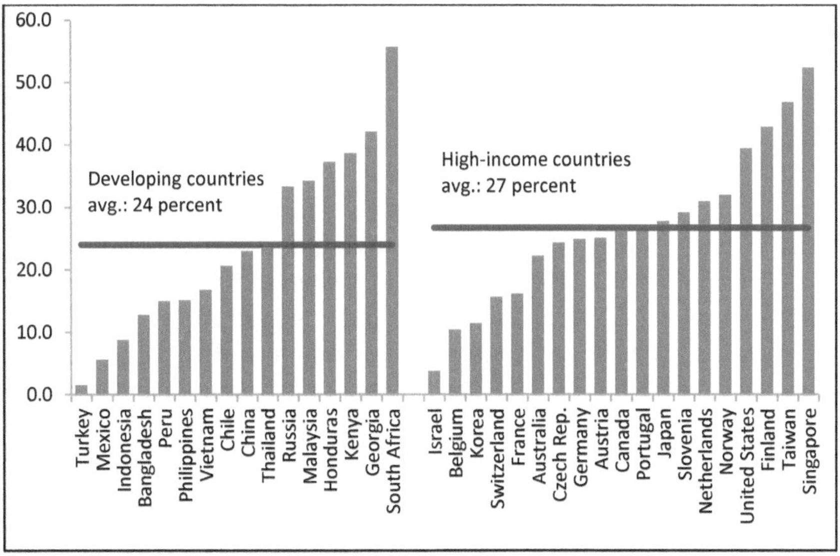

Sources: Authors' calculations based on Zhang et al. (2010) and IMF country reports (Chile and Peru)

Analysis of the latest available health and education spending estimates published in the World Bank's *World Development Indicators* further supports these earlier findings of increased social assistance (Table 9). When comparing the average expenditure trends during the first phase of the crisis (2008-09) with those during the pre-crisis phase (2005-07), spending in the health and education sectors increased by approximately 0.2 and 0.1 percent of GDP, on average, among developing countries with available data; for HICs, this amounted to 0.3 and 0.1 percent of GDP, respectively. In terms of real expenditure, health and education spending grew by an average of 21.3 and 15.1 percent, respectively, over the two time periods in developing countries, but less so in developed countries (13.2 and 8.6 percent, respectively).

Table V.9. Health and Education Spending Trends,
2008-09 avg. versus 2005-07 avg.

Developing Region / Income Group	Change (percent of GDP)		Real Growth (as a percent)	
	Health	Education	Health	Education
CEE/CIS	0.3	0.4	30.2	31.9
EAP	-0.0	0.1	14.5	14.7
LAC	0.3	-0.2	19.4	9.0
MENA	0.3	-0.6	21.3	-10.6
South Asia	0.2	0.8	21.7	29.3
SSA	0.2	0.1	21.2	13.5
All developing (n=)	**0.2 (133)**	**0.1 (39)**	**21.3**	**15.1 (39)**
Low	0.1	0.3	20.6	16.9
Lower-middle	0.1	0.2	21.6	18.0
Upper-middle	0.3	-0.2	21.5	10.5
High	**0.3**	**0.1**	**13.2**	**8.6**
All countries (n=)	0.2 (180)	0.1 (46)	19.2 (46)	14.1 (46)

Source: Authors' calculations based on World Bank's *World Development Indicators* (2011)

Available data, however, do preclude a complete understanding of actual social spending trends during the first phase of the crisis. While there is evidence of moderate upticks in resources allocated to two key social sectors in 2008-09, the data do not cover all social expenditure categories, such as social protection. For example, if social protection spending increased, these allocations may not be captured in health and education estimates due to classification and reporting differences at the national level. The relatively small sample size of countries with education spending estimates through 2009 also falls short of offering a full picture of actual investment trends (39 countries versus 133 with health expenditure data). Lastly, additional research hints that fiscal stimulus packages may not have benefitted certain social sectors to the degree that the earlier presented studies have suggested.[2]

In sum, when taken together as a whole, evidence suggests that governments did, on the aggregate, increase levels of support to several social sectors during 2008-09. The general increases in social sector allocations were largely facilitated by the expansionary fiscal stance as described in Section 2.2.1 and likely reflected a greater policy emphasis on protecting vulnerable populations from the negative shocks of the crisis. Moving to the second phase of the global economic crisis, what type of related conclusions, if any, can be purported?

3.3.   Crisis phase II, 2010- : Reduced public support

Recent surveys suggest a bleak outlook for social expenditures during the second phase of the crisis.[3] Kyrili and Martin (2010), for example, find that two-thirds of 56 LICs surveyed were cutting budget allocations in 2010 to one or more pro-poor sectors, which included education, health, agriculture and social protection. They further confirmed that while expenditures on infrastructure, health and agriculture rose in 2009, they fell in 2010, with social protection allocations contracting in 2010 and ending the period more than 0.2 percent of GDP lower than in 2008, on average. Willem et al. (2009) also observed significant reductions in planned social spending allocations for the 2010 budgets among many of the 10 developing countries in their sample. Moreover, Chubrik et al. (2011) conclude that four of six countries studied in the former Soviet Union were expected to decrease education expenditure in terms of GDP between 2009 and 2010, with Kyrgyzstan and the Russian Federation undergoing real declines in education spending.

---

[2] See, for example, Brumby and Verhoeven (2010), which conclude that growth in health and education spending fell below 2 percent during 2009 after averaging nearly 10 percent between 2005 and 2008 in a sample of 108 developing countries.

[3] Data shortcomings at the time of writing make it impossible to assess actual levels of social spending during since 2010. Although the IMF publishes current and projected fiscal data, there are no near real-time data series on social expenditures. Similarly, the World Bank's *World Development Indicators* compiles expenditures by health and education sectors, but there is a lag time of more than two years before the data become available. While such numbers did offer a picture—although imperfect—of these social spending categories for the earlier phase of the crisis, there is no such information to appraise trends during the latter period. As a result, this section focuses on alternative information sources.

In contrast to these findings, policy discussions described in recent IMF country reports indicate a greater emphasis on safeguarding pro-poor or 'priority' spending than in the past, most notably in LICs supported under the IMF's new lending framework.[4] However, there are major problems associated with definitions of 'priority' spending. This begins with the different budget classifications at the national level (e.g., functional versus economic) and is further complicated by the wide variety of spending categories that are commonly included as 'priority,' such as defense-related (Box 1).

Data and definition constraints aside, social spending cuts are a major concern for countries characterized by a climate of intensifying fiscal contraction. Moreover, even where governments have an explicit policy intention of safeguarding 'priority' pro-poor spending, there is still a heightened risk of social spending and service delivery falling below the levels needed to adequately support vulnerable populations. The following sections highlight these various risks by first identifying the policy choices that governments are adopting to achieve planned expenditure contraction and then detailing their potentially adverse impacts on children and poor households.

Box V.1. Problems of Data and Definitions for 'Priority' Social Spending

There are different approaches to budgeting. For instance, public expenditures are often presented using a *functional classification*, which is the amount allocated to different sector ministries (education, health, social security/welfare, agriculture, transport, energy, defense, etc.). In general, social spending includes education, health, social security and labour, and, in some instances, housing and water. However, updated and accurate information on sector expenditures is not easily available in many countries.

IMF reports, on the other hand, contain timely information on public expenditures using an *economic classification*, which is based on aggregate spending amounts across ministries (e.g., wage bill, transfers, goods and services, and investments). According to this classification, the wage bill (payroll of civil servants) is usually the largest component of public expenditures in LICs and, accordingly, is one of the first items to be considered for cuts during adjustment periods. It is important to note that these classifications do not take into account distributional impacts.

---

[4] See Section 4.1 for details on the methodology used to reach this conclusion.

National plans and policy discussions often identify the need to protect 'priority' pro-poor social expenditures. Pro-poor indicates some consideration of distributional impacts. However, there is no universally-accepted definition of pro-poor social expenditures, and the definition changes from country to country.

In practice, primary education and basic health are common elements of *'priority' pro-poor social expenditures*, but other investments with positive distributional impacts on vulnerable children and poor households may not be included if they are not viewed as priority by the government, such as social protection, water supply and sanitation, or public housing. Policy discussions in recent IMF country reports also suggest that a wide variety of spending categories—such as electricity, judiciary and, in some cases, defense-related—were included in 'priority' social spending to be protected under country programs. These approaches raise questions about the effectiveness of priority setting in safeguarding those areas of social spending that are most essential for directly supporting vulnerable populations.

UNICEF, and the UN as a whole, uses a multidimensional approach to child well-being. The Convention of the Rights of the Child (1990), which has been ratified by 193 countries, clearly states the obligation to invest in eradicating all child deprivations. Children have a right not only to basic education and health, but also to food, clean drinking water, sanitation, shelter and other necessary investments for their families, including those related to basic livelihoods.

4.   Main Adjustment Measures during 2010-12

4.1.   Methodology

How are governments achieving fiscal adjustment? To answer this question, Section 4 looks at policy discussions and other information contained in IMF country reports, which cover Article IV consultations, reviews conducted under lending arrangements (e.g., Stand-by Arrangements and Extended Credit Facility) and consultations under non-lending arrangements (e.g., Staff Monitored Programs). Overall, 158 country reports are reviewed, all of which were published between January 2010 and February 2012 (see Annex 2 for details). Two caveats warrant mentioning. First, the findings are solely based on the authors' interpretation of IMF country reports. And second, to the extent that measures eventually adopted by governments may differ from those under consideration, this analysis is only indicative, and actual outcomes require verification.

4.2.   Results

A review of the latest IMF country reports indicates that five main adjustment policies are being considered to achieve fiscal consolidation. Each of the different adjustment measures is briefly summarized in the following, and the complete list of countries is provided in Table 10 at the end of this section.

First, *cutting or capping the wage bill* emerges as one of the most popular austerity measures. As recurrent expenditures, like salaries, tend to be the largest component of national budgets, an estimated 73 countries are looking to reduce the wage bill, which is often carried out or planned as a part of civil service reforms. This policy stance emerges more or less equally across all developing regions as well as among HICs.

A second widespread policy option to reduce government spending is *phasing out or removing subsidies*. Overall, 73 countries appear to be reducing or eliminating subsidies, predominately on fuel, but also on electricity and food items. While reducing fuel and energy subsidies is being adopted across all regions, with the exception of HICs, it appears especially dominant in Sub-Saharan Africa, where 18 governments are considering this consolidation measure. The removal of public support for food items is also most commonly found in Sub-Saharan Africa and in the Middle and North Africa.

Further targeting social protection emerges as a third common policy channel to contain overall expenditures and achieve cost savings. The review of IMF country reports indicates that 55 countries are rationalizing and further targeting their spending in social protection systems. This includes some developing countries that are under tight fiscal pressures, such as the Philippines, as well as those that have a legacy of extensive social welfare systems, such as Mongolia. This option also appears prominently across HICs (19 in total).

Fourth, many governments are *reforming old-age pensions* to scale back public spending. Approximately 52 countries are discussing different changes to their pension systems, such as through raising contribution rates, increasing eligibility periods, prolonging the retirement age and/or lowering benefits, among others. In broader terms, many of the alterations to pension systems are also linked to public health sector reforms. Among developing countries, this adjustment measure most commonly surfaces in policy discussions in MICs, especially in Eastern Europe and Latin America, which had already reformed their pension systems in recent years. Similar to the case of further targeting, a large number of HICs (23) are also pursuing pension reforms as a main cost-cutting strategy.

Lastly, in response to fiscal pressures, many countries are considering *altering consumer-oriented taxes on basic goods*, either through increasing or expanding VAT rates or sales taxes or, alternatively, by removing exemptions. Importantly, this approach differs from the options identified earlier because it impacts revenue rather than spending. Nonetheless, it is important to highlight because some 71 governments are employing some form of change to their consumption-based tax codes, making this one of the most common adjustment measures under consideration. Of particular concern to vulnerable populations, policy discussions in IMF country reports reveal that basic food items could be subjected to higher taxes (e.g., Ethiopia, Jordan and Moldova) as well as fuel and energy products (e.g., the Dominican Republic, Jordan, Kyrgyz Republic, Mexico and Turkey).

Overall, at least one policy option is being discussed in 138 countries worldwide, with two or more options being considered in 96 countries and four or more in 22 countries. Even more astounding, all five of the main fiscal adjustment measures are being discussed and/or implemented in 15 countries, including Greece, India, Ireland, Italy, Jordan, Malaysia, the Netherlands, Nicaragua, Portugal, Romania, Slovak Republic, Spain, St. Kitts and Nevis, Tunisia and the United Kingdom—a list which includes all of the major European countries that are facing or in the midst of a sovereign debt crisis. Although fewer, a number of countries are also contemplating or planning alternative policy options during the recovery by expanding wages, subsidies, social transfers or pension benefits and/or lowering taxes on basic goods, despite fiscal constraints (Table 11).

Table V.10. Selected Adjustment Measures Considered, 2010-12

Wage Bill Cuts or Caps	Reduce or Eliminate Subsidies	Further Target Social Protection	Old-Age Pension Reform	Increase Consumption Taxes
Algeria	Algeria	Albania	Albania	Antigua & Barbuda
Antigua & Barbuda	Angola	Algeria	Antigua & Barbuda	Armenia
Bahamas	Austria	Antigua & Barbuda	Austria	Belize
Belarus	Bangladesh	Belarus	Belarus	Bhutan
Belize	Belarus	Bolivia	Belgium	Botswana
Benin	Bolivia	Bosnia and Herz.	Belize	Colombia
Bosnia and Herz.	Burundi	Bulgaria	Benin	Costa Rica
Botswana	Cameroon	Cambodia	Bosnia and Herz.	Czech Republic
Bulgaria	Cape Verde	Cyprus	Bulgaria	Djibouti
Burundi	Central Afr. Rep.	Czech Republic	Canada	Dominican Rep.
Cambodia	Congo, Dem. Rep.	Denmark	Cyprus	Egypt
Chad	Dominican Rep.	Dominica	Czech Republic	Ethiopia
Chile	Egypt	Egypt	Egypt	Fiji
Costa Rica	El Salvador	El Salvador	Estonia	France
Côte d'Ivoire	Fiji	Fiji	France	Gambia
Cyprus	Gabon	France	Greece	Germany
Djibouti	Ghana	Germany	Guyana	Ghana
Estonia	Greece	Greece	Honduras	Greece
Fiji	Grenada	Grenada	India	Guatemala
Gabon	Guinea-Bissau	Hungary	Ireland	Guinea-Bissau
Greece	Haiti	India	Italy	Guyana
Grenada	Honduras	Indonesia	Jamaica	India
Guinea-Bissau	India	Ireland	Japan	Iran
Haiti	Indonesia	Italy	Jordan	Ireland
Honduras	Iran	Japan	Korea, Rep. of	Italy
Hungary	Iraq	Jordan	Lebanon	Jamaica
India	Ireland	Kazakhstan	Lithuania	Japan
Ireland	Italy	Lebanon	Mali	Jordan
Italy	Jordan	Malaysia	Mexico	Kenya
Jamaica	Kiribati	Mauritania	Micronesia	Kiribati
Jordan	Korea, Rep. of	Mauritius	Montenegro	Korea, Rep. of
Kazakhstan	Kosovo	Moldova	Morocco	Kyrgyz Republic
Kiribati	Lesotho	Mongolia	Netherlands	Liberia
Lebanon	Liberia	Morocco	New Zealand	Lithuania
Lithuania	Macedonia, FYR	Mozambique	Nicaragua	Malaysia
Macedonia, FYR	Malaysia	Nepal	Norway	Mali
Maldives	Maldives	Netherlands	Portugal	Mexico
Marshall Islands	Mali	Nicaragua	Romania	Micronesia
Mexico	Mauritius	Norway	Russia	Moldova
Micronesia	Mexico	Paraguay	Serbia	Montenegro
Moldova	Morocco	Peru	Singapore	Netherlands
Montenegro	Mozambique	Philippines	Slovak Republic	New Zealand
Morocco	Nepal	Portugal	Slovenia	Nicaragua
Mozambique	Netherlands	Romania	Spain	Pakistan
Netherlands	Nicaragua	Russia	St. Kitts and Nevis	Panama
Nicaragua	Niger	Slovak Republic	St. Lucia	Poland
Nigeria	Nigeria	Slovenia	St. Vincent	Portugal
Palau	Norway	Spain	Tunisia	Qatar
Poland	Pakistan	St. Kitts and Nevis	Uganda	Romania
Portugal	Palau	St. Vincent	Ukraine	Russia
Romania	Philippines	Sudan	United Kingdom	Saudi Arabia
Samoa	Portugal	Timor-Leste	United States	Seychelles
Serbia	Qatar	Tunisia		Slovak Republic

Wage Bill Cuts or Caps	Reduce or Eliminate Subsidies	Further Target Social Protection	Old-Age Pension Reform	Increase Consumption Taxes
Slovak Republic	Romania	United Kingdom		Spain
Slovenia	Saudi Arabia	United States		Sri Lanka
Solomon Islands	Serbia			St. Kitts and Nevis
South Africa	Sierra Leone			St. Lucia
Spain	Singapore			Sudan
St. Kitts and Nevis	Slovak Republic			Suriname
St. Lucia	Spain			Swaziland
St. Vincent	St. Kitts and Nevis			Tanzania
Swaziland	Sudan			Thailand
Tajikistan	Suriname			Togo
Tanzania	Tanzania			Tunisia
Timor-Leste	Thailand			Turkey
Tonga	Timor-Leste			Uganda
Tunisia	Togo			United Kingdom
Turkey	Tunisia			Uruguay
Tuvalu	Turkey			Vanuatu
	Tuvalu			Vietnam
	Ukraine			Yemen
	United Kingdom			
	Yemen			

Source: Authors' analysis of 158 IMF country reports (see Annex 2 for details)

Table V.11. Alternative Policy Options Considered, 2010-12

Increase Wage Bill	Increase or Introduce Subsidies	Expand Social Protection	Introduce or Expand Old-Age Pensions	Lower Consumption Taxes
Benin	Bangladesh	Antigua & Barbuda	Argentina	Antigua & Barbuda
Bhutan	Georgia	Armenia	Bolivia	Colombia
Bolivia	Liberia	Bolivia	Chile	Haiti
Cameroon	Mali	Burundi	China	Kenya
Central Afr. Rep.	Mauritania	China	El Salvador	Liberia
China	Mozambique	Dominican Rep.	Georgia	Mongolia
Dominican Rep.	Nicaragua	Fiji	Guyana	Senegal
El Salvador	South Africa	Guyana	Hungary	Solomon Islands
Equatorial Guinea	Togo	Haiti	Kosovo	Ukraine
Haiti	Zambia	Indonesia	Kyrgyz Republic	Uruguay
Kosovo		Iran	Macedonia, FYR	
Kyrgyz Republic		Iraq	Mongolia	
Lao PDR		Kenya	Mozambique	
Lesotho		Kyrgyz Republic	Panama	
Mongolia		Mauritania	Poland	
Namibia		Mozambique	Seychelles	
Niger		Panama	Sudan	
Panama		Philippines	Tajikistan	
Philippines		Senegal	Turkey	
Russia		St. Kitts and Nevis	Zimbabwe	
Sierra Leone		Sudan		
Suriname		Ukraine		
Uruguay				
Zimbabwe				

Source: Authors' analysis of 158 IMF country reports (see Annex 2 for details)

5.   Budget Cuts and Vulnerable Populations: The Risks

The previous sections presented evidence that aggregate budget cuts have intensified across most countries since 2010 and identified the main policies that are being adopted to achieve those cuts. Both of these trends can have a direct impact on the overall level and quality of public assistance and, hence, threaten vulnerable populations, especially for those residing in developing countries whose well-being and survival depends on public support. As a result, this section takes a close look at the risks facing children and poor households by first discussing the more general impact on total social expenditures and then by looking at the specific austerity measures. While this is clearest in cases of scaling down targeted benefits, such as cash transfers or subsidies on which vulnerable groups depend on to meet basic consumption needs, other measures can involve more indirect tradeoffs that also have adverse consequences (e.g., public sector wage cuts can affect private spending, reduce overall aggregate demand and, ultimately, hinder economic recovery, with slower growth weighing most heavily on the poor). Note that the aim of this section is not to assess the appropriateness of adjustment policies but rather to highlight their potential to adversely impact children and poor households.

5.1.   General reductions in social spending

As described in Section 3.2, data shortcomings make it difficult to measure actual social spending trends since 2010. However, when viewed in an overall contractionary fiscal environment at the aggregate level (see Section 2.2.2), there is a heightened risk of social spending and service delivery falling below the levels needed to adequately support vulnerable populations, even in countries with a policy intention of safeguarding 'priority' spending.

One of the ongoing effects of the global economic crisis in developing countries, in particular, is increased uncertainty in budget planning and implementation, which compounds existing weaknesses in social spending and service delivery. For example, where recovery in fiscal revenue is slow and the demand for government assistance remains high, inadequacies in social spending and service delivery can be quickly exacerbated. The expansion of social protection coverage, which was observed in a sizable number of developing and developed countries during the 2008-09 period as part of the initial crisis response, also risks losing momentum, as more governments are increasingly targeting benefits and focusing budget allocations to sectors that can jumpstart economic growth, such as infrastructure and energy.

The heightened risk of inadequate social spending is further reflected by other factors. A reported or budgeted increase in 'priority' spending may not cover certain social spending areas that are essential to vulnerable children and their families (see Box 2). Moreover, cash management difficulties and capacity limitations can cause substantial delays in disbursements and implementation, even when budgeted amounts are preserved or increased. For example, in Pakistan, spending on the Benazir Income Support Program amounted to only 10.4 billion rupees in the first quarter of 2009-10 compared to the 14 billion rupees planned under the program (IMF 2010).

There are other concerns. Seguino (2009), for instance, summarizes some of the likely impacts of health spending cuts among certain developing countries. In particular, given that more than half of public health budgets in Sub-Saharan Africa depend on foreign aid, funding shortfalls in the Global Fund to Fight HIV/AIDs, Tuberculosis and Malaria, as just one example, signify increasing stress on women who are the predominant caretakers of sick persons. As further highlighted by the case of Tanzania, which was the first country in Sub-Saharan Africa to cut its annual HIV/AIDS budget—and by an astounding 25 percent—there are also significant health sector risks in terms of human resources, service delivery and long-term planning.[5]

Moreover, there is ample evidence from HICs indicating that children and their families are disproportionately affected by reduced social expenditures. Typical adjustment measures include increased user fees or charges for health and education services, higher pupil-teacher ratios in schools, reductions in medical personnel and/or their time, discontinuation of allowances, including child benefits, and reductions in housing support, among others. For instance, a Gender Audit of the June 2010 Budget in the United Kingdom carried out by the House of Commons Library shows that women are bearing 72 percent of the burden of national cuts. Fewer housing benefits, lower pensions and

---

[5] Palitza, K. 2009. "Global Financial Crisis Leads to HIV Budget Cuts." *Inter Press Service News Agency*, May 18.

decreased child-related support, including pregnancy health services, maternity grants and child benefits, are among the principal threats resulting from social spending cuts, which reverberate across children. Mapson (2011) highlights additional austerity risks to British children and women. In terms of education, higher fees and reduced assistance make it more difficult for women to study, thus reducing their job prospects and earning potential and furthering gender inequities. Budget cuts to primary schools also disproportionately impact both children and their mothers who tend to be the primary caretakers. Increased violence and abuse against children and women was another serious risk linked to funding cuts in social protection services and legal aid. These experiences from the United Kingdom underscore some of the potential dangers that could be replicated in other countries— developed and developing alike—that have scaled back social spending as part of fiscal consolidation efforts. This section now looks at the specific dangers associated with each of the austerity measures that are being commonly discussed worldwide.

Box V.2. Expenditure Contraction and Social Spending: Ghana's Experience

Ghana's economy came under severe distress in 2008 as a result of expansionary fiscal policy and the impact of the global crisis. The government, in response, sought fiscal consolidation and tighter real expenditure in the 2009 and 2010 budgets. At the same time, macroeconomic difficulties coupled with higher local food prices and weakening economic activity threatened to push more Ghanaians into poverty (UNICEF Ghana 2010). Studies by local researchers calculated that monetary poverty among children would be 30 percent higher in 2011, and that hunger among children would rise an additional 7 percent (from 58 to 65) in 2011 due to the crisis. The impact may be especially acute in the three northern regions where poverty remained high despite the dramatic reduction in national poverty levels.

The IMF-supported program provides a floor for poverty-reducing budget expenditure, which was programed to increase from 8.7 percent of non-oil GDP in 2008-09 to 8.8 percent in 2010-11, while total expenditure was planned to contract by about 3 percent. Ghana's public audit accounts show that the poverty-reducing expenditures in 2009 went mostly to the Ministries of Education (69 percent of total poverty-reduction expenditure) and Health (19 percent), followed by the Ministry of Interior (7.3 percent), the Ministry of Food and Agriculture (3.7 percent), and the Ministry of Roads and Highways (1.1 percent).

However, other social ministries with a key role in supporting vulnerable children and their families appear to form a trivial part of this protected spending category. For example, the Ministry of Employment and Social Welfare accounted for less than 0.3 percent of the total poverty reducing expenditure, and the Ministry of Women and Children Affairs, as well as the Ministry of Water, Works and Housing, comprised about 0.1 percent each. Further, when measuring social spending by the share of all relevant social ministry budgets in the total government budget, the social spending allocation appeared to be falling during 2010 (Figure 5).

While positive steps have been taken by the government (e.g., continued expansion of the cash transfer program and free school uniforms to poor children), greater expenditure allocation to essential social areas are required to ensure that children and their families can survive the adverse impacts, including hunger, despite the contraction in public spending.

Figure V.5. Ghana: Percent Share of Social Sector Budget in Total Discretionary Budget

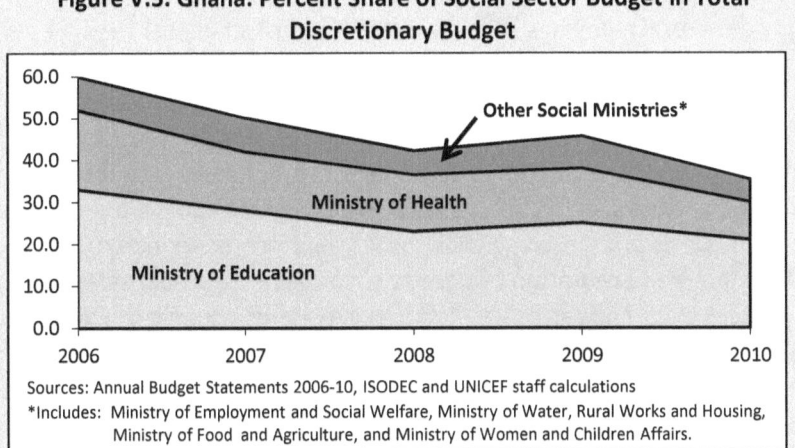

Sources: Annual Budget Statements 2006-10, ISODEC and UNICEF staff calculations
*Includes: Ministry of Employment and Social Welfare, Ministry of Water, Rural Works and Housing, Ministry of Food and Agriculture, and Ministry of Women and Children Affairs.

5.2.   Wage bill cuts or caps

If well designed and executed, fiscal savings can be generated and used for raising low wages for essential public service providers and/or for expanding essential posts, such as those required to meet the MDGs.[6] For instance, wage and employment reforms in Gabon, which include freezing public sector salaries and cutting annual hiring by half, are being complemented by increasing health and education personnel.

---

[6] According to UNESCO (2010), the rate at which teaching posts are created will need to increase if universal primary education is to be achieved by 2015.

Similarly, Burundi is expected to maintain a hiring freeze, which was enacted on civil servants in 2010, but will expand recruitment for priority sectors, including health, education and justice.

However, at least in the short term, there are risks that wage bill cuts or caps may translate into salaries being reduced or eroded in real value, payments in arrears, hiring freezes and/or employment retrenchment, which can adversely impact the delivery of basic social services, especially in high poverty areas (Box 3). UNICEF analysis (Chai et al. 2010) of salary information for primary teachers and nurses shows that their pay in real terms was significantly diminished by increases in local prices during 2009 in about one-third of the developing countries surveyed. The data further suggest that teachers and nurses are not adequately compensated when comparing their pay with at least one income or cost of living benchmark. Such findings were also echoed in a study of several countries in the CEE/CIS (Chubrik et al. 2011).

As low pay is a key factor behind absenteeism, informal fees and brain drain, it is imperative that the number of positions and level of compensation of essential public sector employees are protected, including teachers, medical staff, and social welfare and child protection workers. Decisions on wage bills must therefore ensure that the pay, employment and retention of priority social sector staff are safeguarded to protect child and family-related services—and enhanced when fiscal situations improve—in order to support human capital development for long-term growth. Wage bill decisions must also be based on gender analysis since women can suffer disproportionately from job cuts and public sector pay freezes as highlighted by recent evidence from the United Kingdom (Mapson 2011). Chapter IV complements this section with labour market flexibility reforms being adopted during the period of fiscal contraction.

Box V.3. Cambodia's Wage Bill Cuts in 2010

In Cambodia, the number of poor people is estimated to have increased by at least 200,000 in absolute terms as a result of the recent crises (World Bank 2009). Confronted by a growing fiscal deficit, the government announced that it would be reducing the number of contracted and temporary staff in all sector ministries by 50 percent in fiscal year 2010. Part of the logic to reduce Cambodia's wage bill was to create fiscal space for priority social investments. However, after discussions with sector ministries and development partners, an exception was granted to the health and education sectors since it would be impossible to deliver social services without necessary staff. Yet it remains enforced for other ministries, some with long-term implications for equity in service delivery, such as the Ministry of Social Affairs where social worker coverage was already low before reductions were imposed (one per 25,000 persons). To further contain the expansive wage bill, the government also announced that salary supplementation, allowances and incentive schemes for civil servants would be cancelled and replaced by a new streamlined system. UNICEF, along with other development partners, has pointed to the potential unintended consequences of removing salary incentives on the quality of service delivery. For instance, incentives can double the base salary for certain civil servant categories in Cambodia, such as health sector staff, and shortly after their discontinuation, UNICEF site surveys showed increased staff absenteeism and reduced working hours (UNICEF 2010c).

5.3.   Limiting subsidies

The removal or reduction of subsidies is often accompanied by the development of more targeted social safety nets as a way to compensate the poor. This is largely driven by the logic that generalized subsidies can be ineffective, costly and inequitable, while replacing them with targeted transfers can remove market distortions and more effectively support vulnerable groups (Coady et al. 2010). However, governments must carefully assess the human development and economic impacts of lowering or altogether removing food or fuel subsidies and ensure that any such policy change is accompanied by measures that adequately safeguard the access and well-being of vulnerable populations and overall recovery prospects.

Some countries have removed food subsidies at a time when there is still a high level of need for public nutrition assistance (Box 4). As detailed in Chapter III, local food prices remained at historic highs at the start of 2012 in a large sample of developing countries. Until a tested, well-functioning social safety net is in place, there is a strong case for extending general consumer subsidies, which can be possibly modified to encourage pro-poor self-selection (e.g., providing subsidies on food items that the poor tend to consume disproportionately more) as a short-term measure to protect children and poor households from unaffordable food costs. Moreover, while subsidies are often withdrawn quickly, a functioning targeting mechanism takes a considerable amount of time to design and roll out. This means that any timing mismatch immediately threatens the most vulnerable groups, especially infants and young children who can experience irreversible, long-term adverse effects from nutritional shortfalls.

A review of latest IMF country reports also shows that many countries are contemplating reducing fuel and energy subsidies in order to cut public expenditures. Indeed, the wide fluctuations in international oil prices can make fuel and energy subsidies costly and, therefore, an obvious target during fiscal austerity. However, the negative ripple effects of reversing this policy should be carefully examined. First, cutting fuel subsidies can have a disproportionate negative impact on vulnerable groups, whose already limited incomes are further eroded by any of the resulting inflationary effects on basic goods and services. Second, removing fuel subsidies can hinder overall economic growth, since higher costs of goods and services drag down aggregate demand. Third, any slowdown in economic growth will lower tax receipts and create new budgetary pressures—which is ironically the original impetus of the subsidy policy reversal.

Box V.4. Too Soon to Remove Food Subsidies?

During the food and fuel crisis, many developing countries increased subsidies or cut taxes on food and/or fuel between 2006 and 2008 (IMF 2008a). However, upon the easing in international commodity prices in late 2008, several African countries, including Burkina Faso, the Niger, Senegal and Seychelles, reversed the temporary measures of food subsidies and duty exemptions (IMF 2009), despite the lack of a clear indication that a compensatory safety net measure had successfully been put in place.

UNICEF staff analysis (Chai 2009), along with evidence presented in Chapter III, shows that many African countries continued to experience substantial local food price increases well after the international food commodity prices tapered off, and the high inflation in local food prices had been prolonged, lasting eight months on average. Consequently, the cumulative increases in local food prices outpaced those in per capita GDP, suggesting that, on average, populations in these countries were less able to afford the same amount of food than before (Figure 6).

Figure V.6. Africa: Food Prices and GDP per Capita, May 2007-May 2009
(percent change over the 24-month period)

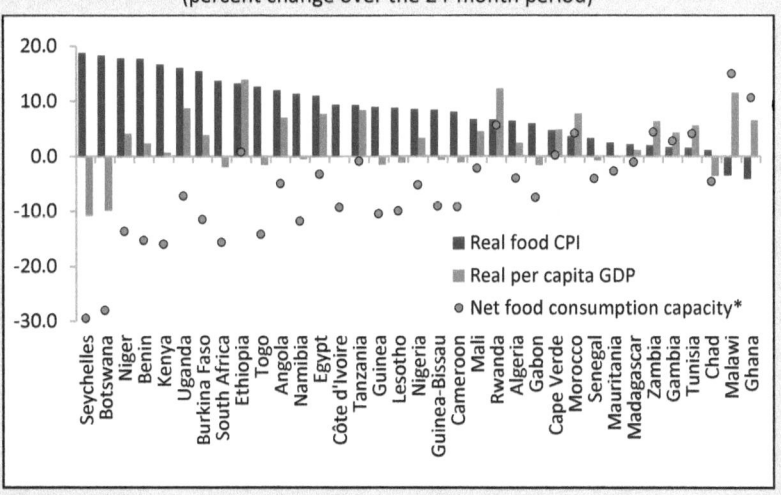

Source: Chai (2009)
* Calculated as the difference between real per capita GDP and real food CPI.

As the poor tend to be disproportionately affected by food price shocks and associated negative coping methods (e.g., cutting back on education and health expenditures), prolonged high food prices can inflict particularly severe and potentially irreversible damage on poor children and pregnant women. Careful analysis of the local realities facing the poor, prior to the removal of the subsidies, is thus important to avoid jeopardizing the long-term development of human capital. In the short term, while more cost-effective safety net measures are being developed, better designed food subsidies or custom tax exemptions may be warranted, which could be cost effective when combined with nutrition interventions such as micronutrient and weaning supplements. A poverty and social impact analysis for Senegal, for example, concluded that maintaining the tax suspension for rice in the short term, while simultaneously expanding existing school lunch and primary healthcare programs, would benefit the poor (IMF 2008b).

5.4.   Further targeting social protection

As a way to reconcile poverty reduction with fiscal austerity, economists often advise governments to better target their spending when budget cuts are called for (Ravallion 1999). Indeed, further targeting can yield fiscal savings over the medium term. In the short term, however, there are limitations inherent to designing and implementing new targeting schemes, which can result in the unintended effects of further excluding marginalized children and their families, especially where poverty is widespread. Overall, policymakers should consider that, in times of crisis, it is important to scale up social investments instead of scaling down, as further targeting is a *de facto* reduction in coverage.

One major constraint is that means-tested targeting is often costly and requires a high level of civil service capacity. Many studies document the considerable administrative costs of accurately identifying the poor (e.g., Coady et al. 2004 and Srivastava 2004). While self-selection and community-based mechanisms can lower overhead, they may fail to protect populations in need. Targeting schemes also have higher administrative costs than universal ones. Cost concerns are further complicated by overall weak public institutions that characterize many developing countries, which are often unable to manage the detailed administrative requirements of selective policies (Mkandawire 2005).

Another serious danger to targeting reforms is that they can result in large under-coverage. Due to a confluence of budgetary and political economy considerations, the scope of the target often falls short of adequately covering vulnerable populations and, instead, tends to focus only on the extreme poor or the poorest, such as in Moldova (Box 5). This leaves many vulnerable persons, especially poor children and women, excluded from receiving any type of cash benefit at a time when their need for public assistance is high. Thus, a strong case may be made to extend universal transfers (e.g., to families with children or to female-headed households) or to carry out some form of geographic targeting to provide immediate support to vulnerable groups facing unexpected and prolonged shocks until administrative capacity is developed to effectively implement more sophisticated systems.

Furthermore, current practices of targeting by income or consumption poverty do not adequately take into account other dimensions of poverty, such as lack of ready access to schools, clean water, health facilities or sanitation systems, among others. As a result, those children whose families meet the minimum consumption criteria but remain vulnerable to dropping out of school, malnutrition and/or mortality due to the deprivations of a safe and enabling environment are at risk of being left out. Several studies (e.g., Alkire and Seth 2008, Coulombe and Chai 2010) show that this exclusion risk could be empirically significant, which indicates the need for setting targeting criteria beyond consumption or income measures, including gender dimensions.

The UN has recently called for a social protection floor, below which nobody should fall, to provide a minimum set of social services and transfers for all persons (ILO 2011). By facilitating access to essential services and decent living standards, social protection is essential to accelerate progress toward achieving the MDGs with equity. Social protection contributes to six different MDGs,[7] with strong impacts for disadvantaged children (Ortiz et al. 2010). At this juncture, it is imperative that governments focus on expanding social protection coverage rather than improving the targeting of existing programs.

Box V.5. Targeting Social Assistance: The Case of Moldova

In 2008, Moldova reformed its social assistance system, moving gradually from a system of category-based nominal compensations for individuals (disabled children and adults, lone pensioners, war veterans, multi-children families, etc.) to poverty-targeted cash benefits for households. Under the previous system, the benefits were small, and less than half of the poorest Moldovans were covered. The new social assistance system is designed to target the poorest households while also increasing the benefit provided.

However, extensive delays occurred in implementing the new system, which were compounded by complicated application procedures and confusion among qualified households. As a result, less than half of the eligible beneficiaries had applied for support one year after the launch. Moreover, households that enrolled in the new system were required to re-apply after a period to continue receiving benefits; one-third of eligible households failed to do so. The government has since taken actions to improve the system.

---

7 MDG 1: Eradicate extreme poverty and hunger; MDG 2: Achieve universal primary education; MDG 3: Promote gender equality and empower women; MDG 4: Reduce child mortality; MDG 5: Improve maternal health; MDG 6: Combat HIV/AIDS, malaria and other diseases.

Moldova's experience underscores the risks of targeting-based reforms. Above all, means-testing is complex to implement and often leads to delays and/or under-coverage. In this example, barely 40 percent of targeted beneficiaries were receiving support 18 months after the launch of the new system, and this was only expected to increase to two-thirds after more than two years (Figure 7). The protracted start-up time also meant that most vulnerable families had to cope with multiple income shocks with little or no assistance.

Figure V.7. Beneficiaries under New Social Assistance System in Moldova
(in thousands of persons)

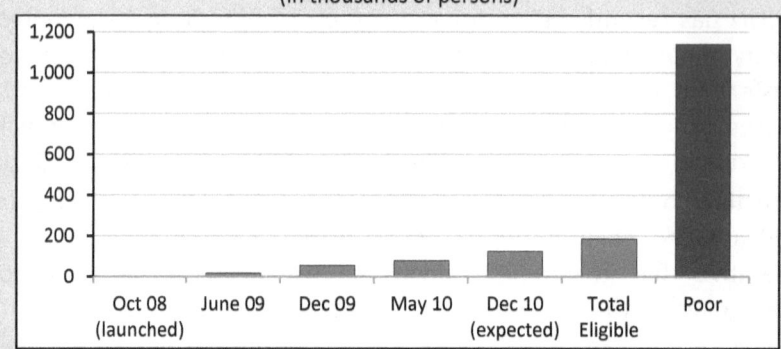

Another major risk of targeting-based reform is not to include, by design, the majority of vulnerable populations. While the scope of the targeted population is often a difficult policy decision for governments, in Moldova the safety net is being targeted to the bottom poorest, compared to 26.4 percent of the population that are below the poverty line. This means that many poor people are excluded from any type of cash benefit despite their continued need for public assistance.

Sources: Barca et al. 2010, Malhotra et al. 2009, and Olteanu and Trigano 2009

5.5.   Old-age pension reform

Cost-saving pension and healthcare policies are being adopted in many countries. Common reforms include prolonging retirement ages, reducing or eliminating benefits, and increasing payroll contributions; many countries are also revising eligibility criteria for disability allowances. The main risk of this policy choice is straightforward: vulnerable groups are either excluded from receiving benefits or critical assistance is diminished at a time when these groups are most in need. For poor households, having an older person at home who receives a pension is an asset, since it is a source of income to sustain the basic needs for the whole family, including children and women (Figure 8).

Figure V.8. How the Elderly Poor Spend their Pensions in Brazil
(as a percent of total pension)

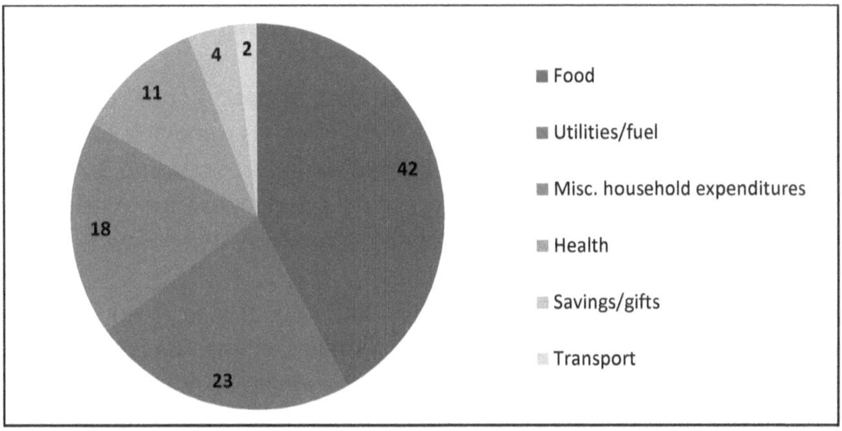

Source: HelpAge International (2004)

Moreover, since women are more dependent on public support and more likely to face pensioner poverty than men, pension cuts are likely to have a disproportionate negative impact on women and further gender disparities (UK Women's Budget Group 2010). As a result, it is imperative that policymakers complement any systematic pension reforms with specific measures that safeguard income support and the delivery of essential services, especially health, to older persons and their families. Given that reducing pensions, wages and social protection schemes decreases household income, which, in turn, will reduce aggregate demand and delay recovery, governments should consider rationalizing expenditures that have less severe social and economic consequences.

Interestingly, a small number of countries are reversing earlier pension reforms, including Argentina, Bolivia, Chile, Hungary and Poland, which had privatized their pension systems in the 1990s. The transition from a public to a privately-funded system has proved costly and difficult for many countries to afford, especially in the current setting of austerity. In particular, the administrative costs of private insurance and pension fund companies tend to be very high, which result in lower overall returns. Another major drawback is that pensioners bear all of the financial risks, which can effectively wipe out their life savings during market collapses, as has recently happened. In several countries, the state (e.g., the taxpayer) was forced to act as a guarantor of last resort, bailing out private companies and providing a tax-funded solidary pension for older persons (Riesco and Durán 2010).

5.6.   Increasing consumption taxes on basic goods

Above all, tax policies that increase the cost of basic goods, especially on food and transportation, have the same effect as removing subsidies. As a result, the same dangers highlighted earlier in Section 5.3 remain relevant, with poor families facing grave risks in the absence of effective safety nets and a strong, resilient economic recovery underway.

Increasing consumption-based taxes on basic goods also raises concern because this shifts the tax burden to families in the bottom income quintile of the distribution. Contrary to progressive taxes, such as taxes on income, taxing goods—especially basic food and household items—can be regressive since it does not discriminate between high-income and low-income consumers. For example, given that poor families spend a higher proportion of their disposable income on food items, applying or increasing consumption taxes on basic food items means that relatively more of their income is subjected to product taxes. Thus, consumption-based taxes can have a disproportionate negative impact on poorer households, reducing their already limited disposable income and further exacerbating existing inequalities.

As in the other adjustment measures, levying or increasing consumption taxes or VATs can be a very prudent policy objective and strengthen fiscal space for ramped up social spending. Different consumption taxes can be progressively designed by allowing exemptions for necessary basic goods that many low-income families depend on while setting higher rates for luxury goods that are principally consumed by wealthier families (see Schenk and Oldman 2007 for discussion). In the current policy environment, examples abound. For instance, Antigua and Barbuda is introducing sales tax exemptions for basic commodities, Kenya is lowering taxes on fuel and food staples consumed by vulnerable populations, and the Solomon Islands is reducing taxes on food and fuel items. Many developing countries also appear to be considering tax increases on luxury items, like vehicles, such as in Ghana and in the Republic of Congo.

6.   Conclusion

Most governments moved swiftly to counter the effects of the global economic crisis by introducing fiscal stimulus packages during 2008-09, which included increased assistance to social sectors. In a second phase of the crisis, however, most countries began to cut deficits and reduce overall expenditures. This chapter confirmed that the scope of austerity widened quickly, with 106 countries worldwide reducing total spending by 2.3 percent of GDP, on average, during 2010, and 133 countries (or roughly 75 percent of the total sample) expected to reduce annual expenditures in 2012 by close to 2 percent of GDP, on average. Moreover, comparing the 2010-12 and 2005-07 periods suggests that one-third of all governments are undergoing excessive contraction. Even more alarming, spending projections for 2013 indicate that fiscal consolidation will continue to characterize public policies worldwide into the foreseeable future.

In terms of their impact on the level and quality of essential public assistance, fiscal consolidation poses clear risks to children and poor households. First, aggregate budget contractions during 2010-12 have likely affected social sector spending allocations and jeopardized the ability of social protection systems to provide adequate support to vulnerable children and their families, even in countries with a policy intention of safeguarding 'priority' spending. Second, the different cost-cutting measures being adopted by governments are expected to be disproportionately felt by poor children and their families: wage bill reductions can hamper the delivery and quality of essential health, education and social protection services, especially in rural areas; subsidy reversals and higher consumption taxes can make food, transport, medicines and other basic goods unaffordable, further eroding the already diminished levels of disposable household incomes; and rationalizing social protection schemes, including reduced pension benefits, runs a high risk of exclusion at a time when children and poor households are most in need. Revenue side measures being implemented to achieve fiscal targets, including higher consumption taxes on basic goods, are also likely to be disproportionately shouldered by the poorest families and further constrain their limited resources.

The severity of the different adjustment risks is perhaps best illustrated by their potential to inflict lasting damage to children. In particular, the limited window of intervention for fetal development and for growth among infants and young children means that deprivations today, if not addressed promptly, can have irreversible impacts on their physical and intellectual capacities, which will, in turn, lower their productivity and income-earning potential in adulthood; this is an extraordinary price for a country to pay.

It is, however, possible to protect children and poor families in times of austerity and avert such adverse outcomes. In Table 12 below, the risks of the main adjustment measures being considered are presented alongside a series of alternative options, which, if adopted, can ensure that the poorest are safeguarded even in an environment of public sector belt-tightening.

Table V.12. Adjustment Risks and Alternative Policy Measures

Adjustment Risks	Alternative Options
Wage bill cuts/caps: As recurrent expenditures like salaries tend to be the largest component of national budgets, many countries are looking to reduce the wage bill, often as a part of civil service reforms. In the short term, however, wage bill changes may translate into salaries being reduced or eroded in real value, payments in arrears, hiring freezes and/or employment retrenchment, all of which can adversely impact the delivery of social services, especially in high poverty areas. Since low pay is a key factor behind absenteeism, informal fees and brain drain, this option poses a high risk to rural areas.	Wage bill decisions must consider the impact of staff in essential social services, such as teachers, healthcare professionals and social protection workers, especially in disadvantaged areas. While the number of related personnel and their salaries should be safeguarded at all times to ensure that vulnerable families have access to quality basic services, they should also be increased whenever possible.
Removing/reducing subsidies: Governments must carefully assess the human and economic consequences of reversing food or fuel subsidies. - Some countries have removed food subsidies at a time when there is still a high need for food support, threatening infants and young children who can experience irreversible, long-term adverse effects from alimentary deficiencies. - In terms of fuel subsidies, reducing price support can have a disproportionate negative impact on vulnerable groups as a result of rising costs of cooking fuel or transport, among others. A careful examination on who benefits from current subsidies is necessary. - Higher fuel prices also negatively impact general economic activity and, therefore, employment and livelihoods.	- As food and energy prices hover near record highs, scaling back consumer subsidies should be avoided unless a well-functioning social protection system is already in place that can protect children and poor households. - Subsidies should not be removed to build a new social protection system, as this takes time and populations will be left unprotected during a period of exceptional vulnerability. - Except for luxury items, consumer subsidies could be maintained to support social and economic recovery.

Adjustment Risks	Alternative Options
Further targeting social protection: There are significant limitations inherent to designing and implementing a new means-tested targeting scheme: - This tends to lead to under coverage, particularly at a time of high social needs and civil unrest. - Means-testing can be expensive to implement. - This requires a high level of civil service capacity. - Common targeting practices do not adequately take into account non-income dimensions of poverty (access to schools, clean water, health facilities, etc.), thus increasing the risk of exclusion.	Rather than further targeting social protection systems for cost savings over the short term—that is, scaling down in times of crisis—there is a strong case for scaling up and expanding a universal social protection floor or for providing immediate support to vulnerable geographic areas or groups (e.g., older persons , orphans, women-headed households, persons with disabilities).
Pension reform: The main options being considered by governments include raising contribution rates, prolonging the retirement age and lowering benefits, many of which are linked to reforms of the public health sector. The key concerns of this policy are that vulnerable groups are excluded from receiving benefits or that critical assistance is diminished at a time when vulnerable groups are most in need, which can further impact poor households who commonly depend on elderly income for basic consumption needs.	- Any systematic pension reform should be complemented by measures that safeguard income support and the delivery of basic services to elder persons and their families. - Given that reducing wages, pensions and household income will reduce demand and delay recovery, consider rationalizing expenditures that have less severe social and economic consequences.
Increasing or expanding VATs: The potential negative implications for vulnerable families are clear: - Tax policies that increase the cost of basic goods can lead to nutrition shortfalls and further deteriorate the already limited income of vulnerable populations and slow overall economic growth, with poorer families facing the gravest risks in the absence of effective social protection and an employment-led economic recovery. - Since increasing consumption-based taxes on basic goods does not discriminate between high- and low-income consumers, this approach can also be regressive, shifting the tax burden to families in the bottom income quintiles of society and exacerbating inequalities.	- Consider other possible tax options, such as taxes on corporate profits, financial activities, personal income, luxury items, property, natural resource extraction, alcohol and tobacco, imports/exports, etc. - Strengthen the efficiency of tax collection methods and overall compliance. - Consumer-oriented tax changes must be progressively designed by allowing exemptions for goods and services that low-income families depend on while setting higher rates for luxury goods that are principally consumed by wealthier households.

But shielding the poorest households from austerity plans is simply insufficient to generate social development. Policymakers must, instead, significantly ramp up pro-poor investments. While this may appear challenging in an environment of increasing fiscal constraints, there is, in fact, a wide variety of options for governments to boost pro-poor investments today, even in the poorest countries (as described at length in Chapter VI).

Protecting vulnerable populations is critical to equitably sharing the adjustment costs and avoiding detrimental or even irreversible effects on children and the poor. However, macroeconomic and fiscal decisions are often taken without comprehensive assessment of their potential impacts on employment, human development, and inclusive and sustainable growth. In particular, some question the logic of using micro-level interventions to support the poorest while adopting macroeconomic policies that principally benefit the wealthy (United Nations 2010a and UNRISD 2010). Such studies look at the wider distributional impacts of economic decision-making and reflect calls by the UN Secretary-General for macroeconomic policies to focus on supporting real output growth, employment and social development rather than debt stabilization and inflation targets (United Nations 2010b).

Moreover, just as stress tests are widely accepted to test financial sector vulnerabilities, they can likewise be used to assess the potential social consequences of macroeconomic policies, as well as the capacity of social protection systems to address them (Kanbur 2010). There are precedents in distributional analysis, poverty and social impact analyses, and studies and evaluations of equitable policies, which expanded from the late 1990s (Ortiz 2008). In addition, more and better data and analysis are needed, especially in terms of collecting real-time information and assessing alternative scenarios to simulate impacts on social and labour market indicators both with and without policy responses (Islam and Chowdhury 2010). If properly designed and executed, such analyses can alert policymakers on the potential distributional impacts of different policy options, including fiscal adjustment measures.

Some potential questions for policymakers to consider may include:

-   Is the fiscal adjustment trajectory—in terms of scope, pace and magnitude—conducive to achieving development targets and equitable long-term economic growth?

-   Are indicators for economic recovery, often the basis for fiscal policy decisions, inclusive of social and economic conditions faced by the poor? Are they taking into account the longer-term impacts of high unemployment, rising food and energy prices, and social inequalities on children and poor households?

-   To what extent is spending on services and programs essential to children a part of 'priority' spending? What is 'non-priority' social spending? Will the protection of 'priority' spending still lead to declines in social expenditures?

-   What are the social impacts of macroeconomic policy decisions, including the opportunity cost of not scaling up equity-based interventions and social protection programs, both which are essential for a *'Recovery for All'*? Have 'stress tests' been carried out to assess the capacity of social protection systems to withstand ongoing and future shocks?

-   Given the limitations and exclusion risks of common targeting practices, are alternative approaches—such as a social protection floor—fully considered in order to better achieve the objectives of protecting the vulnerable, increasing their resilience, and maximizing their human development potential and economic participation?

-   Have all possible alternative measures to expand fiscal space been fully explored and discussed in an open, national dialogue in order to support a socially-responsive recovery?

References

Alkire, S., and S. Seth. 2008. "Measuring Multidimensional Poverty in India: A New Proposal." OPHI Working Paper 15, Oxford Poverty and Human Development Initiative (OPHI).

Barca, V., L. Carraro and A. Sinchetru. 2010. "Study into Reasons for Low Take-Up and Retention." OPM/Every Child, UNICEF/Oxford Policy Management.

Brumby, J. and M. Verhoeven. 2010. "Public Expenditure after the Global Financial Crisis." In *The Day After Tomorrow: A Handbook on the Future of Economic Policy in the Developing World*. Washington, D.C.: World Bank.

Chai, J. 2009. "Crisis Impact on Child Nutrition: How Much has the Risk to Long-term Development Increased in Africa?" Paper presented at AERC Conference in Nairobi, Kenya.

Chai, J., I. Ortiz and X. Sire. 2010. "Protecting Salaries of Frontline Teachers and Health Workers." Social and Economic Policy Working Brief, UNICEF.

Chubrik, A., M. Dabrowski, R. Mogilevsky and I. Sinitsina. 2011. *The Impact of the Global Financial Crisis on Education and Health in the Economies of the Former Soviet Union*. CASE Network Reports No. 100. Warsaw: Center for Social and Economic Research (CASE).

Coady, R., M. Grosh and J. Hoddinott. 2004. "Targeting Outcomes Redux." *The World Bank Research Observer* 19(1): 61-85.

Coady, D., R. Gillingham, R. Ossowski, J. Piotrowski, S. Tareq and J. Tyson. 2010. "Petroleum Product Subsidies: Costly, Inequitable and Rising." IMF Staff Position Note No. 10/05, IMF.

Cornia, G.A., R. Jolly and F. Stewart. 1987. *Adjustment with a Human Face: Protecting the Vulnerable and Promoting Growth*. Oxford: Oxford University Press.

Coulombe, H. and J. Chai. 2010. "Multi-dimensional Poverty Map: An Illustration Using Mongolia Census Data." Social and Economic Policy Working Paper, UNICEF.

HelpAge. 2004. *Age and Security: How Social Pensions can Deliver Effective Aid to Poor Older People and their Families*. London: HelpAge International.

Hicks, N. 1991. "Expenditure Reductions in Developing Countries Revisited." *Journal of International Development* 3(1): 29-37.

ILO and WHO. 2011. *Social Protection Floor for a Fair and Inclusive Globalization*. Report of the Advisory Group chaired by Michelle Bachelet. Geneva: ILO and WHO.

IMF. 2011. *World Economic Outlook: Slowing Growth, Rising Risks, September 2011*. Washington, D.C.: IMF. http://www.imf.org/external/pubs/ft/weo/2011/02/weodata/index.aspx (accessed December 2011).

_____. 2010. "Pakistan: Third Review under Stand-By Arrangement." IMF Country Report No. 10/6, IMF.

_____. 2009. *Regional Economic Outlook: Sub-Saharan Africa*. Washington, D.C.: IMF.

_____. 2008a. *Food and Fuel Prices: Recent Developments, Macroeconomic Impact, and Policy Responses—An Update*. Washington, D.C.: IMF.

_____. 2008b. "Senegal: Selected Issue Paper." IMF Country Report No. 08/221, IMF.

Islam, I. and A. Chowdhury. 2010. "Managing Macroeconomic Risks and Protecting the Vulnerable." *VoxEU.org*, August 14.

Kanbur, R. 2010. "Protecting the Poor against the Next Crisis." Presentation in the Distinguished Lectures Series of the Egyptian Centre for Economic Studies in Cairo, Egypt.

Kyrili, K. and M. Martin. 2010. *The Impact of the Global Economic Crisis on the Budgets of Low-income Countries*. Oxford: Oxfam GB.

Malhotra, D., A. Hurrell and A. Thompson. 2009. "The Evolution of the Policy Framework Governing Cash Transfers in Moldova." Support to the Delivery of Effective and Sustainable Social Assistance Services Project, UNICEF/Oxford Policy Management.

Mapson, A. 2011. *Cutting Women Out in Bristol: A Report of the Human Rights and Equality Impact Assessment of the Public Sector Spending Cuts on Women in Bristol*. Bristol: Fawcett Society Bristol Local Group.

Mkandawire, T. 2005. "Targeting and Universalism in Poverty Reduction." Social Policy and Development Program Paper No. 23, UNRISD.

Olteanu, C. and R. Trigano. 2009. *Assessment of Law No. 133/2008 on the Social Support in the Republic of Moldova, 2009 First Semester*. Chişinău: Government of the Republic of Moldova.

Ortiz, I. 2008. "Social Policy." In *National Development Strategies, Policy Notes*. New York: UN-DESA.

Ortiz, I., G. Fajth, J. Yablonski and A. Rabi. 2010. "Social Protection: Accelerating the MDGs with Equity." Social and Economic Policy Working Brief, UNICEF.

Paxson, C. and N. Schady. 2005. "Cognitive Development among Young Children in Ecuador: The Roles of Wealth, Health and Parenting." Working Paper 239, Princeton University.

Ravallion, M. 2002. "Are the Poor Protected from Budget Cuts? Evidence for Argentina." *Journal of Applied Economics* 5(1): 95-121.

_____, M. 1999. "Is More Targeting Consistent with Less Spending?" *International Tax and Public Finance* 6(3): 411-419.

Riesco, M. and F. Durán. 2010. *Resultados para sus Afiliados de Laqs AFP y Compañías de Seguros Relacionadas con la Previsión: 1982-2008*. Santiago de Chile: Centro de Estudios Nacionales de Desarrollo Alternativo (CENDA).

Seguino, S. 2009. "The Global Economic Crisis, Its Gender Implications and Policy Responses." Paper prepared for Gender Perspectives on the Financial Crisis Panel at the 53rd Session of the Commission on the Status of Women in New York City.

Schenk, A. and O. Oldman. 2007. *Value Added Tax: A Comparative Approach*. Cambridge: Cambridge University Press.

Srivastava, P. 2004. "Poverty Targeting in Asia: Country Experience of India." ADB Institute Discussion Paper No. 5, ADB.

UK Women's Budget Group. 2010. *A Gender Impact Assessment of the Coalition Government Budget*. London: UK Women's Budget Group.

UNESCO. 2010. *Education for All Report*. Paris: UNESCO.

UNICEF Ghana. 2010. "Ghana Must Protect and Maximise Investment in Social Services to Stem the Impact of the Economic Crisis." Unpublished Advocacy Note, UNICEF Ghana.

UNRISD. 2010. *Combating Poverty and Inequality*. Geneva: UNRISD.

United Nations. 2010a. *Rethinking Poverty: Report of the World Social Situation 2010*. New York: UN-DESA.

_____. 2010b. *Keeping the Promise: A Forward-looking Review to Promote an Agreed Action Agenda to Achieve the Millennium Development Goals by 2015*. New York: United Nations.

Willem, D. et al. 2009. "The Global Financial Crisis and Developing Countries: Synthesis of the Findings of 10 Country Case Studies." Working Paper No. 306, Overseas Development Institute.

World Bank. 2009. *Transforming the Rebound into Recovery: Economic Update for the East Asia and the Pacific Region*. Washington, D.C.: World Bank.

Yang, Y., N. Mwase, P. Dudine, P. Mitra, E. Kvintradze and S. Das. 2010. *Creating Policy Space in Low-income Countries during the Recent Crises*. Washington, D.C.: IMF.

Zhang, Y., N. Thelen and A. Rao. 2010. "Social Protection in Fiscal Stimulus Packages: Some Evidence." UNDP/Office of Development Studies Working Paper, UNDP.

Annex 1: Projected Changes in Total Government Expenditures in 179 Countries, 2005-12

A. Change, as a percent of GDP

Country	Annual Change								Period Change		
	2005	2006	2007	2008	2009	2010	2011	2012	2008-09 vs. 2005-7	2010-12 vs. 2008-09	2010-12 vs. 2005-07
Afghanistan	1.5	4.3	0.5	0.3	-0.1	-0.5	3.1	1.9	2.0	2.1	4.1
Albania	-1.1	0.8	-0.1	2.6	1.6	-3.4	-0.6	0.6	3.6	-2.8	0.8
Algeria	-3.6	1.6	4.7	4.7	3.6	-3.2	5.5	-3.2	10.1	1.2	11.2
Angola	-1.0	3.6	-3.9	7.5	-2.6	-4.3	0.8	-0.2	4.9	-5.1	-0.2
Antigua & Barb.	0.2	5.6	-2.7	-0.6	9.3	-14.6	0.0	-0.8	4.1	-10.2	-6.2
Argentina	-0.9	-0.2	2.8	0.6	3.7	0.8	0.8	-0.9	4.3	2.9	7.2
Armenia	...	0.1	2.4	-0.2	6.3	-2.7	-0.6	-1.8	4.6	-0.5	4.1
Australia	-0.2	0.4	-0.4	0.3	3.4	-0.5	-0.5	-0.4	1.9	0.8	2.7
Austria	-3.9	-0.8	-0.6	0.3	3.7	-0.1	-1.1	-0.3	1.5	0.9	2.4
Azerbaijan	-3.2	4.7	-1.5	5.2	3.7	-4.0	1.2	-1.0	7.6	-1.7	5.9
Bahamas	0.6	0.5	1.8	0.4	2.0	0.2	1.3	0.0	2.7	2.0	4.7
Bahrain	-0.9	-1.4	-0.7	0.0	3.0	1.7	3.0	-2.1	0.5	4.5	5.0
Bangladesh	0.5	-0.1	-0.7	2.5	-1.4	0.1	1.5	1.9	1.3	1.0	2.3
Barbados	4.0	-0.4	7.5	0.0	-3.3	-1.2	-3.1	0.4	3.1	-4.8	-1.7
Belarus	0.9	0.2	-0.2	0.0	-1.2	-2.3	-4.1	-0.8	-0.6	-5.8	-6.4
Belgium	2.7	-3.4	-0.2	1.7	4.0	-1.1	-0.5	-0.2	2.4	0.5	2.9
Belize	-3.2	2.1	-0.8	-0.6	-0.1	0.7	1.3	-0.3	-0.5	1.5	1.0
Benin	0.9	-1.9	4.0	-2.0	3.7	-4.6	2.5	-0.5	1.8	-1.3	0.5
Bhutan	5.5	-2.1	-0.8	-0.4	-1.4	5.1	5.7	-6.4	-2.3	6.1	3.8
Bolivia	0.8	-3.3	2.0	2.8	0.9	-4.3	1.4	0.7	3.4	-2.6	0.8
Bosnia & Herz.	0.3	0.2	0.8	3.0	0.7	0.0	-0.7	-1.6	3.9	-0.7	3.2
Botswana	-4.2	-2.7	2.1	8.2	6.2	-6.9	-2.1	-5.4	11.9	-7.0	4.9
Brazil	1.6	0.2	-1.1	-0.6	1.0	1.7	-1.2	0.0	-0.8	1.4	0.6
Brunei	-4.5	-1.4	1.7	-2.4	8.5	1.4	-3.5	1.7	2.6	3.9	6.5
Bulgaria	-0.6	-1.5	1.3	0.2	1.0	0.5	-1.7	0.7	1.1	0.1	1.2
Burkina Faso	0.0	0.8	3.1	-5.2	3.5	1.0	0.6	-2.9	-1.2	2.2	1.0
Burundi	-3.1	1.4	15.8	2.8	-6.0	4.0	-7.3	-5.2	10.8	-5.6	5.1
Cambodia	-1.5	0.6	1.6	0.0	4.8	0.3	-2.1	0.4	3.6	1.4	5.0
Cameroon	-1.4	-0.1	1.2	2.8	-0.1	0.1	1.0	-0.6	3.5	0.6	4.1
Canada	-0.5	0.1	-0.1	0.4	4.5	-0.2	-1.5	-0.4	2.6	0.9	3.5
Cape Verde	1.8	-0.4	-3.7	1.1	0.4	3.6	0.5	-2.7	-1.3	3.2	1.9
Central Afr. Rep.	3.1	-3.0	-0.7	2.9	0.0	1.4	-1.0	0.1	1.5	0.8	2.3
Chad	-1.3	-0.3	9.7	2.3	6.1	1.0	-3.1	-2.4	11.7	1.2	12.9
Chile	-0.6	-1.3	0.7	2.4	3.6	-1.3	-0.5	-0.4	4.2	0.1	4.3
China	0.5	0.3	0.0	1.1	3.1	-0.4	-0.2	0.1	2.8	1.0	3.8
Colombia	-0.3	2.3	0.1	-1.9	2.8	-1.6	0.8	-0.9	0.3	0.0	0.3
Comoros	-0.2	1.3	1.0	3.4	-2.8	0.9	-0.2	-0.4	3.1	-0.7	2.4
Congo, Dem.	10.3	-6.1	0.3	4.1	4.3	2.4	5.0	-2.3	4.4	7.1	11.5
Congo, Rep. of	-2.6	3.6	2.1	-6.2	1.0	-3.2	2.3	0.5	-3.1	-0.9	-4.1
Costa Rica	-0.4	-1.0	-0.5	1.0	1.6	1.7	0.3	0.4	1.1	2.8	3.9
Côte d'Ivoire	-0.2	1.0	-0.3	0.6	-0.1	0.9	4.3	-3.6	0.7	2.6	3.3
Croatia	-1.1	-0.1	0.7	-1.5	1.7	-0.3	-0.8	-0.8	-0.2	-0.3	-0.5

Country	Annual Change								Period Change		
	2005	2006	2007	2008	2009	2010	2011	2012	2008-09 vs. 2005-7	2010-12 vs. 2008-09	2010-12 vs. 2005-07
Cyprus	1.3	-0.3	-1.8	0.3	4.1	0.8	0.9	-0.9	1.0	3.2	4.1
Czech Republic	-0.2	-1.2	-1.2	0.4	3.1	-0.7	-0.2	-0.2	0.7	0.6	1.2
Denmark	-1.7	-1.8	-0.5	1.0	6.5	-0.4	-1.2	-0.9	3.3	1.7	5.1
Djibouti	-0.7	0.6	0.4	2.9	1.0	-5.6	-0.3	-0.4	3.8	-5.4	-1.6
Dominica	0.8	-1.3	4.1	0.9	2.1	-2.7	-1.2	-1.2	4.3	-2.9	1.4
Dominican Rep.	-0.7	1.0	-0.5	2.3	-1.7	-1.1	-0.7	-0.5	1.5	-2.5	-1.0
Ecuador	0.8	-0.1	3.8	6.5	0.5	1.3	2.8	-0.7	9.3	3.2	12.5
Egypt	-0.6	4.5	-2.5	0.3	-1.0	-1.2	1.5	-0.4	-0.4	-0.7	-1.1
El Salvador	0.3	0.7	-0.8	0.7	2.2	0.4	0.1	-0.9	1.5	1.2	2.7
Equatorial	-3.4	3.2	1.7	2.7	27.3	-13.8	-2.9	-0.4	18.5	-2.3	16.3
Eritrea	2.6	-16.3	-1.2	2.2	-11.5	4.0	-1.0	-2.9	-9.8	-3.3	-13.2
Estonia	0.6	-0.6	0.8	6.2	6.0	-2.1	-2.3	-0.1	9.5	-0.6	8.9
Ethiopia	-0.3	-0.8	-1.6	-1.8	-1.7	1.4	1.5	1.0	-3.9	1.9	-2.1
Fiji	-0.1	1.7	-2.0	-1.9	4.9	-1.5	-0.3	0.3	-0.2	0.9	0.7
Finland	0.1	-1.1	-1.8	1.9	6.5	-0.5	-1.2	-1.0	3.5	1.6	5.2
France	0.3	-0.6	-0.4	0.7	3.5	-0.1	-0.1	-0.7	2.0	1.3	3.3
Gabon	0.1	-0.2	-1.6	-0.6	4.9	0.0	-1.5	0.6	0.7	1.6	2.3
Gambia	-0.4	0.9	-5.0	0.4	3.6	0.9	1.6	-2.8	-0.8	2.8	2.0
Georgia	2.8	1.1	5.1	4.2	3.1	-2.8	-2.6	-1.6	9.6	-3.5	6.1
Germany	-0.2	-1.7	-1.9	0.3	4.1	-1.0	-1.2	-0.6	0.5	0.1	0.5
Ghana	-1.0	2.2	1.3	1.4	-2.2	1.8	-1.1	-1.7	2.0	-0.6	1.3
Greece	-1.6	1.2	1.5	3.0	3.2	-3.4	-1.4	-0.5	6.0	-2.9	3.1
Grenada	0.6	4.9	-3.9	0.1	0.2	-1.2	-1.0	-0.3	-0.8	-1.9	-2.7
Guatemala	0.3	1.0	-0.4	-0.6	0.6	0.4	-0.2	-0.4	-0.3	0.4	0.1
Guinea	-1.1	2.1	-4.2	2.7	6.6	6.1	3.0	-14.7	3.9	6.5	10.4
Guinea-Bissau	-3.2	-0.9	0.9	2.4	-2.5	-1.3	0.9	-0.3	1.4	-2.0	-0.6
Guyana	5.7	0.7	-5.2	-1.3	1.6	-1.9	2.9	-1.4	-3.7	0.4	-3.3
Haiti	4.6	-0.7	0.4	2.4	4.4	5.2	-6.3	11.4	4.6	7.0	11.6
Honduras	-0.9	0.4	0.0	2.2	1.6	-2.0	-1.8	-0.5	3.1	-2.6	0.5
Hong Kong	-1.6	-1.7	-0.4	3.4	-1.3	0.4	3.2	-2.2	1.9	1.2	3.1
Hungary	1.4	1.9	-2.1	-1.2	1.7	-1.7	1.8	-4.1	-1.0	-1.0	-2.0
Iceland	-3.7	-0.6	0.6	2.3	5.1	-2.0	-2.3	-1.7	5.1	-1.6	3.5
India	-0.7	-0.1	0.4	1.9	0.3	-1.1	-0.5	0.2	2.2	-1.3	0.9
Indonesia	-1.2	1.4	0.2	1.0	-3.0	0.0	1.2	-0.9	0.0	-1.0	-0.9
Iran	5.4	1.1	-6.1	2.9	-2.0	-0.7	2.5	-1.1	-1.7	-0.4	-2.1
Iraq	...	-28.1	-0.8	15.2	15.3	-17.6	-1.9	-1.9	12.9	-11.9	1.0
Ireland	0.3	0.6	2.2	6.0	6.2	18.1	-21.0	-1.1	10.8	6.8	17.6
Israel	-2.1	-0.6	-0.9	-0.2	-0.2	-0.4	-0.5	0.4	-1.0	-0.7	-1.7
Italy	0.4	0.6	-0.8	1.0	3.0	-1.3	-0.6	-0.7	2.1	-0.4	1.7
Jamaica	-2.1	1.4	0.4	3.0	3.7	-5.5	-1.0	0.2	5.6	-4.2	1.4
Japan	0.0	0.5	-1.3	2.4	4.3	-0.3	1.9	-0.4	3.8	3.0	6.9
Jordan	1.1	-2.5	0.6	-2.6	0.6	-4.7	3.8	-3.6	-2.7	-3.1	-5.8
Kazakhstan	0.2	-2.4	4.3	2.6	-3.3	-1.0	0.3	0.1	3.1	-2.4	0.7
Kenya	1.6	0.8	1.4	1.5	0.4	2.7	1.5	-0.8	2.9	3.6	6.5
Kiribati	-12.5	-8.8	-10.1	8.4	0.7	-0.8	3.7	2.0	-0.9	2.7	1.8
Korea, Rep. of	-0.2	0.7	0.4	0.5	0.6	-1.8	-0.3	-0.5	1.3	-1.9	-0.6

Country	Annual Change								Period Change		
	2005	2006	2007	2008	2009	2010	2011	2012	2008-09 vs. 2005-7	2010-12 vs. 2008-09	2010-12 vs. 2005-07
Kosovo	-1.7	-3.7	-1.0	5.4	5.2	0.5	1.7	-1.1	6.1	3.8	9.9
Kuwait	-6.1	3.8	-1.8	9.9	0.8	-2.8	-3.1	1.3	10.4	-4.0	6.4
Kyrgyz Republic	0.3	0.6	1.9	-2.1	4.5	4.4	4.9	-2.3	1.6	9.1	10.7
Lao PDR	1.5	0.0	0.3	1.4	4.4	-0.9	-1.9	-0.1	3.9	0.0	3.8
Latvia	1.4	0.0	-1.0	7.3	1.2	0.0	-2.1	-3.1	7.2	-1.8	5.4
Lebanon	-1.4	4.6	-0.6	-1.6	-0.9	-3.6	1.6	0.5	-1.0	-2.8	-3.7
Lesotho	3.5	2.6	0.0	6.1	9.1	-9.6	6.9	-5.4	11.5	-2.2	9.2
Liberia	-0.6	-1.2	6.9	17.7	4.2	0.0	-7.7	-3.0	24.0	-4.0	20.0
Lithuania	0.3	0.2	1.1	2.5	6.6	-2.4	-2.3	-1.2	6.6	-1.1	5.6
Luxembourg	-1.0	-2.9	-2.4	0.7	5.3	-0.9	-1.3	0.4	0.8	1.0	1.7
Macedonia, FYR	-1.2	-1.5	-0.9	1.8	-0.2	-0.6	0.8	0.3	0.6	-0.1	0.5
Madagascar	-3.9	0.1	-2.8	0.0	-3.3	-2.7	0.7	1.2	-3.6	-3.5	-7.1
Malawi	-1.8	1.6	2.5	0.5	-1.4	-0.1	-3.0	-0.5	2.0	-3.0	-1.1
Malaysia	-1.6	0.5	0.8	0.9	4.1	-1.9	-0.1	-0.6	3.7	-0.1	3.6
Maldives	18.0	-3.1	-0.1	2.0	-1.2	-3.9	2.1	0.4	0.3	-3.1	-2.8
Mali	0.8	0.2	-0.4	-3.3	4.6	-3.3	0.8	0.0	-1.2	-0.5	-1.6
Malta	-0.8	-0.2	-1.8	1.0	-0.4	-0.3	-1.6	-0.2	-0.5	-1.6	-2.1
Mauritius	0.5	-0.9	-1.3	0.2	2.4	0.6	0.8	-0.6	0.2	2.2	2.4
Mexico	1.6	0.2	0.1	1.6	2.9	-0.8	-1.5	0.0	3.2	-0.2	3.0
Moldova	2.4	2.8	2.1	-0.4	3.7	-4.4	-2.1	-0.2	3.8	-4.1	-0.3
Mongolia	-7.5	-1.3	9.1	2.3	-2.4	0.1	2.3	0.2	6.8	0.5	7.3
Montenegro	-1.5	2.8	1.1	6.7	0.8	-2.9	-0.3	-0.9	8.7	-3.0	5.7
Morocco	4.2	-1.6	-0.4	3.5	-1.2	0.5	3.2	-1.8	2.0	1.4	3.4
Mozambique	-1.9	4.1	1.2	-0.3	4.8	-0.1	1.7	0.6	4.2	3.6	7.8
Myanmar	-0.3	1.8	-0.7	-1.4	1.8	1.4	-0.7	-0.4	-0.3	1.7	1.4
Namibia	-1.6	-0.8	-0.3	1.7	3.4	2.0	-2.0	-1.5	2.9	1.8	4.7
Nepal	0.5	-1.2	2.5	1.1	3.2	-0.3	1.1	1.1	4.0	2.5	6.5
Netherlands	-1.4	0.8	-0.7	0.9	4.8	-0.4	-0.7	-0.1	3.2	1.5	4.6
New Zealand	0.9	1.4	-0.1	1.8	1.6	0.7	-0.1	-1.9	3.0	0.8	3.8
Nicaragua	0.5	0.8	0.4	0.9	1.5	-1.0	1.2	0.3	2.2	0.7	2.9
Niger	-0.5	-0.4	3.4	-0.4	1.8	-3.1	2.5	-1.1	2.7	-0.9	1.8
Nigeria	4.9	-9.8	5.6	0.1	2.3	2.6	-4.0	-2.8	1.8	0.2	2.0
Norway	-3.2	-1.5	0.7	-0.5	6.6	-0.7	-0.9	0.5	2.8	2.2	4.9
Oman	-4.1	-0.6	0.9	-6.0	10.0	-5.5	0.6	1.4	-0.6	0.4	-0.3
Pakistan	0.8	1.2	2.4	1.5	-2.4	0.4	-0.6	-1.7	2.3	-1.8	0.5
Panama	-1.0	0.2	-0.4	1.1	1.0	1.0	1.9	-0.3	1.5	2.7	4.2
Papua New Gui.	2.0	-1.8	-2.4	1.8	7.0	-4.3	-0.4	-1.3	3.1	-1.5	1.6
Paraguay	1.0	0.4	-1.4	-1.7	4.8	-1.1	1.8	0.8	-0.1	2.8	2.7
Peru	0.5	-0.9	-0.4	1.2	1.8	-0.3	-0.7	0.0	1.5	0.1	1.6
Philippines	-0.5	-0.3	-0.2	-0.3	1.3	-0.9	-0.3	0.0	0.2	-0.4	-0.2
Poland	0.8	0.4	-1.7	1.0	1.3	1.2	0.1	-1.2	0.7	1.5	2.2
Portugal	1.0	-1.6	3.5	0.3	5.2	0.8	-2.6	-1.3	4.7	1.3	6.0
Qatar	0.3	-0.5	-1.4	-2.1	5.3	-1.8	-3.4	0.9	-0.6	-1.1	-1.7
Romania	-1.2	1.6	1.7	1.6	1.7	0.7	-1.4	-1.3	4.1	0.1	4.3
Russia	1.1	-1.7	2.0	1.2	7.1	-2.9	-0.3	-0.6	5.5	0.3	5.8
Rwanda	2.0	-1.6	1.3	1.7	-0.5	2.1	2.2	-2.3	1.8	2.6	4.4

Country	Annual Change								Period Change		
	2005	2006	2007	2008	2009	2010	2011	2012	2008-09 vs. 2005-7	2010-12 vs. 2008-09	2010-12 vs. 2005-07
Samoa	3.8	-3.7	3.5	-3.0	5.6	12.5	-6.9	-3.8	0.9	9.4	10.3
São Tomé & Prí.	-8.7	6.9	-10.9	-9.6	14.9	1.2	0.6	-9.8	-7.1	5.9	-1.3
Saudi Arabia	-4.0	-0.1	2.6	-3.0	14.0	-3.4	-0.8	-1.7	5.7	2.5	8.2
Senegal	0.9	3.0	0.9	-1.0	0.2	0.6	0.7	-1.0	0.7	0.8	1.5
Serbia	-1.0	3.3	0.1	-0.5	1.2	-1.4	-1.7	-0.1	1.2	-2.0	-0.7
Seychelles	-3.0	8.8	-5.2	-11.2	5.8	0.5	1.4	-3.4	-8.8	3.2	-5.6
Sierra Leone	-0.3	-1.8	-5.9	3.9	2.2	4.4	-0.2	-8.3	0.5	2.6	3.1
Singapore	-2.0	0.5	-0.9	5.0	0.4	-1.8	1.7	-0.1	4.8	-0.5	4.3
Slovak Republic	0.3	-1.4	-2.3	0.6	6.6	-0.5	-2.7	-0.9	1.9	0.7	2.6
Slovenia	0.2	-0.2	-2.3	1.1	5.0	0.0	0.3	-1.5	2.0	2.2	4.3
Solomon Islands	8.6	3.2	-0.9	4.7	4.2	5.3	2.6	-3.6	7.3	7.9	15.2
South Africa	0.2	-0.2	1.3	2.5	2.7	-0.3	-0.3	-0.4	4.6	0.7	5.3
Spain	-0.4	-0.1	0.8	2.1	4.5	-0.8	-2.0	-0.9	4.9	-0.2	4.6
Sri Lanka	1.0	0.4	-0.8	-0.9	2.3	-2.0	-0.8	-0.7	-0.2	-1.7	-1.8
St. Kitts and	1.7	-0.4	-1.9	-0.7	2.1	1.9	-0.7	-1.8	-1.0	1.9	0.8
St. Lucia	0.0	-0.5	-5.1	1.7	2.6	1.6	3.4	-4.3	-0.5	3.7	3.2
St. Vincent & Gr.	1.6	-0.7	0.9	1.5	3.2	-0.2	-2.3	1.2	3.4	0.3	3.7
Sudan	4.8	0.2	0.7	-2.2	-3.0	-2.2	0.6	-4.1	-3.2	-4.7	-7.9
Suriname	1.1	-3.0	2.1	-2.3	7.3	-3.2	-2.3	-1.6	1.7	-1.6	0.1
Swaziland	0.1	-2.5	-0.9	6.8	4.9	-2.8	-5.7	-2.2	7.7	-4.9	2.9
Sweden	-0.3	-1.1	-1.8	0.7	3.5	-2.1	-2.7	-1.2	0.8	-2.5	-1.7
Switzerland	-0.3	-1.8	-1.0	-2.0	1.8	-0.1	0.1	0.0	-2.4	0.8	-1.6
Syria	-3.2	-1.5	-0.9	-2.8	3.8	0.1	5.2	-1.7	-2.0	4.9	2.9
Taiwan	0.3	-1.7	-0.1	1.0	2.0	-2.1	-0.5	-0.8	1.4	-1.7	-0.3
Tajikistan	2.7	-1.1	6.1	-0.8	1.5	-2.5	1.3	-0.7	3.6	-1.2	2.4
Tanzania	2.3	1.1	0.2	-0.2	3.3	1.5	2.2	-0.1	1.9	4.5	6.5
Thailand	0.4	-1.0	1.2	-0.1	2.8	-0.5	0.1	-0.6	1.8	0.7	2.5
Togo	2.7	1.9	-0.8	-2.5	3.4	1.2	3.7	0.6	-0.7	5.6	4.9
Tonga	4.5	0.2	-1.7	0.4	4.0	1.7	-3.9	-4.4	1.4	-0.4	1.0
Trinidad & Tob.	1.5	4.6	-2.6	1.9	8.1	1.0	0.7	-0.7	5.8	5.3	11.0
Tunisia	0.1	-0.1	0.3	1.1	0.3	0.1	3.4	-0.8	1.4	2.2	3.6
Turkey	-2.5	0.2	0.5	0.5	3.8	-2.1	-0.8	-0.2	2.8	-0.8	2.1
Turkmenistan	0.8	-4.7	-1.5	-2.6	3.7	1.0	2.6	-1.4	-3.3	4.2	0.8
Uganda	0.4	-1.5	-0.4	0.2	-1.1	2.4	4.0	-0.7	-1.1	4.3	3.2
Ukraine	2.6	0.5	-0.8	3.6	1.1	-0.1	-3.5	-1.6	3.8	-2.4	1.4
United Arab Em.	-2.9	-0.3	0.7	2.2	8.4	-1.1	-2.1	0.1	6.7	1.7	8.5
United Kingdom	0.8	0.0	-0.3	2.3	4.5	-0.3	-1.2	-1.2	4.4	0.7	5.1
United States	0.3	-0.3	0.8	2.6	4.8	-2.8	0.0	-0.7	5.4	-0.6	4.8
Uruguay	-0.7	0.4	-0.7	-0.4	1.8	0.4	-0.1	0.0	0.2	1.3	1.5
Uzbekistan	-2.0	-0.5	1.4	-0.4	3.6	0.8	2.2	-0.7	2.1	3.8	6.0
Vanuatu	-0.2	1.7	1.8	5.9	-0.3	0.1	-2.2	-0.9	7.5	-1.8	5.7
Venezuela	1.6	5.6	-3.0	-1.8	-1.3	3.9	2.5	1.2	-2.6	5.3	2.7
Vietnam	2.9	-1.5	1.4	-0.5	5.4	-1.6	-1.9	0.1	2.6	-0.2	2.4
Yemen	2.6	0.6	3.0	0.9	-6.0	-5.4	-2.4	2.7	0.1	-9.1	-9.0
Zambia	-0.6	-2.6	0.8	-0.4	-2.4	1.3	1.6	3.0	-1.9	2.1	0.2

Source: Authors' calculations based on IMF's *World Economic Outlook* (September 2011)

B. Real Growth, as a percent*

Country	Annual Growth								Period Growth		
	2005	2006	2007	2008	2009	2010	2011	2012	2008-09 vs. 2005-7	2010-12 vs. 2008-09	2010-12 vs. 2005-07
Afghanistan	20.3	34.8	11.8	-4.6	34.0	5.0	22.4	15.1	30.9	45.6	90.5
Albania	2.2	8.9	6.3	18.4	8.4	-6.7	0.6	6.3	32.0	-0.5	31.3
Algeria	6.7	16.9	22.5	28.3	-4.7	2.8	32.3	-6.1	49.6	19.3	78.3
Angola	18.5	33.0	10.6	47.5	-21.7	-1.4	14.9	6.6	52.7	-2.6	48.8
Antigua & Barb.	9.6	37.7	1.4	-3.0	23.9	-43.6	1.8	-2.7	20.6	-37.3	-24.4
Argentina	5.3	10.3	24.4	19.2	15.8	16.5	14.3	4.8	52.4	39.2	112.2
Armenia	...	15.8	27.1	3.1	9.2	-5.8	-0.5	-1.6	31.2	-2.5	27.8
Australia	4.4	5.6	5.5	5.5	8.7	3.4	1.8	0.1	16.1	9.0	26.5
Austria	-4.9	2.2	2.4	1.5	3.7	1.8	0.3	1.0	5.8	4.2	10.2
Azerbaijan	17.3	66.9	22.9	33.1	0.2	5.8	15.9	-1.6	73.7	16.5	102.3
Bahamas	7.3	7.3	11.8	-0.9	4.9	-3.6	5.2	3.4	11.6	3.3	15.3
Bahrain	13.3	9.8	10.1	15.7	-5.9	21.4	26.3	-4.4	23.2	36.1	67.7
Bangladesh	8.1	4.4	-0.7	25.9	-2.5	4.9	13.6	19.5	25.5	20.6	51.3
Barbados	17.5	-3.2	16.8	-8.9	-10.6	-2.7	-7.6	1.0	-5.6	-12.5	-17.4
Belarus	22.4	14.4	12.6	16.4	-8.5	4.7	-3.4	-0.9	25.5	-2.6	22.2
Belgium	7.2	-4.1	3.0	2.0	6.1	-0.5	2.0	1.6	5.6	4.4	10.3
Belize	-7.9	11.4	0.3	-3.7	-1.9	7.0	7.9	0.9	-1.1	11.9	10.7
Benin	6.5	-6.0	27.7	-4.8	20.0	-16.5	16.8	1.6	20.1	1.9	22.3
Bhutan	24.1	1.7	9.1	5.6	-1.6	23.0	24.4	-6.3	11.5	38.7	54.7
Bolivia	7.7	2.7	10.1	11.8	0.1	-2.8	12.8	5.4	20.1	7.5	29.2
Bosnia & Herz.	4.6	6.3	13.2	12.3	-1.2	-0.5	-1.4	0.0	23.4	-2.0	21.0
Botswana	-6.6	0.3	17.5	25.7	3.9	-4.1	0.6	-9.7	42.5	-5.0	35.3
Brazil	8.0	6.4	5.2	6.0	2.8	14.7	0.4	3.3	13.5	17.8	33.6
Brunei	3.4	9.7	5.8	0.4	-2.8	11.5	2.7	3.6	5.8	13.3	19.9
Bulgaria	5.8	1.4	12.2	3.5	-1.0	1.5	-1.9	5.4	11.5	1.4	13.1
Burkina Faso	5.7	11.6	16.1	-17.6	21.2	16.1	7.4	-6.0	3.8	30.8	35.7
Burundi	-4.3	11.1	46.1	10.5	-4.6	13.5	-7.0	-5.6	40.8	3.7	46.1
Cambodia	0.5	14.7	22.1	3.7	31.9	4.1	-6.5	7.0	42.5	15.9	65.1
Cameroon	-5.8	1.8	11.6	21.1	-4.7	5.7	10.5	1.3	27.8	10.9	41.7
Canada	2.7	3.7	3.0	3.4	6.0	3.8	-1.4	0.7	9.8	6.1	16.5
Cape Verde	9.7	6.6	-4.9	5.9	8.2	17.5	5.7	-2.3	8.9	25.8	37.0
Central Afr. Rep.	26.1	-16.4	-0.6	22.2	1.8	12.4	-1.3	6.1	15.3	14.7	32.2
Chad	15.0	-4.2	103.6	13.8	2.5	33.4	-6.7	-12.4	72.5	23.9	113.7
Chile	7.0	6.6	9.3	7.0	14.9	8.0	5.3	3.8	24.3	21.1	50.6
China	16.6	17.1	17.2	18.3	26.0	10.9	8.0	9.5	55.4	34.5	108.9
Colombia	4.0	17.7	6.7	-2.8	12.1	-0.6	10.5	1.2	13.1	12.9	27.8
Comoros	2.4	6.8	6.3	18.5	-10.2	7.8	0.6	1.9	19.6	3.1	23.3
Congo, Dem.	75.1	-17.2	8.7	27.9	11.2	14.8	25.1	-2.3	33.7	39.9	87.1
Congo, Rep. of	15.4	38.3	4.3	-1.4	-14.7	8.9	23.3	2.2	3.3	16.8	20.6
Costa Rica	0.7	1.9	4.5	8.4	8.6	16.3	5.5	6.3	17.2	28.2	50.2
Côte d'Ivoire	0.4	7.6	1.0	7.2	2.3	7.5	-15.2	25.9	11.8	5.7	18.2
Croatia	1.7	5.5	8.2	-1.4	-1.2	-2.0	-1.7	0.5	5.0	-3.5	1.3
Cyprus	7.6	4.1	3.1	5.0	7.4	2.3	1.9	-0.9	12.5	7.0	20.4
Czech Republic	3.7	2.4	3.6	-1.0	4.2	-1.9	1.0	1.7	4.3	1.4	5.8

Country	Annual Growth								Period Growth		
	2005	2006	2007	2008	2009	2010	2011	2012	2008-09 vs. 2005-7	2010-12 vs. 2008-09	2010-12 vs. 2005-07
Denmark	0.3	0.1	1.2	1.3	5.7	2.1	0.2	-0.4	5.0	4.9	10.2
Djibouti	1.3	6.4	6.1	11.3	7.5	-10.4	4.1	4.1	22.5	-3.4	18.4
Dominica	3.7	0.6	20.4	3.3	7.7	-9.3	-4.4	-2.0	21.2	-9.3	9.9
Dominican Rep.	3.3	15.2	5.0	19.1	-4.4	0.0	-1.6	1.9	25.8	-2.7	22.3
Ecuador	14.7	8.9	24.0	35.9	-7.3	11.8	16.4	2.6	54.2	20.3	85.6
Egypt	0.2	25.1	1.5	8.6	-2.7	0.2	5.3	0.8	15.9	2.6	18.9
El Salvador	5.3	8.2	-0.5	2.9	6.8	3.3	2.4	-1.6	8.8	7.8	17.3
Equatorial	19.1	36.2	28.2	49.6	47.9	-17.0	7.2	-3.6	136.5	2.4	142.3
Eritrea	2.9	-31.4	-3.4	-7.9	-26.5	14.4	5.1	-4.0	-32.3	-1.1	-33.0
Estonia	12.9	12.6	13.5	8.2	-1.3	-2.8	-0.6	2.4	21.1	-3.1	17.3
Ethiopia	13.7	6.1	4.9	5.3	-9.7	20.1	16.3	11.2	5.4	31.3	38.3
Fiji	2.4	7.0	-11.8	-7.0	12.3	-7.3	3.2	3.4	-7.3	1.4	-6.0
Finland	2.9	1.6	2.9	3.3	4.0	1.4	0.7	1.5	7.9	4.4	12.7
France	2.4	1.6	2.6	0.6	4.0	0.4	0.5	0.3	4.8	2.8	7.8
Gabon	19.7	9.8	-1.9	8.0	-3.2	24.2	9.3	1.4	8.2	30.3	41.0
Gambia	-2.2	5.0	-18.6	8.8	31.2	11.0	12.7	-7.9	11.0	32.9	47.5
Georgia	25.3	14.0	37.7	17.2	1.6	-0.6	-4.5	1.1	50.0	-2.5	46.3
Germany	-1.0	-1.4	-1.7	-0.3	4.6	1.0	-1.2	-0.4	0.4	2.4	2.8
Ghana	-0.5	20.0	18.5	18.8	-7.3	23.1	9.8	-0.3	34.8	26.1	70.0
Greece	-1.9	7.9	7.8	6.5	4.2	-12.4	-9.4	-3.6	17.0	-17.2	-3.1
Grenada	16.3	14.0	-8.3	1.6	-7.5	-4.2	-3.2	0.1	-3.8	-9.8	-13.2
Guatemala	2.3	11.0	3.8	-3.1	6.3	6.6	3.0	1.3	6.0	12.5	19.3
Guinea	-6.0	17.9	-27.3	19.4	38.0	33.0	13.3	-41.0	20.4	44.1	73.5
Guinea-Bissau	-7.3	-4.4	8.9	14.2	-5.1	-1.9	10.4	3.2	16.0	3.3	19.8
Guyana	16.8	6.4	-7.3	-1.2	7.6	1.2	14.1	1.2	-0.5	15.2	14.6
Haiti	44.6	-1.6	5.2	14.7	27.9	17.9	-19.1	62.0	34.4	37.5	84.9
Honduras	0.8	7.9	6.1	8.9	-0.8	-3.2	-2.2	-0.2	15.6	-5.0	9.8
Hong Kong	-4.6	-4.6	1.5	28.7	-7.7	0.7	20.0	-4.9	23.0	7.7	32.4
Hungary	4.9	7.9	-5.1	-2.7	-3.3	-4.0	4.4	-6.4	-5.2	-4.9	-9.9
Iceland	-2.2	5.2	8.2	6.4	0.2	-6.3	-3.4	-1.2	14.0	-8.6	4.2
India	7.0	8.1	10.2	11.6	7.2	2.9	2.3	5.1	26.3	10.0	38.9
Indonesia	2.9	14.2	12.7	19.5	-7.3	9.1	13.5	1.5	29.6	15.0	49.0
Iran	37.0	12.2	-7.7	7.0	-11.9	0.8	15.0	-2.2	-0.9	3.0	2.0
Iraq	...	-32.5	-18.3	70.3	-12.5	2.0	24.6	1.7	18.7	11.5	32.3
Ireland	7.1	8.1	10.5	7.4	4.2	36.0	-32.1	-0.8	20.0	8.9	30.7
Israel	0.0	4.2	3.3	0.4	2.0	2.5	6.2	4.5	5.0	9.4	14.9
Italy	1.4	2.8	0.2	0.0	2.1	-2.3	-1.1	-1.1	2.1	-2.3	-0.3
Jamaica	-9.3	9.8	4.6	0.7	9.2	-18.1	-2.6	1.9	11.8	-15.4	-5.5
Japan	1.0	2.3	-2.2	3.4	6.0	1.8	3.1	1.3	5.7	7.4	13.5
Jordan	9.8	5.4	10.4	4.8	11.1	-8.7	14.7	-7.9	20.0	2.6	23.2
Kazakhstan	20.7	10.7	36.2	21.7	-14.6	14.6	12.7	2.0	41.2	15.3	62.7
Kenya	8.0	10.0	14.7	3.7	4.4	15.8	4.8	4.6	19.3	24.0	48.0
Kiribati	-5.6	-5.5	-10.5	3.1	-4.2	2.9	7.2	4.7	-8.2	7.2	-1.6
Korea, Rep. of	0.8	5.9	6.3	2.9	3.9	-1.5	1.3	1.8	11.3	1.9	13.3
Kosovo	-2.5	-12.5	-1.0	32.6	26.3	5.1	8.5	2.3	42.3	25.0	77.8
Kuwait	6.4	37.5	-1.1	47.5	-22.8	8.0	9.6	3.7	42.8	1.4	44.8

Country	Annual Growth								Period Growth		
	2005	2006	2007	2008	2009	2010	2011	2012	2008-09 vs. 2005-7	2010-12 vs. 2008-09	2010-12 vs. 2005-07
Kyrgyz Republic	3.7	9.2	20.4	-0.9	15.9	10.7	13.6	-0.6	23.9	29.3	60.1
Lao PDR	17.8	14.7	12.0	13.8	28.1	1.1	-1.5	8.4	45.9	15.5	68.5
Latvia	18.6	15.6	16.9	14.6	-19.6	-1.5	-2.0	-5.4	19.5	-14.9	1.6
Lebanon	-3.4	11.6	5.5	3.3	11.6	-4.4	5.4	4.9	17.2	6.2	24.5
Lesotho	13.2	11.5	7.0	17.7	21.5	-6.8	22.1	-2.7	41.0	16.1	63.8
Liberia	4.3	-4.3	64.7	84.6	6.7	4.9	-12.3	5.1	155.4	1.0	157.8
Lithuania	12.9	11.5	16.4	8.9	-7.2	-3.5	1.0	0.9	19.7	-6.2	12.3
Luxembourg	5.0	1.4	1.3	4.2	9.5	4.4	0.0	4.6	10.6	10.9	22.6
Macedonia, FYR	4.1	0.5	8.5	10.0	-0.1	0.5	6.6	6.5	16.2	7.2	24.6
Madagascar	-11.4	6.1	-8.4	6.9	-21.4	-17.1	6.8	14.2	-8.2	-20.1	-26.6
Malawi	0.9	12.7	23.3	10.8	4.9	7.7	-4.9	-0.9	34.5	6.3	43.0
Malaysia	0.9	8.1	13.0	13.3	3.8	4.5	4.7	3.4	28.0	11.0	42.2
Maldives	49.1	18.2	9.7	10.6	2.6	-6.1	10.2	0.3	25.3	1.7	27.4
Mali	7.0	10.1	3.8	-9.5	29.0	-5.6	10.5	5.8	9.5	16.1	27.1
Malta	2.4	1.8	2.8	5.8	-3.6	3.4	-0.6	2.1	6.4	1.9	8.4
Mauritius	3.0	-1.3	-0.5	3.3	11.1	5.7	5.9	0.7	8.2	15.9	25.4
Mexico	11.6	9.3	5.1	9.8	4.0	2.7	-1.7	3.1	19.0	4.6	24.5
Moldova	12.3	13.5	11.9	3.5	4.6	-0.1	2.9	3.3	18.4	5.3	24.7
Mongolia	-9.6	32.0	53.3	11.2	-11.4	16.3	22.5	6.4	46.5	28.5	88.3
Montenegro	1.0	23.6	22.9	23.1	-5.0	-5.1	-0.8	0.6	45.7	-7.8	34.3
Morocco	21.4	-0.2	2.9	21.7	1.0	5.5	16.1	-1.1	24.6	17.0	45.7
Mozambique	2.5	23.7	11.1	3.7	25.6	4.1	13.0	9.7	33.5	30.2	73.8
Myanmar	18.2	32.7	-3.1	-14.3	28.3	19.5	-2.3	0.8	4.5	32.5	38.5
Namibia	2.1	7.4	7.5	11.0	9.7	11.9	-2.5	-0.6	24.9	14.9	43.5
Nepal	8.6	-5.6	25.3	12.7	28.2	6.7	9.5	9.5	45.9	31.6	92.0
Netherlands	0.1	5.4	2.7	3.8	5.1	1.2	-0.7	0.6	10.2	3.4	13.9
New Zealand	5.4	6.1	4.9	4.9	3.6	4.5	2.1	-2.8	12.3	6.7	19.9
Nicaragua	6.4	5.9	3.7	1.3	3.4	2.0	8.5	3.0	7.5	10.7	19.0
Niger	5.1	4.9	26.3	4.1	10.1	-5.1	18.6	7.3	28.9	14.6	47.7
Nigeria	26.5	-18.6	32.5	5.9	-1.6	15.9	-0.4	-8.0	17.6	11.6	31.2
Norway	2.1	4.5	6.2	5.3	5.6	3.0	2.5	3.1	14.2	8.6	24.1
Oman	10.1	13.2	10.3	6.4	0.3	2.9	13.1	3.6	18.1	13.5	34.1
Pakistan	10.7	16.3	19.1	13.1	-8.1	6.3	0.6	-5.2	27.2	0.4	27.7
Panama	1.7	9.2	9.1	12.0	6.4	12.2	14.1	5.6	25.8	29.0	62.3
Papua New Gui.	17.2	3.4	1.8	10.2	18.6	-4.5	11.5	1.9	23.2	12.3	38.4
Paraguay	9.5	5.2	1.8	-0.7	18.6	8.9	13.7	6.9	11.6	32.1	47.5
Peru	11.2	7.9	6.4	11.6	9.7	10.3	3.8	5.2	24.9	20.4	50.3
Philippines	0.2	1.9	5.7	0.9	8.9	2.8	2.9	4.8	10.0	11.0	22.0
Poland	6.1	7.7	4.2	6.5	4.9	5.5	1.8	0.1	14.8	9.4	25.5
Portugal	3.5	-2.7	11.9	-0.3	10.4	2.7	-9.1	-5.0	12.0	-0.4	11.5
Qatar	29.2	18.3	12.9	0.1	21.3	27.4	8.3	3.9	26.1	49.3	88.2
Romania	3.2	17.5	20.9	20.0	-4.1	-1.1	-4.2	0.5	39.3	-5.7	31.3
Russia	16.4	7.8	20.4	12.7	1.5	0.9	8.7	2.2	31.0	8.4	42.0
Rwanda	19.7	1.9	16.2	16.6	2.5	16.7	16.9	-2.1	30.9	30.5	71.0
Samoa	14.9	-5.5	15.8	-5.0	-0.1	35.1	-11.8	-6.9	2.5	21.6	24.7
São Tomé & Prí.	-19.0	20.1	-15.7	-18.6	61.3	3.0	3.2	-16.9	0.4	22.4	23.0

Country	Annual Growth								Period Growth		
	2005	2006	2007	2008	2009	2010	2011	2012	2008-09 vs. 2005-7	2010-12 vs. 2008-09	2010-12 vs. 2005-07
Saudi Arabia	11.2	10.0	12.3	2.9	8.6	4.4	16.3	-5.4	19.3	18.2	41.1
Senegal	10.5	17.5	7.9	0.2	3.7	6.6	6.6	1.1	12.7	13.7	28.2
Serbia	1.5	11.7	9.2	2.7	-3.2	0.5	-2.8	3.0	10.9	-2.0	8.7
Seychelles	-0.9	37.3	3.1	-31.7	11.0	9.4	8.4	-6.6	-19.2	18.8	-4.0
Sierra Leone	6.9	1.4	-21.8	26.0	10.1	21.3	0.2	5.5	12.2	29.6	45.3
Singapore	-3.6	13.9	5.9	22.3	7.4	-0.3	12.2	3.6	37.2	13.0	55.0
Slovak Republic	7.1	3.3	2.8	6.7	10.8	2.5	-5.7	0.0	15.7	3.6	19.9
Slovenia	3.7	5.0	1.7	5.0	5.1	0.1	2.1	-1.6	10.7	3.5	14.5
Solomon Islands	35.1	9.0	17.2	6.6	9.2	18.9	7.2	-1.9	26.9	29.3	64.0
South Africa	8.7	7.8	11.0	8.7	7.7	6.5	3.1	3.3	23.7	14.0	41.0
Spain	3.4	4.4	6.2	4.5	7.7	-3.0	-5.0	-1.0	14.5	-3.1	11.0
Sri Lanka	10.5	10.9	1.8	-3.4	16.7	0.5	2.7	3.4	9.4	11.5	22.0
St. Kitts and	9.7	5.1	-0.2	0.7	-0.2	5.2	-1.1	-4.3	2.1	2.8	5.0
St. Lucia	3.6	5.2	-12.4	5.1	9.9	9.5	13.0	-9.9	2.5	20.4	23.4
St. Vincent & Gr.	9.5	4.5	8.5	-2.4	6.0	0.6	-8.3	7.0	7.6	0.0	7.6
Sudan	37.5	9.9	13.1	1.2	-18.2	1.7	-4.4	-26.9	2.6	-19.0	-16.9
Suriname	14.0	-3.9	15.2	1.4	36.5	-4.3	-0.6	0.1	29.8	10.1	42.9
Swaziland	5.0	-0.2	2.7	19.9	12.5	-3.7	-15.9	-7.2	29.7	-10.9	15.5
Sweden	2.6	2.6	0.7	0.6	1.1	0.9	-0.9	1.4	2.4	1.3	3.8
Switzerland	0.7	-0.4	2.4	-3.9	4.2	1.7	2.6	1.4	-0.5	6.1	5.6
Syria	-0.3	-3.1	9.3	-6.2	16.8	5.4	22.8	-6.0	6.7	28.1	36.7
Taiwan	2.4	-3.9	3.0	-1.1	8.8	-1.3	3.4	0.3	3.8	5.3	9.3
Tajikistan	23.4	11.6	55.6	11.1	15.9	2.7	17.4	7.4	62.1	26.2	104.6
Tanzania	23.1	12.9	8.7	7.5	18.4	8.9	15.6	4.2	28.9	32.3	70.4
Thailand	6.9	1.3	11.9	4.0	10.3	6.1	4.0	2.8	18.2	15.4	36.4
Togo	18.6	11.1	0.0	-5.5	23.0	8.2	20.3	6.9	9.0	38.9	51.3
Tonga	17.3	12.4	-9.8	2.4	11.3	4.1	-8.1	-12.9	4.8	-0.6	4.2
Trinidad & Tob.	18.6	25.2	0.2	17.0	-1.7	-12.4	-0.2	1.6	24.6	-12.8	8.6
Tunisia	5.9	4.5	6.4	9.7	3.6	3.6	12.2	1.8	17.9	14.7	35.3
Turkey	-0.3	7.2	3.9	3.7	4.9	1.0	4.7	1.9	11.4	7.4	19.6
Turkmenistan	13.8	-12.5	2.7	29.3	47.6	10.1	32.9	-1.2	55.6	59.3	147.9
Uganda	-1.4	-1.4	7.0	8.8	1.3	19.4	27.0	1.3	14.0	42.5	62.5
Ukraine	19.6	14.3	15.4	13.7	-14.9	9.4	0.6	2.5	20.2	1.9	22.5
United Arab Em.	-3.6	10.0	9.9	24.2	25.1	6.1	5.9	2.7	53.2	23.7	89.6
United Kingdom	4.3	3.6	2.6	5.0	4.4	0.3	-1.9	-0.6	10.4	1.0	11.5
United States	3.8	1.8	4.3	5.0	9.8	-3.9	0.6	0.0	14.0	1.0	15.1
Uruguay	1.2	6.8	6.2	6.7	7.2	8.5	5.0	4.3	17.4	17.6	38.1
Uzbekistan	10.4	12.2	26.6	17.3	27.5	18.1	14.0	4.9	60.5	47.2	136.2
Vanuatu	3.1	20.6	17.0	34.5	-0.6	2.7	-4.3	0.4	57.0	-0.4	56.4
Venezuela	29.5	33.1	-4.0	0.0	-20.6	26.1	11.4	2.9	-4.7	21.4	15.6
Vietnam	20.3	2.2	13.9	3.6	24.9	4.0	-1.4	6.8	27.6	17.0	49.3
Yemen	22.6	7.4	14.7	7.2	-21.9	2.7	-9.2	7.1	6.7	-13.5	-7.7
Zambia	2.0	-0.6	11.9	3.9	-6.7	17.3	14.3	18.4	7.9	32.0	42.5

Source: Authors' calculations based on IMF's *World Economic Outlook* (September 2011)
* in billions of local currency/average consumer prices

Annex 2: IMF Country Reports Reviewed, 2010-12

The identification of possible adjustment measures considered by governments is inferred from policy discussions and other information contained in IMF country reports, which cover Article IV consultations, reviews conducted under lending arrangements (e.g., Stand-by Arrangements and Extended Credit Facility) and consultations under non-lending arrangements (e.g., Staff Monitored Programs). Overall, 158 IMF country reports were reviewed to develop Tables 10 and 11 in Chapter V, all of which were published between January 2010 and February 2012. The complete list of countries, along with corresponding region, report number and date, is provided below.

Country	Region	Report #	Date Published
Afghanistan	South Asia	10/22	January 2010
Albania	Europe and Central Asia	11/313	October 2011
Algeria	Middle East and North Africa	11/39	February 2011
Angola	Sub-Saharan Africa	11/51	February 2011
Antigua and Barbuda	Latin America and Caribbean	10/279	September 2010
Armenia	Europe and Central Asia	11/178	July 2011
Australia	High-income	11/300	October 2011
Austria	High-income	11/275	September 2011
Azerbaijan	Europe and Central Asia	10/113	May 2010
Bahamas	High-income	11/338	December 2011
Bangladesh	South Asia	11/314	November 2011
Belarus	Europe and Central Asia	11/66	March 2011
Belgium	High-income	11/81	April 2011
Belize	Latin America and Caribbean	11/18	January 2011
Benin	Sub-Saharan Africa	11/60	March 2011
Bhutan	South Asia	11/123	June 2011
Bolivia	Latin America and Caribbean	11/124	June 2011
Bosnia and Herz.	Europe and Central Asia	10/348	December 2010
Botswana	Sub-Saharan Africa	11/248	August 2011
Bulgaria	Europe and Central Asia	11/179	July 2011
Burundi	Sub-Saharan Africa	11/199	July 2011
Cambodia	East Asia and Pacific	11/45	February 2011
Cameroon	Sub-Saharan Africa	10/259	July 2010
Canada	High-income	11/364	December 2011
Cape Verde	Sub-Saharan Africa	11/254	August 2011
Central African Rep.	Sub-Saharan Africa	10/332	October 2010
Chad	Sub-Saharan Africa	10/196	June 2010
Chile	Latin America and Caribbean	11/260	August 2011
China	East Asia and Pacific	11/192	July 2011
Colombia	Latin America and Caribbean	11/224	July 2011
Comoros	Sub-Saharan Africa	11/72	March 2011

Country	Region	Report #	Date Published
Congo, Dem. Rep. of	Sub-Saharan Africa	11/190	July 2011
Congo, Republic of	Sub-Saharan Africa	11/255	August 2011
Costa Rica	Latin America and Caribbean	11/161	July 2011
Côte d'Ivoire	Sub-Saharan Africa	11/194	July 2011
Cyprus	High-income	11/331	November 2011
Czech Republic	High-income	11/83	April 2011
Denmark	High-income	10/365	December 2010
Djibouti	Middle East and North Africa	10/277	September 2010
Dominica	Latin America and Caribbean	10/261	August 2010
Dominican Republic	Latin America and Caribbean	11/177	July 2011
Egypt	Middle East and North Africa	10/94	April 2010
El Salvador	Latin America and Caribbean	11/90	April 2011
Equatorial Guinea	Sub-Saharan Africa	10/103	May 2010
Estonia	High-income	11/333	November 2011
Ethiopia	Sub-Saharan Africa	10/339	November 2010
Fiji	East Asia and Pacific	11/85	April 2011
Finland	High-income	10/273	September 2010
France	High-income	11/211	July 2011
Gabon	Sub-Saharan Africa	11/97	May 2011
Gambia	Sub-Saharan Africa	11/22	January 2011
Georgia	Europe and Central Asia	11/146	June 2011
Germany	High-income	11/168	July 2011
Ghana	Sub-Saharan Africa	11/128	June 2011
Greece	High-income	11/351	December 2011
Grenada	Latin America and Caribbean	10/139	May 2010
Guatemala	Latin America and Caribbean	10/309	October 2010
Guinea-Bissau	Sub-Saharan Africa	11/119	May 2011
Guyana	Latin America and Caribbean	11/152	June 2011
Haiti	Latin America and Caribbean	11/106	May 2011
Honduras	Latin America and Caribbean	11/101	May 2011
Hungary	High-income	12/13	January 2012
India	South Asia	11/50	February 2011
Indonesia	East Asia and Pacific	10/284	September 2010
Iran	Middle East and North Africa	11/241	August 2011
Iraq	Middle East and North Africa	11/75	March 2011
Ireland	High-income	11/356	December 2011
Italy	High-income	11/173	July 2011
Jamaica	Latin America and Caribbean	11/49	February 2011
Japan	High-income	11/181	July 2011
Jordan	Middle East and North Africa	10/297	September 2010
Kazakhstan	Europe and Central Asia	11/150	June 2011
Kenya	Sub-Saharan Africa	11/165	July 2011
Kiribati	East Asia and Pacific	11/113	May 2011
Korea, Rep. of	High-income	11/246	August 2011
Kosovo	Europe and Central Asia	11/210	July 2011
Kyrgyz Republic	Europe and Central Asia	11/155	June 2011
Lao PDR	East Asia and Pacific	11/257	August 2011

Country	Region	Report #	Date Published
Lebanon	Middle East and North Africa	10/306	October 2010
Lesotho	Sub-Saharan Africa	11/88	April 2011
Liberia	Sub-Saharan Africa	11/174	July 2011
Lithuania	Europe and Central Asia	10/201	July 2010
Macedonia, FYR	Europe and Central Asia	11/42	February 2011
Malaysia	East Asia and Pacific	10/265	August 2010
Maldives	South Asia	10/167	June 2010
Mali	Sub-Saharan Africa	11/141	June 2011
Marshall Islands	East Asia and Pacific	11/43	February 2011
Mauritania	Sub-Saharan Africa	11/189	June 2011
Mauritius	Sub-Saharan Africa	11/96	May 2011
Mexico	Latin America and Caribbean	11/250	August 2011
Micronesia	East Asia and Pacific	11/43	February 2011
Moldova	Europe and Central Asia	11/200	July 2011
Mongolia	East Asia and Pacific	11/76	March 2011
Montenegro	Europe and Central Asia	11/100	May 2011
Morocco	Middle East and North Africa	11/341	December 2011
Mozambique	Sub-Saharan Africa	11/149	June 2011
Namibia	Sub-Saharan Africa	10/269	September 2010
Nepal	South Asia	10/185	July 2010
Netherlands	High-income	11/142	June 2011
New Zealand	High-income	11/102	April 2011
Nicaragua	Latin America and Caribbean	11/118	May 2011
Niger	Sub-Saharan Africa	11/357	December 2011
Nigeria	Sub-Saharan Africa	11/57	February 2011
Norway	High-income	12/25	February 2012
Pakistan	South Asia	10/384	December 2010
Palau	East Asia and Pacific	11/43	February 2011
Panama	Latin America and Caribbean	10/314	October 2010
Papua New Guinea	East Asia and Pacific	11/117	May 2011
Paraguay	Latin America and Caribbean	11/238	August 2011
Peru	Latin America and Caribbean	10/98	April 2010
Philippines	East Asia and Pacific	11/59	March 2011
Poland	High-income	11/166	July 2011
Portugal	High-income	11/363	December 2011
Qatar	High-income	12/18	January 2012
Romania	Europe and Central Asia	11/158	June 2011
Russia	Europe and Central Asia	10/246	July 2010
Rwanda	Sub-Saharan Africa	11/19	January 2011
Samoa	East Asia and Pacific	10/214	July 2010
São Tomé & Príncipe	Sub-Saharan Africa	10/100	April 2010
Saudi Arabia	High-income	11/292	September 2011
Senegal	Sub-Saharan Africa	11/139	June 2011
Serbia	Europe and Central Asia	11/213	July 2011
Seychelles	Sub-Saharan Africa	11/134	June 2011
Sierra Leone	Sub-Saharan Africa	11/361	December 2011
Singapore	High-income	10/226	July 2010

Country	Region	Report #	Date Published
Slovak Republic	High-income	11/122	June 2011
Slovenia	High-income	11/121	May 2011
Solomon Islands	East Asia and Pacific	11/180	July 2011
South Africa	Sub-Saharan Africa	11/258	July 2011
Spain	High-income	11/215	July 2011
Sri Lanka	South Asia	10/333	October 2010
St. Kitts and Nevis	Latin America and Caribbean	11/270	September 2011
St. Lucia	Latin America and Caribbean	11/278	September 2011
St. Vincent and Gren.	High-income	11/343	December 2011
Sudan	Sub-Saharan Africa	11/86	April 2011
Suriname	Latin America and Caribbean	11/256	August 2011
Swaziland	Sub-Saharan Africa	11/84	April 2011
Sweden	High-income	11/171	July 2011
Switzerland	High-income	11/115	May 2011
Tajikistan	Europe and Central Asia	11/130	June 2011
Tanzania	Sub-Saharan Africa	11/105	May 2011
Thailand	East Asia and Pacific	10/344	December 2010
Timor-Leste	East Asia and Pacific	11/65	March 2011
Togo	Sub-Saharan Africa	11/240	August 2011
Tonga	East Asia and Pacific	11/110	May 2011
Tunisia	Middle East and North Africa	10/282	September 2010
Turkey	Europe and Central Asia	12/16	January 2012
Tuvalu	East Asia and Pacific	11/46	February 2011
Uganda	Sub-Saharan Africa	11/308	October 2011
Ukraine	Europe and Central Asia	11/52	February 2011
United Kingdom	High-income	11/220	August 2011
United States	High-income	11/201	July 2011
Uruguay	Latin America and Caribbean	11/62	March 2011
Vanuatu	East Asia and Pacific	11/120	May 2011
Vietnam	East Asia and Pacific	10/281	September 2010
Yemen	Middle East and North Africa	10/300	September 2010
Zambia	Sub-Saharan Africa	11/196	July 2011
Zimbabwe	Sub-Saharan Africa	11/135	June 2011

VI. IDENTIFYING FISCAL SPACE: OPTIONS FOR SOCIO-ECONOMIC INVESTMENTS IN CHILDREN AND POOR HOUSEHOLDS

Isabel Ortiz, Jingqing Chai and Matthew Cummins

"Do not let this economic crisis do not let short-term austerity deflect you from your long-term commitment to the world's poorest people."

UN Secretary-General's remarks to High Level Forum on Aid Effectiveness in Busan, Republic of Korea on November 30, 2011

"At the G20 Summit meeting this weekend, you are likely to hear leaders of the world stress the need for austerity and budget consolidation at a time of crisis. I will argue exactly the opposite: that we can't afford not to invest in the developing world... In our efforts to eradicate poverty, create jobs and control disease, years of experience has shown us what works and what doesn't work. Our challenge now is to scale up our commitment. Let us all be architects of a brighter, more sustainable future... I count on your leadership and commitment for a better future for all."

UN Secretary-General's address to the Global Compact Leaders Summit in New York City on June 24, 2010

1.   Introduction

It is often argued that social and economic investments that benefit children and poor households are not affordable or that government expenditure cuts are inevitable during adjustment periods. But there are alternatives, even in the poorest countries. Finding fiscal space for critical social and economic investments is necessary for sustained equitable results for children and human development, particularly during downtimes. This rationale is not only based on the complementary effects of human and physical capital more generally, but also on the fact that children's deprivations can have irreversible adverse impacts on their future capabilities and, in turn, the long-term economic prospects of their countries. Moreover, the need to identify fiscal space for social and economic investments has never been greater. As documented in the previous chapters, poor children and their families continue to face the barrage of food, employment and fiscal austerity shocks.

The increasing and widespread adoption of expenditure contraction worldwide reflects the common perception that fiscal space has diminished in countries due to lower revenues and rising debt. However, this view is limiting and counterproductive because fiscal space is not just financing that is readily available today, but also the dynamic outcome of policy actions and reforms that governments may aggressively pursue to enhance resource mobilization. In this sense, it is feasible to find fiscal space for increased social spending and economic investments, even in the poorest countries.

To start, it is important to understand that government spending and revenue choices vary widely across the globe. For example, total public expenditure in the Republic of Korea is expected to reach 20 percent of GDP in fiscal year 2012 compared to 40 percent in the United States and nearly 56 percent in France, all of which are HICs (Figure 1). As in spending decisions, there is a similar disparity in how governments raise resources for social and economic development. While some governments utilize all possible options, others may not. Indeed, many countries—including some of the poorest—have succeeded in mobilizing significant resources for public investments during downturns. By utilizing all possible options to expand fiscal space and invest in their people, these countries have achieved a virtuous circle of sustained growth and further expansion of fiscal space; they set inspiring examples to others who have remain trapped in limited fiscal space, low social investments and weak economic growth. Acknowledging the risks of premature and/or excessive fiscal consolidation, the new Managing Director of the IMF, Christine Lagarde, called for "aggressive exploration of all possible measures that could be effective in supporting short-term growth."[1]

---

[1] Lagarde, C. 2011. "Don't Let the Fiscal Brakes Stall Global Recovery." *Financial Times*, August 15.

Figure VI.1. Total Government Expenditures in Selected Countries, 2012
(in percent of GDP)

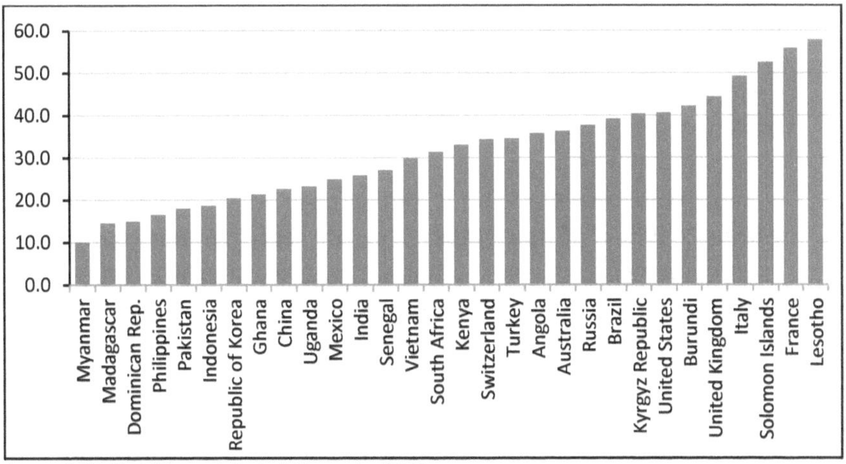

Source: IMF's *World Economic Outlook* (September 2011)

This chapter is intended to serve as a guide for governments and development partners to identify possible funding avenues to boost investments in children and poor households today in support of a *'Recovery for All.'* It is not meant to be exhaustive, nor does it address the distinct risks and trade-offs that are associated with each of the different options. As such, this chapter should be viewed as an overview of fiscal space-enhancing opportunities that are to be further explored at the country level. Given the priority of the UN to support human development, this chapter ties many of the different options together by making comparisons in health spending in order to illustrate the possible benefits of increasing investments in key human development areas.[2]

The structure is straightforward: each section describes one of six options that are available to governments to expand fiscal space today, even in the poorest countries. These different areas are summarized below, all of which are supported by policy statements of the UN and international financial institutions:[3]

---

[2] The option of privatizing public assets, services and enterprises is not considered in this paper given the remaining limited scope for privatization in most developing countries and the potential problems associated with earlier privatizations, namely, the loss of future revenues and the lack of extension of coverage of services, as well as the general absence of results to provide more affordable services.

[3] See, for example, Development Committee (2006), Roy et al. (2007), IMF (2009), United Nations (2009a), UNICEF (2009), ILO (2010), UNDP (2010), UNESCO (2010) and WHO (2010).

i. *Re-allocating current public expenditures:* This is the most orthodox option, which includes assessing ongoing budget allocations through public expenditure reviews and thematic budgets, replacing high-cost, low-impact investments with those with larger socio-economic impacts, eliminating spending inefficiencies and/or tackling corruption (Section 2).

ii. *Increasing tax revenue:* This is a main channel achieved by altering different types of tax rates—e.g., on consumption, corporate profits, financial activities, personal income, property, imports or exports, etc.—or by strengthening the efficiency of tax collection methods and overall compliance (Section 3).

iii. *Increased aid and transfers:* This requires either engaging with different donor governments in order to ramp up North-South or South-South transfers, or reducing South-North transfers, such as illicit financial flows (IFFs) (Section 4).

iv. *Using fiscal and central bank foreign exchange reserves:* This includes drawing down fiscal savings and other state revenues stored in special funds, such as sovereign wealth funds, and/or using excess foreign exchange reserves in the central bank for domestic and regional development (Section 5).

v. *Borrowing or restructuring existing debt:* This involves active exploration of domestic and foreign borrowing options that are at low costs, if not concessional, following a careful assessment of debt sustainability. For those countries under high debt distress, restructuring existing debt may be possible and justifiable if the legitimacy of the debt is questionable and/or the opportunity cost in terms of worsening deprivations of children and other vulnerable groups is high (Section 6).

vi. *Adopting a more accommodating macroeconomic framework:* This entails allowing for higher budget deficit paths and higher levels of inflation without jeopardizing macroeconomic stability (Section 7).

The uniqueness of each country requires that fiscal space options be carefully examined at the national level and fully explored in an inclusive dialogue of recovery alternatives. A good starting point for country-level analysis may be a summary of the latest fiscal space indicators, which is provided in Annex 1 for 184 countries and offers a general overview of which funding possibilities may or may not be potentially feasible for a given country. Box 1 illustrates how a rapid fiscal space analysis could be performed.

Box VI.1. Identifying Fiscal Space: How to use Annex 1

Annex 1 provides a snapshot of different fiscal space indicators for 184 countries and can be used as a resource to carry out a rapid analysis of resource options that may be available to a particular government. It is important to note that Annex 1 only serves as a reference starting point. It is therefore critical to acquire the latest available figures, as well as projections, for relevant indicators and to perform in-depth analysis and outcome assessments for all possible scenarios. Moreover, such exercises should be carried out in consultation with development partners and key stakeholders.

The data below are extracted from Annex 1 and represent examples of two developing countries from different continents: Bangladesh and Guatemala. Examination of their different fiscal space indicators reveals numerous opportunities to boost social and economic investments today.

Country	(i) Govt. Expends.				(ii) Revenue		(iii) ODA	(iv) Illicit Fin. Flows	(v) Foreign Reserves	(vi) Debt			(vii) Budget Deficit	(viii) Inflation
	Total	Health	Educ.	Military	Total	Tax				External stocks	Total	service		
Bangladesh	16.1	1.1	2.4	1.1	12.7	8.6	1.4	2.5	7.8	24.0	1.0		-3.4	10.1
Guatemala	14.4	2.6	3.2	0.4	11.4	10.4	1.0	4.5	12.7	38.8	4.6		-3.0	6.3
Global avg.	34.2	4.0	4.9	2.2	32.5	16.9	6.6	7.9	21.3	45.1	4.0		-1.6	6.6

Source: Annex 1 (all figures in percent of GDP, unless otherwise noted, for 2011 or latest available)

i.   In terms of **government spending**, countries can consider reallocating expenditures from areas with limited development returns to social and economic investments that benefit children and households. For instance, military expenditures in Bangladesh equal total public investments in health, suggesting that a reallocation of current spending is an area for further analysis. For both Bangladesh and Guatemala, deeper examination of the budget is required to understand the distributional impacts of current allocations and to identify spending inefficiencies as well as more effective investments (Section 2).

ii.   In terms of **tax revenue**, Bangladesh and Guatemala rank among the lowest levels of tax intake as a percent of GDP among the 184 countries with data. The revenue fiscal indicator thus indicates that deeper investigation of tax codes and collection methods is warranted in both countries, as well as improving other revenue streams or identifying new ones. Generally, it is advisable to have lesser reliance on consumer taxes, which tend to be regressive on households (e.g., VATs), and expand other types of taxation—on corporate profits, financial activities, personal income, wealth, property, tourism, imports or exports, etc.—without jeopardizing employment-generating investments. For instance, taxes on natural resource extraction have secured national development programs in many countries (e.g., Mongolia—a low-income country—financed a child benefit with a tax on copper exports) (Section 3).

iii.   At around 1 percent of GDP, levels of **official development assistance (ODA)** in Bangladesh and Guatemala point to ample scope to lobby for increased aid and transfers. As a first step, these governments could develop an enhanced aid strategy tailored to bilateral partners. Both countries could also explore enhancing South-South development cooperation with strategic emerging donors (e.g., China and India in the case of Bangladesh; Brazil, Mexico and Venezuela in the case of Guatemala) (Section 4).

iv.   The estimated size of **IFFs** is significant in both countries (2.5 percent of GDP in Bangladesh and 4.5 percent of GDP in Guatemala). In-depth analysis of IFFs could therefore identify policy changes that can re-direct these resources to achieve more public resources for children (see Section 4).

❖   The limited availability of data inhibits an assessment of **fiscal reserves** as a potential source for either country, and further investigation is required. Here, the primary concern is that many governments channel a part of their fiscal reserves into special funds, which often invest in capital markets in higher-income economies instead of using these resources for national and regional socio-economic development (Section 5).

v.   In terms of **foreign exchange reserves**, central banks in Bangladesh and Guatemala do not appear to be holding excessive levels, and other fiscal space options should be prioritized (Section 5 describes how reserves can be channeled into national development initiatives that benefit children and poor households, and includes details on the implied impacts on the money supply and/or debt).

vi.   Regarding **debt**, Guatemala's annual service payments approach 5 percent of GDP, which nearly equals the total spent on education and health combined, suggesting that strategies to lower payments through debt restructuring may be worth examining to achieve more public resources for children. At less than 25 percent of GDP, Bangladesh's moderate level of external debt, on the other hand, points to additional borrowing as a potential option, such as through concessional or commercial lending or issuing government securities, if possible. However, caution is necessary, as debt service can quickly escalate; it is important to carry out a comprehensive debt sustainability assessment (DSA) before assuming additional government liabilities (Section 6).

vii.   At around 3 percent of GDP, Bangladesh and Guatemala are forecasted to run relatively tame **budget deficits**, suggesting that there may be space to allow for an increasing degree of deficit spending to ramp up public investments in children and poor households (Section 7).

viii.   In terms of **inflation**, Guatemala is maintaining inflation levels around 6 percent, which is beneath the world average, and may have room for expansionary monetary policy, if warranted. For Bangladesh, inflation is over 10 percent, suggesting that it would be prudent to analyze other options first (Section 7).

In sum, this rapid fiscal space analysis identifies preliminary areas that can be further examined in order to boost investments in social and economic development today, even in the poorest countries.

2.   Re-prioritizing Public Sector Spending

Rethinking sector-specific allocations within existing budgets is one strategy to increase social expenditures. The chapter opens with this option since it is normally the first to be considered. However, based on experiences from the 1990s and early 2000s, the re-prioritization of public spending has proven to be a contentious and difficult approach to fight for increased investments in poor households and children. This reflects the underlying assumption that no extra resources are available and, therefore, other sectors or subsectors must be reduced in order to allow for increased social investments—these sectors often represent important vested interests in a country (e.g., military). In other words, this approach presumes that the budget is fixed and a zero-sum game.

The extensive literature on public choice and public finance describes how different interest groups within and outside of government compete to influence public policies and budget allocations (e.g., Buchanan and Musgrave 1999). In cases where social sector ministries and groups representing or comprised of poor and marginalized sectors are incapable of garnering the support of policymakers or of society at large, the result is a collapse in allocations for pro-poor budget items. Moreover, even in situations where there is broad consensus that pro-poor expenditures should be boosted, policymakers often fail to agree on specific sectors to sacrifice (e.g., defense/security, commerce/finance). This debate is often imbalanced. For instance, when arguing that social expenditures may be part of the cause of large deficits, there is little or no debate on the role of military or other essentially non-productive expenditures (Figure 2).

Figure VI.2. Military and Health Spending in Selected Developing Countries, 2006-09*
(average values)

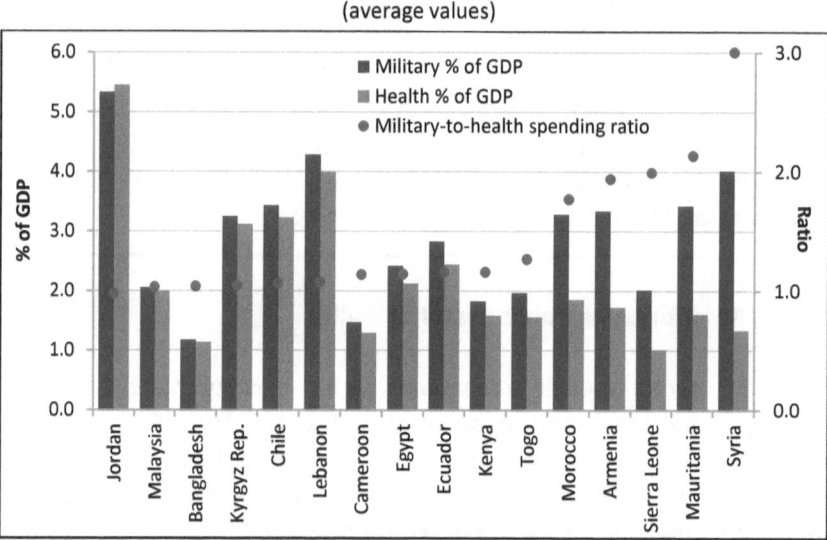

Source: Authors' calculations based on World Bank's *World Development Indicators* (2011)
* Only includes countries with no major armed conflict since 2000 based on Uppsala Conflict Data Program *Armed Conflict Dataset* (December 2011).

More importantly, various studies have highlighted the risks of pro-poor budget items being the most affected during budget consolidation (e.g., Cornia et al. 1987, Hicks 1991, Ravallion 2002, 2004 and 2006). Evidence from the recovery period following the debt crisis of the 1980s shows that social sector budgets, on average, received among the highest cuts when governments in Latin America scaled back on expenditures—just behind that of infrastructure budgets and expenditures for industrial and agricultural development; defense budgets, on the other hand, were highly protected (Hicks 1991:33).

Still there are ways of prioritizing socially-responsive expenditures even when overall budgets are contracting. This re-prioritization requires, first and foremost, that governments have their budget priorities in place. For example, governments in Cambodia and Sri Lanka recently decided to reduce expenditures in the defense and security sectors in favor of increased spending in social sectors.[4] The political and technical challenges of identifying sectors/subsectors that can be reduced to promote fiscal space can be overcome through the following strategies (see Ortiz 2008a for further details):

- *Re-prioritizing through public expenditure reviews and thematic budgets:* These are well-developed approaches to public financial management that bring evidence and rationality to public policymaking by showing the distributional impacts of current budgetary allocations. A common exercise is to examine budgets from a child and/or gender perspective. Given that children and youth comprise nearly half of the population of many developing countries, as do females, public budgets should support these groups proportionally.

- *Replacing high-cost, low-impact investments:* Whether or not these investments are in social sectors, all new public investments can be re-examined. For instance, the social impact of a cardiology center in a national capital tends to be small and carries a high operational cost. Rural or slum area health interventions, conversely, tend to have much larger positive social impacts. To offer an example in the energy sector, the opportunity cost of building a nuclear power plant is usually very high when compared to investing in rural electrification systems that serve poorer populations. Similar trade-offs exist in the water and sanitation sectors. Public debates that include relevant stakeholders and civil society organizations are one strategic tool to replace high-cost, low-impact interventions, which

---

[4] IMF Country Report No. 11/45 (February 2011) and IMF Country Report No. 10/333 (October 2010).

can help to minimize the possible influence of powerful lobbying groups on public policymaking.

- *Eliminating inefficiencies:* Although linked to the previous point, deeper analysis of sector investments is required to eliminate inefficiencies. In particular, the overall cost-effectiveness of a specific program or policy should be impartially evaluated according to various factors. These include: (i) coverage (beneficiaries and benefits); (ii) total cost (as a percent of GDP, public expenditure and sector expenditure); (iii) administrative costs (as a percent of total costs and how these costs compare with other programs—for example, means-testing targeting is typically expensive); (iv) long-term social benefits and positive externalities; and (v) opportunity cost (how a specific policy/program compares to alternatives). Making sector allocations more efficient also involves strengthening supervision and inspection as well as reducing other leakages, especially corruption (see below).

- *Fighting corruption:* Corruption can also be a significant source of waste and inefficiencies within sector budgets. This most commonly affects extra-budgetary accounts (where there is less transparency), the selection of investment projects, and the procurement of goods and services (either overpriced or simply non-existent, such as 'ghost' local investments or workers). Tackling corruption requires strategies that address both supply and demand factors, and, ultimately, strengthening transparency and good governance practices can increase the availability of resources for social and economic development.[5]

While reducing intra-sector inefficiencies is the most commonly used strategy since it avoids political tensions, *expenditure reforms take time to advance and are unlikely to yield significant, immediate resources for social and economic recovery in the near term.* In addition, expenditures aimed at social and economic recovery may be increased slightly, but their relative weight vis-à-vis other forms of investment may be too small to ensure a *'Recovery for All.'* Thus, while the re-

---

[5] Specific strategies to address corruption are widely documented by international agencies and development partners. See, for example, the UN (http://www.unodc.org/unodc/en/treaties/CAC/index.htm), Transparency International (http://www.transparency.org/) and the World Bank (http://wbi.worldbank.org/wbi/topic/governance).

prioritization of public sector spending may be a good starting point to expand fiscal space, other options should be examined in parallel.

3.   Increasing Tax Revenues

Increasing tax compliance and/or raising tax rates are potential strategies to mobilize additional public resources without necessarily sacrificing other spending priorities. Moreover, new taxes, when well designed and executed, improve government revenues without increasing debt.[6] Aside from strengthening a country's overall fiscal position, new tax revenue can potentially support equity objectives, especially in situations of widespread disparities. For example, if income tax rates are increased among the richest groups of a country (known as progressive taxes), additional revenues can be generated and invested in the poorest households, which promotes poverty-reducing economic growth and sustains growth in the long run.

There are many types of taxes. Some of the most common include: (i) consumption or sales taxes (e.g., on goods and services or on any operation that creates value—these are applied to everybody); (ii) corporate taxes (applied to businesses); (iii) income taxes (e.g., on persons, corporations or other legal entities); (iv) inheritance taxes (applied when a person dies); (v) property taxes (e.g., applied to owners of private property); (vi) social security taxes (applied to the wages/salaries of formal workers to provide income and health benefits to retirees); (vii) tariffs (e.g., taxes levied on imports or exports); and (viii) tolls (e.g., fees charged to persons traveling on roads, bridges, etc.).

In recent history, increasing progressive taxation from the richest income groups to finance social and pro-poor investments has been uncommon. This is largely the result of the wave of liberalization and de-regulation policies that swept across most economies beginning in the early 1990s. These led many developing countries to offer tax breaks and subsidies to attract foreign capital, as well as scale back income taxes applied on wealthier groups and businesses to further

---

[6] It is important, however, to carefully scrutinize the risks of reforms involving changes to tax rates. Some of the main arguments against raising taxes include the potential of: (i) *political risks* (higher income or business taxes are unpopular and can reduce the support of influential voters and campaign contributions); (ii) *inflation* (higher taxes on products are often passed on to consumers); and (iii) *increasing poverty* (higher sales taxes, such as through VATs, absorb a higher percentage of the income of the poor).

encourage domestic investment. Moreover, to counter the revenue losses associated with these tax policies, many countries levied different consumption taxes.

The tax policy framework associated with liberalization and de-regulation continues to typify most governments today. Contrary to progressive, equity-based policies, many current tax regimes may be characterized as regressive since they take a larger percentage of income from poor households than rich households. In particular, a large number of governments rely heavily on VATs for revenues, which tend to weigh most heavily on the poor since they spend a higher share of their income on basic goods and services when they are not exempted. In light of this reality, it is imperative that distributional impacts are at the forefront of tax policy discussions—across income groups, regions, gender and age.

In the present context, and given the urgency to increase fiscal space for equitable development, the UN and other international organizations are working with many developing country governments to boost tax revenues. For example, the review of 158 IMF country reports in Chapter V indicates that tax reforms are being undertaken in virtually all developing countries during 2010-12. Indeed, efforts to develop collection capacities and broaden the tax base are to be applauded, especially those aimed at cracking down on evasion, which has been estimated to result in annual revenue losses of US$285 billion for developing countries as a whole (Cobham 2005). Strengthening domestic tax and collection systems can also foster good governance by enhancing citizen-state dialogue on how taxes are spent, as well as increase incentives to pay taxes, thereby enforcing accountability and creating a demand for greater provision of public services (Brautigam et al. 2008).

The following considers six broad tax categories that governments can adjust to increase revenue streams, which include tariffs, consumption/sales taxes, income taxes, corporate taxes, natural resource extraction taxes and other taxes that use more innovative approaches.

3.1.   Tariffs

By some measures, developing countries appear to have steadily reduced tariff rates since the 1990s, implying lowered capacity to generate revenues from trade. The financial implications of this trend are likely greater for LICs, which have sliced tariffs by more than half—from 27 to 13 percent between 1996 and 2009, on average—compared to a 6 percent average cut in MICs (Figure 3). Several countries stand out, such as India, whose average tariff rate fell from 71 to 13 percent between 1994 and 2009, and Brazil, whose average tariff rate dropped from 51 to 14 percent between 1987 and 2009 (WTO 2010).

Figure VI.3. Tariff Rates by Income Groups, 1996-2009*
(as a percent)

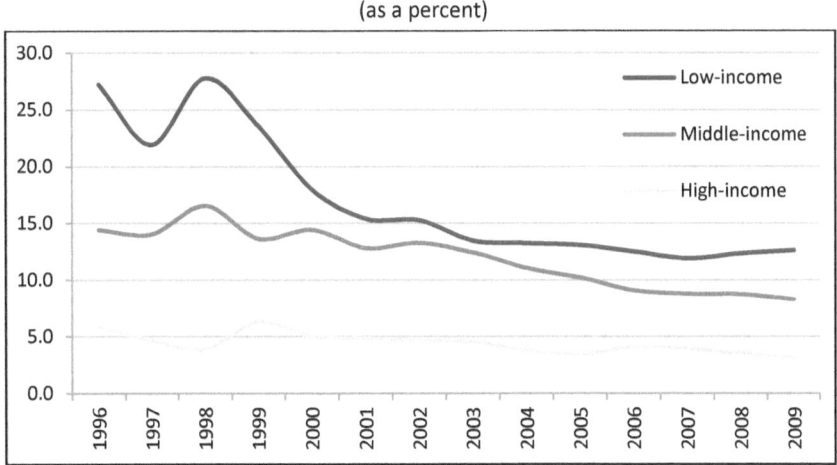

Source: World Bank's *World Development Indicators* (2011)
* Values reflect unweighted average of applied rates for all traded products subject to tariffs.

Such declines in tariff revenue have at times been associated with trade liberalization. In theory, the overall gains to free trade were supposed to outweigh the loss of tariff revenues, but, in practice, less developed countries tend to have limited ability to recover foregone revenues, which results in net revenue losses. For example, Baunsgaard and Keen (2005) find that while rich countries have been able to offset reductions in tariff revenues by increasing their domestic tax revenues, this has not occurred in most developing countries. MICs were found to recover only up to 60 cents of each dollar of tariff revenue lost, and LICs recovered no more than 30 cents.

Consequently, in many developing countries there may be a good rationale to examine current tariff levels, at least until domestic tax collection mechanisms are strengthened, to sustain or increase levels of revenue. In countries such as Brazil and India, there may be ample scope to raise tariffs since prevailing levels are far below the WTO-bound tariff rate ceilings agreed to in the 1995 Uruguay Round of trade negotiations (Gregory et al. 2010).

Moreover, for countries undergoing export-driven commodity booms, fiscal space could be enhanced for social investments by introducing or raising export tariffs. In many Latin American countries, for instance, special funds and laws have been created to govern the use of revenue derived from price increases in commodities exports (Gallagher and Porzecanski 2009). One of the most well-known examples is Venezuela, where an increasingly progressive windfall tax is levied on oil exports to fund social development projects.[7] To highlight the overall potential of commodity export taxes, a 2-5 percent tax on oil exports from petroleum-exporting developing countries could generate anywhere from US$48 billion to US$119 billion in additional resources to support social and economic investments in children and poor households during 2012.[8]

3.2.   Consumption/sales taxes

By some accounts, many developing countries have introduced more consumption or sales taxes, such as VATs, over the past decade. According to the World Bank's *World Development Indicators*, between 2000 and 2009, the overall share of consumer-related taxes increased by over 1 percent in LICs and by 3.2 percent in MICs, on average, in terms of total revenue, while this share slightly declined in higher-income economies (Figure 4). Within the cohort of developing countries, it also appears that these new taxes have been a source of a

---

[7] Taxation News and Information. 2011. "Venezuelan Oil Taxes to Reach up to 95%." *Taxation News and Information*, April 26.

[8] Estimates reflect the 2009 average barrels per day of oil exports from Algeria, Angola, Iran, Iraq, Kazakhstan, Libya, Nigeria, the Russian Federation and Venezuela as reported by the United States Energy Information Administration (combined total of 21.6 million barrels) and the forecasted price of crude oil for 2012 (US$110/barrel of Brent crude) according to the Economist Intelligent Unit's Global Forecasting Service (both estimates as of February 2012).

steady increase in overall tax revenues.[9] While there is limited data for developing countries prior to 2000, which likely hides much of the marked increase, available information shows that the contribution of new consumption taxes to overall revenue increased from around 10 percent of GDP in 2000 to 14 percent in 2009 for MICs, on average, with a slightly lower increase for LICs.

Figure VI.4. Taxes on Goods/Services and Overall Tax Revenue by Income Groups, 2000-09*

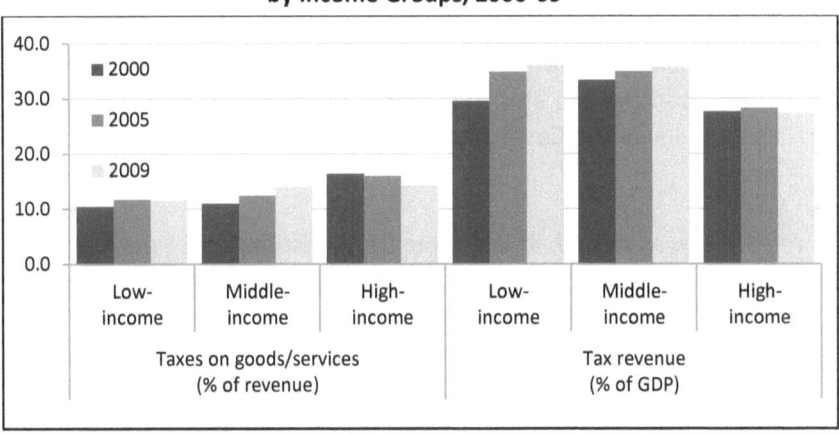

Source: World Bank's *World Development Indicators* (2011)
* Tax revenue refers to compulsory transfers to the central government for public purposes and does not include social security contributions; Taxes on goods/services include general sales and VATs, selective excises on goods, selective taxes on services, and taxes on the use of goods or property, among others.

If the distributional impact of such a change in tax policy is not properly addressed, there is the additional concern of worsening inequity by disproportionately shifting the tax burden to families in the bottom income quintiles of society. Contrary to progressive taxes, universal taxes on goods, especially on basic food and household items, can be regressive since they do not discriminate between high-income and low-income consumers. For example, given that poor families spend a higher proportion of their disposable income on food items, applying or increasing consumption taxes on basic food items means that relatively more of their income is subjected to product taxes.

However, as in the other tax measures, levying or increasing consumption taxes or VATs can be a prudent policy objective and

---

[9] This may reflect in part strengthened collection of existing taxes, the extent of which cannot be ascertained due to a lack of consistent data.

strengthen fiscal space if targeted to the products that the better-off consume disproportionately more. For example, it is possible to exempt necessary basic goods that many low-income families depend on while setting higher rates for luxury goods that are principally consumed by wealthier families. In this manner, progressively designed consumption taxes can increase public resources and protect the most vulnerable (see Schenk and Oldman 2007 for discussion). For instance, according to the latest IMF country reports, Antigua and Barbuda is introducing sales tax exemptions for basic commodities, Kenya is lowering taxes on fuel and food staples consumed by vulnerable populations, and the Solomon Islands is reducing taxes on food and fuel items. At the same time, many developing countries are also considering tax increases on luxury items, such as cars, including Costa Rica, Ghana, Kosovo and the Republic of Congo.

More recently, as described in Chapter V, an estimated 71 governments worldwide have adopted or are planning to impose higher consumption taxes, either through increasing or expanding VAT rates or sales taxes or, alternatively, by removing exemptions. However, the potential ripple effects of this policy change must be carefully examined. First, tax policies that increase the cost of basic goods, such as on food and fuel or energy items, may enhance the vulnerability of poor households by further reducing their already limited disposable incomes. Second, there is a risk of weakening aggregate demand, which is important for solidifying still fragile growth. And third, a slowdown in economic growth will lower tax receipts and create new budgetary pressures.

Another type of consumption tax that can be used to increase fiscal space is an excise tax, which is collected on goods such as alcohol, cigarettes and petroleum whose consumption creates negative social externalities (e.g., the cost of the good does not factor in the negative side effects to third parties or society that result from its consumption). The advantage of increasing so-called 'sin' taxes is that they may be more politically acceptable, especially if the revenue is directed toward social expenditure. Based on current tax proceeds, the World Health Organization (WHO) (2009a) estimates that a 5-10 percent increase in the tobacco tax rate could net up to US$1.4 billion per annum in additional revenue in LICs and US$5 billion in MICs; raising tobacco taxes by 50 percent could cover nearly half of public health expenditures in a number of developing countries. Given the public health spillovers and revenue potential associated with new or higher 'sin' taxes, many governments appear to be considering this option in the current policy environment, including Antigua and Barbuda, Jamaica, Kyrgyz Republic, Liberia, the Republic of Congo and Turkey, according to IMF country reports.

3.3.   Income taxes

In contrast to taxes on goods and services, income taxation is often progressive—that is, people in higher income brackets pay higher tax rates than those in the bottom. According to data gathered by the World Bank's *World Development Indicators*, with the exception of the CEE/CIS and Sub-Saharan Africa, developing countries have, on average, increased personal and corporate income taxes, as well as those levied on capital gains, since 2001. The rise in various income taxes is likely to have led to enhanced revenue streams for most of these governments.

However, this progressive trend hides important disparities within income tax policies. In particular, a number of developing countries have reduced income tax rates on the wealthiest groups (Table 1). In terms of individual income taxes, 12 of the 39 countries with data (or 31 percent of the sample) had lowered the tax rates applied to the highest income earners in 2009 when compared to the 2005-08 period. Of the 71 developing countries that offer corporate income tax data, 33 (or nearly half) had reduced the tax rate applied to the top income bracket in 2009 when compared to previous years. For these countries, expanding the income tax base through more efficient collection, especially through eliminating evasion, or by decreasing the income required to qualify for higher tax brackets, could increase available fiscal space over the short term.

Furthermore, there is an urgent need to introduce increasingly progressive income taxes to counter current trends in inequality. The large income disparities that characterize most developing countries— especially MICs—are being exacerbated during 2011 due to the three persisting shocks as described in this book (e.g. high food and fuel prices, unemployment and reduced public support), all of which have a disproportionate, negative impact on the bottom quintiles of the income distribution (Ortiz and Cummins 2011). As a result, income taxes—which are the principal redistribution tool available to policymakers—should be examined on both fiscal space and equity grounds in order to enlist the political support of citizens, safeguard children's lives, nutrition and basic education, and engender social stability.

Table VI.1. Developing Countries that Lowered Individual and Corporate Income Tax Rates for the Top Income Brackets, 2009*

Individual Income Tax	Corporate Income Tax		
Bulgaria	Albania	Ghana	Romania
Colombia	Bangladesh	India	Russian Federation
Egypt	Bosnia and Herzegovina	Indonesia	Serbia
Indonesia	Bulgaria	Kazakhstan	South Africa
Kazakhstan	China	Kenya	Swaziland
Lithuania	Colombia	Macedonia, FYR	Thailand
Malaysia	Costa Rica	Malaysia	Tunisia
Mauritius	Côte D'Ivoire	Mauritius	Uganda
Mexico	Congo, Dem. Rep. of	Mexico	Venezuela
Pakistan	Dominican Republic	Papua New Guinea	
Papua New Guinea	Ethiopia	Peru	
Vietnam	Fiji	Philippines	

Source: Authors' calculations based on World Bank's *World Development Indicators* (data extracted in Jan. 2010)
* A country is included if its highest marginal tax rate in 2009 was lower than the 2005-08 avg. rate.

3.4.   Corporate taxes

Increasing business taxes is another possible strategy to generate additional fiscal revenues. Developing countries across all regions decreased commercial tax rates, on average, between 2005 and 2010. The CEE/CIS and Middle East and North Africa regions underwent the largest reductions according to data from the *World Development Indicators*. East Asia and the Pacific, Latin America and Sub-Saharan Africa also lowered commercial tax rates by 3-5 percent, on average, over the same time period.[10]

The logic behind lowering corporate taxes and related license costs and fees was to encourage entrepreneurial risk-taking and generate new economic activity. However, the potential trade-off needs to be carefully balanced, to ensure that the gains from increased economic activity do not come at the expense of foregone essential investments in human and social development. This may be particularly important in those countries that have undergone major reductions—e.g., Belarus,

---

[10] Authors' calculations based on World Bank's *World Development Indicators* (2011).

Georgia, Mauritania, Sierra Leone, Timor-Leste and Uruguay, all of which reduced commercial tax rates by more than 25 percent between 2005 and 2010—as well as those that have among the world's lowest commercial tax rates—e.g., Georgia, Kosovo, Macedonia, Maldives, Namibia, Vanuatu, Timor-Leste and Zambia, all of which had commercial tax rates under 17 percent as of 2010.[11]

The former logic is being questioned in many countries following the global economic crisis, particularly related to the financial sector. Different financial sector tax schemes may offer another possible revenue stream for stepped up social investments, provided that their impact on financial sector development is carefully evaluated. Many countries are considering special taxes on the profits and remuneration of financial institutions. For instance, Turkey taxes all receipts of banks and insurance companies, and, in the United Kingdom and France, all bonus payments in excess of €25,000 were taxed by 50 percent (IMF 2010a). Another example is a bank debit tax in Brazil, which charged 0.38 percent on online bill payments and major cash withdrawals; before its discontinuation in 2008, it raised an estimated US$20 billion annually and financed healthcare, poverty alleviation and social assistance programs. And Argentina operates a 0.6 percent tax on purchases and sales of equity shares and bonds, which, in 2009 accounted for more than 10 percent of overall tax revenue for the central government (Beitler 2010).

In addition to altering corporate tax rates, governments can also increase fiscal space by taking concerted actions to minimize tax evasion and/or aggressive avoidance of taxes on the part of large companies. Transnational corporations, in particular, commonly shift profits and losses around so that they are recorded in different jurisdictions in order to minimize overall tax liabilities. Such practices are difficult to track, but estimates suggest that total lost revenues could amount to US$50 billion per year among developing countries (Cobham 2005). Proposals have been put forward to increase the transparency of transnational corporations and hold them accountable for their tax obligations, such as reporting profits, losses and taxes paid in each location where the company does business (see Kar 2011 for details).

---

[11] Authors' calculations based on World Bank's *World Development Indicators* (2011).

3.5.   Natural resource extraction taxes

Developing countries that rely on non-renewable natural resources as a main source of wealth should consider applying extraction taxes or introducing specific windfall taxes to support social and economic development initiatives. In terms of finite assets, including energy, minerals and forests, governments face a limited window of opportunity to use these for national development aims. There are also significant environmental and social externalities associated with natural resources, such as the impacts on local communities, which, if not adequately addressed, serve as a subsidy to extracting companies and further distort the true cost of development.

A government may raise revenues either by extracting the natural resources through a state-owned enterprise or by selling off the exploitation rights and taxing the profits, both of which can provide significant revenues for social and economic development. Regarding the former, a number of countries have effectively managed their natural resources through public companies, including Botswana (diamonds), Brazil (oil), Indonesia (oil and gas) and Malaysia (forestry, tin, oil and gas) (Chang 2007). In terms of the latter approach, ample care must be taken to find the right types of contracts, including licenses, joint venture, production-sharing arrangements, etc. (Radon 2007). While Norway's approach of taxing oil profits and storing the revenues in the Petroleum Fund[12] is perhaps the best-known case, developing countries offer several innovative examples of channeling natural resource revenue streams for social development. In Peru, for example, the government recently expanded taxes levied on the mining sector whose proceeds are being invested in health and education programs.[13]

Given the volatile nature of primary commodity prices, many governments have created 'stabilization funds' based on windfall taxes. Such funds allow governments to smooth their income and expenditure, keeping savings in years of bonanza for 'rainy days' when prices of commodity exports may be low, and hence ensuring that investments in social and economic development remain constant. Chile's Copper

---

[12] Now called the Government Pension Fund Global.
[13] Peruvian Times. 2011. "Peru Organization Says New Mine Tax to Make Important Dent in Social Breaches." *Peruvian Times*, August 30.

Stabilization Fund, Iran's Oil Stabilization Fund, Papua New Guinea's Mineral Resources Stabilization Fund and the Stabilization Fund of the Russian Federation are among the many examples. During the recent economic downturn, a number of countries have accessed these 'rainy day' funds to finance stimulus measures and increase social protection.

3.6.   Other taxes

Alternative tax options could also help to raise public revenues for investments in poor households and children, several examples of which are described below.

-    *Property taxes:* Higher real estate and inheritance taxes are a form of progressive levies that require large landowners and wealthier generations to contribute more to government revenues. There are many advantages to such taxes, including fairness, evasion difficulties and an impact on those with assets whose value is increased by public services and infrastructure. In many developing countries, higher property taxes could transform into a robust source of funding for local governments. For example, a 2.5 percent property tax in Thailand is estimated to be able to finance all local government spending (Hall 2010:41). According to the latest IMF country reports, many countries appear to be considering introducing or increasing property or real estate taxes in the current policy environment, including Costa Rica, Kosovo, the Russian Federation and St. Lucia. Land taxes are another example, which are a broader form of property tax applied to all land, not just buildings. Campaigns for land taxes have surfaced in many developing countries recently. In Latvia, for instance, a group of economists and other activists argued for the introduction of a land tax as an alternative to deep public spending cuts (Strazds 2010); similar discussions are also occurring in parts of Southern Africa.

-    *Airline and/or hotel taxes:* Many developing countries have recently increased taxes charged at airports or on the sale of airline tickets. As demonstrated in recent IMF country reports, this has been most commonly observed in small island states, like Antigua and Barbuda and the Maldives, as well as in emerging tourist destinations, such as Ghana and Liberia—the latter which increased taxes on airlines and hotels by 3 percent in fiscal year 2012.[14]

-   *Linking taxes to social programs*: Another strategy to enhance fiscal space for social and economic development is to tie the revenues raised from new or existing tax measures to the financing of specific social programs, which can help to secure resources and make them less volatile, as well as ensure wider public support. For example, Mexican lawmakers agreed to raise VATs by 1 percent (from 15 to 16 percent) and the top income tax rate by 2 percent (from 28 to 30 percent), in addition to increase taxes on beer producers and on certain bank deposits, with all of the proceeds specifically earmarked to support anti-poverty programs.[15] Ghana has also introduced links between taxes and public services: 2.5 percent of the VAT is reserved for education, another 2.5 percent of the VAT is allocated for social health insurance, and 20 percent of a communication service tax is directed to a national youth employment scheme (Hall 2010:40-41). And in India, an education cess of 2 percent is levied on corporate income taxes, service taxes, and excise and customs duties.[16]

-   *Remittance taxes*: Some countries have introduced taxes on remittance inflows to support social and economic development. Such tax schemes vary widely. For instance, remittances were subjected to a 0.004 and 0.1 percent tax rate in Colombia and Peru, respectively; a 12 percent VAT was applied to remittances in Ecuador; Georgia and Poland imposed income tax rates on remittance inflows; and, in the Philippines, banks deducted withholding taxes for interest earned on deposited remittances (de Luna 2006). However, a wide body of literature suggests that lowering transaction costs and even subsidizing remittances may do more social good than taxing inflows and directing the revenue to specific development uses (see, for instance, Inter-American Dialogue 2007, Ratha 2007, Rosser 2008, Barry and Øverland 2010). This conclusion is generally attributed to the following factors: (i) migrants have already paid income and sales tax in the host country

---

[14] IMF Country Report No. 11/174 (July 2011).
[15] Gutierrez, M.A. 2009. "Mexico Lawmakers Adopt Tax Plan—Raise VAT, Income Tax." *Reuters*, November 01.
[16] Embassy of India. 2011. "Taxation System in India." *Embassy of India*, September.

on money remitted; (ii) taxes reduce incentives to remit; (iii) taxes lower the value of funds received by poor households; (iv) remittance taxes encourage informal transfers and financial exclusion; (v) countries with overvalued official exchange rates already implicitly tax remittances by requiring recipients to convert at uncompetitive official exchange rates; (vi) remittance tax policies are difficult to administer; and (vii) remittance taxes are regressive. As a result, developing countries should look to other options to create fiscal space before considering remittances taxes.

In short, it is critical to take into account the distributional impacts of tax systems and to support tax reforms and tax collection that benefit children and poor households. Sound tax approaches are progressive, broad-based and reliant on multiple sources, especially in MICs.

4.   Increased Aid and Transfers

Governments have three main options for increasing net international transfers in order to support socio-economic investments today: (i) lobby for further North-South aid flows; (ii) lobby for additional South-South transfers and development assistance; and (iii) curtail South-North financial flows.

4.1.   More North-South transfers: ODA

In principle, ODA is a first option for expanding fiscal space for LICs, in particular. However, there is significant uncertainty surrounding future aid flows in a climate of fiscal consolidation that is increasingly taken hold of many traditional donor countries during 2011-12.[17] There is also concern over aid commitments more generally. In particular, current aid levels remain far below the 0.7 percent of gross national income (GNI) threshold that was first agreed to by wealthy countries in 1970 and which has been repeatedly re-endorsed at the highest levels, most recently at the G8 Gleneagles Summit and the UN World Summit in 2005.

---

[17] World Bank analysis of historical ODA flows from donor countries during past crises suggests that aid could drop 20-25 percent (relative to the counterfactual) and recover only after about a decade (Dang et al. 2009). Preliminary data, however, show that net aid flows appear to have increased by 6.5 percent in 2010, at least (OECD 2011).

The justification for meeting the 0.7 percent GNI aid target has never been greater. Global inequality is staggering: the top 20 percent of the global population enjoys more than 70 percent of total world income, contrasted by 2 percent for those in the bottom population quintile (Ortiz and Cummins 2011). Given the stark disparities at the global level, ODA serves as the main redistributive channel to ensure equity. However, current international redistributive flows are simply insufficient. As of 2009, net ODA amounted to only 4.7 percent of total GDP in Sub-Saharan Africa followed by 1.3 percent of GDP in the Middle East and North Africa and far below 1 percent of GDP in all other developing regions.[18] Moreover, as an outflow, OECD countries contributed a meager 0.23 percent of their GDP to developing countries.[19] In short, meeting aid targets is a matter of global justice, and the failure of donors to provide additional development support indicates that globalization continues to benefit a privileged few.

In its current form, foreign aid is characterized by problems of size, transaction costs, limited predictability, macroeconomic impacts ('Dutch disease'), being tied, lack of policy coherence, fungibility and conditionality (see Ortiz 2008b). Concentration of ODA is another major problem, which has direct implications for fiscal space. Given limited development resources and increasing bilateralism, donors oftentimes pick their favorite allied developing countries and those in which they perceive to be strategic interests (often referred as the problem of aid 'orphans' and aid 'darlings'). When measuring average global aid flows between 2005 and 2009, among the list of 'darlings' includes Afghanistan, the Democratic Republic of Congo, Ethiopia, Iraq, Nigeria, Pakistan, the Sudan, Tanzania, Vietnam, and the West Bank and Gaza (Table 2). Overall, 15 countries receive more than 50 percent of all international assistance. On the other end of the spectrum, many of the neediest countries are virtually left out of aid flows (the 'orphans'). As Table 2 demonstrates, 20 of the world's poorest countries received a combined total of only 10 percent of all ODA; indeed, there is a strong case for the so-called 'orphans' to lobby for increased North-South assistance.

---

[18] Authors' calculations based on World Bank's *World Development Indicators* (2011).

[19] These estimates differ from those of the OECD due to differences in the base value year of the US dollar as well as those between GDP and GNI—OECD (2011) estimates total net aid outflows to be 0.31 percent of GNI in 2009.

Table VI.2. Aid Concentration and Neglect, 2005-09
(average values)

	Country	% of Global Aid	Aid Volume*	Aid per Capita**	GDP per Capita**	Infant Mortality Rate†	Aid, % of GDP	Health Spending, % of GDP
Significant Aid Flows	Iraq	12.3	10.6	352	1,891	35	18.5	2.6
	Nigeria	5.3	4.55	31	1,085	86	2.8	1.9
	Afghanistan	4.8	4.13	146	354	134	40.9	1.8
	Ethiopia	3.2	2.73	35	254	67	13.5	2.4
	Vietnam	2.9	2.51	30	871	20	3.4	2.4
	Tanzania	2.7	2.28	55	433	68	13.1	3.3
	Sudan	2.5	2.13	53	1,095	69	4.8	1.9
	Pakistan	2.4	2.06	13	865	71	1.5	0.8
	West Bank/Gaza	2.3	2.00	525	1,123	25	49.9	...
	Congo, Dem. Rep.	2.2	1.91	31	152	126	20.0	3.2
	India	2.1	1.83	2	997	50	0.2	1.2
	Mozambique	2.0	1.74	79	377	96	21.0	3.7
	Uganda	1.8	1.58	52	397	79	12.9	1.7
	Bangladesh	1.7	1.47	9	455	41	2.0	1.1
	China	1.7	1.42	1	2,722	17	0.0	2.0
	Total/Average	50.0	42.9	94	871	66	13.6	2.1
Limited Aid Flows	Gambia	0.10	0.09	53	391	78	13.5	3.0
	Guinea-Bissau	0.13	0.11	72	461	115	15.5	1.6
	Central Afr. Rep.	0.21	0.18	42	399	112	10.5	1.6
	Eritrea	0.21	0.18	39	306	39	12.5	1.3
	Togo	0.26	0.22	35	398	64	8.8	1.5
	Guinea	0.27	0.23	24	370	88	6.4	0.7
	Timor-Leste	0.27	0.23	219	394	48	55.2	11.3
	Tajikistan	0.33	0.28	42	559	52	7.5	1.3
	Chad	0.47	0.40	38	631	124	6.0	2.9
	Sierra Leone	0.47	0.41	75	302	123	24.8	1.2
	Burundi	0.54	0.47	59	132	101	44.9	5.0
	Zimbabwe	0.58	0.50	40	412	56	9.7	...
	Niger	0.62	0.53	38	309	76	12.1	3.2
	Nepal	0.72	0.62	22	371	39	5.9	1.9
	Cambodia	0.75	0.64	45	598	68	7.5	1.6
	Malawi	0.87	0.74	51	249	69	20.5	4.8
	Haiti	0.87	0.75	77	572	64	13.4	1.3
	Rwanda	0.88	0.75	79	405	70	19.4	4.2
	Madagascar	0.90	0.77	41	383	41	10.7	2.7
	Total / Average	10.1	8.7	63	392	75	19.3	2.9

Source: Authors' calculations based on World Bank's *World Development Indicators* (2011)
* billions of current US dollars, ** in current US dollars, † per 1,000 live births.

There is also the issue of where bilateral assistance is actually invested. Figure 5 reflects the three-year average values of ODA flows alongside health spending during 2007-09 in a select group of developing countries, many of which rank among the aid 'darlings.' The striking feature is that health spending tends to pale in comparison to overall aid volumes, thus suggesting that social sectors are not a major priority area for foreign assistance in many countries. This is perhaps best illustrated by Afghanistan and Sierra Leone. Although these countries rank among the worst in the world in terms of infant mortality rates and public health expenditures, the average aid that they received during 2007-09 was more than 25 times the size of overall public investments in the health sector.

Figure VI.5. ODA and Health Spending in Selected Developing Countries, 2007-09
(average values)

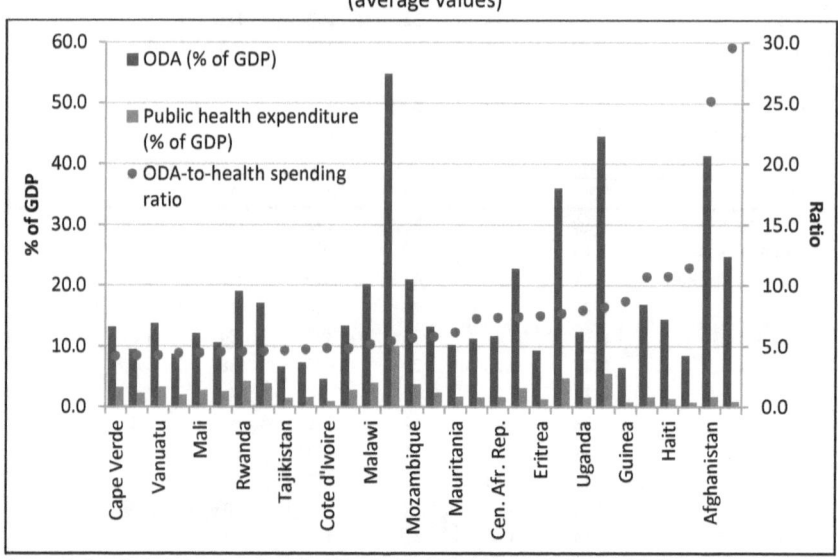

Source: Authors' calculations based on World Bank's *World Development Indicators* (2011)

But where is the ODA directed when it actually reaches recipient countries? Following a comprehensive study of aid in Sub-Saharan Africa, the IMF's Independent Evaluation Office found that nearly three-quarters of aid given to poor countries between 1999 and 2005 was used to accumulate reserves and pay off debt rather than invest in much needed social and economic programs (Figure 6). Such a strategy implies high human development opportunity costs, as vulnerable groups in Sub-Saharan Africa suffer from food insecurity, poor basic services and nutritional deprivations.

Figure VI.6. Use of ODA in Sub-Saharan Africa, 1999-2005
(in percent of anticipated aid increase)

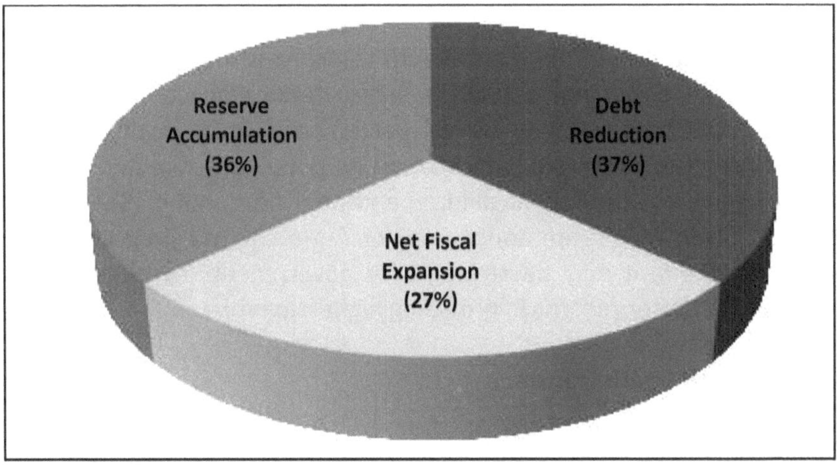

Reserve
Accumulation
(36%)

Debt
Reduction
(37%)

Net Fiscal
Expansion
(27%)

Source: IMF (2007:42)

For developing countries not among the 'darlings' or 'orphans,' donor resources tend to move in and out together, causing herd-like behavior (Khamfula et al. 2006, Desai and Kharas 2010, and Frot and Santiso 2011). Poverty Reduction Strategy Papers (PRSP) and Country Policy and Institutional Assessments (CPIA),[20] which are performed by international financial institutions, function like rating signals for donors—similar to international credit rating agencies for private investors. Sometimes there are good reasons for donor withdrawal, such as when the policymaking process is captured by an interest group that benefits disproportionately from public policies rather than ensuring development for the majority of the population. On other occasions, however, ratings are based on compliance with orthodox conditionality

---

[20] The CPIAs are the base of the World Bank's Resource Allocation Index for International Development Association (IDA) eligible countries (concessional loans). Countries are ranked against a set of 16 criteria grouped in four clusters: economic management, structural policies, policies for social inclusion and equity, and public sector management and institutions. Designing a universal rating system for allocating resources is very correct, but criticisms naturally accompany criteria. For instance, macroeconomic criteria measure whether aggregate demand policies are consistent with macroeconomic stability, whether monetary and exchange rate policies ensure price stability, and whether private sector investment is crowded out. In terms of trade, criteria include measuring tariff levels, which need to be less than 12 percent, on average, and never exceed 20 percent, as well as evaluating internal tax policies to ensure that they do not discriminate heavily against imports (World Bank 2010a). Many argue that these criteria are based on contractionary policies that, combined with trade liberalization, are obstacles to inclusive growth and job generation in developing countries. Even the Independent Evaluation Group questions whether these criteria lead to growth and has recommended a series of revisions (2010:59-64).

(e.g., fiscal and monetary austerity measures), which do not always allow for policy flexibility (Ortiz 2008b).

A final important point on North-South transfers is that only about half of traditional donor aid actually reaches developing countries. Data from the OECD shows that just 54 percent of ODA is in the form of country programmable aid, which could be potentially directed toward development investments in children and poor households (Benn et al. 2010).[21] Given that some donors deliver more country programmable aid than others, it may be strategic for governments to target those donors with better records in providing higher volumes.

4.2.   South-South transfers

For governments, South-South transfers are a clear avenue to tap into regional and cross-regional resources for social and economic development. South-South transfers are becoming increasingly important and take place through three main channels of cooperation: (i) bilateral aid; (ii) regional integration; and (iii) regional development banks.

As a first major channel of South-South transfers, bilateral aid (non-OECD donors) is led by Brazil, China, India, Kuwait, Saudi Arabia, South Africa, the United Arab Emirates and Venezuela (in alphabetical order). Data on South-South transfers are disparate and unreliable, and further difficult to compare in the absence of a universally-agreed definition of ODA. Nevertheless, estimates suggest that total worldwide ODA provided by non-OECD and non-EU member countries leaped from US$8.6 billion in 2006 to US$15.3 billion in 2008 (or from about 7 to 10 percent of total global development cooperation) (United Nations 2010a). If such estimates are at all indicative of actual flows, South-South aid offers a fast-growing opportunity for developing countries to finance social investments in children and poor households.

Two examples underscore the potential of South-South transfers. Given the magnitude of its investments in developing countries, especially in Sub-Saharan Africa and neighboring East Asian countries, the case of China must be highlighted. The Export-Import Bank of China, in

---

[21] The rest is spent on humanitarian aid (11 percent), in-donor costs (10 percent), debt relief (10 percent), and NGOs and local government (3 percent), with another 12 percent simply unallocated.

particular, plays a strategic role, lending mostly to large infrastructure projects. Another case is oil-rich Venezuela, which has funded numerous social and economic investments in neighboring countries, including through the *Petrocaribe* Initiative. One of the largest projects, Project Grand National, was launched in 2007 and supports everything from literacy programs, regional universities and radio/TV media with indigenous content to energy generation and distribution. It is important to note that about 90 percent of South-South cooperation is in the form of country programmable aid, which means that assistance from these 'emerging' donors can play a significant role in increasing fiscal space (United Nations 2010a:15).

A second channel is regional integration, which is a major form of South-South cooperation. Regional trading strategies can be an effective means of protecting, promoting and reshaping a region's division of labour, trade, production and consumption. Regional integration can also help to redress social asymmetries and raise living standards through social spending, public investment, and macroeconomic policies geared toward employment and the expansion of national markets. The EU is the best existing example of how regional solidarity may be articulated, but there are increasing experiences in developing countries. In fact, virtually every country in the world belongs to a regional block: the Association of South East Asian Nations (ASEAN), the African Union, the Andean Community (CAN), the Caribbean Community (CARICOM), the League of Arab States, the South Asian Association for Regional Cooperation (SAARC) and the Southern Africa Development Community (SADC), to name a few. In terms of fiscal space, regional formations can offer a means of 'locking in' finance for the development of member countries, which can be achieved through regional transfers or through regional development banks (see below).

A third major avenue of South-South transfers is regional development banks. The earliest South-South multilateral banks were founded in the Arab and Islamic world, where institutions were established in the 1970s as vehicles to transfer resources from the oil-rich countries to poorer countries. One such example is the Islamic Development Bank, whose objective is to foster the economic development and social progress of Muslim communities in accordance with the principles of Islamic law (*shari'ah*). In 2006, it announced a major funding operation in support of MDG-related expenditures among its member states. The second-largest regional development bank is the Arab Fund for Economic and Social Development, which provides soft lending for Arab League countries, but mostly for infrastructure projects. There are many successful cases outside of the Islamic world, such as the Andean Development Corporation (CAF), whose portfolio of US$3.0 billion, mostly in infrastructure, has largely surpassed investments by the World Bank and the Inter-American Development Bank in the South American sub-region. Also from Latin America, countries are collaborating to create alternative regional development banks, such as the Bank of the Bolivarian Alternative for Latin America (ALBA) and Bank of the South.

Box VI.2. South-South Cooperation in Guinea-Bissau

Traditionally, the main development partners of Guinea-Bissau have been the EU, European bilateral donors, and multilateral organizations such as the World Bank, the African Development Bank, the UN and the Economic Community of West African States (ECOWAS). During 2000-09, among donors that report to the OECD-Development Assistance Committee, the EU (US$294 million), Portugal (US$132 million), the World Bank (US$125 million), Italy (US$78 million) and Spain (US$55 million) provided the most development assistance to Guinea-Bissau. Not captured in these figures, however, is development assistance from key providers of South-South cooperation. Providers of South-South cooperation in Guinea-Bissau have typically provided project financing, often for infrastructure, as well as technical assistance, and include Angola, Brazil and China.

Angola provided a US$12 million (about 1.3 percent of GDP) grant in February 2011, which the authorities intend to use to finance roads and agriculture projects and to pay previous years' arrears to the private sector. In October 2010, Angola announced that it would open a US$25-million line of credit to support entrepreneurs from both countries who want to invest in Guinea-Bissau. In 2008, Angola provided US$10 million in budget support. In addition to financial assistance, Angola has been actively involved in security reform.

Brazil has cooperated with Guinea-Bissau across several sectors. It has provided technical assistance to increase agricultural production; established training centers for the military, the police, teachers, and ex-combatants; and helped build capacity to combat HIV/AIDS. The UNDP estimates that Brazil's bilateral assistance to Guinea-Bissau totaled US$6.2 million during 2006-09.

China has realized several large projects in Bissau, including a 20,000-seat stadium, the National Assembly building (US$6 million), a new government office (US$12 million) that houses 12 ministries and a hospital (US$8 million). China has also provided technical assistance to improve rice production.

Source: Adapted from IMF Country Report No. 11/119, May 2011, p. 7

4.3.   Curtailing South-North transfers

Net financial flows between the South and North show a different picture: debt interest payments, profit remittances and public/private investments in capital markets in developed economies largely offset net financial inflows to developing countries. According to the United Nations (2011), net financial flows out of developing economies totaled $557 billion in 2010, which is below the peak of US$881 billion reached in 2007 but significantly above trends from the late 1990s (Table 3). Most of this goes to the United States, which accounts for two-thirds of global savings, followed by other HICs like the United Kingdom, Spain and Australia. In sum, poor countries are transferring resources to rich countries, not vice versa.[22]

Table VI.3. Net Transfer of Financial Resources to
Developing Economies, 1998-2010
(in billions of US dollars)

Developing Region	1998	2000	2002	2004	2006	2008	2010
Africa	2.9	-13.7	-4.2	-34.5	-108.3	-99.1	-35.3
Sub-Saharan Africa*	11.5	2.3	4.4	3.5	-10.5	-4.8	14.6
East and South Asia	-129.8	-122.8	-149.2	-183.4	-385.7	-481.3	-352.9
Western Asia	34.5	-35.3	-23.2	-76.3	-175.6	-222.5	-112.7
Latin America	41.5	-4.2	-33.6	-85.4	-138.0	-73.5	-56.1
All developing countries	-41.0	-194.0	-210.2	-379.5	-807.8	-876.4	-557.0

Source: United Nations (2011:71)
* Excludes Nigeria and South Africa.

In addition to legal financial flows, curtailing IFFs could also free up additional resources for critical social and economic investments in many developing countries. IFFs involve capital that is illegally earned, transferred or utilized and include, *inter alia*, traded goods that are mispriced to avoid higher tariffs, wealth funneled to offshore accounts to evade income taxes and unreported movements of cash. More than US$1.3 trillion in IFFs are estimated to have moved out of developing countries in 2009, mostly through trade mispricing, with nearly two-thirds ending up in HICs (Kar et al. 2010). Overall, the average annual outflow of illicit capital is estimated to surpass 10 percent of GDP in 28

---

[22] Indeed, some of these flows are private or public savings in developing countries that are chasing safe investment returns in capital markets in developed countries. Nevertheless, global savings are flowing in the wrong direction, and countries need to ensure that more of their savings are directed toward domestic and regional development objectives rather than being exported to rich countries. Reversing the outflow of financial resources may require an overhaul of the financial system to provide greater banking stability and foster confidence in financial institutions.

developing countries—a truly staggering amount, especially when compared to health spending (Table 4)—and more than 5 percent of GDP in 64 developing countries.[23] Moreover, as of 2009, IFFs amounted to more than 10 times the total aid received by developing countries (Figure 7). To put this in perspective, the net effect would be that for every one dollar that developing countries receive in ODA, they are giving back about seven dollars to wealthy countries via illicit outflows.

Table VI.4. Exporting Illicit Capital and Health Spending, latest available
(in percent of GDP)

Country	IFFs (2005-08 avg. annual value)	Public health spending (2009 or latest available)	Country	IFFs (2005-08 avg. annual value)	Public health spending (2009 or latest available)
Panama	29.4	5.9	Nigeria	17.0	2.1
Seychelles	29.3	3.1	Lao PDR	15.5	0.8
Malaysia	28.1	2.2	Estonia	15.3	5.3
Guinea	26.7	0.9	Philippines	15.1	1.3
Honduras	26.6	3.4	Venezuela	12.8	2.4
Costa Rica	26.3	7.1	Madagascar	12.0	2.8
Kazakhstan	25.1	2.7	Zimbabwe	11.9	...
Azerbaijan	22.1	1.4	China	11.6	2.3
St. Vincent	21.3	3.2	Namibia	11.4	4.0
Samoa	20.7	6.1	Bulgaria	11.4	4.4
Nicaragua	20.5	5.4	Belarus	11.1	4.1
Djibouti	18.6	5.3	Mali	10.8	2.7
Trinidad & Tob.	17.9	2.7	Lithuania	10.7	4.5
Slovenia	17.7	6.4	Ukraine	10.6	3.8

Source: Authors' calculations based on Kar & Curcio (2011) and World Bank's *World Development Indicators* (2011)

Figure VI.7. Illicit Financial Flows (IFFs) versus ODA, 2000-09*
(in billions of current US$)

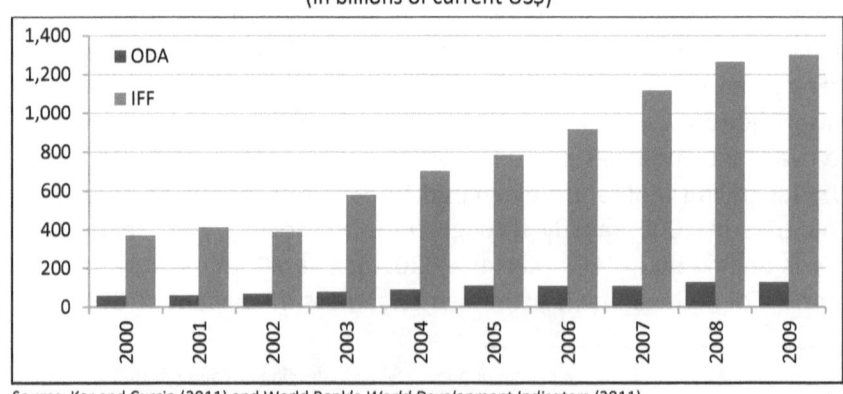

Source: Kar and Curcio (2011) and World Bank's *World Development Indicators* (2011)
* Only includes ODA given by OECD countries.

---

[23] Authors' calculations based on Kar and Curcio (2011) and World Bank's *World Development Indicators* (2011).

Given the vast amount of resources that illegally escape developing countries each year, policymakers should crack down on IFFs. Tax evasion, money laundering, bribery, trade mispricing and other financial crimes are illegal and deprive governments of revenues needed for social and economic development. To limit IFFs, there are several broad areas that policymakers can focus on, which include:

-   *Curtailing trade mispricing:* This can be achieved through strengthening legal institutions and attacking corruption, while, at the same time, empowering regulatory agencies to exercise adequate oversight over the financial system, the customs authorities, multinational and domestic companies, and the collection of direct and indirect taxes. Here, one concrete policy goal is to ensure that customs officials are able to effectively check the declared price of goods being transacted against international benchmark prices.

-   *Reducing bribery in public contracts:* To this end, policy measures should focus on enhancing the transparency and accountability of contracting processes according to international best practices.

-   *Reducing tax evasion:* At the national level, efforts must aim to widen the tax base and maximize compliance while also reducing indirect taxes; at the international level, consensus is needed to counter tax havens and forge global tax cooperation (see OECD's Centre for Tax Policy and Administration and Kar 2011 for a detailed discussion on policy options).

4.4.   New international sources of development finance

Given the failure of most donors to meet their aid commitments of 0.7 percent of GNI, many alternative sources of development finance have been proposed. Most of these involve taxing luxury activities or those that have negative social or environmental externalities (Atkinson 2004), and developing countries and partners could advocate for novel or 'innovative' sources of development finance. Several of the more popular ideas to increase financing for development are summarized below.

- *Currency transactions taxes:* Applying a 0.005 percent single-currency transaction tax on all four major currencies could yield up to US$33 billion per year for developing country assistance. And if applied more broadly to cover all financial transactions globally, a 0.01 percent tax could raise over US$1 trillion annually (Leading Group on Innovating Financing for Development 2010).

- *International transportation taxes*: Taxing fuel emissions for cargo transports could raise between US$2-19 billion a year in maritime receipts and US$1-6 billion a year in aviation receipts (Institute for Policy Studies 2011).

- *Carbon taxes:* Charging a flat fee for every ton of CO_2 emitted could lead to up to US$10 billion a year in development financing (Institute for Policy Studies 2011).

- *Arms trade taxes*: A 10 percent tax on the international arms trade could accrue up to US$5 billion annually in new development revenue (WHO 2009b).

- *Airline taxes:* A number of countries have implemented an air ticket solidarity levy that is charged to all passengers taking off from their national airports. In France, for example, this raised €160 million for additional development assistance in 2009 (Leading Group on Innovating Financing for Development 2010).

- *Global lottery:* The idea of a global lottery for development financing was widely touted following the introduction of the MDGs, but its popularity has since waned. Nonetheless, introducing national versions of a global lottery game, or a single global lottery sold worldwide and run by one organization, still has immense potential— it has been valued at US$6.2 billion annually (Carnegie Council 2005 and Inwent 2005).

In summary, there are ample opportunities for developing countries to increase fiscal space through strategies to increase North-South and South-South transfers, as well as capture and re-direct illicit funds into development aims. Similarly, there is an array of innovative sources of development financing available to donor countries, which means that there are no longer any excuses for falling short on aid commitments.

And for all countries—rich and poor—fiscal and foreign exchange reserves present additional creative options to boost fiscal space.

5.   Using Fiscal and Foreign Exchange Reserves

Fiscal reserves and central bank foreign exchange reserves (also known as international reserves) offer other potential sources of financing for investments in children and poor households today. Fiscal reserves are accrued through government budget surpluses, profits of state-owned companies or other government net income (the classic example is export revenues from state-owned natural resources, such as oil). Foreign exchange reserves, on the other hand, are accumulated through foreign exchange market interventions by central banks within the context of current account surpluses and/or capital inflows.

It is important to note the conceptual difference between fiscal reserves and central bank reserves. While fiscal reserves provide additional fiscal resources for the government and can be spent without incurring debt, central bank reserves are financed by issuing bonds or currency and do not constitute 'free fiscal assets' since they have counterpart liabilities (e.g., currency or bonds). Regarding the latter, it follows that if a government wishes to 'spend' central bank reserves, it must borrow to cover its new liabilities or otherwise creates new monetary liabilities (Park 2007).

5.1.   Fiscal reserves

For most developing countries, it is difficult to identify the overall levels of fiscal reserves, largely due to transparency issues as well as differing central bank and government accounting methods. However, given that many governments channel at least a part of their fiscal reserves into special funds, the most popular being sovereign wealth funds (SWFs), it is possible to broadly identify certain countries that could potentially access such resources for social and economic development. SWFs are state-owned investment funds composed of different financial assets that seek to maximize returns according to set levels of risk. SWFs have existed since the 1950s, but have grown rapidly over the past decade, reaching a record US$4.2 trillion in assets in 2010 (Figure 8).[24]

There are two main types of SWFs: commodity and non-commodity. About two-thirds of all assets in SWFs are funded by commodity exports (copper, gas, oil, phosphates, etc.), which is why they are commonly referred to as oil or natural resource funds. The two largest commodity-based SWFs are the Abu Dhabi Investment Authority (US$627 billion) and Norway's Government Pension Fund Global (US$572 billion) (SWF Institute 2011). Non-commodity SWFs, in contrast, can be funded through government budget surpluses, profits of state-owned companies and foreign aid. Singapore is home to two of the most well-known non-commodity SWFs—Temasek Holdings and the Government of Singapore Investment Corporation—which managed more than US$400 billion in combined assets in 2011 (SWF Institute 2011).

**Figure VI.8. Assets under Management by Sovereign
Wealth Funds (SWFs), 2000-12**
(in billions of current US$)

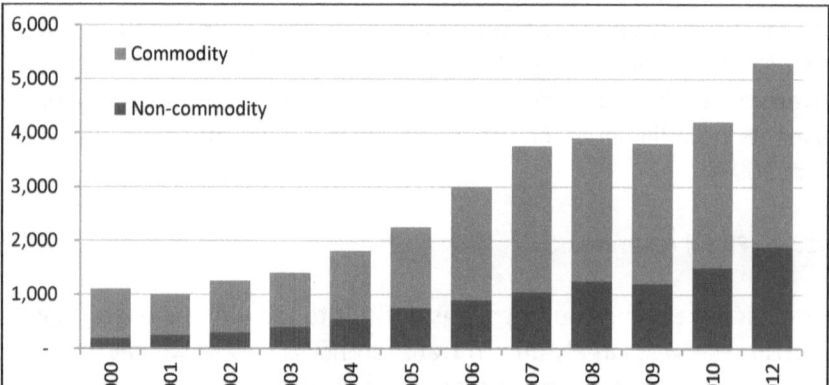

Source: TheCityUK (2011)

As evidenced by recent and projected trends in SWFs, many developing countries appear well endowed with fiscal reserves. Some of the more notable candidates are identified in Table 5 below, with the Russian Federation topping the list at more than US$140 billion in fiscal reserves followed by Libya, Algeria, Kazakhstan, Malaysia and Azerbaijan, all of

---

[24] An additional $6.8 trillion was held in other sovereign investment vehicles (e.g., pension reserve funds).

which had more than US$30 billion in 2011. Importantly, no least developed countries appear on this list.

Table VI.5. Sovereign Wealth Funds (SWFs) based on Fiscal Reserves
in Selected Countries, 2011

Country	Fund Name	Assets*	Inception	Origin
Russia	National Welfare Fund	142.5	2008	Oil
Libya	Libyan Investment Authority	70.0	2006	Oil
Algeria	Revenue Regulation Fund	56.7	2000	Oil
Kazakhstan	Kazakhstan National Fund	38.6	2000	Oil
Malaysia	Khazanah Nasional	36.8	1993	Non-Commodity
Azerbaijan	State Oil Fund	30.2	1999	Oil
Iran	Oil Stabilisation Fund	23.0	1999	Oil
Chile	Social and Economic Stabilization Fund	21.8	1985	Copper
Brazil	Sovereign Fund of Brazil	11.3	2008	Non-Commodity
Botswana	Pula Fund	6.9	1994	Diamonds/Minerals
Timor-Leste	Timor-Leste Petroleum Fund	6.3	2005	Oil and Gas
Mexico	Oil Revenues Stabilization Fund	6.0	2000	Oil
Venezuela	Macroeconomic Stabilization Fund	0.8	1998	Oil
Vietnam	State Capital Investment Corporation	0.5	2006	Non-Commodity
Kiribati	Revenue Equalization Reserve Fund	0.4	1956	Phosphates
Indonesia	Government Investment Unit	0.3	2006	Non-Commodity
Mauritania	Natl. Fund for Hydrocarbon Reserves	0.3	2006	Oil and Gas
Total		452.4		

Source: SWF Institute (2011)
* in billions of current US dollars.

The logic behind SWFs is to maximize financial returns, normally in international capital markets. A great deal of attention has been devoted to the fact that SWFs from the South are buying assets, real state, sovereign and corporate debt, private equity, hedge funds and commodity stocks in the North. Many have questioned the logic of investing earned public income for capital market growth to spend at some future point when those resources could be invested in needed social and economic goods and services at home, today.

Venezuela, for example, has used its fiscal reserves to finance a number of development objectives both domestically and internationally. At home, the government has fostered local development since 2001 through the Bank for Economic and Social Development of Venezuela (BANDES), which offers concessional rates to public and social enterprises (such as state-owned and community/family enterprises as well as cooperatives), supporting everything from milk producers to health services. In neighboring Latin American countries, Venezuela has channeled its fiscal reserves in support of social and economic development through the *Petro-Caribe* and *Petro-Andes* Initiatives. However, it is also important to understand the capacity issues that underlie a government's ability to spend fiscal reserves, as evidenced by the case of Timor-Leste (Box 3).

Box VI.3. When Resources and Poverty Abound:
The Paradox of Timor-Leste

A number of countries are sitting atop abundant natural resource funds, yet social indicators and progress toward development objectives remain dismal. One such case is Timor-Leste. For example, the share of people living in poverty increased from 36 to 50 percent between 2001 and 2007, levels of underweight children and maternal mortality remain unacceptably high, and it ranks in the bottom 30 percentile of all countries in terms of the Human Development Index (HDI). At the same time, however, Timor-Leste has an estimated US$6.3 billion stored in a sovereign wealth fund. If these funds were simply divvied up amongst the populace, they could, in effect, increase the average Timorese per capita income by more than 11-fold, to US$5,500 per person. So why isn't the government using the available resources to ramp up investments in its people?

Timor-Leste's government faces many development challenges. In addition to rampant poverty and unemployment, infrastructure remains dilapidated following years of conflict, and, despite vast petroleum reserves, it is the most oil dependent country in the world. Perhaps the biggest challenge, however, is the lack of institutional capacity, which makes it difficult for the government to effectively deliver public goods and services, especially to the poorest groups. As a result, present spending levels have stretched administrative capacities and created bottlenecks in the economy. The government has recognized the existing constraints and developed a plan to address budget under-execution and to build administrative capacities; possibilities for procuring external capacities are also being explored for areas that are locally unavailable. With capacity development—especially 'investing in investing'—now at the fore of the government's agenda, further tapping into available fiscal reserves could lead to a big return on socio-economic investments in the near future for Timor-Leste.

Sources: Gomes and Hailu (2009), World Bank (2010b) and IMF Country Report No. 11/65 (February 2011)[25]

---

[25] See also United Nations. 2010. "Timor-Leste's Economy at 'Turning Point,' Says Top UN Envoy." *United Nations News Centre*, April 07.

5.2. Central bank foreign exchange reserves

Foreign exchange reserves accumulated at central banks have increased dramatically in many developing countries over the past decade and offer creative opportunities to finance social and economic investments. On a global level, the accumulation of foreign exchange reserves more than quadrupled between 2000 and 2011, reaching 17 percent of global GDP in 2011.[26] Several developing regions, however, experienced elephantine growth. For example, total foreign exchange reserves leaped by 15-fold in the CEE/CIS, by 12-fold in East Asia and the Pacific, and by more than seven-fold in South Asia and the Middle East and North Africa, on average (Figure 9).

Figure VI.9. Foreign Exchange Reserve Accumulation by Developing Region, 1993-2011
(in millions of current US dollars; excluding gold)

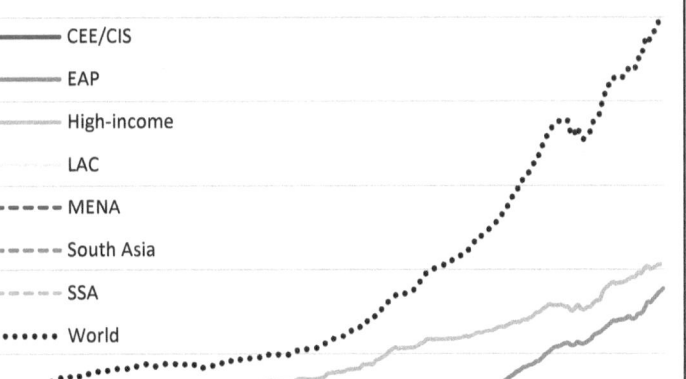

Source: World Bank's *Global Economic Monitor* (2011)

The massive accumulation of foreign exchange reserves is largely attributed to two strategies. On the one hand, some countries stockpile reserves to self-insure against economic and financial shocks, notably those that lead to capital flight and/or severe external imbalances. While this trend is most obvious in emerging market economies, especially in Asia, it is increasingly applicable to a number of LICs. In

---

[26] Authors' calculations based on World Bank's *Global Economic Monitor* (2011).

Sub-Saharan Africa, for example, more than one-third of foreign aid received between 1999 and 2005 was used to accumulate reserves (IMF 2007:42). On the other hand, countries also stockpile foreign exchange reserves as part of broader efforts to stabilize the macro economy, especially exchange rates. This is most commonly linked to export-led growth strategies that are based on exchange rate regimes with *de jure* or *de facto* pegs to the US dollar or currency baskets.

The strategy of reserve accumulation as self-insurance has been questioned by many, from the UN to the IMF. However, until better international solutions are put in place, some basic indicators point to the need to explore the use of foreign exchange reserves for social and economic development. For instance, according to the most popular gauge—the number of months for which a country could support its current level of imports if all other capital flows were to suddenly stop—62 developing countries with recent reserves data boasted more than one-and-a-half times the three-month safe level benchmark (e.g., more than 4.5 months). Using another standard indicator—the ratio of short-term debt-to-foreign exchange reserves—58 developing countries had short-term debt-to-reserve levels that were under 25 percent in 2011, which far exceeds the so-called Greenspan-Guidotti rule of thumb that advises countries to hold enough foreign reserves to cover total short-term external debt obligations. When combining these indicators, 33 developing countries with corresponding data exceeded both of the safe-level benchmarks during 2011 (Table 6).

So what are developing countries doing with their vast arsenals of foreign exchange reserves? In practice, most governments invest their reserves in Treasury Bills issued by the United States due to their safety (they were considered the least risky investment available, at least until August 2011) and high liquidity (they have maturity dates as short as four weeks). However, given the extremely low yields that are offered on these investments, there is definitely room for central banks in some developing countries to re-assess their current risk portfolios. It is also important for developing countries to question the logic of investing excess foreign reserves overseas when social and economic investments are needed at home.[27]

---

[27] While central bank reserves are not 'free' resources, they can be used as foreign currency liquidity guarantees to lower the costs of external borrowing for financing domestic development projects or strategic businesses.

Table VI.6. Foreign Exchange Reserve Adequacy in Selected
Developing Countries, 2011 (or latest available)
(excluding gold)

Country	Reserves (in months of imports)	Short-term Debt (as % of reserves)	Country	Reserves (in months of imports)	Short-term Debt (as % of reserves)
Algeria	51.3	1.0	Kyrgyz Republic	11.9	5.1
Angola	15.1	19.3	Lebanon	26.4	7.9
Azerbaijan	8.6	15.1	Madagascar	4.8	23.0
Bolivia	13.4	6.5	Malaysia	6.7	24.5
Brazil	17.9	16.7	Mongolia	6.6	5.4
Burundi	5.0	2.3	Morocco	6.6	9.2
Cambodia	5.2	8.1	Nigeria	8.2	7.7
Cameroon	8.2	0.6	Pakistan	4.9	10.8
China	20.4	9.8	Paraguay	4.5	19.5
Colombia	6.9	16.4	Peru	15.2	14.2
Congo, Rep. of	16.7	5.6	Philippines	10.3	9.1
Côte d'Ivoire	4.5	3.0	Russia	17.7	7.0
Egypt	8.1	7.3	Thailand	8.8	20.1
Gabon	7.6	5.4	Uganda	10.4	7.9
Guatemala	5.1	23.6	Uruguay	8.5	14.0
India	7.9	15.1	Yemen	6.9	6.3
Jordan	8.7	9.5			

Source: Authors' calculations based on World Bank's *World Development Indicators* (2011) and *Global Economic Monitor* (2011)

One strategy to foster local development using surplus foreign exchange reserves is to finance domestic projects. India stands as an innovative example, as it strategically uses a portion of its foreign reserves—without the risk of monetary expansion—to support one of the country's biggest development needs: infrastructure investment (Park 2007:21-22). To do so, India's government created two subsidiaries that borrow foreign exchange reserves from the central bank. The foreign exchange is then: (i) directly on-lent to Indian companies for capital expenditures outside India; (ii) used to co-finance the external commercial borrowings of Indian companies; or (iii) invested in highly rated collateral securities to enhance the credit ratings of Indian companies that raise funds in international capital markets. The central government plays an important role by guaranteeing the loans from the central bank, which, in turn, is assured a higher return on domestic highways, for instance, than would otherwise be achieved on short-term government bonds from the United States. In addition to more traditional productive sectors, such as infrastructure, India's approach could also be applied to facilitate private sector borrowing for different social investments, such as education and health facilities.

In addition to financing domestic projects, developing countries can also pursue longer-term investment returns on their excess foreign exchange through regional South-South cooperation. For example, since the major oil boom in the 1970s, many countries in the Middle East have invested surplus foreign exchange reserves in the Islamic Development Bank to foster social and economic development in poorer communities (Ortiz 2008b). The CAF, the Bank of ALBA and the Bank of the South are examples from Latin America where countries are channeling extra foreign exchange reserves to support regional investments. And in Asia, 13 countries contributed US$120 billion to the Chiang Mai Initiative in 2010, which serves as a reserve-pooling mechanism to help manage short-term liquidity problems in the region.

In sum, fiscal and foreign exchange reserves present creative possibilities for governments to enhance fiscal space for social and economic investments, although a careful assessment of their potential impact on monetary expansion or public debt impact is merited.

6.   Borrowing and Debt Restructuring

Sound debt management is a key principle of a stable macroeconomic policy framework. Studies have shown that high debt distress can restrict capital market access, disrupt financial intermediation and/or hinder economic activities. Yet for countries that have some scope for additional borrowing, this offers another source of financing for social and economic investments. For those countries that may have elevated levels of sovereign debt, it may also be possible to restructure existing obligations either by debt re-negotiation, debt relief/forgiveness, debt swaps/conversion or debt repudiation, especially when the legitimacy of the debt is questionable and/or the opportunity cost in terms of worsening child outcomes is high.

6.1.   Borrowing

Many developing countries, having strengthened their national financial markets, show capacity to engage in further borrowing, both domestically and externally. These may include loans, either from commercial or development banks or funds, or through issuing government securities, such as bonds. International commercial bank loans are a least preferred option for governments to expand fiscal space due to associated fees and higher interest rates. Tanzania stands as one recent example, as its government borrowed US$1.5 billion from local and foreign banks to boost its 2011 budget and cover a deficit left by an unexpected withdrawal of donor support.[28]

Loans from development banks and funds, as well as bilateral loans from donors, may be at commercial or concessional interest rates. If debt is perceived as a strategic option to boost social and economic spending, concessional loans are a much better option than loans with commercial rates since they offer beneficial conditions to developing countries. For example, the World Bank's International Development Association (IDA) lends money to the poorest countries without interest along with long grace periods (usually 10 years) and 35 to 40-year repayment periods. Concessional borrowing is generally available from regional development banks (e.g., the African, Asian, Inter-American and Islamic Development Banks), specialized funds (e.g., the OPEC Fund for International Development or the Arab Fund for Economic and Social Development) and from bilateral loans from donor countries.

Government bonds are another market-based borrowing option and generally cheaper when compared to commercial bank loans. While European governments have been issuing bonds to support public spending since the dawn of modern history, financial liberalization coupled with the rise of creditworthiness among emerging markets has made the issuance of public bonds increasingly popular since the 1990s.

Total public bonds issued annually by developing country governments increased markedly during the 1990s, reaching close to US$500 billion in 2009 (Figure 10). Latin America is the region that has experienced the largest growth, issuing nearly double the amount of debt as the next highest region, the CEE/CIS, as of 2009. Although bonds appear less common in other regions, they are still viable options for many lower-income countries. For example, Ghana and Senegal tapped international debt markets in 2007 and 2009, respectively (Gueye and Sy 2010). In addition to bonds at the national level, municipal or sub-national bonds

---

[28] Liganga, L. and B. Kagashe. 2010. "Tanzania: World Bank Faults Government's Borrowing Plan." *The Citizen*, June 05.

are another alternative for local governments, which are typically issued for specific purposes, such as for developing an urban area or expanding school, water supply or transportation systems (Ortiz 2008b).

Figure VI.10. Public Bonds by Developing Regions, 1980-2009*
(in billions of current US dollars)

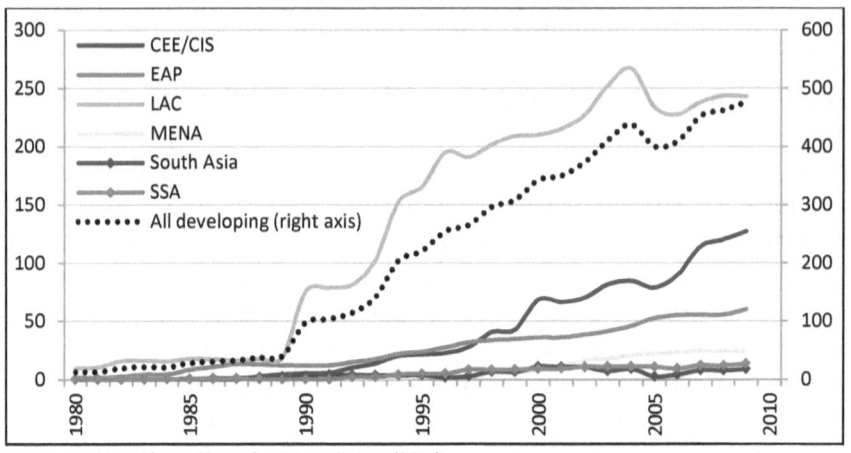

Source: World Bank's *World Development Indicators* (2011)
* Includes public and publicly guaranteed debt from bonds that are either publicly issued or privately placed.

How much public debt is sustainable? The IMF (2010b) uses a 40 percent long-term debt-to-GDP ratio as the ceiling that developing countries should not exceed in order to ensure fiscal sustainability and macroeconomic stability. Others suggest a higher threshold (e.g., 60 percent according to Reinhart and Rogoff 2010). Still another approach is to view an optimal debt-to-GDP ratio as arbitrary since public debt can be beneficial over the long term if interest payments are less than the annual increase in nominal GDP (see Chapter 3 of UNCTAD 2011).

So which countries might have room to borrow? Applying even the most conservative parameters, many developing countries appear well-positioned to tap into debt markets. Figure 11 lists 29 countries that had total external debts under 20 percent of GDP through 2009. This list is, of course, only indicative, as debt levels have likely increased in many countries since then due to debt-financed fiscal stimulus packages.

However, to determine the feasibility of increasing public debt for a given country, it is important to carry out a comprehensive and dynamic analysis, such as the IMF-World Bank debt sustainability assessments (DSA) framework. DSAs seek to determine, going forward, if a country's overall debt level would be too big to be serviceable under a given set of assumptions, which include the projected fiscal and GDP growth paths.[29] However, DSA conclusions reflect the underlying assumptions, and depending on how conservative or ambitious those underlying assumptions may be, a rather different picture on the level of debt distress may emerge. Another key limitation of DSAs is that GDP growth projections only take into account returns from investments in physical capital (airports, roads etc.) but not returns from investments in human or social capital (e.g., spending on primary/secondary education, health and social protection), which are vital to sustained growth in the longer run. Thus, while current DSA frameworks should be viewed as a good starting point of analysis, they can be enhanced by relaxing certain assumptions and accounting for both social and economic returns.

Figure VI.11. Possible Borrowing Candidates, 2009[30]
(total external debt as a percent of GDP)

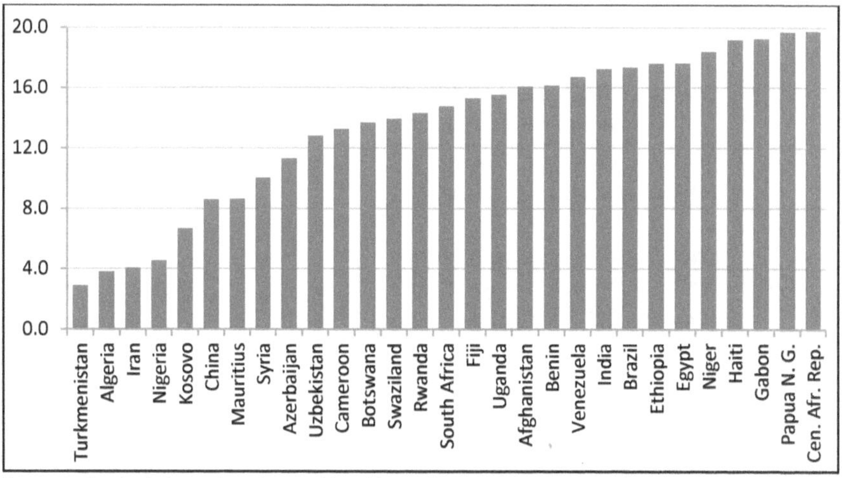

Source: Authors' calculations based on World Bank's *World Development Indicators* (2011)

---

[29] The DSA approach includes four steps: (i) a five-year forecast of variables that impact external debt (e.g., the primary account, GDP, interest rates, exchange rates and inflation); (ii) an examination of the evolution of debt as a percent of GDP over the next five years; (iii) different stress tests to evaluate the impact of adverse shocks on the different forecasted variables in step i; and (iv) evaluation of whether current debt loads are sustainable based on the stress tests.

[30] Figure 11 only captures external public debt. While domestic debt is generally a smaller proportion of total public debt in developing countries, this is certainly not true for all countries. It is, however, more difficult to assess domestic debt levels since they are not tracked by major databases (e.g., by the IMF or World Bank), and detailed information is often unavailable to policymakers and analysts (Panizza 2008). Moreover, the gravity of domestic debt can be high in developing countries, many of which have replaced external debt with more expensive domestic debt in recent years. When performing country level analysis, it is therefore imperative to assess the composition of both domestic and foreign public debt.

6.2.   Debt restructuring

Debt restructuring is the process of reducing existing levels of debt or debt service. While some developing countries have space for additional borrowing, debt restructuring has become an increasingly common strategy to alleviate fiscal pressures for other countries, especially those suffering from exorbitant sovereign debt levels. Figure 12 highlights the gravity of the external debt burden facing a number of developing countries. Overall, 33 countries (only 20 are displayed) have a three-year average external debt-to-public health spending ratio greater than 1.75; in other words, debt payments in these countries are nearly double or more than the amount of public money invested in the health of their populaces, with Kazakhstan spending a staggering 13 times more on external debt than on health. When sovereign debt payments crowd out essential social expenditures, there is a strong case for policymakers to explore the restructuring of their obligations to their creditors.

Figure VI.12. Debt and Health Spending, 2007-09*
(average values, based on current US dollars)

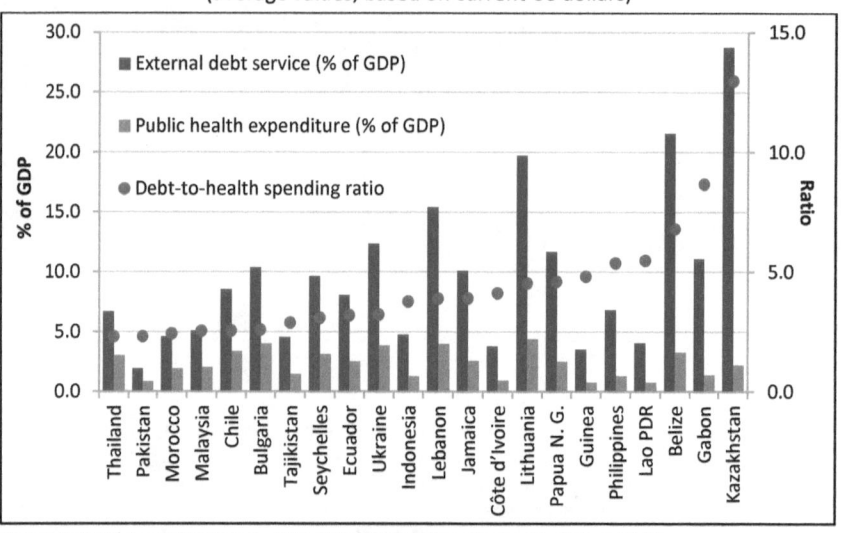

Source: Authors' calculations based on World Bank's *World Development Indicators* (2011)
* This figure only includes external public debt (see footnote for Figure 11).

In recent years, many—including some official creditors such as Norway—have raised the issue of creditor co-responsibility as a way of promoting responsible lending practices. The Monterrey Consensus additionally opened up the debate on the issue of creditor co-responsibility for what is termed 'illegitimate debt,' as well as the need to find a fair and durable solution to the debt crisis. In particular, the UN Secretary-General and the UN Independent Expert on debt and human rights note that creditor and debtor countries are both equally responsible for preventing and resolving unsustainable debt situations.

The concept of illegitimate debt refers to a variety of debts that may be questioned, including, *inter alia*: (i) debt incurred by authoritarian regimes; (ii) debt that cannot be serviced without threatening the realization or non-regression of basic human rights; (iii) debt incurred under predatory repayment terms, including usurious interest rates; (iv) debt converted from private (commercial) to public debt under pressure to bail out creditors; (v) loans used for morally reprehensible purposes, such as the financing of a suppressive regime; and (vi) debt resulting from irresponsible projects that failed to serve development objectives or caused harm to the people or the environment (United Nations 2009a).

In practice, there are five main options available to governments to restructure sovereign debt, which include re-negotiating debt, pursuing debt relief/forgiveness, debt swaps/conversions, repudiating debt and defaulting. These are briefly summarized in the following.

- *Debt re-negotiation:* A first option is to restructure debt via voluntary negotiations and collective action clauses. Voluntary negotiations have mostly applied to bank loans, as demonstrated by the more than 60 countries that have successfully re-negotiated terms between 1990 and the early 2000s (Bai and Zhangy 2010). These processes, however, take an average of five years, which carry a high re-negotiation cost since governments cannot resume international borrowing during that period. Collective action clauses are most commonly used to restructure government bonds and take much less time than voluntary negotiations (about one year on average); through collective action clauses included in bond contracts, many countries have successfully reached agreements with commercial creditors to lengthen the maturity and lower the coupon of outstanding bonds.

- *Debt relief/forgiveness:* A second option is to negotiate debt forgiveness. This has happened through creditor-led forums, such as the Paris and London Clubs, which are used to restructure or cancel bilateral and commercial debt, respectively, as well as the Heavily Indebted Poor Countries (HIPC) Initiative that is managed by the IMF and World Bank. The HIPC Initiative has been the most prominent option for debt relief. Launched in 1996, 32 of the 39 eligible LICs had reached their completion points as of early 2012 by meeting debt relief criteria. While earlier these countries were spending more on debt service than on health and education combined, on average, social spending now accounts for roughly five times their amount of debt-service payments (IMF 2011a). However, debt forgiveness has been slow to deliver (Figure 13), and the benefits of agreed debt reduction have proven far less than hoped for in most cases (UNCTAD 2008:139-141).

Figure VI.13. Poor Country Debt at a Glance
(in billions of current US$)

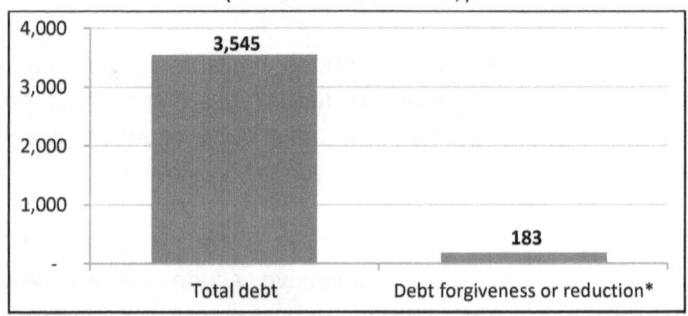

Source: World Bank's *World Development Indicators* (2011)
* Since 2000.

- *Debt swaps/conversions*: A debt swap or debt conversion is the sale of a debt by a creditor to an investor (usually a non-profit organization) who purchases the debt at a discounted price and then exchanges it with the indebted government for shares in a state-owned company or for domestic currency to finance a specific project. More than 50 developing countries have undertaken debt swaps with different aims. They emerged in the 1980s as a strategy to improve the fiscal solvency of governments, mostly in Latin America, and to give them access to new international finance. Countries such as Argentina and Chile carried out debt-for-equity swaps, exchanging external private debt for shares in state-run companies. Debt-for-nature swaps soon followed in which a portion of a developing country's foreign debt was exchanged for investments in environmental conservation measures. During the 1990s, UNICEF facilitated several private debt swaps to support child-related aid programs. Although most swaps have been conducted within the framework of the HIPC Initiative, there are a variety of swap options available to governments to enhance fiscal space. The Debt2Health initiative of the Global Fund is a recent debt swap initiative that converts debt repayments into health expenditures in countries that are ineligible for debt relief.[31] For smaller island states, there are debt conversions for climate change adaptation (Hurley 2010). There are also opportunities to negotiate other types of swaps/conversions to enhance fiscal space, including: debt-for-children/education/health/environment, debt-for-equity, debt-for-exports, debt-for-offsets and even debt-for-debt (Ruiz 2007).

- *Debt Repudiation:* Another option is repudiation. History shows examples of governments repudiating debt, such as the United Kingdom after the Boer War or the United States' repudiation of Cuban debts owed to Spain following the Spanish-American War. Given that the high cost of debt servicing limits public investments in essential social and economic goods and services, repudiation has been increasingly considered by developing countries in recent years. Christian Aid (2007) outlines a number of practical steps that debtor countries can follow to determine if debt repudiation is a sensible option: (i) assess the impact that debt servicing has on the financing of basic services; (ii) carry out a full debt audit to identify which parts are odious or illegitimate; (iii) identify what portion of the legitimate debt can be serviced without jeopardizing essential public services; (iv) hold a moratorium on servicing illegitimate debt and discuss with creditors; (v) depending on the progress of discussions, examine the possibility of withholding payments in order to increase investments in basic services; and (vi) open debt contraction processes to full democratic scrutiny. The recent referendum in Iceland (Box 4) and public debt audits, such as in Ecuador (Box 5), underscore the idea that citizens have valid concerns about illegitimate sovereign debt and the high social costs.

---

[31] http://www.theglobalfund.org/en/innovativefinancing/debt2health/.

Box VI.4. Debt Repudiation: Iraq and Iceland

Two recent examples of sovereign debt repudiation are Iraq and Iceland. Iraq's 80 percent debt cancellation was a result of international political pressure; the United States was at the forefront of negotiating for a full-scale write-off of loans undertaken by foreign creditors to the Saddam Hussein regime after its overthrow in 2003. Iceland, on the other hand, pursued repudiation through public consultation. In March 2010, a national referendum was called that allowed Icelandic citizens to vote on whether and how the country should repay a nationalized private debt that was claimed by the Netherlands and the United Kingdom. This was not a sovereign debt issue; private Icelandic banks held €6.7 billion in deposits from British and Dutch banks, and, when they collapsed, the government decided to assume the private obligations as a public debt. According to the IMF, this debt was a result of privatization and deregulation of the banking sector, which was facilitated by easy access to foreign funding; the growing imbalances went undetected by Iceland's financial sector supervisory. In the referendum, voters delivered a resounding 'no' (more than 90 percent) to reimburse the Dutch and British banks along with the orthodox policies that would have accompanied the debt repayment plan. After massive international pressure, a second referendum was called in April 2011; Icelanders again rejected a proposed repayment plan. Despite pressures and threats due to the government's heterodox policies (e.g., debt repudiation, capital controls and currency depreciation), Iceland is recovering well from the crisis. Not only has it regained access to international capital markets, but it has also preserved the welfare of its citizens, with support from the IMF (de Bruijn et al. 2010, IMF 2010c).

Box VI.5. Debt Audits: The Case of Ecuador

Some developing countries have re-examined their accumulated debt from the 1970s in order to decrease outstanding obligations. In 2008, Ecuador became the first country to hold an official audit to assess the legitimacy of its sovereign debt. The government-commissioned, two year-long investigation concluded that some of its foreign debts had broken multiple principles of international and domestic law and were therefore deemed 'illegitimate'— these were mostly private sector debts that had been nationalized by former governments. While Ecuador respected all of the debt that had contributed to the country's development—the so-called 'legitimate' debt—it defaulted on its alleged illegitimate debt in November 2008 and bought this back at 35 cents to the US dollar just a few weeks later. Based on the experience of Ecuador, as well as Norway, a special UN Commission of Experts on Reforms of the International Monetary and Financial System came out in support of public debt audits as a mechanism for transparent and fair restructuring of debts (United Nations 2009b:125). Debt audits are ongoing in several other countries, such as Bolivia, Brazil, Greece, Ireland and the Philippines.

Box VI.6. The Need for an International Debt Work-out Mechanism

In practice, all of the different sovereign debt restructuring options are politically difficult, as governments that initiate such processes are often under enormous pressure by creditors. This reality, coupled with the increasing prevalence of sovereign debt crises in the current environment, underscores the pressing need for an international judicial body that can resolve issues between sovereign borrowers and their lenders. Since the pioneering proposals for an International Chapter 9 Insolvency by Raffer (1993), the international financial institutions, the UN and different civil society organizations have been advocating for an international debt-work out mechanism. More recently, the IMF proposed a Sovereign Debt Restructuring Mechanism, which would have created a process for 'sovereign bankruptcy' to give states a new beginning, much like a corporation or individual who files for bankruptcy. In the same line, the Jubilee Campaign (Pettifor 2002) and Eurodad (2009) have identified principles for a sovereign debt work-out procedure, many of which are supported by the UN. Current proposals to operationalize these principles include an International Debt Court and/or an International Mediation Forum (United Nations 2010b).

- *Default:* Overall, some 20 countries have defaulted on their sovereign debt since 1999, which includes debt denominated in both local and foreign currencies.[32] At US$82 billion and US$73 billion, Argentina and the Russian Federation, respectively, stand as the largest sovereign defaulters in history. The widely used term 'haircut' refers to investor losses as a result of debt restructuring. While this was an estimated 75 percent in the case of Argentina in 2005 and 55 percent for the Russian Federation in 1999-2000, the average haircut in more recent forced restructurings has been between 25 and 40 percent (Sturzenegger and Zettelmeyer 2005). Outright default may be viewed as disorderly debt restructuring since the immediate aftermath can be severe as foreign investments flee and capital inflows cease, which could hurt domestic employment and economic activities, the extent of which depends on the openness of the economy. However, history shows that countries that defaulted have been able to regain capital market access, achieve stable macroeconomic conditions and

---

[32] According to Standard & Poor's (2011) and Moody's (2008), this list includes: Antigua (2006), Argentina (2001), Belize (2006), the Dominican Republic (1999, 2005), Ecuador (2008), Gabon (1999, 2002), Grenada (2004), Indonesia (1999, 2000 and 2002), Côte d'Ivoire (2000), Jamaica (2010), Moldova (2002), Pakistan (1999), Paraguay (2003), Peru (2000), the Russian Federation (1999), Seychelles (2008), Ukraine (2000), Uruguay (2003) and Venezuela (2005).

increase fiscal space for social and economic development in a relatively short amount of time (Lora and Olivera 2006, Weisbrot and Sandoval 2007).

7.   A More Accommodating Macroeconomic Framework

The goals of macroeconomic policy are multiple, from supporting growth, price stabilization or inflation control, to smoothing economic cycles, reducing unemployment and poverty, and promoting equity. In the last decades, macroeconomic frameworks have placed a strong emphasis on short-term stabilization measures, such as controlling inflation and fiscal deficits, as part of broader efforts aimed at economic liberalization, integrating into global markets and attracting investment. While these macroeconomic objectives are not necessarily problematic, there is an increasing risk in many developing countries that other important objectives, such as employment-generating growth and social development, become secondary and underemphasized.

Many of these orthodox approaches have since been questioned, including through UNICEF's work on *Adjustment with a Human Face* in the 1980s and the broader advocacy efforts of the UN to advance human development and human rights since the 1990s. Others (e.g., Chowdhury and Islam 2010) have argued that higher fiscal deficits do not necessarily lead to higher interest rates, higher inflation rates or higher current account deficits if there is unemployment or spare capacity in an economy. More recently, as the multiple shocks of the global economic crisis unfolded and intensified, support shifted from restrictive and narrow macroeconomic frameworks to a more accommodating one, a change that has since been reflected in the statements of senior leaders in various organizations, including the IMF (2009 and 2011b). In practice, this means that the conditions for more maneuver in policymaking and resource mobilization could be achieved through both fiscal and monetary policies, which are discussed in the following sections.

7.1.   More accommodative fiscal policy

The first channel to achieve a more accommodative macroeconomic framework is through expanding government expenditures to influence the economy. As part of the crisis response, there has been a growing recognition of the need to ease budget constraints and allow for an increasing degree of deficit spending, especially to support socially relevant investments. By doing so, more resources can be allocated to address the impacts of the crisis and support poverty-reducing and employment-generating economic growth (IMF 2009).

To demonstrate the potential size of resources that could be freed up for social spending through larger—albeit reasonable—fiscal deficits, consider Sub-Saharan Africa. Of the 42 developing countries in the region for which there is fiscal balance data, 35 were forecasted to run fiscal deficits in 2011. If each of these countries increased the size of their current deficit by 2.5 percentage points, public health spending could jump by more than 5 percent, on average. Some countries, however, could experience vast increases in available resources for public health. For example, expanding the fiscal deficit by 2.5 percent could lead to a roughly 10 percent increase in the health budget in all of the countries listed in Table 7, and more than 30 percent in Eritrea. Notably, many of these countries contain some of the highest under-5 mortality rates in the world (Column D).

Table VI.7. Real Fiscal Deficits and Health Spending in 35 Sub-Saharan African Countries, fiscal year 2011

Country	(A) Fiscal Balance (% of GDP)*	(B) Health Spending (2007-09 avg.) % of GDP	(B) % of budget	(C) 2.5% Real Increase of Deficit (in % of health budget)**	(D) Under-5 Mortality Rate, 2010 (per 1,000 births)
Cape Verde	-11.8	3.2	10.4	9.2	36
Côte d'Ivoire	-3.9	0.9	4.5	10.6	123
Eritrea	-16.2	1.3	3.2	32.3	61
Guinea	-3.9	0.8	4.3	12.9	130
Kenya	-5.4	1.5	5.9	8.8	85
Lesotho	-14.5	4.9	8.2	7.4	85
São Tomé and Príncipe	-7.4	3.1	13.2	6.0	80
Sierra Leone	-4.0	0.9	4.2	11.7	174
Swaziland	-9.0	3.7	9.3	6.0	78
Uganda	-6.8	1.6	10.6	10.9	99

Sources: IMF's *World Economic Outlook* (September 2011) for fiscal balance, real GDP and inflation; World Bank's *World Development Indicators* (2011) for health expenditure; and the UN Inter-agency Group for Child Mortality Estimation for under-5 mortality estimates
* Includes grants.
** Estimate based on real value (local currency value/avg. consumer price) of fiscal balance and health expends.

While many developing countries are already running deficits, a number of others were forecasted to have fiscal surpluses in 2011 (Figure 14). In these cases, allocating surplus funds to public health could lead to extraordinary gains. In the Republic of Congo, for example, significant progress in health outcomes could be made if even a small portion of surplus funds were directed to the health sector together with appropriate reforms to strengthen service delivery institutions. And for the 16 developing countries that were projected to benefit from a positive fiscal balance in 2011, surplus budget funds could ramp up health spending by about four times the current levels, on average.

Figure VI.14. Fiscal Surplus and Health Spending, 2011

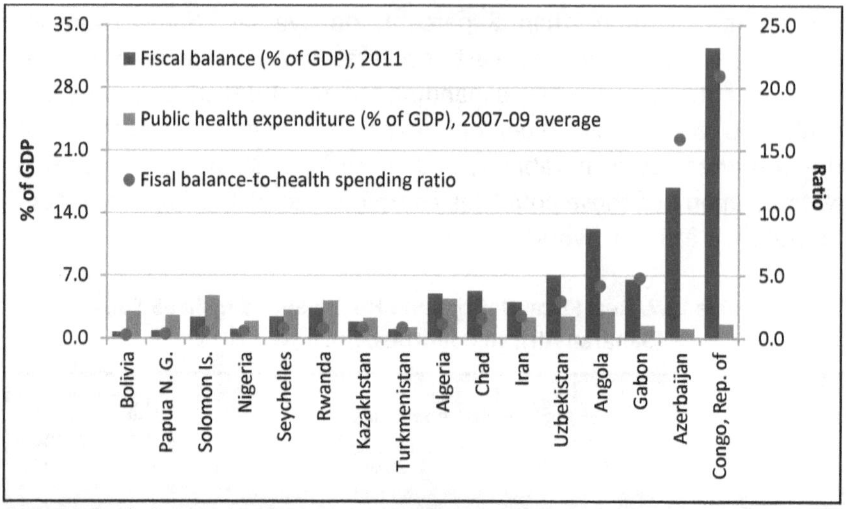

Sources: Authors' calculations based on IMF's *World Economic Outlook* (September 2011) for fiscal balance data and World Bank's *World Development Indicators* (2011) for health expenditure

The analysis of Sub-Saharan African countries serves to illustrate the potential of any government's fiscal position—deficit or surplus—to impact essential social and economic spending. However, it is important to carry out a rigorous assessment of fiscal sustainability at the country level, taking into account not only economic aspects, such as debt burden, revenue generation capacity and likely GDP growth trajectory, but also the potential opportunity cost of foregoing spending on children and other vulnerable populations. By doing so, many governments may be able to pursue an alternative fiscal adjustment path to ramp up needed and urgent investments today (Figure 15).

**Figure VI.15. Projected Fiscal Deficits and Alternative
Adjustment Path, 2007-16**
(as a percent of GDP)

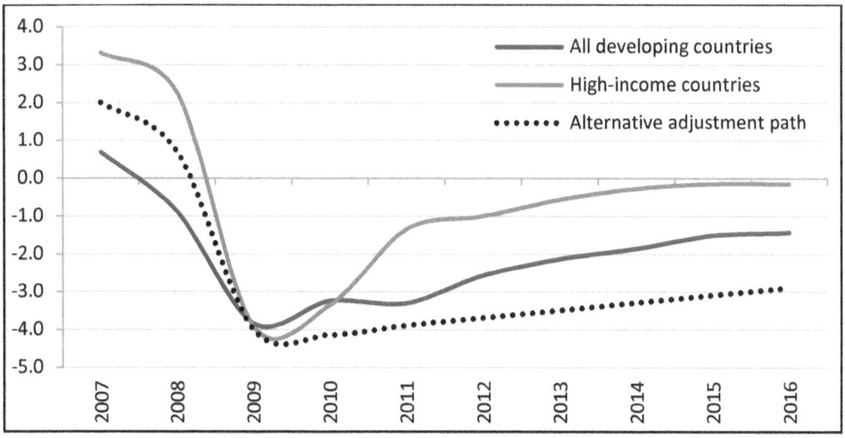

Source: Authors' calculations based on IMF's *World Economic Outlook* (September 2011)

7.2.   More accommodative monetary policy

The second channel to achieve a more accommodative macroeconomic framework is through expansionary monetary policy. There are two schools of thought regarding how authorities should control the money supply in an economy. On the one hand, some argue that the ultimate aim of monetary policy should be to achieve low inflation.[33] Here, since high inflation creates uncertainties about the future and depresses investment, low inflation is viewed as a key component of macroeconomic stability and growth, and is a goal in itself. This faction also underscores the dangers of high inflation on poor households, which erodes their disposable incomes and makes it more difficult for them to purchase essential goods and services.

On the other side of the spectrum are those who view excessive inflation control as a danger to poverty and economic growth. This school of thought argues that certain measures, such as higher interest rates, can lead to increasing unemployment, lower aggregate demand and weaker growth. High interest rates are especially bad for small producers and those who already have limited access to finance, including women and persons with limited assets. The resulting declines

---

[33] This view is more controversial, as it has been found that a certain amount of inflation (moderate inflation, not very high inflationary episodes) may be necessary to fuel more economic activity.

in output and employment can also weaken workers' bargaining positions and depress wages, therefore indirectly increasing poverty. All of these, in turn, weaken the capabilities of households to provide for and invest in children. Acknowledging the potential risks of low inflation on growth and poverty, the IMF advised governments to raise inflation above the standard 5 percent benchmark during 2009 in order to respond to the food, fuel and financial shocks (IMF 2009). However, it is important to underscore that there are diverse views on what constitutes an 'acceptable' level of inflation (Table 8).

Table VI.8. Safe Inflation Thresholds for Developing Countries

Source	Author(s)	Inflation Threshold (%)
Academic Papers	Fischer (1993)	15-30
	Bruno (1995)	20
	Barro (1996)	10-20
	Bruno and Easterly (1998)	40
	Gylfason and Herbertsson (2001)	10-20
	Rousseau and Watchel (2002)	13-25
	Burdekin et al. (2004)	3
	Gillman et al. (2004)	10
	Sepehri and Moshiri (2004)	5-15
	Pollin and Zhu (2006)	14-16
	Li (2006)	14
	Vaona and Schiavo (2007)	12
	US GAO (2009)	5-12
	Bick (2010)	12
	Kremer et al. (2011)	17
IMF Papers	Sarel (1996)	8
	Ghosh and Phillips (1998)	>5
	Kochar and Coorey (1999)	5
	Khan and Senhadji (2001)	11-12
	Selassie et al. (2006)	5
	Espinoza et al. (2010)	10
	Blanchard et al. (2010)	4

Source: Authors' literature review

In general, flexibility to pursue expansionary monetary policy is strongly related to the extent to which wages and incomes are 'indexed'—in other words, automatically adjusted to changes in overall prices, at least to some extent. In developing countries where most incomes, including wage incomes, tend to move along with prices, there can be social tolerance of fairly high rates of inflation, especially if it still allows people to continue to consume essential goods and services. But in other developing countries where wage incomes and the earnings of the self-employed do not increase much when overall price levels rise, even relatively low inflation rates can cause social havoc, especially if the inflation is not accompanied by higher employment. They can also immediately and directly affect the well-being of children; this is especially true for food inflation, which continues to be a significant challenge to many developing countries (Chapter III).

Ultimately, this means that inflation thresholds are policy choices based on particular conditions in different societies, and monetary policies should be designed to encourage employment creation. Bearing this in mind, the IMF forecasted that 65 developing countries will have inflation rates at or below 5 percent during 2012, 47 of which exercise independent monetary policy (Table 9). In such cases, an expansionary monetary policy could be explored as a potential option to support increased social and economic investments among the poorest and most disadvantaged populations. For other developing countries that are also experiencing low inflation rates but belong to monetary unions—such as the Eastern Caribbean Currency Union, the Economic and Monetary Community of Central Africa, and the West African Economic and Monetary Union—there may be scope to discuss the loosening of monetary policy as a block of countries.

Table VI.9. Developing Countries with Inflation Rates at or below Five Percent, 2012 forecasts
(in percent change, year on year average consumer prices)

Country	Inflation Rate	Country	Inflation Rate
St. Vincent and Grenadines*	1.4	Armenia	3.3
Liberia*	1.6	China	3.3
Dominica*	1.9	Comoros	3.3
Djibouti	1.9	Belize	3.3
Burkina Faso*	2.0	Gabon*	3.4
Guinea-Bissau*	2.0	Albania	3.5
Macedonia, FYR	2.0	Panama	3.5
Montenegro	2.0	Myanmar	3.7
Niger*	2.0	Tunisia	4.0
Latvia	2.3	Thailand	4.1
Mali*	2.3	Antigua and Barbuda*	4.1
Peru	2.4	Philippines	4.1
Senegal*	2.5	Algeria	4.3

Country	Inflation Rate	Country	Inflation Rate
Bosnia and Herzegovina	2.5	Romania	4.3
Cameroon	2.5	Serbia	4.3
Côte d'Ivoire*	2.5	Seychelles	4.6
Malaysia	2.5	St. Kitts and Nevis*	4.7
St. Lucia*	2.5	Bolivia	4.8
Kosovo	2.6	Tonga	4.8
Tuvalu	2.6	El Salvador	4.9
Lithuania	2.6	Ecuador	4.9
Central African Republic*	2.6	Cape Verde*	4.9
Morocco	2.7	Lebanon	5.0
Togo*	2.8	South Africa	5.0
Vanuatu	2.9	Bhutan	5.0
Bulgaria	2.9	Chad*	5.0
Colombia	2.9	Fiji	5.0
Benin*	3.0	Georgia	5.0
Samoa	3.0	Iraq	5.0
Chile	3.1	Kiribati	5.0
Mexico	3.1	Syria	5.0
Afghanistan	3.2	Solomon Islands	5.0
Grenada*	3.2		

Source: IMF's *World Economic Outlook* (September 2011)
* Country belongs to a monetary union.

8.   Conclusion

As the number of countries expected to adopt fiscal contraction in 2012 increases dramatically, there are grave concerns that many are doing so prematurely and even excessively (see Chapter V). Aside from the direct impact on essential social expenditures, the different austerity measures being considered pose immense risks to vulnerable populations whose need for public assistance remains significant. The drive toward fiscal consolidation is further impeding critical investments to achieve food security (Chapter III) and create decent employment opportunities (Chapter IV), as well as hindering economic recovery.

This chapter has shown that governments, even in the poorest countries, have multiple options to invest in the neediest and jumpstart long-term inclusive and sustainable growth. The broad areas that warrant further exploration by policymakers, development partners and civil society stakeholders include reallocating existing resources, tax policies, foreign aid and transfers, fiscal and foreign exchange reserves, debt policy, and fiscal and monetary policies. While specific options are unique to each country and have associated risks and trade-offs, they should be carefully examined at the national level and considered in an inclusive dialogue.

Some questions for policymakers to consider in terms of public spending trends may include:

- Are current spending priorities and decisions considering the longer-term impacts of high unemployment, rising food and energy prices, and social inequities on children and poor households? What are the long-term opportunity costs of not scaling up equity-based interventions, social protection programs and productive social sector investments during the economic recovery?

- Is the current fiscal adjustment trajectory—in terms of scope and pace—conducive to adequately investing in the most vulnerable groups and achieving the MDGs? Are current and medium-term expenditure frameworks based on both social and economic indicators that are sufficiently disaggregated to capture the conditions of the poor and the most disadvantaged, including children?

- Have all possible fiscal scenarios been fully explored—or fiscal sustainability assessment exercises been carried out—and discussed in an open, national dialogue in order to support a socially-responsive recovery? More specifically:

  i. Can government expenditures be re-allocated to free up additional space for high-priority socio-economic investments that benefit poor households? Are current military expenditures, or expenditures to support the commercial sector, justified in light of existing poverty rates and overall levels of vulnerability among poor populations, especially during the recovery? Is it possible to enhance the efficiency of existing investments?

  ii. Have *all* tax codes and possible modifications been considered and evaluated to maximize public revenue without jeopardizing private investment? Are personal income and corporate tax rates designed to support equitable outcomes? What specific taxation collection methods could be strengthened to enhance overall revenue streams? Could minor tariff adjustments increase the availability of resources for social investments? Can tax policies better respond to 'boom' and 'bust' cycles? Have financial transaction taxes been considered to support productive and social sector investments?

iii.   Is the government lobbying for increased North-South (ODA) or South-South transfers? Are there efforts to fight and re-channel IFFs?

iv.   Are there fiscal reserves, for example, sitting in SWFs that could be invested in children and poor families today? Are excess foreign exchange reserves being maximized and fostering local and regional development investments?

v.   Have debt options been thoroughly examined for increased social and economic investments today? Have different maturity and repayment terms been discussed with creditors? Has a public audit been carried out to examine the legitimacy of existing debts? What are the distributional impacts of financing additional government expenditures by borrowing?

vi.   Could relaxing the fiscal deficit ceiling by just a few percentage points significantly increase health and education spending allocations and better protect the most vulnerable? Are current inflation levels unduly restricting employment growth?

References

Atkinson, A. (ed.). 2004. *New Sources of Development Finance*. Oxford: Oxford University Press.

Bai, Y. and J. Zhangy. 2010. "Duration of Sovereign Debt Renegotiation." University of Michigan Working Paper No. 593, University of Michigan.

Barro, R. 1996. "Inflation and Growth." *Federal Reserve Bank of St. Louis Review* (78): 153-169.

Barry, C. and G. Øverland. 2010. "Why Remittances to Poor Countries Should Not Be Taxed." *New York University Journal of International Law and Politics* 42(4): 1181-1207.

Baunsgaard, T. and M. Keen. 2005. "Tax Revenue and (or?) Trade Liberalization." IMF Working Paper No. 05/112, IMF.

Beitler, D. 2010. *Raising Revenue: A Review of Financial Transaction Taxes throughout the World*. A Report for Health Poverty Action and Stamp Out of Poverty. London: Just Economics.

Benn, J., A. Rogerson and S. Steensen. 2010. "Getting Closer to the Core: Measuring Country Programmable Aid." OECD-DCD Development Brief, OECD Development Co-operation Directorate.

Bick, A. 2010. "Threshold Effects of Inflation on Economic Growth in Developing Countries." *Economic Letters*, 108(2): 126-129.

Blanchard, O. G. Dell'Ariccia and P. Mauro. 2010. "Rethinking Macroeconomic Policy." IMF Staff Position Note No. 10/03, IMF.

Brautigam D., Fjeldstad, O. and M. Moore. 2008. *Taxation and State-Building in Developing Countries: Capacity and Consent*. Cambridge: Cambridge University Press.

Bruno, M. 1995. "Does Inflation Really Lower Growth?" *Finance and Development* 32(3): 35-38.

Bruno, M. and W. Easterly. 1998. "Inflation Crises and Long-run Growth." *Journal of Monetary Economics* 41(1): 3-26.

Buchanan, R. and R. Musgrave. 1999. *Public Finance and Public Choice: Two Contracting Visions of the State*. Cambridge: MIT Press.

Burdekin, R., C.K. Denzau, T. Arthur, M. Keil, T. Sitthiyot and T. Willett. 2004. "When does Inflation Hurt Economic Growth? Different Nonlinearities for Different Economies." *Journal of Macroeconomics* 26(3): 519-532.

Carnegie Council. 2005. "Financing Global Development: Key Proposals and Recommendations." Global Policy Innovations Policy Brief, Carnegie Council for Ethics in International Affairs.

Chang, H.J. 2007. "State Owned Enterprise Reform." In *National Development Strategies, Policy Notes*. New York: UN-DESA.

Chowdhury, A. and I. Islam. 2010. "Is There an Optimal Debt-to-GDP Ratio?" *VoxEU.org*, November 09.

Christian Aid. 2007. *Debt: The Repudiation Option*. London: Christian Aid.

Cobham, A. 2005. "Tax Evasion, Tax Avoidance and Development Finance." Queen Elisabeth House Working Paper No. 129, University of Oxford.

Cornia, G.A., R. Jolly and F. Stewart. 1987. *Adjustment with a Human Face: Protecting the Vulnerable and Promoting Growth*. New York: Oxford University Press.

Dang, H., S. Knack and H. Rogers. 2009. "International Aid and Financial Crises in Donor Countries." World Bank Policy Research Working Paper No. 5162, World Bank.

de Bruijn, K., J. Kaiser, N. Dearden, Ø. Brynildsen and N. Molina. 2010. "Europe Needs Fair and Transparent Debt Work-Out Mechanisms: Lessons from the Icelandic Case." ETUI Policy Brief, European Trade Union Institute (ETUI).

de Luna Martínez, J. 2006. "Workers' Remittances to Developing Countries: A Survey with Central Banks on Selected Public Policy Issues." World Bank Policy Research Working Paper No. 3638, World Bank.

Desai, R.M. and H. Kharas. 2010. "The Determinants of Aid Volatility." Brookings Global Economy and Development Working Paper No. 42, Brookings.

Development Committee. 2006. "Fiscal Space Policy for Growth and Development: An Interim Report." Background paper for the Development Committee Meeting, IMF and World Bank.

Espinoza, R., H. Leon and A. Prasad. 2010. "Estimating the Inflation-Growth Nexus: A Smooth Transition Model." IMF Working Paper No. 10/76, IMF.

Eurodad. 2009. *A Fair and Transparent Debt Work-Out Procedure: 10 Core Civil Society Principles*. Brussels: European Network on Debt and Development (Eurodad).

Fischer, S. 1993. "The Role of Macroeconomic Factors in Growth." *Journal of Monetary Economics* 32(3): 485-512.

Frot, E. and J. Santiso. 2011. "Herding in Aid Allocation." *Kyklos* 66(1): 54-74.

Gallagher, K. and R. Porzecanski. 2009. "China and the Latin America Commodities Boom: A Critical Assessment." Political Economy Research Institute Working Paper Series No. 192, University of Massachusetts Amherst.

Ghosh, A., and S. Phillips. 1998. "Warning: Inflation May be Harmful to Your Growth. IMF Staff Papers, Vol. 45, IMF.

Gillman, M., M. Harris and L. Matyas. 2004. "Inflation and Growth: Explaining a Negative Effect." *Empirical Economics* 29(1): 149-167.

Gomes, R. and D. Hailu. 2009. "One Instrument, Many Targets: Timor-Leste's Macroeconomic Policy Challenge." One pager, No. 93, UNDP International Policy Centre for Inclusive Growth.

Gregory, R., C. Henn, B. McDonald and M. Saito. 2010. "Trade and the Crisis: Protect or Recover." IMF Staff Position Note, IMF.

Gueye, C. and A. Sy. 2010. "Beyond Aid: How Much Should African Countries Pay to Borrow?" IMF Working Paper, IMF.

Gylfason T. and T.T. Herbertsson. 2001. "Does Inflation Matter for Growth?" *Japan and the World Economy* 13(4): 405-428.

Hall, D. 2010. *Why We Need Public Spending*. London: University of Greenwich.

Hicks, N. 1991. "Expenditure Reductions in Developing Countries Revisited." *Journal of International Development* 3(1): 29-37.

Hurley, G. 2010. "Achieving Debt Sustainability and the MDGs in Small Island Developing States." UNDP Discussion Paper, UNDP.

Inwent. 2005. *New Sources of Development Financing*. Development Policy Forum Summary Report. Bonn: Deutsche Gesellschaft für Internationale Zusammenarbeit (GIZ).

ILO. 2010. *World of Work Report 2010: From One Crisis to the Next?* Geneva: ILO.

IMF. 2011a. "Debt Relief under the Heavily Indebted Poor Countries (HIPC) Initiative." IMF Factsheet, March 31, IMF.

_____. 2011b. *World Economic Outlook: Slowing Growth, Rising Risks, September 2011*. Washington, D.C.: IMF. http://www.imf.org/external/pubs/ft/weo/2011/02/weodata/index.aspx (accessed December 2011).

_____. 2010a. *Financial Sector Taxation*. IMF's Report to the G20. Washington, D.C.: IMF.

_____. 2010b. "From Stimulus to Consolidation: Revenue and Expenditure Policies in Advanced and Emerging Economies." IMF Working Paper, IMF.

_____. 2010c. "Iceland Article IV Consultation and Third Review under Stand-By Arrangement." IMF Country Report No. 10/305. Washington D.C.: IMF.

_____. 2009. *Creating Policy Space: Responsive Design and Streamlined Conditionality in Recent Low-income Country Programs*. Washington, D.C.: IMF.

_____. 2007. *The IMF and Aid to Sub-Saharan Africa*. Washington, D.C.: IMF.

Independent Evaluation Group. 2010. *The World Bank's Country Policy and Institutional Assessment: An Evaluation*. Washington, D.C.: World Bank.

Institute for Policy Studies. 2011. *Innovative Mechanisms of Development Finance: Some Key Options for Public Revenue Streams*. Washington, D.C.: Institute for Policy Studies.

Inter-American Dialogue. 2007. *Making the Most of Family Remittances: Second Report of the Inter-American Dialogue Task Force on Remittances*. Washington, D.C.: Inter-American Dialogue.

Kar, D. 2011. "Illicit Financial Flows from the Least Developed Countries: 1990-2008." UNDP Discussion Paper, UNDP.

Kar, D. and K. Curcio. 2011. *Illicit Financial Flows from Developing Countries: 2000-2009, Update with a Focus on Asia*. Washington, D.C.: Global Financial Integrity.

Kar, D., D. Cartwright-Smith and A. Hollingshead. 2010. *The Absorption of Illicit Financial Flows from Developing Countries: 2002-2006*. Washington, D.C.: Global Financial Integrity.

Khamfula, Y., M. Mlachila and E. Chirwa. 2006. "Donor Herding and Domestic Debt Crisis." IMF Working Paper No. 109, IMF.

Khan, M., and A.S. Senhadji. 2001. "Threshold Effects in the Relation between Inflation and Growth." IMF Staff Papers, Vol. 48, IMF.

Kochar, K. and S. Coorey. 1999. "Economic Growth: What Has Been Achieved So Far and How?" In H. Bredenkamp and S. Schadler (eds.), *Economic Adjustment and Reform in Low-income Countries*. Washington, D.C.: IMF.

Kremer, S., A. Bick and D. Nautz. 2011. "Inflation and Growth: New Evidence from a Dynamic Panel Threshold Analysis." SFB 649 Discussion Paper 2009-036, Humboldt University.

Leading Group on Innovating Financing for Development. 2010. *Globalizing Solidarity: The Case for Financial Levies*. Report of the Committee of Experts to the Taskforce on International Financial Transactions and Development. Paris: French Ministry of Foreign and European Affairs.

Li, M. 2006. "Inflation and Economic Growth: Threshold Effects and Transmission Mechanisms." University of Alberta Working Paper, University of Alberta.

Lora, E. and M. Olivera. 2006. "Public Debt and Social Expenditure: Friends or Foes?" IADB Working Paper 563, Inter-American Development Bank (IADB).

Moody's. 2008. *Sovereign Default and Recovery Rates, 1983-2007*. Moody's Global Credit Research. New York: Moody's.

OECD. 2011. *Development Aid Reaches an Historic High in 2010*. Paris: OECD.

Ortiz, I. 2008a. "Social Policy." In *National Development Strategies, Policy Notes*. New York: UN-DESA.

_____. 2008b. "Financing for Development." In K. Hujo and S. McClanahan (eds.), *Financing Social Policy*. Basingtoke: UNRISD/Palgrave Macmillan.

Ortiz, I. and M. Cummins. 2011. "Global Inequality: Beyond the Bottom Billion – A Rapid Review of Income Distribution in 141 Countries." Social and Economic Policy Working Paper, UNICEF.

Panizza, U. 2008. "Domestic and External Public Debt in Developing Countries." UNCTAD Discussion Paper No. 188, UNCTAD.

Park, D. 2007. "Beyond Liquidity: New Uses for Developing Asia's Foreign Exchange Reserves." ERD Working Paper No. 109, ADB.

Pettifor, A. 2002. *Chapter 9/11? Resolving International Debt Crises – the Jubilee Framework for International Insolvency*. London: Jubilee Research/New Economics Foundation.

Pollin, R., and A. Zhu. 2006. "Inflation and Economic Growth: A Cross-country Nonlinear Analysis." *Journal of Post-Keynesian Economics* 28(4): 593-614.

Radon, J. 2007. "How to Negotiate your Oil Agreement." In M. Humphreys, J. Sachs and J. Stiglitz (eds.), *Escaping the Resource Curse*. New York: Columbia University Press.

Raffer, K. 1993. "What's Good for the United States Must Be Good for the World: Advocating an International Chapter 9 Insolvency." In B. Kreisky (ed.), *From Cancún to Vienna, International Development in a New World*. Vienna: Bruno Kreisky Forum for International Dialogue.

Ratha, D. 2007. "Leveraging Remittances for Development." Policy Brief, Migration Policy Institute.

Ravallion, M. 2006. "Who is Protected? On the Incidence of Fiscal Adjustment." In A. Mody and C. Pattillo (eds.), *Macroeconomic Policies and Poverty Reduction*. London: Routledge.

_____. 2004. "Who is Protected from Budget Cuts?" *Journal of Policy Reform* 7(2): 109-22.

_____. 2002. "Are the Poor Protected from Budget Cuts? Evidence for Argentina." *Journal of Applied Economics* 5(1): 95-121.

Reinhart C. and K. Rogoff. 2010. "Growth in a Time of Debt." *American Economic Review* 100(2): 573-578.

Rosser, E. (2008). "Immigrant Remittances." *Connecticut Law Review* 41(1): 1-62.

Rousseau, P.L. and P. Watchel. 2002. "Inflation Thresholds and the Finance-Growth Nexus." *Journal of International Money and Finance* 21(6): 777-793.

Roy R., A. Heuty and E. Letouzé. 2007. "Fiscal Space for What? Analytical Issues from a Human Development Perspective." Paper for G20 Workshop on Fiscal Policy, UNDP.

Ruiz, M. 2007. *Debt Swaps for Development: Creative Solution or Smoke Screen?* Brussels: European Network on Debt and Development (Eurodad).

Sarel, M. 1996. "Nonlinear Effects of Inflation on Economic Growth." IMF Working Paper No. 95/56, IMF.

Schenk, A. and O. Oldman. 2007. *Value Added Tax: A Comparative Approach*. Cambridge: Cambridge University Press.

Selassie, A.A., B. Clements, S. Tareq, J.K. Martijn and G. di Bella. 2006. "Designing Monetary and Fiscal Policy in Low-income Countries." IMF Occasional Paper No. 250, IMF.

Sepehri, A. and S. Moshiri. 2004. "Inflation-Growth Profiles across Countries: Evidence from Developing and Developed Countries." *International Review of Applied Economics* 18(2): 191-207.

Standard & Poor's. 2011. "Sovereign Defaults and Rating Transition Data, 2010 Update." RatingsDirect on the Global Credit Portal, Standard & Poor's.

Strazds, A. (ed.). 2010. *Economic Development Program: Latvia Renewed*. Riga: Concord Centre.

Sturzenegger, F. and J. Zettelmeyer. 2005. "Haircuts: Estimating Investor Losses in Sovereign Debt Restructurings." IMF Working Paper No. 05/137, IMF.

SWF Institute. 2011. "Sovereign Wealth Fund Rankings, June 2011." Las Vegas: SWF Institute. http://www.swfinstitute.org/fund-rankings/ (accessed December 2011).

TheCityUK. 2011. "Sovereign Wealth Funds." Financial Markets Series, TheCityUK.

UNCTAD. 2011. *Trade and Development Report, 2011*. Geneva: UNCTAD.

_____. 2008. *Trade and Development Report, 2008*. Geneva: UNCTAD.

UNDP. 2010. *Beyond the Midpoint: Achieving the Millennium Development Goals*. New York: UNDP.

UNESCO. 2010. *Education for All Global Monitoring Report 2010: Reaching the Marginalized*. Paris: UNESCO.

UNICEF. 2011. *Child Info: Monitoring the Situation of Children and Women database*. http://www.childinfo.org/ (accessed December 2011).

_____. 2009. *Fiscal Space for Strengthened Social Protection: West and Central Africa*. Nairobi: UNICEF.

United Nations. 2011. *World Economic Situation and Prospects 2011*. New York: UN-DESA.

_____. 2010a. *Development Cooperation for the MDGs: Maximizing Results.* New York: UN-DESA.

_____. 2010b. "Till Debt do us Part: the Urgency of a Sovereign Debt Workout Mechanism." UN-DESA Policy Brief No. 29, UN-DESA.

_____. 2009a. "Effects of Foreign Debt and other Related International Financial Obligations of States on the Full Enjoyment of All Human Rights, particularly Economic, Social and Cultural Rights." Note by the United Nations Secretary-General, A/64/289, United Nations.

_____. 2009b. *Report of the Commission of Experts of the President of the United Nations General Assembly on Reforms of the International Monetary and Financial System.* New York: United Nations.

Uppsala Conflict Data Program. 2010. *UCDP/PRIO Armed Conflict Dataset, Version 4.* http://www.prio.no/CSCW/Datasets/Armed-Conflict/UCDP-PRIO/ (accessed December 2011).

US GAO. 2009. *International Monetary Fund: Lending Programs Allow for Negotiations and are Consistent with Economic Literature*. Report to the Chairman, Committee on Financial Services, House of Representatives. Washington, D.C.: United States Government Accountability Office (US GAO).

Vaona, A. and S. Schiavo. 2007. "Nonparametric and Semiparametric Evidence on the Long-run Effects of Inflation on Growth." *Economics Letters* 94(3): 452-458.

Weisbrot, M. and L. Sandoval. 2007. "Argentina's Economic Recovery: Policy Choices and Implications." Washington, D.C.: Center for Economic and Policy Research.

World Bank. 2011. *World Development Indicators (WDI) database.* http://databank.worldbank.org/ddp/home.do?Step=12&id=4&CNO=2 (accessed December 2011)

_____. 2010a. "Country Policy and Institutional Assessments: 2010 Assessment Questionnaire." World Bank.

_____. 2010b. "A 2009 Update of Poverty Incidence in Timor-Leste Using the Survey-to-Survey Imputation Method." World Bank.

WHO. 2010. *World Health Report 2010 – Health Systems Financing: The Path to Universal Coverage.* Geneva: WHO.

_____. 2009a. *Raising and Channeling Funds.* Taskforce on Innovative Financing for Health Systems, Working Group 2 Report. Geneva: WHO.

_____. 2009b. *Public Health, Innovation and Intellectual Property.* Report of the Expert Working Group on Research and Development Financing. Geneva: WHO.

_____. 2010. *Tariff Profiles.* Geneva: WTO.

Annex 1. Selected Fiscal Space Indicators for 184 Countries, 2011 or latest available

(in percent of GDP, unless otherwise noted)

Country	(i) Government Expenditures				(ii) Revenue		(iii) ODA Received 2009*	(iv) Illicit Fin. Flows 2008**	(v) Foreign Reserves 2011***	(vi) Debt (% of GNI) 2009*		(vii) Budget Deficit 2011	(viii) Inflation (% Δ) 2011
	Total 2011	Health 2009*	Educ. 2009*	Milit. 2009*	Total 2011	Tax 2009*				External Stocks	Total Service		
Afghanistan	24.7	1.6	...	1.9	24.7	5.2	...	0.1	...	...	...	0.0	8.4
Albania	29.4	2.8	...	2.1	25.6	...	3.0	1.4	18.6	40.3	2.2	-3.7	3.9
Algeria	43.9	5.0	4.3	3.8	41.3	34.3	0.2	2.0	97.1	3.8	0.7	-2.6	3.9
Angola	36.0	4.1	...	4.2	43.9	...	0.3	9.2	25.7	28.2	5.1	7.9	15.0
Antigua & Bar.	20.8	3.8	2.7	...	20.5	...	0.5	3.7	10.5	...	...	-0.4	3.7
Argentina	39.6	6.3	5.4	0.8	37.6	...	0.0	4.2	10.4	40.1	4.1	-2.0	11.5
Armenia	25.3	2.0	4.4	4.1	21.4	16.7	6.2	8.6	19.3	55.3	4.9	-3.8	8.8
Australia	36.7	5.6	4.4	1.9	32.8	22.1	...	...	2.6	...	...	-3.9	3.5
Austria	51.8	8.2	5.5	0.9	48.3	18.7	...	...	2.7	...	...	-3.5	3.2
Azerbaijan	32.0	1.4	2.8	3.5	41.7	16.7	0.5	22.1	8.6	12.1	1.0	9.8	9.3
Bahamas	22.4	3.2	...	...	17.8	16.0	...	2.3	14.2	...	...	-4.7	2.5
Bahrain	35.1	3.1	2.9	3.6	27.4	1.5	...	12.5	...	...	...	-7.7	1.0
Bangladesh	16.1	1.1	2.4	1.1	12.7	8.6	1.4	2.5	7.8	24.0	1.0	-3.4	10.1
Barbados	40.2	4.4	6.7	...	36.8	33.2	0.3	4.3	19.0	...	...	-3.4	6.9
Belarus	39.7	4.1	4.5	1.8	39.0	19.3	0.2	11.1	5.4	35.6	2.5	-0.7	41.0
Belgium	52.4	8.1	6.5	1.1	48.9	24.0	...	...	3.4	...	...	-3.5	3.2
Belize	30.2	3.6	5.7	1.1	28.6	...	2.1	5.2	15.6	...	8.1	-1.6	2.1
Benin	22.9	2.3	4.5	1.0	21.2	16.1	10.3	0.9	15.3	16.1	0.6	-1.7	2.8
Bhutan	44.1	4.5	4.8	...	39.5	9.2	9.9	...	57.8	57.7	6.1	-4.6	6.5
Bolivia	32.6	3.1	...	1.6	34.5	...	4.2	2.9	38.5	34.5	3.5	1.8	9.8
Bosnia & Herz.	49.7	6.7	...	1.5	46.2	19.6	2.4	3.9	24.7	54.6	3.7	-3.5	4.0
Botswana	36.5	8.2	7.9	3.2	30.3	...	2.4	4.2	54.3	14.1	0.4	-6.1	7.8
Brazil	39.2	4.1	1.9	1.6	36.7	15.6	0.0	0.5	13.9	17.9	2.8	-2.5	6.6
Brunei Darussalam	36.6	2.6	...	3.1	61.0	...	...	45.2	11.1	...	...	24.4	1.8
Bulgaria	35.0	4.4	4.4	2.3	32.5	21.0	...	11.4	28.5	90.4	11.1	-2.5	3.8
Burkina Faso	26.5	3.9	...	1.3	22.2	12.9	13.3	1.4	10.1	22.9	0.5	-4.3	1.9
Burundi	47.4	6.0	8.3	3.8	44.3	...	42.3	5.4	20.6	38.9	1.5	-3.1	8.7
Cambodia	17.4	1.6	2.1	1.2	15.3	9.6	6.9	5.8	26.3	45.0	0.5	-2.2	6.4
Cameroon	19.5	1.6	3.6	1.5	18.1	...	2.9	...	13.3	13.6	1.8	-1.4	2.6
Canada	42.3	7.5	4.8	1.4	38.0	11.8	...	...	3.7	...	...	-4.3	2.9
Cape Verde	39.1	2.9	5.9	0.6	28.8	19.9	12.3	3.5	16.7	47.2	2.1	-10.2	5.0
Central Afr. Rep.	16.6	1.6	1.3	1.8	14.7	...	12.2	4.9	7.9	20.0	1.6	-2.0	2.8
Chad	27.4	3.9	3.1	6.4	29.7	...	8.2	0.0	8.0	28.6	1.3	2.3	2.0
Chile	24.7	3.8	4.0	3.1	26.1	15.6	0.0	9.0	15.9	46.7	10.2	1.4	3.1
China	22.4	2.3	...	2.0	20.9	10.3	0.0	11.6	46.1	8.7	0.8	-1.6	5.5
Colombia	28.3	5.4	4.7	4.1	25.3	11.8	0.4	1.9	9.8	23.6	3.9	-3.0	3.3
Comoros	22.0	2.1	7.6	...	20.4	...	9.5	1.1	27.9	51.0	2.2	-1.6	5.8
Congo, Dem. Rep.	36.9	4.9	...	1.1	29.1	...	21.0	8.3	8.2	121.4	6.7	-7.7	14.8
Congo, Rep. of	23.8	1.6	...	1.2	43.4	...	3.0	6.7	39.9	83.8	2.4	19.5	5.9

Country	(i) Government Expenditures				(ii) Revenue		(iii) ODA Received 2009*	(iv) Illicit Fin. Flows 2008**	(v) Foreign Reserves 2011***	(vi) Debt (% of GNI) 2009*		(vii) Budget Deficit 2011	(viii) Inflation (% Δ) 2011
	Total 2011	Health 2009*	Educ. 2009*	Milit. 2009*	Total 2011	Tax 2009*				External Stocks	Total Service		
Costa Rica	19.7	7.1	6.3	...	14.1	13.9	0.4	26.3	11.9	28.1	4.3	-5.6	5.3
Côte d'Ivoire	26.3	1.0	4.6	1.6	17.8	16.6	10.3	7.9	18.6	53.0	5.0	-8.5	3.0
Croatia	41.4	6.6	4.6	1.8	35.6	19.0	0.3	5.1	24.1	...	...	-5.7	3.2
Cyprus	47.5	2.5	7.4	2.2	40.8	25.8	...	12.2	2.2	...	...	-6.6	4.0
Czech Republic	45.0	6.1	4.1	1.5	41.2	13.5	...	6.7	18.7	...	...	-3.8	1.8
Denmark	56.6	9.0	7.8	1.4	53.6	34.6	...	...	23.9	...	...	-3.0	3.2
Djibouti	35.7	5.3	...	3.7	36.1	...	15.5	18.6	18.1	67.2	2.6	0.4	7.1
Dominica	33.1	4.1	4.7	...	31.3	...	9.6	0.5	16.1	69.9	5.0	-1.8	4.2
Dominican Rep.	15.4	2.4	2.3	0.6	13.8	14.9	0.3	3.5	5.7	24.6	3.0	-1.6	8.3
Ecuador	38.6	2.9	...	3.7	37.5	...	0.4	5.7	3.5	23.3	11.4	-1.0	4.4
Egypt	35.0	2.1	3.8	2.1	24.7	15.7	0.5	7.5	7.7	17.6	1.6	-10.3	11.1
El Salvador	21.9	3.8	3.6	0.6	18.3	12.5	1.3	4.6	8.2	54.3	6.0	-3.5	4.6
Equatorial Guinea	32.2	3.4	...	...	29.1	...	0.3	8.0	16.4	...	...	-3.1	7.3
Eritrea	33.7	1.0	...	...	17.4	...	7.8	...	4.6	...	1.2	-16.2	13.3
Estonia	43.2	5.3	5.7	2.3	43.1	17.6	...	15.3	0.9	...	...	-0.1	5.1
Ethiopia	20.1	2.0	...	1.3	18.0	...	12.0	7.1	...	17.6	0.3	-2.1	18.1
Fiji	28.2	2.5	...	1.4	25.4	...	2.5	0.9	27.8	14.2	0.9	-2.8	5.5
Finland	53.9	7.0	6.1	1.5	52.9	21.3	...	...	3.0	...	...	-1.0	3.1
France	56.5	9.0	5.6	2.4	50.6	19.8	...	...	1.9	...	...	-5.9	2.1
Gabon	23.6	1.7	...	...	28.8	...	0.7	6.0	15.1	22.3	4.7	5.2	2.3
Gambia	23.6	3.0	3.8	...	20.2	...	17.5	3.6	19.9	75.3	3.7	-3.4	5.9
Georgia	30.4	2.9	3.2	5.6	28.2	23.1	8.4	7.2	19.9	40.0	2.5	-2.2	9.6
Germany	45.8	8.6	...	1.4	44.1	12.0	...	...	1.8	...	...	-1.7	2.2
Ghana	23.0	3.1	...	0.4	18.8	12.5	6.0	0.3	...	37.3	0.9	-4.2	8.7
Greece	48.1	6.7	...	4.0	40.1	19.3	...	...	0.5	...	...	-8.0	2.9
Grenada	26.1	3.8	...	...	20.8	...	7.8	4.3	16.1	92.0	3.5	-5.3	4.2
Guatemala	14.4	2.6	3.2	0.4	11.4	10.4	1.0	4.5	12.7	38.8	4.6	-3.0	6.3
Guinea	33.1	0.9	2.4	...	20.9	...	5.2	26.7	...	48.3	3.5	-12.2	20.6
Guinea-Bissau	21.6	1.6	...	...	19.6	...	17.6	2.7	25.0	253.2	1.2	-1.9	4.6
Guyana	33.9	7.2	3.4	...	31.5	...	8.6	...	34.0	...	0.8	-2.4	5.8
Haiti	21.3	1.4	...	...	21.5	...	17.3	1.0	19.9	...	0.7	0.2	7.3
Honduras	26.0	3.4	...	0.8	22.9	14.4	3.2	26.6	15.3	25.9	3.0	-3.1	7.8
Hong Kong	21.2	...	4.5	...	23.9	12.8	...	...	114.3	...	...	2.7	5.5
Hungary	50.7	5.1	5.1	1.3	52.7	23.5	...	...	29.7	...	...	2.0	3.7
Iceland	45.4	6.7	7.6	0.1	41.3	21.5	...	...	54.0	...	...	-4.1	4.2
India	25.5	1.4	...	2.7	17.8	9.8	0.2	1.9	15.3	18.2	1.2	-7.7	10.6
Indonesia	19.5	1.2	2.8	0.9	17.7	11.4	0.2	6.0	12.9	30.2	4.8	-1.8	5.7
Iran	24.3	2.2	4.7	2.7	26.7	9.3	0.0	2.8	...	4.1	0.8	2.4	22.5
Iraq	82.8	2.8	...	6.4	74.1	...	4.3	0.1	49.6	...	...	-8.7	5.0
Ireland	44.9	7.8	5.6	0.6	34.6	21.3	...	...	0.7	...	...	-10.3	1.1
Israel	43.6	4.5	5.9	6.9	40.8	23.0	...	2.0	31.1	...	...	-2.8	3.4
Italy	50.0	7.3	4.6	1.7	45.9	23.0	...	...	2.3	...	...	-4.0	2.6
Jamaica	31.6	2.8	5.8	0.6	27.2	21.1	1.2	7.7	16.9	77.8	12.1	-4.4	8.1

| Country | (i) Government Expenditures | | | | (ii) Revenue | | (iii) ODA Received 2009* | (iv) Illicit Fin. Flows 2008** | (v) Foreign Reserves 2011... | (vi) Debt (% of GNI) 2009* | | (vii) Budget Deficit 2011 | (viii) Inflation (% Δ) 2011 |
	Total 2011	Health 2009*	Educ. 2009*	Milit. 2009*	Total 2011	Tax 2009*				External Stocks	Total Service		
Japan	41.7	6.7	3.4	1.0	31.4	8.7	...	...	21.5	...	...	-10.3	-0.4
Jordan	34.0	6.0	...	5.5	27.8	16.2	3.0	3.5	44.2	28.3	2.3	-6.2	5.4
Kazakhstan	22.8	2.7	...	1.2	24.5	8.1	0.3	25.1	15.8	113.0	39.7	1.8	8.9
Kenya	33.9	1.5	...	1.9	28.0	19.6	6.1	0.6	11.6	26.5	1.3	-5.9	12.1
Kiribati	93.9	10.3	...	...	77.6	...	21.2	...	...	...	...	-16.3	7.7
Korea	20.9	3.5	4.8	2.9	22.9	15.4	...	...	25.7	...	...	2.1	4.5
Kosovo	32.0	...	4.3	...	27.1	21.1	14.5	...	...	6.4	4.1	-5.0	8.3
Kuwait	34.9	2.8	...	4.1	58.6	1.1	...	41.4	15.0	...	...	23.6	6.2
Kyrgyz Republic	42.7	3.5	5.9	3.6	34.7	15.0	6.7	1.5	31.9	65.8	8.0	-8.0	19.1
Lao PDR	21.8	0.8	2.3	0.4	19.4	12.2	6.9	15.5	8.9	95.5	4.1	-2.3	8.7
Latvia	42.0	3.9	5.7	2.6	37.5	12.7	...	16.4	23.9	...	...	-4.5	4.2
Lebanon	30.4	4.0	1.8	4.1	22.6	17.1	1.8	5.5	76.4	70.7	12.4	-7.8	5.9
Lesotho	63.2	5.6	13.1	2.6	48.4	59.8	7.2	9.4	...	33.2	1.7	-14.9	6.5
Liberia	34.2	5.3	2.8	0.8	30.6	0.3	58.3	6.6	36.3	257.5	8.7	-3.6	8.8
Libya	n/a	2.6	...	1.2	n/a	...	0.1	0.1	145.2	...	...	...	n/a
Lithuania	39.3	4.5	4.9	1.7	34.1	14.0	...	10.7	18.5	85.3	17.4	-5.3	4.2
Luxembourg	39.9	5.8	...	...	39.2	24.1	...	...	1.6	...	...	-0.7	3.6
Macedonia, FYR	33.4	4.6	...	2.1	30.9	19.1	2.1	8.2	20.9	62.2	6.0	-2.5	4.4
Madagascar	13.3	2.8	3.2	1.1	12.0	13.0	5.2	12.0	13.4	...	0.5	-1.3	10.3
Malawi	34.6	3.6	...	...	30.2	...	16.3	0.1	4.0	24.7	0.8	-4.4	8.6
Malaysia	31.0	2.2	4.1	2.0	26.0	15.7	0.1	28.1	52.4	35.8	5.9	-5.1	3.2
Maldives	41.2	5.2	10.3	...	26.2	15.7	2.5	1.3	15.7	60.0	5.5	-15.0	12.1
Mali	23.3	2.7	4.4	2.0	21.0	14.7	11.0	10.8	13.5	29.6	0.9	-2.3	2.8
Malta	41.2	5.6	...	0.6	38.3	28.2	...	15.2	4.8	...	...	-2.9	2.6
Mauritania	29.0	1.6	...	3.8	26.2	...	9.5	6.6	10.3	66.6	2.5	-2.8	6.2
Mauritius	26.2	2.1	3.2	0.2	21.5	18.6	1.8	1.7	23.1	8.4	1.4	-4.8	6.7
Mexico	24.8	3.1	...	0.5	21.6	...	0.0	6.5	11.0	22.3	4.6	-3.2	3.4
Moldova	38.7	6.4	9.6	0.5	36.8	17.7	4.5	8.9	27.4	59.7	6.7	-1.9	7.9
Mongolia	37.7	4.0	5.6	...	38.6	16.5	8.1	7.6	28.5	55.8	2.5	0.9	10.2
Montenegro	45.7	6.7	...	1.4	42.3	...	1.8	0.7	...	56.4	1.7	-3.4	3.1
Morocco	32.2	1.9	5.6	3.3	25.4	23.8	1.0	3.3	22.1	26.4	3.8	-6.8	1.5
Mozambique	34.2	4.1	...	0.9	28.1	...	20.6	3.1	20.6	43.0	0.4	-6.1	10.8
Myanmar	10.4	0.2	...	...	7.2	...	...	2.5	...	...	...	-3.2	6.7
Namibia	31.1	4.0	6.4	3.3	26.7	...	3.6	11.4	14.0	...	...	-4.4	5.0
Nepal	20.7	2.1	4.6	1.5	18.6	11.8	6.6	5.8	17.5	28.7	1.4	-2.1	9.5
Netherlands	49.5	8.3	5.5	1.5	45.7	22.6	...	...	2.4	...	...	-3.8	2.5
New Zealand	35.0	7.8	6.4	1.1	28.8	...	...	...	12.8	...	...	-6.2	4.4
Nicaragua	34.8	5.4	...	0.7	34.6	17.5	12.5	20.5	24.2	76.2	8.3	-0.2	8.3
Niger	24.0	3.5	4.5	...	21.8	...	8.9	0.0	11.4	18.8	0.9	-2.2	4.0
Nigeria	29.0	2.1	...	0.9	29.4	0.3	1.0	17.0	14.5	5.1	0.3	0.4	10.6
Norway	45.5	7.6	6.4	1.5	57.5	25.6	...	...	9.8	...	...	12.0	1.7
Oman	34.4	2.4	4.5	8.6	46.2	...	0.5	10.6	19.4	...	...	11.8	3.8
Pakistan	19.7	0.9	2.7	3.0	13.2	9.3	1.7	1.7	7.7	31.3	2.1	-6.5	13.9

Country	(i) Government Expenditures				(ii) Revenue		(iii) ODA Received 2009 *	(iv) Illicit Fin. Flows 2008 **	(v) Foreign Reserves 2011 ***	(vi) Debt (% of GNI) 2009*		(vii) Budget Deficit 2011	(viii) Inflation (% Δ) 2011
	Total 2011	Health 2009*	Educ. 2009*	Milit. 2009*	Total 2011	Tax 2009*				External Stocks	Total Service		
Panama	28.4	5.9	3.8	...	26.5	...	0.3	29.4	6.6	52.5	4.3	-1.9	5.7
Papua New Guin.	32.4	2.5	...	0.5	33.4	...	5.2	3.8	28.1	19.9	6.9	1.0	8.4
Paraguay	23.4	3.0	...	0.9	23.8	13.0	1.0	7.4	21.7	29.5	3.2	0.3	8.7
Peru	19.7	2.7	2.5	1.2	20.4	13.7	0.3	1.8	28.1	24.8	3.1	0.6	3.1
Philippines	16.6	1.3	2.8	0.8	13.7	12.2	0.2	15.1	31.8	39.2	5.9	-2.9	4.5
Poland	45.8	4.9	...	2.0	40.3	16.3	...	6.7	17.6	...	...	-5.5	4.0
Portugal	48.0	7.9	4.9	2.0	42.2	19.5	...	...	1.0	...	...	-5.9	3.4
Qatar	24.8	2.0	...	...	32.4	19.8	...	38.3	10.2	...	...	7.6	2.3
Romania	37.9	4.3	...	1.4	33.5	17.9	...	4.7	22.7	71.6	10.0	-4.4	6.4
Russia	38.2	3.5	4.1	4.4	37.1	13.0	...	6.2	24.8	31.9	5.7	-1.1	8.9
Rwanda	28.7	3.9	3.9	1.4	27.1	...	17.8	4.1	13.8	14.9	0.5	-1.5	3.9
Samoa	44.0	6.1	5.7	...	35.7	...	15.6	20.7	31.9	49.0	1.8	-8.2	2.9
São Tomé & Prín.	47.3	2.9	...	...	29.9	...	16.2	0.1	...	94.8	1.8	-17.4	11.4
Saudi Arabia	41.4	3.3	5.6	11.1	50.8	...	...	13.6	95.3	...	...	9.4	5.4
Senegal	28.0	3.1	6.0	1.6	21.8	...	8.0	0.1	17.8	27.1	1.6	-6.2	3.6
Serbia	42.9	6.3	4.7	2.3	39.1	21.7	1.5	9.3	30.6	79.7	11.4	-3.8	11.3
Seychelles	38.6	3.1	...	0.8	41.7	27.1	2.9	29.3	26.0	247.8	9.0	3.1	2.6
Sierra Leone	27.1	0.9	4.3	2.3	22.0	11.0	24.3	2.4	20.7	23.4	0.4	-5.1	18.0
Singapore	19.5	1.6	3.0	4.2	22.7	13.7	...	...	90.4	...	...	3.2	3.7
Slovak Republic	38.3	5.7	3.6	1.5	33.4	12.4	...	5.9	0.9	...	...	-4.9	3.6
Slovenia	46.7	6.4	...	1.7	40.6	18.0	...	17.7	1.7	...	...	-6.2	1.8
Solomon Islands	56.0	5.1	...	...	57.7	...	34.2	6.7	46.0	32.4	2.1	1.7	6.0
South Africa	31.8	3.4	5.4	1.4	27.6	25.5	0.4	4.6	10.2	15.1	2.8	-4.2	5.9
Spain	42.9	7.0	4.6	1.3	36.8	8.5	...	...	1.7	...	...	-6.1	2.9
Sri Lanka	22.0	1.8	...	3.5	15.2	13.3	1.7	2.1	13.6	41.5	3.4	-6.8	8.4
St. Kitts and Nevis	37.6	3.6	...	...	34.5	...	1.0	1.8	32.6	44.3	8.4	-3.1	4.7
St. Lucia	35.4	5.4	4.5	...	27.3	...	4.3	5.8	15.6	47.7	5.1	-8.1	2.5
St. Vincent & Gren.	30.3	3.2	6.6	...	27.2	...	5.3	21.3	12.3	37.2	5.6	-3.2	2.5
Sudan	19.6	2.0	...	...	16.7	...	4.2	1.9	1.7	40.5	1.0	-2.8	20.0
Suriname	27.5	3.7	...	...	25.8	...	4.8	0.7	20.7	...	...	-1.7	17.9
Swaziland	34.5	4.0	7.8	...	26.4	...	1.9	6.0	16.3	15.4	1.6	-8.1	8.3
Sweden	48.4	7.8	6.7	1.3	49.2	21.7	...	...	7.6	...	...	0.8	3.0
Switzerland	34.3	6.7	5.4	0.8	35.1	10.9	...	...	48.8	...	...	0.8	0.7
Syria	32.0	0.9	...	4.0	21.0	...	0.5	2.7	25.7	10.3	1.2	-11.0	6.0
Taiwan	21.8	...	...	...	17.5	...	...	...	73.7	...	...	-4.3	1.8
Tajikistan	27.4	1.8	3.5	...	22.5	...	8.2	7.7	...	51.2	9.6	-4.9	13.6
Tanzania	29.7	3.8	6.8	1.0	21.3	...	13.7	1.5	15.0	34.0	0.8	-8.5	7.0
Thailand	23.5	3.3	4.1	1.8	20.9	15.2	0.0	5.5	50.7	23.3	5.0	-2.6	4.0
Timor-Leste	126.7	8.8	16.8	11.0	336.9	...	36.3	...	...	...	...	210.2	10.5
Togo	26.2	1.7	4.6	1.8	22.3	15.4	15.8	9.2	22.7	57.5	2.0	-3.9	4.0
Tonga	28.8	4.9	...	...	25.5	...	12.1	0.3	35.0	32.8	1.2	-3.3	5.9
Trinidad & Tob.	41.2	2.7	...	...	34.8	30.2	0.0	17.9	43.5	...	...	-6.4	9.6
Tunisia	34.3	3.4	6.9	1.2	30.6	19.9	1.1	3.0	16.3	58.2	5.1	-3.7	3.5

Country	(i) Government Expenditures				(ii) Revenue		(iii) ODA Received 2009 *	(iv) Illicit Fin. Flows 2008 **	(v) Foreign Reserves 2011 ***	(vi) Debt (% of GNI) 2009*		(vii) Budget Deficit 2011	(viii) Inflation (% Δ) 2011
	Total 2011	Health 2009*	Educ. 2009*	Milit. 2009*	Total 2011	Tax 2009*				External Stocks	Total Service		
Turkey	34.8	5.1	...	2.8	33.9	18.9	0.2	2.0	11.5	41.2	10.2	-0.9	6.0
Turkmenistan	18.2	1.2	...	...	18.7	...	0.2	0.0	...	3.0	1.0	0.5	6.1
Tuvalu	...	...	...	...	...	...	...	...	...	...	...	...	0.5
Uganda	23.9	1.6	3.2	2.2	16.3	12.2	11.3	6.4	16.7	16.2	0.5	-7.6	6.5
Ukraine	45.0	3.8	...	2.9	42.2	16.4	0.6	10.6	19.1	83.8	18.5	-2.8	9.3
United Arab Emir.	22.6	1.9	1.2	...	32.9	...	...	22.8	15.4	...	...	10.3	2.5
United Kingdom	45.6	7.8	5.4	2.7	37.1	26.0	...	...	3.3	...	...	-8.5	4.5
United States	41.2	7.9	5.5	4.7	31.6	8.3	...	...	0.9	...	...	-9.6	3.0
Uruguay	32.6	4.7	...	1.6	31.0	18.9	0.2	2.0	20.7	34.5	6.2	-1.6	7.7
Uzbekistan	36.6	2.5	...	...	39.9	...	0.6	0.0	...	12.5	1.9	3.3	13.1
Vanuatu	25.5	3.3	4.8	...	24.3	...	16.8	2.7	23.4	20.7	0.9	-1.3	2.2
Venezuela	39.4	2.4	...	1.3	34.2	...	0.0	12.8	3.5	16.7	1.2	-5.2	25.8
Vietnam	29.8	2.8	5.3	2.2	25.9	...	3.9	0.5	11.1	32.3	1.2	-4.0	18.8
Yemen	27.4	1.6	5.2	4.4	20.3	...	1.9	1.9	12.7	25.5	1.1	-7.1	19.0
Zambia	24.3	2.5	0.8	1.7	21.2	...	9.9	8.8	13.9	26.8	1.5	-3.1	9.1
Zimbabwe	31.3	...	...	...	30.4	...	12.6	11.9	...	...	1.9	-1.0	3.6
Global average	**34.2**	**4.0**	**4.9**	**2.2**	**32.5**	**16.9**	**6.6**	**7.9**	**21.3**	**45.1**	**4.0**	**-1.6**	**6.6**

Source: IMF's *World Economic Outlook* (September 2011), unless otherwise noted
* World Bank's *World Development Indicators* (2011)
** Authors' calculations based on Kar and Curcio (2011); Represents 2005-08 average values
*** World Bank's *Global Economic Monitor* (2011)

VII. CONCLUSION

Isabel Ortiz and Matthew Cummins

"The world has changed dramatically since last year's World Economic Forum. Revolution has swept across North Africa and the Middle East, bringing new freedoms and democracy, but also new challenges as well. Issues of economic inequality and social justice have come to dominate the global debate. From North Africa to New York, Athens to Abidjan... people everywhere are demanding change. They call out for dignity. They demand justice... a better and more fair deal. They want jobs, opportunities and global markets that work for all people, not just elites."

UN Secretary-General remarks at the World Economic Forum in Davos, Switzerland on January 27, 2012

1.   Nobody Should be Left Behind

"We, the Peoples" are the first words of the UN Charter. The UN was founded in 1945 and mandated to respond to the needs and rights of all persons, irrespective of gender, age, race, religious affiliation or minority status, in every country of the world. In this spirit of social justice, a real world recovery means a recovery for *all persons*, not simply the recovery of a few economic indicators and companies.

In 2008, the worst global economic crisis since 1929 originated in the United States as a result of irresponsible financial practices; it quickly spread to Europe and then on to the rest of the world. The global economic downturn resulted in a sharp drop in international trade and—despite major bailouts to financial sectors worldwide—credit freezes, which ultimately led to a severe contraction in global aggregate demand. Commodity prices, such as food and fuel, skyrocketed and reached unprecedented highs in 2008 and 2011. Average citizens in high- and low-income countries alike became victims of a crisis that they did not create.

For the poor, the global economic crisis came on top of an existing human crisis. The beginning of the 21st century was characterized by widespread poverty and hunger, few decent work opportunities and millions of children being denied their rights via limited access to health, education, safe drinking water, basic sanitation and/or housing services. Moreover, prior to 2008 half of the world's children were living below the $2/day poverty line.[1]

While there was progress toward reducing poverty, most of the gains reflect global averages, which were heavily influenced by China and East Asia. In absolute terms, the number of people living below the $1.25/day poverty line actually increased in Sub-Saharan Africa and in many developing countries in other regions between 1999 and 2008.[2] Income inequality trends more accurately capture the gross asymmetries associated with pre-crisis global progress. In 2007, the richest 20 percent of the world's population enjoyed more than 70 percent of total global income, contrasted by two paltry percentage points for those poorest persons located in the bottom quintile of the income distribution.[3] Furthermore, despite positive economic growth trends, most countries were unable to generate sufficient employment for poor families and young persons, a phenomenon known as 'jobless growth.' Employment-to-population ratios show that only 60 percent of the world's potential labour force had some type of job, with millions of the employed trapped in conditions of working poverty due to low wages, long hours, dangerous conditions and inadequate social protection.[4]

The arguments of this book are straightforward. First, billions of children and poor families were left behind before the crisis. Second, despite being temporarily supported by fiscal stimulus plans during the

---

[1] Authors' calculations based on 2008 poverty headcount estimates from the World Bank's *PovcalNet* (2012).

[2] Ibid.

[3] Ortiz, I. and M. Cummins. 2011. "Global Inequality: Beyond the Bottom Billion – A Rapid Review of Income Distribution in 141 Countries." Social and Economic Policy Working Paper, UNICEF.

[4] Refers to employment-to-population ratios for adult workers (15 and older) and young adults (15-24 year-old population); authors' calculations based on the ILO's *Key Indicators of the Labour Market database*.

first phase of the crisis (2008-09), vulnerable populations have been severely affected by the multitude of global shocks since 2008. Third, when most governments aggressively moved to implement fiscal austerity and slash budgets in a second phase of the crisis (2010-), children and poor households were again left behind. Fourth, there is a wide range of feasible policy options that can be adopted to foster a socially-responsive economic recovery—even in the poorest countries— and these alternative approaches should be considered by governments in an open and inclusive dialogue.

2.   The Relentless Triple Threat

One of the main messages of this book is that the global-to-local transmission floodgates remain wide open. On the one hand, higher local food prices are eroding purchasing power and causing families to eat fewer and less healthy meals. On the other hand, the jobs crisis continues to squeeze the incomes of workers and further reduce the availability of decent work opportunities. On top of both of these shocks, social assistance is increasingly in jeopardy due to austerity measures that are disproportionately affecting vulnerable children and their families. Each of these ongoing household-level threats is briefly summarized below.

2.1.   High food prices

In 2012, food prices are at near record levels in many countries, especially low-income. After two major international price spikes in 2007-08 and 2010-11, Chapter III described how populations in a sample of 55 developing countries were paying 80 percent more, on average, for basic foodstuffs at the start of 2012 when compared to price levels prior to the 2007-08 crisis (Figure 1). Even more important is the apparent 'stickiness' of local food prices once reaching new highs. While the international food price index dropped by more than 50 percent in 2009 after peaking in early 2008, local food prices fell only minimally and remained elevated. Moreover, after the 2011 peaks, global food prices dropped by 13 percent, but local food prices appear to have retracted by a meager 2 percent. While increases have been particularly steep in Sub-Saharan Africa and the CEE/CIS, country-level data verify that food price shocks have severely affected a large number of developing countries, especially LICs where poverty is most pervasive.

Figure VII.1. Local and Global Food Price Indices, Jan. 2007 to Jan. 2012
(local food prices in unweighted average index values; Jan. 2007=100 for both metrics)

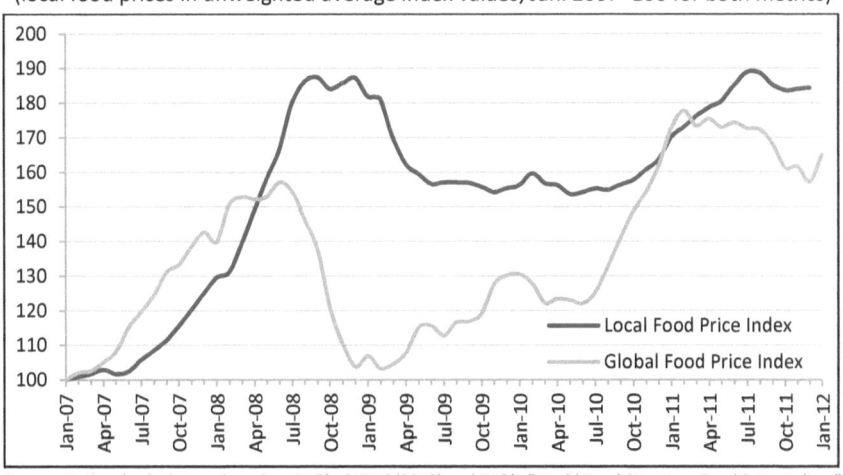

Source: Authors' calculations based on FAO's *GIEWS* (2012) and FAO's "World Food Situation: Food Price Indices" (2012)

2.2. Unemployment and limited decent job opportunities

The jobs crisis is deteriorating amidst the anemic economic growth that continues to besiege much of the globe. While 'jobless growth' patterns characterized most countries prior to the crisis, this trend has since intensified with the weakened demand for labour globally. Of the 102 countries with available estimates for 2012, 35 have unemployment rates in excess of 9 percent, with five countries surpassing 20 percent. Importantly, these aggregate estimates understate the magnitude of the jobs crisis. The employment-to-population ratio, which indicates the employment-generating capacity of a country, further shows that economies are simply not generating sufficient employment opportunities to absorb growth in working-age populations, with two out of every five potential workers in the world unable to find a job.

As described in Chapter IV, labour markets worldwide are characterized by fewer, lower-paying jobs that are increasingly vulnerable and proliferating the incidence of working poverty that had already trapped nearly one billion workers and their families through 2011. The ominous labour market outlook is further exacerbated by alarming rates of youth unemployment and a quickly expanding supply of young labourers in need of work (Figure 2). Due to the demographic trend known as the 'youth bulge,' which is impacting many developing countries, more than

120 million potential new young workers are entering the global labour force each year, 90 percent of them in developing countries. Not coincidentally, countries with large cohorts of young workers who are unable to find decent jobs are among the most vulnerable in terms of political and social instability.

Figure VII.2. Global Youth Employment-to-Population Ratio and Share of Youth in World Population, 1991-2011

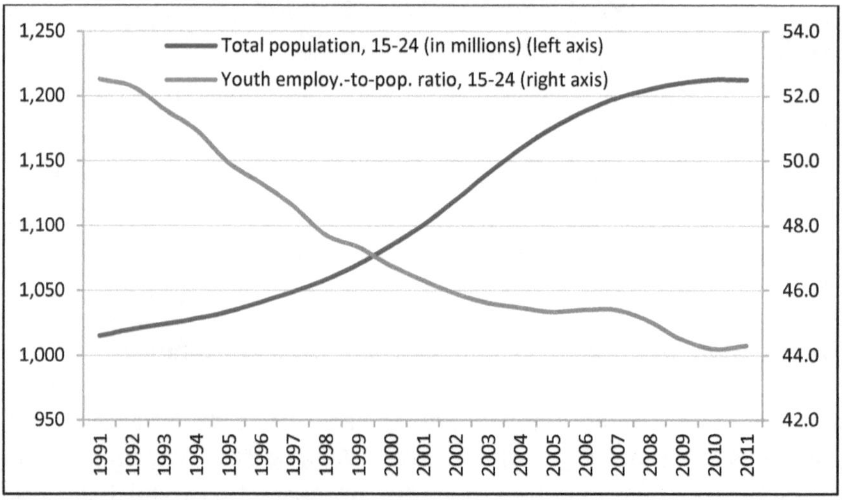

Source: Authors' calculations based on ILO's *Global Employment Trends for Youth* (2010) and United Nation's *World Population Prospects: The 2010 Revision* (2011), medium variant projections

2.3.   Austerity measures

Access to public goods and services is increasingly being challenged in the worldwide drive toward austerity. Using fiscal projections from the IMF, Chapter V looked at the evolution of public expenditures among 179 countries since the start of the global economic crisis. It found that, while most governments introduced fiscal stimulus packages during 2008-09, the majority of governments began to contract overall expenditures in a second phase of the crisis, with serious risks for children and poor households. Both of these distinct phases are outlined below.

Phase I (2008-09), fiscal expansion: During this expansionary phase, the vast majority of governments boosted public expenditures in an attempt to sustain economic growth and buffer the impact of the different global shocks on their populations. When comparing pre-crisis spending levels to those during this first phase of the crisis, nearly three-fourths of developing countries and 90 percent of HICs ramped up public expenditures, with the average expansion amounting to nearly 4 percent of GDP worldwide. Evidence also suggests that social sector investments benefited during this phase; data from the World Bank show that, on average, health and education expenditures rose 19 and 14 percent, respectively, when comparing 2008-09 and 2005-07 spending values among all countries with available estimates.

The expansionary approach starkly differed from orthodox policy reactions to past crises. As explained in Chapter II, counter-cyclical policies re-emerged with force during 2008-09; it was strongly endorsed by the G20, frequently heard from the IMF and even supported by some orthodox economists.

While the size of fiscal stimuli varied by country, in general, the most massive Keynesian macroeconomic packages in history were put in place, including in developing countries. According to UNDP calculations, the total fiscal stimulus size amounted to US$2.4 trillion in a sample of 48 countries, which equaled nearly 4 percent of global GDP in 2008.[5] Importantly, social protection was a critical component of the announced stimulus plans. On average, 25 percent was invested in social protection measures in both high-income and developing countries.[6]

This positive narrative should be nuanced, however, as many have argued that some counter-cyclical policies were inadequate. The experience in Sub-Saharan Africa was diverse, for example, with many countries unable to undertake expansionary policies. Additionally, fiscal stimuli amounts paled in comparison to the elephantine size of funds that were used to bail out financial sectors—the IMF suggests that this amounted to more than US$9 trillion in the G20 countries alone.

Phase II (2010-), fiscal contraction: It was widely recognized that the implementation of counter-cyclical policies during the early stage of the crisis averted an immediate worldwide recession and helped alleviate some of the human costs of the crisis. This expansionary policy stance,

---

[5] Zhang, Y., N. Thelen and A. Rao. 2010. "Social Protection in Fiscal Stimulus Packages: Some Evidence." UNDP/Office of Development Studies Working Paper, UNDP.
[6] Authors' calculations based on ibid and IMF country reports for Chile and Peru.

however, was short-lived. In 2010, 106 governments worldwide scaled back total spending by 2.3 percent of GDP, on average, with 133 countries expected to reduce annual expenditures during 2012 by close to 2 percent of GDP, on average (Table 1). This trend is notably stronger among developing countries, which are contracting more than HICs in terms of GDP. Comparing the 2010-12 and 2005-07 periods further suggests that one-third of all governments (39 in total) are undergoing excessive contraction, defined as cutting expenditures below pre-crisis levels in terms of GDP. Even more unsettling, spending projections for 2013 indicate that fiscal consolidation will continue to characterize public policies globally into the foreseeable future.

Table VII.1. Projected Total Government Spending Trends, 2010-13

Country Category (n=)	Indicator	(A) Change in Spending (year on year, in % of GDP)				(B) Growth of Real Spending (year on year, as a %)			
		2010	2011	2012	2013	2010	2011	2012	2013
All developing (130)	Overall avg.	-0.6	0.2	-1.0	-0.7	5.6	6.4	1.7	2.9
	Avg. contraction	-2.7	-1.8	-1.8	-1.2	-6.7	-5.0	-6.2	-3.3
	# of countries	68	62	94	92	32	36	40	26
High-income (49)	Overall avg.	-0.7	-1.2	-0.6	-0.7	1.8	1.6	0.2	0.6
	Avg. contraction	-1.6	-2.0	-1.0	-1.0	-4.4	-4.7	-2.5	-3.0
	# of countries	38	37	39	39	18	18	20	14
All (179)	Overall avg.	-0.6	-0.2	-0.9	-0.7	4.5	5.1	1.3	2.3
	Avg. contraction	-2.3	-1.9	-1.6	-1.1	-5.8	-4.9	-4.9	-3.2
	# of countries	106	99	133	131	50	54	60	40

Source: Authors' calculations based on IMF's *World Economic Outlook* (September 2011)

The second phase of the crisis saw a sharp shift from fiscal stimulus to fiscal austerity, despite the weakness, unevenness and uncertainty of economic recovery, as well as the continued negative impacts on vulnerable populations, in many countries. Moreover, in terms of social expenditures, recent surveys suggest a bleak outlook during this second phase. A study commissioned by Oxfam found that two-thirds of 56 LICs surveyed were cutting budget allocations in 2010 to one or more pro-poor sectors, which included education, health, agriculture and social protection.[7] Globally comparable data are not yet available in 2012 for a more comprehensive assessment.

To understand how governments are cutting expenditures, Chapter V also reviewed 158 IMF country reports published between January 2010

---

[7] Kyrili, K. and M. Martin. 2010. The Impact of the Global Economic Crisis on the Budgets of Low-income Countries. Oxford: Oxfam International.

and February 2012.[8] The analysis found that, in addition to facing the negative impacts associated with reduced overall public expenditures, children and poor households are also likely to suffer disproportionately from the main austerity measures that many governments are considering. These different austerity measures, along with their potential risks, are summarized below.

- *Wage bill cuts or caps* are under consideration in 73 countries to achieve cost savings, often carried out or planned as a part of civil service reforms. This strategy can jeopardize the delivery of education, health and social services to children and poor families through lower salaries and/or numbers of teachers, medical staff and other civil servants, including social workers. Low pay is also a key factor behind absenteeism, informal fees and brain drain, which can further hinder service delivery, especially in rural areas.

- *Reducing or removing subsidies* is being discussed in 73 countries to contain budgets, predominately on fuel, but also on electricity and food items. When basic subsidies are withdrawn, food and transport costs rise and can become unaffordable for many households; higher energy prices also tend to contract economic activities. Moreover, unless a well-functioning social protection system is in place that can ensure that vulnerable populations have adequate access to food and nutrition, food subsidies are necessary to prevent malnutrition, especially among infants and young children.

- *Further targeting social protection* emerges as a budget-contracting channel in 55 countries. Many governments appear to be rationalizing and targeting social protection systems to the poorest, which is a *de facto* reduction of social protection coverage. This policy approach runs a high risk of excluding large segments of vulnerable households—either through timing mismatches or exclusion errors—at a time when they are most in need and when governments should be considering supporting a social protection

---

[8] The analysis of different adjustment measures is inferred from policy discussions and other information contained in IMF country reports (which cover Article IV consultations, reviews conducted under lending arrangements and consultations under non-lending arrangements); it is important to note that governments may have pursued other policies since the country reports were published.

floor for all, scaling up rather than scaling down social protection systems.

- *Reforming old-age pensions* is another common strategy to reduce government expenditures that is being contemplated in 52 countries, either through raising contribution rates, increasing eligibility periods, prolonging the retirement age and/or lowering benefits. Similar to the case of further targeting, this option can exclude vulnerable groups from receiving benefits or diminish public assistance that is vital to preserve well-being.

- *Increasing consumption taxes on basic goods and services*, such as VATs, is a final widespread austerity tactic that is being discussed in 71 countries. Such measures can further erode the already limited incomes of marginalized groups and stifle economic activity; they can also be regressive, placing a disproportionate and unfair tax burden on poorer households.

Overall, at least one of the above adjustment measures is being considered in 138 countries, with two or more in 96 countries, four or more in 22 countries, and all five in 15 countries, including Greece, India, Ireland, Italy, Jordan, Malaysia, the Netherlands, Nicaragua, Portugal, Romania, Slovak Republic, Spain, St. Kitts and Nevis, Tunisia and the United Kingdom.

3.   The Cumulative Impacts of Multiple Shocks on Households

Various studies highlight the impact of one shock or another on households, but it is important to realize that families have been experiencing the cumulative effects of multiple shocks since 2008, which has exhausted their available coping mechanisms and deepened their hardships. Of particular concern is that many of the coping behaviors have potentially severe and irreversible consequences, especially for infants and young children. Moreover, while the adverse impacts of the different shocks are most pronounced on poorer households in developing countries, they also threaten populations in high-income economies, as summarized below.

- *Hunger and malnutrition:* Higher food prices, fewer and lower-paying jobs, and reduced social support, including the scaling back of subsidies, have limited household spending on food. As families purchase smaller quantities and cheaper food items and subsequently consume fewer meals—sometimes reducing food intake to just once a day instead of three times—and smaller, less nutritious portions, hunger and malnutrition risks have been widely reported across the globe. Importantly, households whose nutritional status was at risk even prior to the crisis appear most likely to modify their dietary intake. Available evidence also suggests that children and women are bearing the brunt of alimentary cutbacks. The impacts of malnutrition are especially acute for children; the limited window of intervention for fetal development and for growth among infants means that food deprivations today, if not addressed promptly, can have irreversible impacts on their physical and intellectual capacities, which will, in turn, lower their productivity and income-earning potential in adulthood.

- *Poor health:* Another common coping mechanism related to the income shocks from the global economic crisis is reduced healthcare expenditures and service utilization. In a number of developing countries, households have consistently reported visiting doctors and medical care facilities less frequently, taking fewer prescription drugs, and increasing self-diagnosis and self-medication practices, such as resorting to folk remedies. These behaviors are most prevalent among the poorest households, which have exposed many vulnerable persons to a higher risk of sickness—and sometimes death; the true health impacts of the crisis, however, appear over time as a result of weakened body defenses. There is also ample evidence that the jobs crisis—via unemployment—is inflicting serious physical and mental damage, including illness, stress, loss of self-esteem, alcohol and substance abuse, clinical depression and even suicide.

- *Lower school attendance and higher rates of child labour:* The increasing need to supplement household income, coupled with the inability to cover the costs of school attendance, has forced many families to pull their children out of school and put them to work. Evidence in rural areas shows that children as young as five years old are increasingly involved in supporting family farms, selling produce in markets and working as apprentices in different trades, especially among boys. It has also been widely documented that many girls in urban centers have stopped going to school in order to help their mothers earn additional income in urban areas.

-   *Domestic violence:* Another negative impact connected to the jobs crisis, specifically, is domestic violence. Job losses coupled with financial stresses have been reported to have increased domestic violence rates in a number of developing and high-income countries.

-   *Unsupervised and abandoned children:* Many parents have been forced to increase their working hours as well as send non-worker members of the household into the labour market, especially mothers. As a result, a well-documented trend of the global economic crisis is the prevalence of children being left at home unattended and unsupervised. Several reports also suggest that children are increasingly being abandoned in orphanages both in low- and high-income countries.

-   *Increased vulnerability to future shocks:* Household incomes are being reduced due to the worsened jobs crisis and austerity measures (e.g., smaller pensions and more targeted social protection). In order to pay for basic goods and services, such as food, rent, electricity, healthcare and education, many households have subsequently resorted to selling assets and borrowing money. Since 2008 families have been widely observed drawing down savings, selling household possessions, such as livestock, and turning to relatives, community groups and banks, where possible, for financial help. However, these informal safety nets for the poor are easily exhaustible. And given that many vulnerable households have been forced to confront an unabated wave of shocks since 2007, the poor increasingly find themselves in situations of extreme vulnerability to any prolonged or renewed shock.

-   *Social instability:* The global economic crisis has led to an outbreak of protests and civil unrest worldwide and further threatened household well-being. While food riots were widespread during the earlier 2007-08 food price spike, 2011 was blanketed with strident reminders of the dangers of unaffordable food, with violent protests erupting in Algeria, Bangladesh, Burkina Faso, Egypt, India, Iraq,

Jordan, Morocco, Mozambique, Nigeria, Senegal, Syria, Tunisia, Uganda and Yemen. The world was also shaken by renewed unrest in 2011 due to the combined effects of high unemployment, worsening living standards, eroding confidence in governments and perceptions that the burden of the crisis is being unequally shared. This was clearly visible in the Arab Spring, the Occupy Wall Street movement in the United States, and the 'indignados' (outraged) in Spain and in other European countries. The ILO's index of social unrest empirically documents the rising levels of worldwide discontent, with the *World of Work Report 2011* warning that social unrest is being aggravated in 45 of the 118 countries surveyed.

In short, children and poor families are bearing the costs of a 'recovery' that has largely excluded them. However, this need not be the case and should be compared with, for example, the near-record bonuses handed out to bank and corporate executives since 2010. To reiterate the sentiments of the UN Secretary-General at the beginning of this chapter, "People everywhere are demanding change. They call out for dignity. They demand justice... a better and more fair deal. They want jobs, opportunities and global markets that work for all people, not just elites."

4.   Policy Responses for a *'Recovery for All'*

The multitude of threats posed by high food prices, the limited supply of decent jobs and public sector belt-tightening are indeed daunting; they further underscore the shortcomings of earlier policy interventions adopted by most governments and the need for urgent change. By adjusting current policy priorities, however, policymakers can effectively invest in children and poor households and achieve an inclusive *'Recovery for All.'* While this requires prioritizing food security, producing employment-generating growth and decent job opportunities, and protecting vulnerable populations,[9] this is also predicated on taking advantage of all available opportunities to expand fiscal space for needed social and economic investments today. Each of these areas is briefly reviewed below.

---

[9] This sub-section presents a synthesis of the empirical findings and policy discussions in this book; clearly the list of policies is not exhaustive, and governments should also consider affordable housing policies, an inclusive financial sector and additional measures described elsewhere.

4.1.   Promoting food security

As presented in Chapter III, national policy responses to the earlier food price spike that began in mid-2007 were primarily focused on short-term mitigation measures:

- *Supporting consumption*: An estimated 75 countries provided food assistance (e.g., through direct food transfers, food stamps/vouchers and school feeding programs), announced price subsidies and controls, introduced or scaled-up cash transfers, reduced consumption taxes and/or initiated food-for-work schemes.

- *Boosting agricultural production*: Some 57 countries attempted to increase food production by providing subsidies for agricultural inputs and reducing taxes on grain producers, although some countries also offered other types of incentives to spur agricultural output, such as credit programs for small farmers.

- *Managing and regulating food markets*: Approximately 76 countries sought to lower domestic food prices by encouraging imports and discouraging exports, most commonly by reducing import tariffs and/or introducing different export restrictions. Building up and releasing strategic food reserves was another frequently employed strategy to stabilize local food prices. A number of governments also intervened in food markets by restricting stockholding by private traders, imposing anti-hoarding measures and restricting futures trading of basic foods.

Regrettably, most policy responses up to 2011 failed to protect populations from future food price increases. Such lessons were quick to bear fruit: local food prices re-ascended quickly in mid-2010 and remained at historic highs at the start of 2012.

This book has argued that governments must move beyond crisis management; high food prices and volatility will continue unless their structural causes are addressed. The UN, in particular, has been calling for the eradication of world hunger for decades. More recently, the UN Secretary-General formed the High-Level Task Force on the Global Food Security Crisis, which proposed a *Comprehensive Framework for Action* to overcome the food crisis. The policy recommendations are based on a twin-track path that includes short-term emergency support alongside longer-term development interventions that are focused on supporting consumption and agricultural production.

However, several UN reports have noted that higher food prices are also a result of speculative activities in commodity derivatives. This argument has been further echoed by the G20 and the EU in 2011, which acknowledged the need for regulation to ensure better functioning and more transparent agricultural financial markets, including OTC trading, to prevent and address market abuses, cross-market manipulations and price volatility.

Ultimately, addressing food insecurity requires action on three fronts. The first is poverty reduction. The principal reason that basic local food items remain unaffordable for vulnerable populations is because of low living standards. As Nobel Laureate Amartya Sen recognized, rather than insufficient food production, a main problem associated with hunger is distribution and access. This may be effectively overcome by introducing or scaling up social protection programs to ensure that vulnerable households have access to affordable and nutritious foods, ultimately moving toward a universal social protection floor. Over the longer term, however, reducing poverty requires comprehensive national policy planning, such as through national development strategies that aim at both employment-generating growth and equitable social development.

The second is focusing on sustainable food production. This requires supporting investment and productivity growth in agriculture, livestock and fisheries, as well as appropriately focusing on women who produce 60 to 80 percent of food in developing countries (90 percent in some countries in Sub-Saharan Africa). Ultimately, effective interventions should support small-scale farming by addressing land redistribution, access to credit, rural extension services, etc. to lift populations out of poverty. Moreover, in a context of climate change and the increasing incidence of floods and droughts, governments should also focus on developing better irrigation and water management systems as well as adopting longer-term commitments to both mitigating and adapting to the impacts of climate change.

And third is effectively managing and regulating food and commodity markets. Regulation can and should play an important role to ensure that markets are well-functioning, that commodity prices remain stable and that consumers are protected. Collective action at the international level is also needed so that global trade policies favor developing countries and the poor.

4.2.   Creating decent jobs

Work is the main source of income for households, especially the poor, and an employment-based recovery is vital to protecting and supporting the most vulnerable populations, including children. Yet current policy stances will only perpetuate ongoing patterns of 'jobless growth.' As described in Chapter IV, in the first phase of the crisis (2008-09), many governments adopted a series of measures to promote employment, which included investing in infrastructure, offering subsidies and tax incentives to SMEs, expanding public employment services and training programs, increasing unemployment benefits and social transfers, and social dialogue with employer and worker organizations.

Beginning in 2010, however, most governments abandoned strategies to create jobs and protect workers, and moved, instead, to cut public spending. In the process, austerity measures have reduced the quantity and quality of employment opportunities and debilitated social protection systems. Many countries, especially in Europe, have also been adopting labour flexibilization reforms since 2011, which is furthering 'precarization' and vulnerable employment, as well as depressing incomes and aggregate demand.

Moving forward, employment growth, especially for youth, must be a top priority for socio-economic recovery. This does not mean returning to pre-crisis policies; since the 1980s economic policy frameworks have, in general, been narrowly focused on growth and macroeconomic stability—employment, equity and social cohesion being only afterthoughts—and failed to maximize synergies between macroeconomic and sectoral policies. As a result, restoring these earlier orthodox policies will not create sufficient job opportunities for the world's labour force.

The UN, particularly the ILO, has consolidated a policy agenda to achieve decent jobs for all persons, especially youth, which was endorsed by all governments at the UN Summit in September 2010. This is based on a combination of macroeconomic and labour policies, which are outlined below.

-   *Macroeconomic and sector policies* must be geared toward fostering aggregate demand, investment and new jobs. An appropriate jobs-creating policy framework requires significant expansion of public investments, which is wholly incongruent with fiscal tightening. It also requires recognizing the multiple inter-linkages between economic and social policies, analyzing labour market dynamics, and strong coordination of all development-related ministries in the design and implementation of employment-generating policies—for instance, ensuring that the financial sector serves the real economy. Three policy areas merit special attention: (i) monetary and fiscal policies should aim to boost aggregate demand and pursue employment targets rather than inflation or budget deficit targets; (ii) sector policies should offer strong incentives to increase investment and employment in both the private and public sectors; and (iii) exchange rate and technology policies should stimulate output growth and be complemented by the gradual and sequential opening of trade.

-   *Active labour market policies and programs:* There is a wide range of options that can be considered based on national circumstances, which can be grouped into four general categories: (i) direct employment generation (promoting SMEs and cooperatives, wage subsidies, public works programs, guaranteed job schemes, etc.); (ii) labour exchanges or employment services (job brokerage and counseling offices); (iii) skills development programs (e.g., training and retraining of labour to enhance employability and productivity); and (iv) special programs for youth and persons with disabilities.

-   *Labour standards*: As presented in Chapter IV, nearly one billion poor persons work long hours but are unable to bring their families out of poverty. As a result, employment policies must not solely focus on creating jobs but also on ensuring adequate wages and working conditions. In addition, legislation and enforcement efforts must prevent child labour and protect women, young people, persons with disabilities and minority groups from discrimination and abuse. Countries must further aim for an appropriate legislative framework that strikes a balance between economic efficiency and labour protection.

- *Social protection:* Since not everybody can or should work, jobs programs and policies must be accompanied by adequate social protection measures, such as the UN and G20-proposed social protection floor. In particular, social protection must aim to prevent child labour and provide adequate income support for the poor, unemployed, older persons, women on maternity leave and persons with disabilities. Moreover, social protection should not be viewed as a cost to society, but rather as an investment—e.g., investing in children has large impacts on human development and productivity, and raising the incomes of the poor expands domestic markets.

- *Social dialogue:* Now, more than ever in recent history, it is indispensable that employers, unions and governments dialogue together about how to achieve socio-economic recovery. Social pacts can be an effective strategy to articulate labour market policies that have positive synergies between economic and social development; they are especially well-suited to arrive at optimal solutions in macroeconomic policy, in strengthening productivity, job and income security, and in supporting employment-generating enterprises.

It is imperative that all of the abovementioned employment strategies are infused with a strong focus on creating opportunities for young workers. More than 120 million new potential workers enter the global labour force each year, nearly 90 percent of which are from developing countries, with nearly 1.1 billion expected between 2012 and 2020. Prioritizing decent jobs for youth can help recoup prior investments in education and health, expand the tax and savings base, and, ultimately, stimulate aggregate demand and socio-economic recovery.

4.3.   Prioritizing recovery for households

Chapter V detailed the marked change in fiscal policy stances between the two phases of the crisis: expansion versus contraction. Indeed, the efforts of governments to shield their populations from the multitude of global shocks during 2008-09 were short-lived, as budget cuts became widespread beginning in 2010.

In 2011, the UN warned of the risks of fiscal consolidation for socio-economic recovery. The simultaneous adoption of fiscal austerity policies in countries worldwide is driving the global economy toward recession; the vicious circle induced by fiscal contraction, weak financial institutions and vulnerable households does not encourage economic activity or job creation, and is detrimental to high-income and developing countries alike.

To avoid repeating the mistakes of the 1930s, world leaders should adopt a coordinated global policy framework that prioritizes employment-generating growth and socio-economic recovery. This requires that policymakers recognize the impacts that different austerity measures have on children and poor households, as well as on decent jobs growth and equitable outcomes. As a result, in addition to considering the set of alternative socially-responsive policies as described in this book, policymakers should also ensure that the following factors are taken into account:

- *Wage bill cuts/caps:* Wage bill decisions impact staff in essential social services, such as teachers, healthcare professionals and social protection workers, especially in disadvantaged areas where wages are traditionally very low. While the number of related personnel and their salaries should be protected at all times to ensure that vulnerable families have access to quality basic services, they should also be increased whenever possible.

- *Removing/reducing subsidies:* As food and energy prices hover near record highs, scaling back consumer subsidies should be avoided unless a well-functioning social protection system is already in place that can protect poor households. It is also important that subsidies are not removed to build a new social protection system—this takes time and populations will be left unprotected during a period of exceptional vulnerability. Lastly, maintaining certain consumer subsidies—except on luxury items—can support aggregate demand and national recovery efforts.

- *Further targeting social protection:* Rather than rationalizing and scaling down social protection investments to achieve cost savings over the short term, there is a strong case for scaling up in times of crisis and expanding a universal social protection floor to provide immediate support to vulnerable geographic areas or groups (orphans, women headed-households, persons with disabilities, etc.).

- *Pension reforms:* Any systematic pension reform should be complemented by measures that safeguard income support and the delivery of basic services to older persons and their families. Given that reducing wages, pensions and household income will reduce demand and delay recovery, policymakers should consider rationalizing expenditures that have less severe social and economic consequences.

- *Increasing or expanding VATs:* Instead of increasing taxes on items that are consumed by the poor and further eroding their already scant disposable income, governments should weigh other options, such as taxes on corporate profits, financial activities, personal income, luxury items, property, natural resource extraction, alcohol and tobacco, imports/exports, etc.; tax revenues can also be increased by strengthening collection systems. It is equally important that consumer-oriented tax changes are progressively designed by exempting goods and services that low-income families depend on while setting higher rates for luxury goods that are primarily consumed by wealthier households.

4.4.   There are alternatives: Fiscal space exists even in the poorest countries

It is often argued that social and economic investments that benefit children and poor households are not affordable or that government expenditure cuts are inevitable during adjustment periods. But there are alternatives, even in the poorest countries. Chapter VI presented six broad areas that governments can explore to expand fiscal space today, which are supported by policy statements of the UN and international financial institutions. These include: (i) re-allocating public expenditures; (ii) increasing tax revenues; (iii) lobbying for increased aid and transfers; (iv) tapping into fiscal and foreign exchange reserves; (v) borrowing and restructuring existing debt; and/or (vi) adopting a more accommodative macroeconomic framework.

- *Re-allocating current public expenditures:* This is the most orthodox option, which includes assessing ongoing budget allocations through public expenditure reviews and thematic budgets, replacing high-cost, low-impact investments with those with larger socio-economic impacts, eliminating spending inefficiencies and/or tackling corruption. Chapter VI showed how much countries spend on health, education and military expenditures; in the context of national debates on budget cuts, the need of non-productive expenditures should be questioned (who benefits?). In terms of this option, two important points should be raised. First, re-prioritizing budgets has proven to be a difficult approach given vested interests in countries. Second, while improving spending inefficiencies is the most common orthodox measure suggested to expand fiscal space, this approach takes time to advance and is unlikely to yield significant, immediate resources for social and economic recovery in the near term. As a result, other strategies should also be considered.

- *Increasing tax revenues:* This is a main channel achieved by altering different types of tax rates or by strengthening the efficiency of tax collection methods and overall compliance. Efforts to develop collection capacities and broaden the tax base are to be applauded, especially those aimed at cracking down on tax evasion, which has been estimated to result in annual revenue losses of US$285 billion for developing countries as a whole, as presented in Chapter VI. This is particularly relevant since, in recent decades, there has been a significant reduction of progressive taxes on personal income, property, corporate profits and imports/exports (including taxes on natural resource extraction), as well as an expansion of regressive VATs and other consumption taxes, which have contributed to rising levels of inequality. It is also noteworthy that few countries have attempted to increase taxes on financial activities. However, there are positive experiences that reverse earlier orthodox approaches, such as raising personal income and capital gains taxes, levying the financial sector during the economic crisis or raising export tariffs in countries undergoing export-driven commodity booms.

Governments should therefore examine the numerous options for progressive taxation on both fiscal space and equity grounds.

- *Increased aid and transfers:* This requires engaging with different donor governments in order to ramp up North-South ODA or South-South transfers. On the one hand, despite fiscal pressures in HICs, the justification for meeting the aid target of 0.7 percent of GNI has never been greater; global inequality is staggering, and developing countries are suffering the consequences of a crisis created by the North. On the other hand, South-South cooperation is an important and burgeoning avenue of development support, which occurs through three principal channels: (i) bilateral aid between developing countries; (ii) regional integration; and (iii) regional development banks. Above all, however, improving the fiscal position of developing countries also requires reducing South-North transfers, including illicit financial flows, which could free up vast resources for critical social and economic investments; in 2009 alone, illicit financial flows amounted to more than 10 times the total aid received by developing countries.

- *Using fiscal and central bank foreign exchange reserves:* This includes drawing down fiscal savings and other state revenues stored in special funds, such as sovereign wealth funds, and/or using excess foreign exchange reserves in the central bank for domestic and regional development. Foreign exchange reserves accumulated in central banks have increased dramatically in most countries over the past decade and offer creative opportunities to finance social and economic investments. A number of countries are also sitting atop abundant natural resource funds, yet social indicators and progress towards development objectives remain dismal (e.g., Timor-Leste).

- *Borrowing or restructuring existing debt:* Some countries have scope for additional borrowing; other countries are highly indebted and should consider restructuring existing debt. For the first group, this involves active exploration of domestic and foreign borrowing options that are at low costs, if not concessional, following a careful assessment of debt sustainability. For those countries under high debt distress, restructuring existing debt may be possible and justifiable if the legitimacy of the debt is questionable and/or the opportunity cost in terms of worsening deprivations of children and other vulnerable groups is compelling. The main strategies adopted by governments to restructure debt in recent years include: (i) debt re-negotiation (60 countries); (ii) debt relief (32 countries through the Heavily Indebted Poor Countries [HIPC] Initiative); (iii) debt swaps or conversions (50 countries); (iv) debt repudiation (e.g., the recent cases of Iceland and Iraq); and (v) default (20 countries since 1999). The increasing prevalence of sovereign debt crises further underscores the pressing need for an international debt work-out mechanism that can resolve issues between sovereign borrowers and their lenders, as called by the UN.

- *Adopting a more accommodating macroeconomic framework:* The goals of macroeconomic policy are multiple, from supporting growth and price stabilization to smoothing out economic cycles, reducing unemployment and poverty, and promoting equity. In the last decades, however, macroeconomic frameworks have placed a strong emphasis on short-term stabilization measures, such as controlling inflation and fiscal deficits, and relegated employment-generating growth and social development to an afterthought. As presented in Chapter VI, this need not be the case: allowing for more flexible budget deficits and inflation targets can be achieved without jeopardizing overall macroeconomic stability in support of a socially-responsive recovery.

In summary, there are ample opportunities for countries to increase fiscal space through a combination of tailored strategies. While some governments utilize all possible options, many do not. Each country is unique, and fiscal space options should be carefully examined—including the potential risks and trade-offs—in an inclusive national dialogue. But even small changes in a variety of measures—that is, combining minor increases in different options—can create substantial resources to support vulnerable populations. Moreover, given the importance of public investment in enhancing the prospects for sustainable growth and social development, including the MDGs, the discussion on policy alternatives to support food security, decent jobs, and social protection systems—both during and after the recovery—can begin today.

5.   The Drive toward Social Justice: A real recovery means a *'Recovery for All'*

Crises oblige policymakers to rethink development models. The 1929 financial crash led to a New Deal that radically altered the development model of the day. As a response, Henry Ford paid his workers a wage that would allow them to buy the cars that they built, and this was only the beginning of a major policy shift globally. At the end of World War II, politicians from advanced economies were determined that unemployment and economic crisis, which fueled the evils of fascism, should never be repeated. They accepted that full employment, political stability and social cohesion must be primary national policy objectives, and, as a result, governments became more involved in education, healthcare, social security and housing assistance, as well as in promoting investment and employment-generating growth. This policy change was highly successful: postwar policies achieved high productivity gains in the workforce, expanded internal markets and increased economic growth, with the populations of Europe, North America, Japan, Australia and New Zealand experiencing unparalleled prosperity.

A comparable policy push is needed today. The current global economic crisis presents an opportunity to rethink socio-economic policies for all persons. This requires shedding the myopic scope of macroeconomic and fiscal policy decisions of recent decades and, instead, basing them on their potential to achieve food security, full employment, human development, and inclusive and sustainable growth. To do so, social and economic investments—such as nutritional assistance, education and health services, social protection and job creation—must be viewed as priority investments within a flexible, longer-term fiscal policy framework and recognize that there are a variety of financing options available to bolster these much needed investments today, even in the poorest countries.

The crisis has already triggered a shift in the way that the international community sees the relationship between growth and public support for the poor. In the Asia-Pacific region, for example, policymakers are increasingly shifting away from unsustainable export-led growth models toward more inclusive employment-intensive recovery strategies that are centered on building internal markets and improving social protection systems. Latin America, another region much affected by financial crises in the 1990s, has pursued regional integration to expand internal markets and invested significantly in social protection systems to improve living standards; indeed, much of the region's relative resilience to the contagion effects of the current crisis is due to these recent policy stances. At the global level, there is also increased awareness of the need to eradicate poverty and the extremes of inequality, and to strike the right balance between growth and inclusive development progress.

The policies outlined in this book to achieve social justice are well-known by governments worldwide; all nations have endorsed them in the UN General Assembly. Whether this remains simply an ideal on paper or is transformed into actual policies, however, depends on global leadership.

For billions of persons, the persistence of the food, unemployment and austerity shocks can only be expected to further the depth and scope of coping mechanisms that households have adopted since 2008, in many cases unabatedly. Poor families are bearing the costs of a 'recovery' that has largely excluded them. Above all, children cannot wait. While an adult may fall into poverty temporarily, falling into poverty in childhood can last a lifetime—few children get a second chance at an education or a healthy start in life. Moreover, even short periods of food deprivation can impact a child's long-term development. If children do not receive adequate nutrition, they grow smaller in size and intellectual capacity, they are more vulnerable to life-threatening diseases, they perform worse in school—if able to attend at all—and, ultimately, they are less likely to be productive adults, reducing their income prospects, and therefore domestic demand. In sum, not only does child poverty threaten the individual child, but it is also likely to be passed on to future generations, entrenching and even exacerbating poverty and inequality across society; this is an extraordinary price for countries to pay.

It is time for global leaders to think about the longer term—about the future we want for our children—and to turn the current vicious circle into a virtuous circle that effectively links economic and human development. Today, another New Deal is warranted, a fair social contract for the 21st century that includes all countries—both high-income and low-income—and all persons—both rich and poor—through increased public investments to boost aggregate demand, catalyze sustainable development and political stability, and achieve long-term global prosperity for all. Ultimately, an inclusive recovery is a matter of social and economic justice: nobody should be left behind. Or, in the words of the UN Secretary-General, "Real recovery means recovery for all."[10]

---

[10] United Nations. 2010. *Voices of the Vulnerable: Recovery from the ground up*. New York: United Nations Global Pulse.

www.ingramcontent.com/pod-product-compliance
Lightning Source LLC
Chambersburg PA
CBHW061335280526
45784CB00001B/18

* 9 7 8 1 1 0 5 5 8 7 5 5 9 *